Community

of Suffering

& Struggle

Community of Suffering & Struggle

Women, Men, and the Labor Movement in Minneapolis, 1915–1945

Elizabeth Faue

The University of
North Carolina Press

Chapel Hill & London

The paper in this book meets the guidelines for permanence and durability of
the Committee on Production Guidelines for Book Longevity of the Council on
Library Resources.

Manufactured in the United States of America

95 94 93 92 91   5 4 3 2 1

Library of Congress Cataloging-in-Publication Data

Faue, Elizabeth.
    Community of suffering and struggle : women, men, and the labor
movement in Minneapolis, 1915–1945 / Elizabeth Faue.
        p.   cm. — (Gender & American culture)
    Includes bibliographical references and index.
    ISBN 0-8078-1945-X (alk. paper).—
    ISBN 0-8078-4307-5 (pbk. : alk. paper)
    1. Trade-unions—Minnesota—Minneapolis—History—20th
century.   2. Women in trade-unions—Minnesota—Minneapolis—
History—20th century.   3. Sex discrimination in employment—United
States—History—20th century.   4. Women—Employment—United
States—History—20th century.   5. Depressions—1929—United States.
I. Title.   II. Series.
HD6519.M6F38   1991
331.4'78'0977657909041—dc20   90-48929
                                                                                    CIP

Portions of Chapters 2 and 6 appeared previously in somewhat different form as
"Women, Family, and Politics: Farmer-Labor Women and Social Policy in the
Great Depression," in *Women, Politics, and Change in Twentieth-Century America*,
edited by Louise Tilly and Patricia Gurin, copyright © 1990 by Russell Sage
Foundation. Reprinted by permission.

Chapter 3 appeared in somewhat different form as "The 'Dynamo of Change':
Gender and Solidarity in the American Labour Movement of the 1930s" in
Gender and History 1, no. 2 (Summer 1990): 138–58. Reprinted by permission.

for my nieces and nephews,

consanguineous and fictive

––––––––––––

Jeremiah, Jennifer,

Stephen, Jessica,

Rebecca, Sarah,

John, and Katherine;

Kristina, Benjamin,

Emilirose, Celia,

William, and Caleb

Contents

Preface   xiii

Acknowledgments   xvii

Introduction: Community and Workplace in the History of U.S. Labor   1

One   Women in the American City, 1910–1940   21

Two   Gender, Politics, and the Labor Movement, 1914–1934   47

Three   Gender, Language, and the Meaning of Solidarity, 1929–1945   69

Four   Women and the Revival of Unionism, 1933–1936   100

Five   The Changing Bases of Labor Solidarity, 1936–1939   126

Six   Gender, Labor, and the State in the WPA Strike of 1939   147

Seven   Working Women and Unions during World War II   168

Conclusion: Women, Labor, and the State in the Twentieth Century   189

Appendix: Social and Economic Data on Minneapolis   195

Notes   203

Bibliography   251

Index   289

Illustrations

70   3.1 Labor Progresses by Struggle

75   3.2 He Goes on Fighting!

76   3.3 Gulliver Awakes!

77   3.4 Safe at Home Plate

78   3.5 And the Fight Has Just Begun!

79   3.6 Look, Pal, Communists!

80   3.7 Come on in out of the Rain, Boys!

81   3.8 The Secondary Defense

84   3.9 Challenge to Public Welfare

85   3.10 The Only Friend Labor Has!

86   3.11 Let's Put Shingles on Our Own Homes!

87   3.12 The Spirit of '36!

88   3.13 The New Crusader

91   3.14 The Eternal Nightmare

92   3.15 Sure . . . She Has Her Choice

93   3.16 What Do You Say, Brother?

102   4.1 The Old Spirit Returns

105   4.2 One of the "Ten Per Cent!"

177   7.1 Brother, I'm In—Every Pay Day!

178   7.2 To the War Bond Ramparts—Modern Molly Pitchers

179   7.3 It's the *Least* I Can Do for You, Son!

184   7.4 Union Gains

A section of photographs will be found following page 125.

Tables, Figures, and Maps

Tables

1.1 Farm Origin and Destination of Migrants, Minneapolis–St. Paul, 1935–1940   27

1.2 Age at First Marriage by Sex, Minneapolis, 1920–1940   33

1.3 Child-Woman Ratios, Minneapolis, 1920–1940   34

1.4 Labor Force Participation by Sex, Minneapolis, 1910–1940   35

1.5 Mean Years in Work Force by Sex, Synthetic Cohort, Minneapolis, 1920–1950   39

1.6 Manufacturing and Clerical Employment by Sex, Minneapolis, 1910–1930   40

1.7 Married Women's Labor Force Participation by Husband's Occupation, Minneapolis–St. Paul, 1940   43

5.1 Employment Class by Sex, Minneapolis, 1937   135

7.1 Changes in Women's Employment by Industry, Twin Cities, 1940–1945   172

7.2 Employment by Sex and Industry, Twin Cities, 1940 and 1945   173

7.3 Changes in Women's Employment in Manufacturing, Twin Cities, April 1940–April 1945   174

A.1 Population, Minneapolis, 1880–1950   195

A.2 Population by Nativity and Race, Minneapolis, 1910–1940   196

A.3 Rural and Urban Population, Minnesota, 1880–1920   196

A.4 National Origin of Foreign-Born Whites, Minneapolis, 1930   197

A.5 Ethnicity of Native Whites of Foreign Parentage, Minneapolis, 1930   197

A.6 Birthplace by Sex, Minneapolis–St. Paul, 1940   198

A.7 Relationship to Head of Household, In-Migrants, Minneapolis, 1935–1940   198

A.8 Labor Force Participation by Sex and Age, Minneapolis, 1930–1940   199

A.9 Female Labor Force Participation by Nativity, Race, and Marital Status, Minneapolis, 1930   199

A.10 Employment by Industry and Sex, Minneapolis, 1930 and 1940   200

A.11 Women in Selected Industries by Marital Status, Minneapolis, 1930   201

A.12 Manufacturing, Wholesaling, and Retailing, Minneapolis, 1929–1937   201

A.13 Relief Cases Opened by Year, Minneapolis, 1928–1935   202

Figures

1.1 Net Migration, Women, Minneapolis, 1920–1940   25

1.2 Net Migration, Men, Minneapolis, 1920–1940   26

1.3 Labor Force Participation by Age, Women, Minneapolis, 1930 and 1940   36

1.4 Labor Force Participation by Age, Men, Minneapolis, 1930 and 1940   37

Maps

1.1 Center City, Minneapolis, 1935   29

1.2 Minneapolis Neighborhoods, 1930   31

4.1 Minneapolis Garment District Businesses   103

Preface

The call for synthesis in the historical profession reached American labor history at a time of tremendous debate over what our story should be. In the past twenty years of scholarship, it is argued, there has been no new formulation beyond the narratives of labor union progress and the absence of socialism; there has only been fragmentation. In light of their collective productivity, labor historians are perplexed by this failure. The 1984 conference on synthesizing labor history was fraught with impatience and despair; the recent publication of its collective findings gives no clue as to the nature of the problem with which historians of the American working class grapple.[1]

The erosion of labor's power in the marketplace and in the political arena has only reinforced this sense of crisis. It has been predicted for over a decade that labor unions are on the verge of disintegration; and unlike other periods of decline in their history, the struggle of the last few years could be the death throes of the labor movement as the voice of the working class. Craft, industrial, and white collar unions have been destroyed or disabled in the convergence of employer hostility, economic recession, and public apathy.

Behind the confusion about the nature of labor history reside two models of unionism that have characterized recent scholarship: concern for community, largely inspired by the work of Herbert Gutman, and focus on workplace struggle, from David Montgomery's studies of shopfloor militancy. The incompatibility of these two major interpretations is often given as the reason that synthetic approaches to labor history have not succeeded. The failure of these schools fully to incorporate or explain women's labor activism is another major problem that divides theorists of labor history and women's history. Surprisingly, only a few scholars have suggested that there might be a connection between the problems of synthesis and the gender-class split in labor history.

At a time when the dismantling of the labor movement is almost universally interpreted as the product of structural shifts in the economy, it seems foolish and even pretentious to argue that gender—in either its structural or ideological manifestations—might have a bearing on the failure of the labor movement. If any cultural explanation is forwarded, it is that Americans as a people are too individualistic and prosperous to embrace the collectivity of unions for very long. The decline of our industrial economy is linked by the same arguments to the unnatural monopoly of labor unions over jobs in the primary labor force. In light of this rhetoric, it is important to note that the battle against labor unions is being fought not only through the economic and political strategies of corporations but on the terrain of rhetoric and culture.

Quite contrary to the emphasis on structural trends one finds in the sociology of work, my perspective is that the recent decline of labor is a cultural crisis with roots in the decade of its most dynamic growth—the 1930s. I argue it in the full knowledge that there are those who can and will debate with me on this ground alone. Even now, as I write my preface, I recognize my enormous intellectual debt to the women historians of labor who have preceded me—from Alice Henry and Theresa Wolfson to Alice Kessler-Harris and Ruth Milkman. In important ways, their mastery of the economic and social changes in the labor movement has allowed me the freedom to write a more political and cultural account. In this, I also must acknowledge the influence of other heroes whose work first prompted me to study women—Adrienne Rich, Mary Heaton Vorse, and Meridel Le Sueur.

The main argument of this book is that women workers, for the major portion of twentieth-century history, were either ignored or alienated by a labor movement that failed to acknowledge the connections between productive and reproductive labor and the importance of women's work to the family economy. This failure was and is rooted first in the male dominance of the public arena of the labor movement and second in labor theory which failed to acknowledge the connections between community and workplace.

As I studied unions and their history, I became increasingly aware of the problems and limitations of the labor movement and its institutions, particularly with regard to women. But even as I must chronicle some of the failures and limitations of the labor leadership and root the decline of contemporary unions in the decisions of the 1930s, so must I claim that it is not the labor ideal itself that has failed but only its practitioners.

On the verge of the Great Depression, Mary Beard wrote, "Even though [the labor movement] may always remain a minority movement in point of membership among workers, it will exercise the power that a minority always exercises in proportion to its clearness of purpose, its efficiency of organization, and the integrity of its directors."[2] Inasmuch as the labor Left demonstrated courage and leadership on the issues of rank and file democracy, control over workplace conditions, and gender and race equality, it had power to change them and American society. Its struggle for autonomy, dignity, and decent standards of living had and still has a heroic quality in a world where poverty, disease, and the increasing control of corporations over our daily lives are reality.

As an author who is both celebratory of labor's potential for change and critical of its policies toward women, I have created a narrative that bears a moral—much like a nineteenth-century novel. I recognize and claim the moral will behind it, which results partly from my reading of Hayden White's theory of emplotment.[3] Reading *Jane Eyre* twice while I was writing this book no doubt also has played a part. In some respects, the romance of the labor movement and the working class bears resemblance to the romance of Jane and Fairfax Rochester. The history of the labor movement is filled with ghosts, a little madness, passion, denial, fall, and redemption. By daring to be critical, I emphasize how this redemption might have been extended to women as well.

Some might argue that the moral is superfluous to *Jane Eyre*. Morals, they say, ought to be banished from writing as just literary convention. But I doubt Charlotte Brontë would have thought so. Inasmuch as her novels are full of storm and emotion, Brontë's gentle wedding of passion and morality seems appropriate in a world where one of the strongest claims of the vulnerable—whether male or female—is their right and will to justice. This history I have written is a small contribution to those struggles.

Acknowledgments

I have been working on the ideas in this book for a few years. Needless to say, the debts I incurred along the way—both personal and intellectual—are far beyond the capacity of this debtor to pay. Acknowledgment can only be a token of my esteem for those who gave freely of their time, ideas, and affection. First, I must thank Sara Evans, who first taught me women's history. She was a model advisor, critiquing initial drafts of the present book and suggesting needed revisions. More than that, she and another scholar, Mary Jo Maynes, taught me something about how one reconciles the contradictory demands of being historians, professionals, and human beings. This book would be a poorer thing if Sara and MJ had not been insightful mentors and careful critics. It might not have been completed at all but for their encouragement.

During my residence in Rochester, Bonnie Smith was a provocative mentor and a good friend. Her careful reading of the manuscript gave me insight into the art and craft of historical writing; it also improved the book. Nell Painter, Ruth Milkman, Daniel Walkowitz, Mari Jo Buhle, Rus Menard, and John Modell read an early version of the manuscript and contributed to refining the study. Ava Baron, Nancy Hewitt, and Angel Kwolek-Folland helped me rethink crucial aspects of the argument; they demonstrated as well that scholarship and sisterhood are mutually reinforcing. Participants in the History and Society Writing Workshop at the University of Minnesota in the winter of 1987 (Kai Eriksen, Barbara Laslett, Allan Isaacman, Ron Aminzade, Barbara Hanawalt, Helga Leitner, and Davida Alperin) extended wise and friendly advice on rewriting the introduction. Paula Baker, Susan Porter Benson, Stanley Engerman, Lynn Gordon, Cathy Kelly, Earl Lewis, Barbara Nelson, Peter Rachleff, Steve Ruggles, Edward Tebbenhoff, Louise Tilly, and Mary Young read parts of the manuscript; the final text benefited from their criticism. With a renewed sense of the importance of good editors, I want to thank mine at the University of North Carolina Press—Iris Hill, Kate Torrey, Sandra Eisdorfer, and Stephanie Sugioka.

I finished revising the manuscript while I was a Susan B. Anthony Post-Doctoral Fellow in Women's Studies at the University of Rochester. Beyond subsistence, the Women's Studies Center provided me with the use of a computer and staff support (the humor and labor of June Miller, Alice Powell, and Elizabeth Ormond). I received additional research support from the Department of History, the College of Liberal Arts, and the Graduate School of the University of Minnesota. The Russell Sage Foundation funded initial research on women in the Farmer-Labor party. For their extraordinary efforts, I want to thank the staff of the Minnesota Historical Society, especially Dallas Lindgren and Debbie Miller; Dave Klaasen of the Social Welfare History Archives at the University of Minnesota; David Rosenberg of the UE Archives at the University of Pittsburgh; Jerry Hess at the National Archives in Washington, D.C.; and Martha Hodges of the Labor-Management Documentation Center at Cornell University.

On a more personal level, I want to thank Paula Nemes and Steven Rasmusson, whose home has been a refuge for an occasionally weary scholar. The poetry group to which both Paula and I belong has been my artistic refuge; Florence Timmerman makes it all possible by providing encouragement and the necessary space. For their companionship in Rochester, I thank Celia Applegate and Stewart Weaver. For their friendship, I celebrate Jan Boyer, Jill Busse, Pat Gaarder, Jo Goodwin, Pat Hanzel, Natalie Reciputi, Mary Ellen Waller, Kimberly Welch, and Anne Winkler. Jeff Stewart and Steve Gross, while they aided my research in other ways, served me best by being fellow buccaneers. Graduate students at the University of Rochester served the project by diverting me with both intellectual engagement and entertainment; in this endeavor, Bill Harkins played a major role. Although Doreen Savage did not live to see the completion of this book, she helped to shape this prose.

My brother Jeffrey, his wife Alice, and my sister Annamarie have given critical support at various stages of this project. My other siblings (Charlotte, Deborah, Gregory, Marcia, and Paul) and their families have been wonderful distractions. My parents, Vincent Faue and Yvonne Skrade, although they haven't always understood or approved, have tolerated and inspired this work. This volume is dedicated to what I perceive as the future: the children of my given and chosen kin.

Community
of Suffering
& Struggle

As long as there is work on wood, on metal, or upon the soil, or as man bears down and changes the nature of his work, and his social relationship, there will be a culture of work and struggle. Community of suffering, of need, of menace, makes the democratic meeting out of which comes the struggle, the organization, the poem, the song.
—Meridel Le Sueur, 1958

Introduction

Community and Workplace in the History of U.S. Labor

That's what I call "the fetish of being outside." It makes a big difference whether you see the world from "inside" or "outside." It affects how you see politics and how you see people.
—Meridel Le Sueur, 1935

"A woman's movement is arising in this country which is among the greatest the world has ever known," wrote journalist Mary Heaton Vorse in *Labor's New Millions*.[1] Vorse was writing in the 1930s, a decade known more for its class than its gender consciousness. Her sense of the possibility of women's empowerment through union organization is puzzling in the light of contemporary feminist evaluations. In the 1930s, however, Vorse's recognition of the strength of the labor movement as a voice for women echoed that of other observers. This was the decade, some argued, that would witness the final triumph of women's struggle for equality.[2] Labor leaders assumed that women would be organized with the men of their class, and the labor movement of the 1930s was celebrated in its time as a democratic movement of workers, egalitarian in spirit if predominantly male in membership.

American City, an account of labor struggle in the 1930s by writer Charles Rumford Walker, presented a different view. While Walker sought to explore "the lives of individuals, in their ways of making a living, in their emotions and in their basic beliefs," he emphasized the "economic bones" of one event: the Minneapolis truckers' strike of 1934. Written in heroic prose, Walker's Minneapolis is the scene of an epic confrontation between the robber barons and the rank and file. This is social history at its most vivid, where the terrain of struggle is located in the hearts and minds of men who work, cuss, marry, play baseball, and—if pushed to the limit—revolt against oppressive and hostile employers. But *American City* is a city of men—unemployed laborers, miners, farmers, and truck drivers; and the women's movement Vorse envisioned disappears in the smoke of battle.

Vorse and Walker presented contrasting perspectives on the political culture of labor. Although both authors emphasized the democratic impulse in the labor-Left coalition of the 1930s, they differed sharply in their perception of class and in their evaluation of labor's strength and goals. For Walker, an educated man who worked in steel and copper mills for a few years and wrote extensively as a journalist, the essence of working-class culture was politics. Walker found evidence of this culture in "a May Day demonstration, the annual union picnic, the Ness Memorial Day demonstration held once a year in the Minneapolis market where Ness was shot."[3]

Behind Walker's deep admiration of working-class organization was the belief that the working class had no internal life of its own. He argued that it mimicked middle-class culture as "in everyday life [the working class] tend[ed] with slenderer means to approximate the social fashions and cultural content handed to it." In Walker's view, "Trotsky's remark that the culture of the working class is *politics* is clearly enough illustrated in Minneapolis. The political and economic ideas, the organizational forms, the speeches, songs and heroes which proceed from its struggles are its only original class contributions to cultural content."[4] Walker argued that only during crises did workers respond with "the faint beginnings of an original culture." Only in the politics of work and struggle did they "produce leaders, think up fresh forms of organization and strategy, and above all scan skeptically their own relation to the rest of society."[5]

In contrast to Walker's narrow vision of labor as a political movement, Vorse recognized that the new unionism of the 1930s "[did] not stop at the formal lodge meeting. It [saw] the union as a way of life which [involved] the entire community."[6] If the factory was "the pivot of all organizational effort," the community was its sustenance. Worker education, the women's auxiliary movement, union culture, and a strong labor press demonstrated how the labor movement was being reborn through the community.[7]

At the heart of this vision was the family. Vorse believed that the desire of workers for a better life for their children was at the root of their militancy and their desperation. In her autobiography, *Footnote to Folly*, she wrote: "For when you come down to it, the labor movement is about children and about homes. In the last analysis, civilization itself is measured by the way in which children will live and what chance they will have in the world. . . . The workers feel this instinctively. Their immediate way of helping children to live in a better world is by a union."[8] During the economic crisis of the 1930s, the family, which was the ultimate reason for labor's victory, also became its primary defense against despair. "In the modern strike," Vorse argued, "all the working community is involved." Women and men, mothers, fathers, daughters and sons played their roles in the drama of labor.[9]

This vision of a community-based labor movement was a product of Vorse's own long experience in that movement. Beginning in 1912 when she first reported on the Lawrence strike, Vorse witnessed the growth, repression, and rebirth of labor unions. She worked as an organizer in the clothing trades and had close ties to the European as well as the American labor movement. In all her writing, Vorse focused consistently on the values and needs of the workers themselves. One critic wrote, "There was very little about her in all that she wrote about the battles, ancient and modern; most of them were, in fact, the records of the ordinary talk of strikers and their wives, spare and low key language, all of it exactly as spoken because Mary Vorse knew that the one thing most dangerous to falsify is the speech of men."[10]

As a woman, Vorse also witnessed a part of the labor struggle invisible to many of her male peers. She had worked in strike commissaries and in workers' homes. Above all Vorse knew the women who supported labor's struggle. For Walker, the central stage of the movement was in the streets, which were an extension of the shopfloor; for Vorse, it was in Pengally Hall (in Flint, Michigan, where the Women's Emergency Brigade met), a community arena where women spoke publicly for the first time in their lives.[11]

These contrasting pictures suggest that even as workers in the 1930s made a common history, they differed in their beliefs concerning the nature of working-class community and the appropriate terrain for labor organization.[12] Vorse and Walker expressed conflicts in attitudes and goals that occurred both between and among working-class men and women. Divided by skill, gender, race, and ethnicity, workers also differed in the solutions they proposed to the problems of community. Solidarity there was, but conflicting opinions fostered a debate about the future that was resolved only when labor unions narrowed their scope of organization and allowed more expansive expressions to be silenced.

This book is about women workers and the various bases for organization in Minneapolis during the most important epoch in United States labor history, the decades between 1915 and 1945. The prospects for a broadly based labor movement looked bleak after the labor insurgency of 1919 to 1922. An open shop campaign, growing nativist and racist activity, a government-led assault on radical organizations, and internal dissent threatened to destroy the labor movement. But, despite the high unemployment and mass suffering of the Great Depression, community-based grassroots militancy revitalized working-class organization as men and women took the path of democratic participation. The 1930s represented a window of opportunity for a labor movement that had struggled against overwhelming odds to retain its institutional existence. Prolonged economic crisis, the growth of the welfare state, and war mobilization changed the context of unionism as the labor movement increasingly developed bureaucratic and routinized relationships with workers and further marginalized the women in its ranks.

Community and Workplace in Labor History

From the origins of working-class politics in the popular protest of the eighteenth century to the emergence of contemporary bureaucratic unions, workers have chosen the terrain of struggle on which to build a labor movement. They have shifted the emphasis toward and away from the community; they have incorporated state strategies and excluded them; they have focused their energies on the narrow terrain of craft identity or extended the arena of activism from shopfloors to streets, churches, homes, and legislatures.

The participation of women and men varied in these configurations of labor. At times, workers' definition of labor solidarity required women's inclusion on an equal basis with men—both as workers and as the wives of workers; at other times, solidarity was seen as incompatible with gender and ethnic competition. People supporting either model of unionism could and did belong to the labor movement at the same time.

One of the major factors determining women's participation was the extent to which the labor movement was defined by community concerns. Community-based unionism emphasized local autonomy and community-level organization even as it opposed bureaucratic unionism. It invested organizing strategies with a reliance on personal networks, on connections with local institutions and especially with citywide labor organizations, and on the use of community as a model to recruit workers into the union. Further, community-based unions developed languages and rituals which embraced a broad definition of solidarity. In turn, women joined workplace and union struggles and brought labor concerns into the community arena.[13]

During the political and economic upheaval in the eighteenth-century United States, free workers organized in defense of community and livelihood without seeing any contradiction in these objectives. As artisans, they made their living in settings where family, work, and community were overlapping realms. The married woman was both productive worker and household manager; the daughter or son both worker and dependent; the male household head both employer and patriarch. Central to systems of production and exchange, kinship networks remained an integral part of the ways in which workers responded to the claims of class and community; the families which recruited and organized labor often mobilized protest as well.[14]

Collective action in these settings was a response to the failure of customary obligations between rich and poor, landed and landless. In the moral economy of village and town, men and women of the poorer classes focused their discontent on reproductive issues like the price of bread and poor law relief. These solidarities bolstered the fainthearted, empowered the weak, and expressed the bonds of community through demands for a just society. The reliance on communal themes is telling; class as a political category had not yet been relegated to the formal public sphere. Bread riots in the late eighteenth century emerged from communal values; rebellions in the British colonies of North America addressed abusive authority which had abrogated its responsibilities. In these communal actions, there were roles for the entire community. Men, women, and children jointly engaged in the conflicts of early modern capitalism.[15]

With the advent of industrial capitalism, changes in the organization of labor and of kinship rewrote the rules of protest. As productive work became divorced from the family household economy, the demand for a just price changed meaning and context. The workshop, not the moral economy of the community nor the increasingly privatized household, was the principal locus of collective action. Women's protest and dissent were defined outside politics, the arena in which men were engaged. Workshop and trade union increasingly monopolized the arena of collective politics; and those who worked in the household—mothers, female relatives, children—were excluded. Community protests over morality, the price or availability of food, the constitution of a community, and ethnic conflict were seen in increasingly private terms—as the quarrels between neighbors, between women, or between private individuals.[16]

For both the white working and middle classes, collective protest became stylized as masculine behavior. The early Victorian period represented a transition between informal communal politics and those in which protest was formally organized. Although it was uncertain how gender roles and expectations would shape the new politics of protest, craft workers proved to be remarkably responsive to the demands of sentimental patriarchy.[17] As artisans, they forged an identity to reinforce the declining power of individual men in an industrializing society, much as their middle-class counterparts did. They accepted the division of the world into male and female realms and identified the trade union as a male sphere. The union increasingly expressed the values of masculine culture; the tavern and saloon were the incubators of much working-class radicalism. Women workers would be defined outside this laboring culture. As the wives of workers, they had no place at all.[18]

Despite this proscription, women workers engaged in both wage work and collective protest, actions which were defined as public and male. The "mill girls" of Lowell and the women shoemakers of Lynn found in the language of artisan republicanism a place for the daughters of freemen. Participating in what was viewed as an unseemly activity, they "made Mary Wollstonecraft speeches," formed trade unions, and signed legislative petitions. Female tailoresses in Baltimore, Philadelphia, and New York were part of the same movement. On the basis of a wage-earning status, they laid claim to a public role.[19]

The radical separation of male trade unions from their communities was the first stage in the development of the labor movement in the United States. By the end of the Civil War, the organization of workers had emerged as a force for unifying community and workplace concerns. With this reunion, women of the working classes—both with men and separately—acted in the public arena as participants in the labor movement. Identified as advocates for the productive classes—not just for members of a skill, trade, or specific shop—the National Labor Union and its successor, the Knights of Labor, were organizations which combined community concerns with specific workplace issues.[20]

This dual concern for the integrity of community and labor had one of its clearest expressions in the Knights of Labor. The Knights envisioned a society of producers that did not recognize competition among workers on the basis of skill, ethnicity, or race. Drawing on a rich base of working-class and ethnic mutual aid societies, the Knights developed an understanding of labor strategy and organization that emphasized community involvement. Highlighting this connection, the Knights promoted the strategies of the boycott and the cooperative factory; they supported political activity and limited use of the state.[21]

For women, the Knights of Labor provided an important arena for organization. Both as wives and as workers, women Knights asserted their right to public equality.[22] In carpet factories in Yonkers and Philadelphia, among women collar makers in Troy, in overall factories in Minneapolis, women organized to protest low wages and poor working conditions. While women workers shared with men similar complaints on wages, hours, and control of production, they also confronted the contradiction of paternal ideology and sexual harassment in the workplace. Embracing an alternative vision of womanhood, one in which the concerns of community and class were empowering, women found in the Knights' ideology of mutuality themes of justice and social honor that ennobled women as well as men.[23]

By the twentieth century, the ways in which workers experienced and expressed solidarity had begun to change. Fraternal organizations supporting unionism had been built around neighborhoods and ethnic identities, but neither the physical city nor its population stayed the same. In place of the Irish, German, and French Canadian workers came new immigrants from Asia and from eastern and southern Europe and migrant laborers from Mexico. But while the old immigrant groups had some acquaintance with the culture of industrialism, new immigrant men and women were less familiar with the technology and scale of modern industry. Many came from peasant and artisan households, lifeways which had already passed into historical memory for native-born American workers. They viewed the new immigrants' customs, languages, and religions as barriers to solidarity.[24]

The threatened displacement of skilled male workers by new immigrants gave new life to nativism and created divisions in a once unified—if not entirely homogeneous—working-class community. In garment shops, textile factories, and steel mills, managers used ethnic antagonisms to reinforce skill hierarchies, divisions which previously existed along gender and age lines. New methods of production and scientific management undercut workers' control in the workplace and their monopoly on skill, especially in the new mass production industries.[25] Moreover, employers created ethnic and racial tensions among workers by recruiting strikebreakers from the most recent arrivals, including eastern Europeans and southern black migrants. To enforce these changes, businessmen united in local and national trade networks, using the tools of police and state control to suppress unionism even as they used divisions among workers to undermine class solidarity.[26]

Other changes in American society accompanied the rapid growth of industry. Working-class communities, built around factories and workshops in walking cities, dispersed as cities acquired new territory and developed streetcar lines and suburbs.[27] The physical proximity of workers to the factory had aided and abetted protest; now the dispersal of workers into separate neighborhoods and their distance from work mitigated expression of discontent. Ethnic and racial hostility prevented many workers from fusing community and work organizations. Further, leisure now became an arena of division and separation; divided by the forces of age and generation, the privatized family and the private individual assumed a new importance in this realm. Solidarity that had begun in communal arenas of leisure and play was now short-circuited by the privatization of these activities.[28]

Among the new workers in the industrial labor force were increasing numbers of women who worked in domestic, industrial, and clerical positions. Although women and men rarely competed for the same jobs, an influx of women workers into some occupations had been followed by the deskilling of labor and deteriorating wages, a trend which craft unionists used as a rationale for excluding women from other trades. Additional factors impeded the participation of women in the labor movement. Migration in particular proved to be an obstacle to the stable growth of labor unions.[29]

As in the earlier period, the female labor force in the early twentieth century was composed of single women workers who were migrant and sporadic wage earners. For those living apart from family, the absence of connections within the city meant isolation from a potential base of support. Historian Jonathan Prude's insight that workers in the early industrial economy often voted with their feet was true of women as well as men. Solidarity there was, but it was solidarity focused in the community. Both women and men formed their allegiances within networks of neighbors and social groups rather than with co-workers. Personal networks could provide the basis for collective action, but women's mobility usually restricted their options socially and politically. The conditions for women's collective organization had to be built from the ground up in a geographically mobile urban society.[30]

Sex-segregated workplaces also restricted the extent to which women could take part in a labor movement defined by skill and workplace organization alone. In addition, women's family obligations and status influenced their willingness to join the labor movement or any collective protest. Women in homework and cottage industry found that isolation and familial authority prevented collective action; women in sales and clerical work established a work culture which often deterred them from identifying with the labor movement.[31]

During this period, as married women were increasingly isolated outside the productive wage economy, their importance in the reproductive realm of family and community grew. Because working-class incomes had to be balanced between precarious resources and constant needs, women's skills as consumers and managers became the margin between mere survival and a decent standard of living. These dynamics took on political shape and meaning in urban communities. As mothers, consumers, and community members, women took to the streets to defend the family against the encroachments of capital. This was not merely the extension of domesticity to the political realm. Rent strikes, meat boycotts, mass demonstrations against police abuses were new forms of protest that pointed to the emergence of class politics in the urban sphere of social reproduction.[32]

Despite this revitalization of urban protest, the vision of the Knights of Labor that "an injury to one is an injury to all" faded into memory. Craft-based unions fought over jurisdictional lines, undermining organizations of unskilled workers. In a work force sharply divided along ethnic, racial, and gender lines, the labor movement's emphasis on skilled workers amounted to the effective exclusion of black and immigrant men and of almost all women workers. Moreover, exclusionary rules often carried over into the sphere of public policy, where unions argued for restriction of immigration, Jim Crow legislation in the trades, and protective legislation for women workers, which amounted to discriminatory constraints on their work force participation.[33]

The American Federation of Labor (AFL) was a central force in these battles. Having gained hegemony during the late nineteenth century, it operated on the assumption that workers could only be organized through the craft brotherhoods. It emphasized the public character of solidarity and the importance of male bonds forged in the workplace. More important, AFL president Samuel Gompers perceived that the wider labor's grasp and the farther its reach beyond the workplace, the more likely it was to be repressed by the state, a policy that historian Bruce Laurie has termed "prudential unionism." The AFL saw its mission as protecting the interests of male craft workers on the shopfloor, a goal which ideally would defend the wages of workers everywhere. In this context, the federation argued that the solution to the economic problems of workers was a family wage for working men.[34]

In the culture of craft solidarity, women were defined outside the sphere of work. Further, the sex-segregated labor force did not provide the preconditions of sexual equality and integration of a class-based labor movement. Finally, control of the labor movement itself—with its system of economic, political, and social rewards—had long been held by men. This fact had established the labor union as a male sphere of activity. As in the political arena, men proved resistant to attempts by women to infiltrate or join the ranks.[35]

One answer to the problem was the creation of autonomous organizations for women workers. The Women's Trade Union League (WTUL) led the way with its support of women's collective organizations in the garment, clerical, and telephone industries. Using tactics which recognized and celebrated difference between men and women workers, the WTUL sought to reshape the experience and meaning of unionism. It sponsored a union journal, *Life and Labor*, which addressed working women specifically; it developed a leadership school and remade the culture of unionism with its attention to educational and cultural programs. To the effort, WTUL women brought a collective identity that crossed class boundaries and a politicized and secular ideal of motherhood grounded in theories of sexual difference. In fact, the WTUL relied on community support for working women's plight, based on their special need for protection. Such a stance implicitly renounced claims of equality within the labor movement and later justified opposition to the Equal Rights Amendment. It also implied that feminine solidarity was neither auxiliary nor complementary to the masculine solidarity of labor; rather it implicitly defined women's activism outside the bounds of the working-class community.[36]

While the AFL refined its workplace strategies and the WTUL created cross-class gender alliances with working women, some workers developed alternatives. The massive influx of immigrant, ethnic, and minority men and women into the labor force created possibilities as well as obstacles for labor organizers. In the absence of any AFL initiative, labor organizers and socialists—prominent among them Western Federation of Miners' Big Bill Haywood, socialist Eugene Debs, and Mother Jones—established the Industrial Workers of the World (IWW) to revive unionism among the unorganized.[37] Carrying the banner of industrial unionism, the IWW organized timber workers and miners, domestic servants, and textile workers—the native-born and the foreign. It called for the opening of the labor movement and its extension beyond business unionism as a movement for all working people. With this as its goal, the IWW made room for the organizing and the unorganized.[38]

Among those embracing the ideal of "One Big Union," harvest workers and western miners provided the initial base for the IWW. Like the craft unions they despised, IWW members, or Wobblies, believed that strength and solidarity could only be constructed at the point of production. Sabotage, not wage negotiation, was the strategy of choice. Wobblies also identified the union with masculine struggle; their popular image was single, transient, and male.[39] Celebrated in the art of *The Masses*, the Wobbly embodied brute labor as well as brute force, engaged in fierce class struggle, unfettered by family ties. As a member of the lumpenproletariat, the Wobbly neither respected nor engaged in the building of community.[40]

As the IWW emerged as a symbol of solidarity, workers from other industries and locals appealed for its help. In joining, they shifted the image and strategy of the union. On the Iron Range in Minnesota, mining unions—unlike their western counterparts—were a product of immigrant communities and ethnic associations. As family men, the Finnish and Slavic miners of the Mesabi found solidarity in the defense of home and with the support of women and children. In the textile strikes in Lawrence, Massachusetts, and Paterson, New Jersey, workers recreated a community-based unionism through the IWW. A range of immigrant groups was represented on the organizing committees; ethnic associations supported the strike; and the organizers themselves came from multilingual communities. Merging the concerns of work and home, gender and ethnicity, these local variations of the Wobbly ideal transformed workplace concerns into community ones.[41]

Unlike the Knights who came before them, the IWWs failed to establish organizations to sustain these connections. Although they believed that the lack of permanent unions would guard against complacency, too often the strategy weakened already fragile bonds between ethnic groups and undermined alliances between skilled and unskilled workers. Further, the absence of an industrial union could lead to the use of organized craft unions to divide the industrial labor force—as in the Paterson strike of 1913 or the Steel Strike of 1919. Conflict over U.S. entry into World War I and the Russian Revolution exacerbated rifts within the working-class community. Repressive labor legislation and threats of deportation during the Palmer raids of 1919–20 removed many industrial and community unionists from active labor organization. Even the mass strikes of 1929, which were constructed on the bases of kinship, community, and union, could not revitalize the communal tradition in labor. Not until the Great Depression did workers, reviving the concept of labor as a community, heal their divisions.[42]

During the 1930s, men and women workers rebuilt the labor movement with a strategy that went beyond both the exclusive craft orientation of the AFL and the corporate unionism of the later years of the Congress of Industrial Organizations (CIO). They rooted unions in the community and directed their attention to what can be described as the reproductive sphere—specifically, consumer concerns, family and community networks, and education. In Minneapolis, San Francisco, Akron, Toledo, Flint, and the cities of New England, the labor movement was strengthened by networks of sociability, ethnic association, and political affiliation. Working-class activism through 1937 was local activism, at times encouraged by but kept at a distance from established bureaucratic union structures.[43]

For women, the new orientation of the labor movement in the 1930s was crucial. During these decades, economic crisis highlighted the importance of their wage and domestic labor to the family economy.[44] Further, women joined the labor force in greater numbers, for a longer period, and increasingly after marriage. These changes opened up an historic opportunity for the integration of women into the labor movement. Encouraged by an egalitarian call to organize the unorganized and make their cities union towns, women joined unions in the workplace and formed auxiliary units. They engaged in strategies of solidarity including strike support, boycotts, union label purchasing, education, and political action in behalf of labor.[45]

The involvement of women in mobilizing labor's new millions varied according to the strength of their organization in the local community. In towns where women had an independent voice, their concerns—which linked labor and social provision, as did the Farmer-Labor movement in Minnesota—formed an integral part of the labor program. But where trade unions dominated, bureaucratic unionism flourished, and women remained in a marginal role. The labor movement of the 1930s thus had tremendous local variations and conflicting and contradictory approaches to women and political activity.[46]

One of the causes of these contradictions was the extent to which the communally based unionism of the 1930s capitalized not on women as workers but rather on their role as nurturers and moral guardians within the working-class community.[47] Women worked in auxiliaries during strikes and supported their male kin, partners, and peers with coffee, donuts, and bandages. Although women often demonstrated their militancy on the picket line, their role in the labor community was basically seen as supportive. As wives and as daughters, they were responsible for the raising of funds and morale. In staffing commissaries and demanding relief for workers during and after strikes, women could express their support for a strong union movement; but they were excluded from participation in decision making.[48]

By the 1940s, the labor movement again became more exclusively tied to the workplace. There had been preexisting tendencies toward bureaucratization within the labor movement, and the length and severity of the economic crisis reinforced the trend. First, national unions reasserted control over unions in the local arena. The appointment of professional organizers, business agents, and educational directors was part of an overall strategy to concentrate labor's power on the national political scene and within the economic structure. Allegiance to the Democratic party put continuous pressure on labor leaders to fill a conciliatory role.[49]

Under the New Deal, the expanded state role in labor relations was crucial to the process of union bureaucratization. New guidelines for arbitration at the National Labor Relations Board straitjacketed community strategies of boycott and political intervention and required unions to specialize in labor law.[50] Beyond the realm of negotiations, labor unions were engaged in the struggle to create federal social insurance. The New Deal coalition sponsored programs for social security, unemployment insurance, and aid to dependent children. Allied with the Democratic party, national unions advocated social support for workers, augmenting union wages with federal entitlement programs.[51]

While the transfer of these functions to the state benefited both men and women workers, it did so unequally. The National Labor Relations Board regularized union elections and disputes but restricted the community-based strategies in which women had been central. Further, the dual-track welfare state privileged skilled, industrial wage earners and disadvantaged those who were not engaged in regular, continuous employment—a category into which the majority of women and minority workers fell. Arguments for the provision of maternity insurance and leave were defeated as impractical and even antifamily; social security was defined narrowly in order to insure its passage in the face of extensive opposition.[52] The success of the welfare program and the New Deal coalition seemed further to cement the control of national labor leaders over local coalitions and community-oriented programs. Finally, the growth of a war economy with the severe regulation of manpower and labor relations encouraged the trend toward corporate unionism.[53]

The decline of community-based unionism and the subsequent invisibility of women in the labor movement can be further explained by the social and cultural upheavals of the depression decade. The crisis reinforced the family's importance as an aspect of the economy and as a metaphor. Widespread unemployment led to both a material and a sentimental dependence on family ties and on the psychological compensation of family authority. Reliance on family, and on the promise of the family wage, exacerbated hostility toward those who fell outside its boundaries. For these reasons, women workers, especially those who were married, sometimes became targets in a working-class politics sparked by prolonged economic crisis.[54]

These themes surfaced in labor's political culture during the 1930s. Employing metaphors of sport and struggle, the labor press portrayed the worker and work as male; it created heroes in a narrative of solidarity born through violence and sacrifice. While the language of labor relied on an understanding of union as brotherhood, the image of masculine solidarity expressed hostility toward and competed with familial metaphors. Departing from a nineteenth-century political culture which integrated women on the basis of their role as Republican mother and workingman's wife, the laboring culture of the 1930s initially excluded women from its icons. In the symbolic discourse of the labor movement, female imagery emerged only to depict victimization and to portray impersonal forces of want and need. Women's absence from labor's language and iconography, remedied only by the emergence of Popular Front ideology in the latter part of the decade, reinforced the institutional marginality of women workers in the labor movement.[55]

Employing a rhetoric of equality that embraced all workers regardless of skill, race and ethnicity, or gender, the labor movement of the 1930s nevertheless encountered the resilience of familial, racial, and political ideology. The exclusion of women thus took place on two different grounds: women were excluded from leadership positions and even union membership, and they were absent from the symbolic system of labor culture. Despite the importance of women's paid employment to the family economy in a time of crisis, the labor movement at the end of the depression decade was only slightly more responsive to women's participation and leadership than its historical predecessors.[56] When bureaucratic and national unionism prevailed under the New Deal, so did women's continued marginality in the labor movement.

Class and Gender in Labor History

The divide between community and workplace organization in the labor movement mirrored social theory. Perceiving the world in terms of a public/private dichotomy, one tradition identified class through formal economic and political struggle; another tradition, predating industrial capitalism, saw class relations as an expression of community concerns.[57] The major question for both was the extent to which production assumed a primary or determining role in the constitution of class. Only in those systems of thought which recognized the centrality of symbolic and biological reproduction was women's activism and participation considered vital.[58]

The meaning of class has changed considerably over time. Early eighteenth-century usage equated class with special interest. The democratic revolutions of the nineteenth century, however, transformed the meaning of work and economy; once recognized as individual and private, they became collective and political terms. For the emergent bourgeois and artisan classes who first experienced industrial change, the arenas of workplace and home became radically separate and distinct.[59]

Class came to be understood solely as the relationship of workers to the means of production. Cultural agency and expression mediated this relationship, but class was fundamentally public—rooted in workplace structure and political participation. Paralleled in the European tradition of social theory, the concept of class was further restricted to its expression through economic and political conflict.[60] This shift in struggle to the point of production, as the working-class center of gravity was removed to the workplace, distorted the relationship between community and work politics.[61]

E. P. Thompson's definition, quoted extensively as the model for the new social history of labor, posits class as a historical relationship created by men (his usage) as they perceive their interests collectively and in opposition to those of other men. In *The Making of the English Working*

Class, Thompson's subject was the formation of working-class consciousness through political activity. Other, more recent works exemplify this equation of class with public and workplace expression, particularly as it affected male workers. In *The Fall of the House of Labor*, David Montgomery characterizes the family as "a nursery of class consciousness"; but at the same time he argues that "working men's experience introduced them to class first and foremost through conflict at the workplace." By associating men with workplace and public activity and women with private and communal mutual aid, Montgomery echoes Thompson's definition. Similarly, in another recent study, we are told that "a job and a workplace give an individual a class identity."[62] These studies assume that class solidarity occurs in the public realm, an arena which in nineteenth-century ideology was increasingly assigned to men. The problem is that the kind of information we have about men and about women differs substantially. We have learned that working-class women framed their work lives and protests in the context of familial obligation; we know less about how men connected their family and work identities.

For working women, the boundaries between home and work, community and polity were not formidable obstacles to action in the public sphere. These barriers, firmly established in modern social theory from Tocqueville and Durkheim to the present day, did not seem unbreachable to working-class women and men. The public character of communal unionism created its own logic of solidarity, parallel to the public notion of a class for itself. More important, one of the preconditions for women's participation in social movements historically has been an understanding of the connection between women's wage labor and their family labor and of the permeability of these aspects of their lives. As historian Louise Tilly has argued, women's collective action must be seen as a continuum of community and workplace protest that varies with the life course and work situation. The same might well be true of men.[63]

There were alternative visions of both class and political struggle in the early nineteenth century. Utopian socialism encouraged the development of broad strategies for social change, incorporating family, community, and workplace organizations. More important, the designation of work as a male activity—and work organization as necessarily male dominated— varied with respect to the family economies of workers. Where the family with only one wage earner dominated, laboring men organized protest almost exclusively through the workplace; where the incomes of wives and children as well as men were necessary to sustain the family, workers were more likely to adopt a strategy of protest which connected community and family.[64]

In socialist thought, the concept of labor could encompass family labor as well as wage labor, a dualism which made sexual and familial issues central to socialism as an ideology. European and American followers of Owen, Fourier, and Saint-Simon experimented with the sexual and social order; moreover, women's concern for public equality was recognized on the Left as literature proliferated on the woman question. Implicit in these arguments was an acceptance of sexual difference in tandem with the contradictory promise of public equality. But although gender ideology and practice were socially constructed in the parameters of the welfare state, the discourse of public morality, and even in the sphere of production as it was defined as both primary and masculine, they remained unexamined in the larger debates over women's equality.[65]

In fact, socialists and trade unionists characterized the bourgeois women's movement as individualist and class oriented, assuming that individual identity—republican virtue and citizenship—was first created in the home and only secondarily in the public sphere. They followed the lead of liberal political theorists in assuming that public behavior was disconnected from power relations in the private realm. The source of women's oppression therefore was widely recognized as the private family, created as a conduit for the transmission of property and the care of children.[66] Outside of this realm, socialists argued, women should be organized with the men of their class. Engaged in the struggle against employers, women workers were assumed to have the same relation to and experience of work as men.

The failure of the community-based tradition of the Left to confront the issue of female subordination had serious consequences for the long-term development of labor ideology. In the first instance, it led to the contradictions the labor movement experienced in the 1930s—the importance of women's work, their presence in the ranks of organized labor, and their marginality to and exclusion from the centers of power.[67] Further, the labor movement carried this intellectual separation between the spheres of home and work into its analysis of how to organize, who should be organized, and whose jobs would be protected.

In the family economy idealized by the labor movement, men and women had differing responsibilities and roles, unaltered by the increased presence of women in the labor force. Despite egalitarian approaches to the organization of the unskilled, unionists believed that the rights of women were different. Women's right to a decent living included the right to carry out their role within the nuclear family to raise and nurture children, but not rights to a job or to pay equity with working men.

Labor's debate over the character and meaning of workplace, community, and political struggle which began in the eighteenth century continued into the twentieth. Faced with an economic crisis of almost unprecedented proportions, one in which men were disproportionately unemployed, the labor movement shifted from advocating the claims of working-class families to advocating the rights of men alone and back again. Throughout its history, labor solidarity took on gendered meanings and forms. The subordination of the family metaphor to the individualist and masculine language of labor was only the temporary intensification and uneasy resolution of a century-long debate over the public meaning of class and the efficacy of workplace struggle.

Scope of the Book

A community-based labor movement arose in Minneapolis during the 1930s. It could be witnessed in the ringing evocation of the "gospel of unity and unionism," in the solidarity of picket lines, and in public rituals such as Labor Day picnics and mass funerals mourning strike victims. This movement grew under the leadership of union activists in the trucking industry and among other leftist labor organizers in the skilled trades, in garment shops and textile factories, and among the unemployed. While it was strongest in the industrial sector, the movement also recruited clerical and service workers, revitalized party politics, and shaped the growth of the welfare state. Its decline in the wake of increasingly bureaucratized, national unions forms the narrative of this book.

The study is organized into three parts. First, it outlines the patterns of women's work and family lives in Minneapolis in the period between 1910 and 1940. It shows the possibilities of both isolation and community as they existed in the city circa 1935. After this foray, it explores the existence and progress of the labor community in Minneapolis from 1915 to 1935. The narrative of political development illuminates the evolving pattern of working-class activism—from the pluralistic design of the prewar labor movement to the Popular Front of the 1930s.

Second, the book focuses on the creation, decline, and rebirth of a community-based labor movement in Minneapolis during the depression decade. It examines the union campaigns of the 1930s and considers the consequences of community-based versus workplace-oriented unionism for women. The activism of the Farmer-Labor Association and its women's federation, the General Drivers' union, and the Communist party helped to set the stage for the rebirth of unionism. Revitalizing unions in the garment and textile industries and organizing clerical and Works Progress Administration (WPA) workers, activist women represented a growing proportion of the female labor force. Despite their presence, the culture of the labor movement and its increasingly violent language defined solidarity in masculine terms.

The connections between gender, work, and solidarity were expressed in the 1939 WPA strike. Initially, the labor movement aided the unemployed in their demands for relief and organizational sanctions. By 1939, however, labor's advocacy shifted away from the rights of the unemployed to the rights of relief workers. During the protest, some of the most violent scenes occurred at places where women were employed. The anger directed at women as strikers and as scabs revealed deep social tensions that had much to do with the collision between gender-neutral ideals of equality and gendered perceptions of difference.

The book concludes by examining the transformation of labor solidarity during World War II. The decline in militancy was reflected in labor's shift away from a community base to a more narrowly defined workplace unionism, a shift rationalized in terms both of efficiency and patriotism. The drive for a war victory justified a more tightly controlled unionism, and the use of national themes in defense of labor's rights and the emphasis on family masked the growing reluctance of the labor movement to foster local autonomy. Despite the occasional emphasis on equality, as in equal pay demands, the departure from local union autonomy alienated those workers—especially women—for whom the laboring community meant reaching beyond the workplace.

This study takes place in the historically specific circumstances of Minneapolis in the years after World War I. Certain features of the city are important to note. While neither its economy nor the composition of its population were unique, they differed from some cities in which unionism has been studied. Most important, minority groups in Minneapolis—as in a few smaller northern cities—constituted only a tiny proportion of the population. Further, Minneapolis had a diverse and commercially based economy, in contrast to single-industry cities such as Detroit, Steelton, and Manchester.[68]

Finally, Minneapolis had a large and politically active ethnic population. Eastern Europeans constituted a small fraction of the ethnic population, but the city had heavy concentrations of first- and second-generation Swedish, Norwegian, and Finnish Americans. These ethnic groups had a strong ideological affinity for democratic socialism, expressed through the Socialist party, the Non-Partisan League and the Farmer-Labor Association, the Communist League (the Socialist Workers' party), and the Communist party.[69] The strength of the Left had an enormous influence on the emergence and success of militant unionism in the 1930s. There was a legacy of consumer cooperation, worker education, and the linking of community and workplace politics.

For these reasons, Minneapolis during the 1930s is an important case study of how women fare in social movements based on class. If women were to be recruited into the labor movement on the basis of equality, it would have been in those areas of the country where both labor unions and female employment were expanding. And yet, as we shall see, women remained in a marginal and subordinated position in that movement, excluded both from the arrangements of power and from the symbolic system of labor. That this happened, in the highly favorable circumstances that prevailed in the 1930s, is testimony to the deeply rooted sexism and racism of the American labor movement and the society in which it operated.[70]

In her essay, "The Fetish of Being Outside," Meridel Le Sueur, a midwestern poet and activist, admonishes us to avoid distancing ourselves from our subjects. This book is in some ways inspired by Le Sueur's dictum to see the world, and especially the people's history, from the inside. Like Mary Heaton Vorse, Le Sueur was a celebrant of the alternative tradition of a working-class movement; family and community were essential to her vision of organizing workers. In Le Sueur's writing, the streets, the homes, the factories, and even the lifeways of workers are part of the same cloth. It is a sentiment that the men and women workers of Minneapolis in the 1930s would have understood and shared.

One

Women in the American City, 1910–1940

Few will dispute that Minneapolis shares a cultural common denominator with all America as surely as any other city. But in other ways I believe her history exemplifies more sharply than most the impact of forces that are typical and universal. . . . Most of the diseases of our economic system visit the city, in a more acute stage— but the maladies are universal ones.
—Charles Rumford Walker, 1937

My mama had told me that the cities were Sodom and Gomorrah, and terrible things could be happening to you, which made me scared most of the time.
—Meridel Le Sueur, 1978

In Meridel Le Sueur's novel, *The Girl*, a young woman migrates to the Twin Cities in the midst of a farm depression. Her family is in desperate circumstances. The farm is failing, and it can no longer support all the family members. As the oldest daughter, the female hero has been her mother's chief aid in making ends meet. Now she must leave the farm so that there will be one less person to feed. Her mother lets the Girl go reluctantly, knowing what the city does to young women; poverty, perhaps even prostitution, will be her daughter's lot as it had been her sister Marilyn's before her. In the cities, the Girl finds a job as a barmaid, learns about sex and abuse from her lover, and gives birth to a child in a community of women on relief.[1]

Le Sueur's story of women in the cities is a narrative of economic and psychological deprivation, sexual awakening and personal loss, and communal struggle. Based on the experiences of women Le Sueur met through her workers' education classes, the novel reveals extreme but real consequences of working-class women's vulnerability in the depression.[2] Most women who migrated to the cities avoided the nightmarish fate of Le Sueur's female protagonist and the dire predictions of her mother. But in the interwar years, urban working women in Minneapolis—single, married, divorced, or widowed; native or foreign born; white or black; migrant or city born—came face to face with economic crisis, exploitation, and the need for collective action. What concerns us in this chapter is the change in men's and women's work and family lives which made activism both possible and significant during the interwar period.

Certainly, one of the most important changes was the increasing role of women as wage earners. Even during the massive unemployment of the Great Depression, women continued to join the labor force in numbers. Despite vocal public opposition to their employment, married women contributed to this trend. Further, in contrast to the declining industrial economy, clerical and sales jobs were on the increase during the twentieth century. It was in these sectors where women worked in sex-segregated employment, outside the traditional domain of the labor movement. The clerical sector, of course, did not employ only women; in fact, white collar employment increased for both sexes. How labor leaders responded to these changes would determine the future of the labor movement and the levels of working men and women's labor activism.

Finally, women's family roles changed significantly. In the period between 1910 and 1940, men and women migrated more often, married younger, divorced more frequently, and had fewer children. The economic crisis of the 1930s intensified and to a certain extent precipitated these trends. Its consequences varied for men and women of different family status, occupation, and class. Single women, especially those who migrated into the cities, faced the impact of unemployment alone or in the company of others who also lacked resources. The poorest among them had little recourse to relief except in the form of domestic jobs. For family women, the depression often meant that a wife sought work to compensate for her husband's layoff, discharge, or desertion. In all respects, women and men found themselves redefining family norms—rejoining households as adult children or postponing family decisions of marriage and childbearing. Over the long term, the durability of the family under economic strain gave a new life to it as metaphor.

Charles Rumford Walker once argued that Minneapolis "exemplifie[d] more sharply than most the impact of forces that are typical and universal."[3] Life in the American city encompassed the full range of experiences that working-class men and women faced during the twentieth century. Migration and immigration; work, unemployment, and family crisis—the transformation of urban life into its contemporary forms—set the stage for the labor upheavals of the 1930s. Through the lens of a single woman's life—that of the fictive Girl—we might be able to glance at the urban world in which workers rebuilt the labor movement in the midst of economic and social upheaval.

Migration and the Working Woman

Like the Girl in Le Sueur's novel, many of the women who came to the cities left rural families and homes. Both men and women moved to the city for work, opportunity, and community. Sometimes this decision was forced upon them by necessity. There was little if any work for women in rural areas either as shop girls or in industry; the agricultural crisis and the subsequent decline in the need for farm labor put young women on the road. Unable to contribute to family income, they could at least avoid being a burden to their farm families, who were struggling against the economic crises of the early twentieth century.

For other women, the decision to move to Minneapolis was simply a personal choice—for independence and excitement.[4] A divorced woman in a small North Dakota town, Marguerite Belton had a daughter to support, and there was no work to be found. Minneapolis could at least offer her the possibility of employment in the garment trade. Staying with her sister after a visit to the city, Elizabeth Banghart actively chose independence and freedom from farm life; even low wages and uncertainty could not dissuade her. She found work in the city as a waitress and later as a garment worker.[5]

From its origins in the mid-nineteenth century, the city of Minneapolis was the destination of many women seeking work.[6] As the center of a large hinterland, the city's economy flourished on agriculture, iron mining, and timber industries. Local labor agents scoured the countryside for manual laborers to work in the region's mines, fields, and forests. At the same time, thousands of men and women workers came to the city to find jobs in the city's manufacturing concerns, which produced boots and shoes, cigars, food stuffs, and garments. Farm hands in the summer, miners and lumberjacks in the fall and winter, immigrant and native-born men congregated in the Gateway District seeking work in flour mills, iron-working shops, and transportation. Women traveled to the cities to be servants and factory operatives, sales women and office workers.[7]

Between 1910 and 1930, substantial numbers of young single women moved to Minneapolis. They were the largest group of migrating workers and outnumbered migrant men in nearly every age group.[8] Among young people aged twenty to twenty-four, nearly twice as many women came to the city as men. This movement to the city was a national trend, in which one in four men and women in their early twenties moved to a city. It depleted the population of the countryside and underscored the markedly different orientation of rural and urban youth.[9] The Girl who came to the city may have traveled singly, but she was not alone in her experience.[10] (See figures 1.1 and 1.2.)

The marginal position of single women in a farm economy was largely responsible for the character of the migration. The mechanization of farms and male inheritance patterns encouraged daughters to leave at an earlier age than sons. In a 1924 study of farm families, only 31 percent of daughters lived at home after age eighteen; 46 percent of sons did. Of those women who left home, nearly three-fourths married. In work or marriage, farm daughters were more likely to live in a city than on a farm. More than 90 percent of single daughters lived in a city; almost 50 percent of married daughters did.[11]

Like their predecessors in the 1920s, those who migrated to the Twin Cities in the depression decade overwhelmingly came from rural areas. Over 75 percent of men and women migrating to Minneapolis and St. Paul between 1935 and 1940 were of farm origins. (See table 1.1.) Moreover, while one in five (19 percent) men left for a farm, only one in seven (14 percent) women did. The number of men and women leaving the countryside declined with the employment crisis of the 1930s, but some still left the farm to look for work in the city. Those migrating to the Twin Cities continued to seek work and marriage in an urban environment.

The rural women who came to the city differed from migrating men in several respects. They migrated in far greater numbers, and they tended to be younger. Overall, they came from shorter distances.[12] It may also be said that the women who came to Minneapolis faced a different set of obstacles and expectations. For young men, the life of the Gateway represented both the temptations and the fears of big city living. As a red-light district, its side streets held countless small dives, bars, and brothels on Washington Avenue and in the Seven Corners area. The Bloody Bucket saloon and Hell's Kitchen were only a few steps away from downtown and the factories, warehouses, and truck garages where working men earned their pay.[13]

This area of the Twin Cities represented the Sodom and Gomorrah of the rural mother's nightmare. If women came by train, they might be met by relatives. Single women could consult the Travelers' Aid Society to find a place to stay and maybe a job in the city, as women had since the turn of the century. A temporary way station might have been the Seventh Street Club for Girls in Minneapolis, which gave food, shelter, and clothing to women in need; in St. Paul, the YWCA filled the same function. Unem-

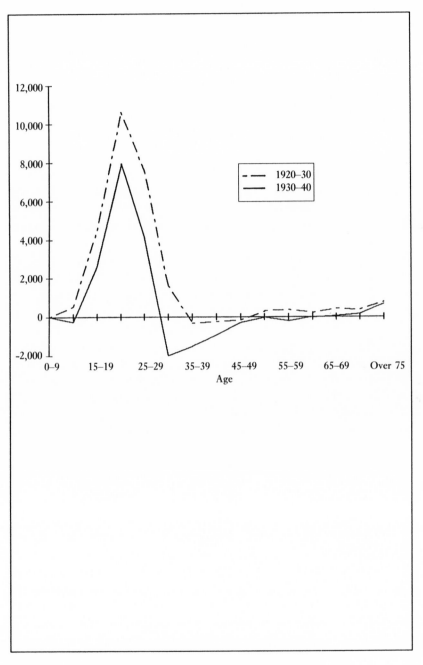

Figure 1.1 Net Migration, Women, Minneapolis, 1920–1940

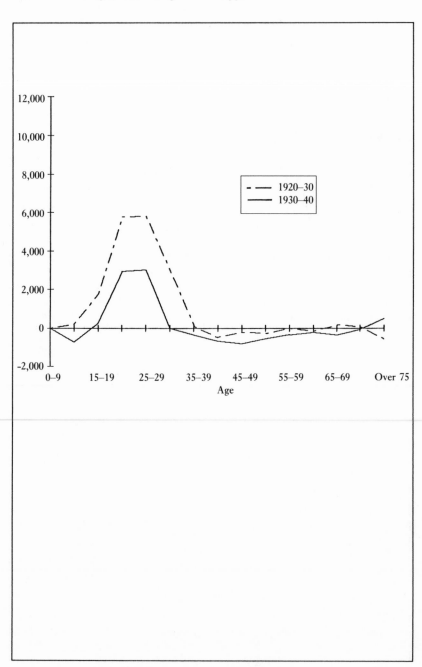

Figure 1.2 Net Migration, Men, Minneapolis, 1920–1940

Table 1.1 Farm Origin and Destination of Migrants, Minneapolis–St. Paul,
1935–1940 (in Percentages)

| | In-Migrants | | Out-Migrants | |
	Men	Women	Men	Women
Farm	75.6	77.2	18.9	14.1
Nonfarm	24.4	22.8	81.1	85.9
Total	46.6	53.4	49.9	50.1
	(n = 348)	(n = 399)	(n = 581)	(n = 617)

Source: U.S. Bureau of the Census, Public Use Sample, Minneapolis–St. Paul
Standard Metropolitan Area (SMA), 1940.

Note: Calculated from census data on SMA in 1935. In-migrants lived outside
the Minneapolis–St. Paul SMA in that year; out-migrants had moved from the
SMA to other regions.

ployed women came from diverse circumstances to the cities, however,
and a temporary agency could not fill all needs.

The most striking difference between men and women migrants was
their family status. Better than three in four men who migrated to the city
came with their families; almost one in two were heads of families. Among
women migrants, however, less than one in ten were household heads, and
over 60 percent were family relatives. More striking were the three in ten
women migrants who came to the city independent of family. Whereas
common wisdom predicted that women would be more likely to migrate in
families than men, a common experience for young women was traveling
to the city alone.[14]

The Seventh Street Club for Girls became a refuge for some of these
women migrants. A twenty-eight-year-old married woman domestic from
Fosston, Minnesota, had only been in the city a short time before she came
to the club for help; a circus performer, twenty years old, stayed at the club
residence after her own interim job as a domestic folded. The Women's
Occupational Bureau found her a waitressing job. A widowed switchboard
operator from Chicago; a domestic from Virginia, Minnesota; a book-
keeper from Wahpeton, South Dakota—all left their rural homes and
migrated to a city where they became part of the thousands of women
seeking work.[15]

The rural men and women who came to Minneapolis changed the

character of the laboring community. In 1940, only two in three adults had been born within the state; a good many of these undoubtedly came from rural towns and villages.[16] Moreover, as immigrant generations became part of the working class, migrants of rural origin took jobs in industry and low-paid clerical work. In one Minnesota study, less than one in five farm sons found their way into professional, clerical, or entrepreneurial positions; nearly three in ten daughters found their way into such positions, but mostly as low-paid teachers and nurses. Overall, the mobility of rural youth was regional and social but not predominantly upward.[17] They became part of the urban working class of diverse origins and identity which found common ground in the labor movement of the 1930s.

What Women Found in the City

Arriving at Union Station on Hennepin Avenue in 1929, a young woman worker would find herself on the edge of the business district facing Bridge Square.[18] It was here that four in five women wage earners worked. As clerks and stenographers in department stores, banks, and insurance offices; as service workers in hotels and restaurants; or as operatives in light manufacturing—women worked within a few miles of the city's center.[19] Most women industrial workers found their jobs in factories in the garment district along First Avenue. There were also other factories. On Lyndale near the city market, the massive Munsingwear factory employed about two thousand workers in the production of underwear and hosiery. Near Sixth and Chicago was the Strutwear plant, employing a thousand workers to produce hosiery. Beyond the garment district were wholesale and market warehouses, with trucks going in and out daily.

Leaving the center city, one would find only a few industrial corridors intruding along Washington Avenue (north), along University Avenue, and along the river front. Other areas of the city were largely residential. As in many cities of the period, central housing districts were deteriorating. Within a short distance of the factory district were boardinghouses and rental units, where many women workers lived. This area was bordered on one side by the largest Jewish neighborhood in the city and on another by a small black neighborhood. Yet another apartment house district centered around Loring Park near the Lake District.[20] (See map 1.1.)

Bohemian Flats was an old ethnic neighborhood built below the bluffs

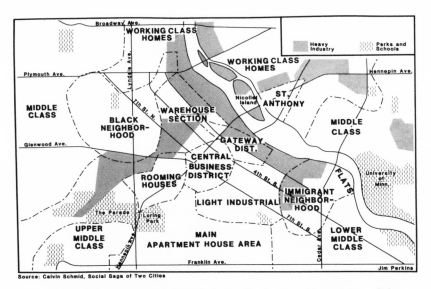

1.1 Center City, Minneapolis, 1935 (map by Jim Perkins, adapted from Calvin Schmid, *Social Saga of Two Cities*)

on the Mississippi river where impoverished eastern European immigrants and their families lived.[21] On Cedar Avenue and stretching into South Minneapolis (Seward and Phillips neighborhoods), Swedish, Norwegian, and Finnish families lived and worked. Another major immigrant enclave was in the Northeast neighborhood. The earliest settlers here had been Norwegian and Swedish; but beginning in the 1880s, communities of eastern and southern Europeans had settled there. By 1920, the neighborhood was predominantly Polish.[22]

Any woman migrant encountering Minneapolis for the first time would be struck by the diversity of people in the city. Immigrant and ethnic, men and women shaped the urban environment in which they lived. A migrant woman might herself be a second generation immigrant, brought up in a rural ethnic community in the Midwest, perhaps attracted to the city by tales of a cousin or aunt. In the period following World War I, men and women of foreign birth or parentage were the vast majority of Minneapolis citizens. In 1920, immigrant men and women accounted for nearly one in four Minneapolis residents. Nearly two-thirds of the city's population were first- or second-generation ethnics. By 1930, immigrants accounted for only 17.4 percent of the city's population, while 41.9 percent were native-born men and women of native parentage. Despite the small number of recent immigrants, ethnicity remained a strong factor in determining where men and women chose to live and work and in the survival of ethnic traditions.[23]

Whether black or white, migrant men and women might have found the absence of a large minority community disturbing. Blacks, Latinos, and Asian Americans numbered less than five thousand individuals and comprised only about 1 percent of the city's population. At a time when southern blacks migrated to northern cities in unprecedented numbers, the Minneapolis black community remained small. Between 1920 and 1930, its population grew by only 6 percent (compared to an overall growth of 22 percent), a fact which suggests that black men and women were probably migrating to other communities.[24]

Among white immigrants, during the late nineteenth and early twentieth centuries, Swedes and Norwegians represented nearly 60 percent of those of foreign birth or parentage. Many of these immigrants came to the Midwest region as farm workers, farmers, and domestic servants.[25] While Germans were not as prevalent among the foreign born (9.3 percent), nearly one in five (18.1 percent) native-born men and women were of German parentage. Another 20 percent of the foreign-born white population had come from eastern and southern Europe. They recreated its diversity in the confines of the central city neighborhoods.[26]

The boundaries of neighborhoods and church communities could almost be marked by the changing languages and customs. Ethnic Russians, Poles, and Ukrainians lived near the Northeast Settlement House; Czechs lived in the Northeast neighborhood and in the Bohemian Flats. In the Beltrami section, Italian immigrants and their families lived near the Margaret Barry Settlement House. Finn Town sprang up in the Bryn Mawr neighborhood. (See map 1.2.)

The proliferation of ethnic churches and ethnic associations enriched urban life as the clustering of first- and second-generation immigrants gave urban neighborhoods their character. Through the mid-twentieth century, men and women of the first and second immigrant generations created rich ethnic subcultures that would support the labor movement of the 1930s. In a 1919 YWCA survey, 43 percent of the city's churches (115 of 267) still held services in foreign languages.[27] Mutual associations, newspapers, unions, and political organizations expressed their immigrant ties. Despite pressures for Americanization after World War I, Scandinavian churches, German newspapers, and Finnish workers' organizations remained vital community institutions.[28]

On the North Side, the community of Romanian Jews organized the

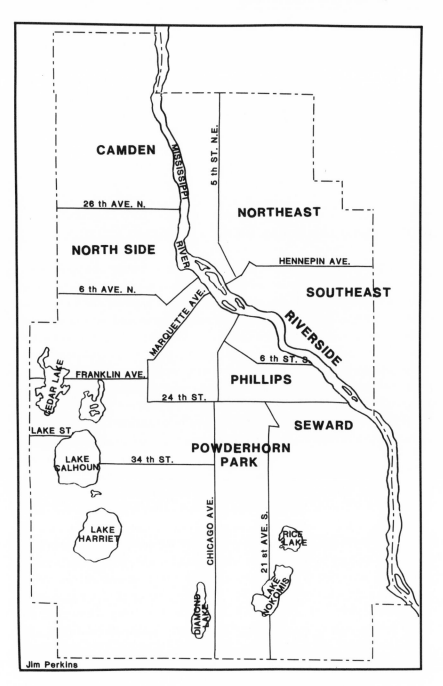

1.2 Minneapolis Neighborhoods, 1930 (map by Jim Perkins)

Apollo Club, the Gymnal Doled Club, the Talmud Torah, and the Emmanuel Cohen Center. During the 1930s, various Jewish labor and political organizations, including the Workmen's Circle, formed the Labor Lyceum for the education of union men and women.[29] The black community supported a newspaper called *The Spokesman*, the Phillis Wheatley House, and a chapter of the Urban League. These organizations provided networks and shelters for black and ethnic rural migrants. The mutuality of ethnic associations could sustain both men and women in the big city— giving aid, companionship, and support for individual lives and political activism.[30]

Gender and Life Course between the Wars

Whether rural migrants, immigrants, or the children of immigrants, women workers had lives that differed substantially from those of their brothers. Marriage, childbearing, and child care placed constraints upon women's capacity and desire for wage work. The majority of women over the course of the twentieth century shared in a pattern of education, early work (preceded for many women by migration from home), marriage, and childbearing. In the 1930s, this was altered by an increasing tendency among women to continue working during early years of marriage and/or to return to work when the children began school.

Urban women were among the first to fit this pattern. In 1920, most women would marry before age thirty-two, with the median age almost twenty-five (see table 1.2). The national average was three years younger. Men married at a median age of twenty-eight in Minneapolis and at twenty-five nationally. By the 1930s, the age range in which men and women married narrowed as had the gap between national and local experience. However, there was only a slight decline in median age at marriage for women, from 24.6 to 24 years; for men, however, marriage age declined to 25.4 years. The migration of women to the city in peak marriage years was a key factor in raising age at marriage. Like other urban areas, Minneapolis also had a higher proportion of men and women who chose not to marry. In the 1930s, while about 15 percent could be expected to remain single during their lifetimes, the national figure was only 10 percent.[31]

Urban patterns which postponed marriage had a significant impact on the familial decisions of working women. As in many urban areas, women

Table 1.2 Age at First Marriage by Sex, Minneapolis, 1920–1940

	Men			Women		
	1920	1930	1940	1920	1930	1940
1st Quartile	22.5	22.4	22.5	19.9	20.3	20.3
Median	27.8	25.4	25.3	24.6	24.0	23.9
3rd Quartile	33.8	29.2	28.7	32.1	28.8	28.9
Percent Ever Married	84.4	84.8	86.7	89.4	87.8	86.7

Source: U.S. Bureau of the Census, *14th Census, 1920*, vol. 2, *General Report and Analysis*, table 16, 496; *16th Census, 1940*, vol. 4, pt. 3, *Characteristics by Age*, table 8, 253.

in Minneapolis had much lower marital fertility than the national average throughout the twentieth century. Between 1920 and 1930 alone, there was a drop of nearly 20 percent. (See table 1.3.) Women who delayed marriage and children were more likely to work, to remain in the labor force longer than the preceding generations, and to entertain the possibility of returning to work when their children were of school age. While there are little reliable data on these connections, the steady increase of women working is a strong indication of a shift in women's generational choice and experience.[32]

During the twentieth century, there has been an incremental growth in the number and proportion of women working, with principal gains occurring among married women and married women with children.[33] Both men and women, however, changed their patterns of work substantially between 1910 and 1940. In Minneapolis, men experienced a decline in overall rates from a high of 88.1 percent in 1920 to 78.6 percent in 1940. By contrast, women were a growing group in the labor force. In 1910, women represented only one in four workers; by 1930, they were three in ten workers; by 1940, they were one in three workers (table 1.4).[34]

The characteristics of women workers were also changing. In the nineteenth century, the typical working woman was young, foreign born, and single. By mid-twentieth century, this composite picture was redrawn: the woman worker, rural migrant or city born, was much more likely to be older, married, and native born. Indeed, there was increasing diversity in age, education, and marital status among women who worked.

By the decade of the 1930s, the decline of immigration and the aging of

Table 1.3 Child-Woman Ratios, Minneapolis, 1920–1940: Children Aged 0–4
per 1000 Married Women Aged 15–44

Year	Marital Fertility
1920	625
1930	496
1940	446

Source: U.S. Bureau of the Census, *14th Census, 1920*, vol. 2, *General Report and Analysis*, table 16, 496; *16th Census, 1940*, vol. 4, pt. 3, *Characteristics by Age*, table 8, 253.

the immigrant population had altered the composition of the labor force in terms of nativity and race. In Minneapolis in 1920, immigrant women formed a much larger proportion of the labor force of married working women than they did in 1930. By the beginning of the depression, women workers were predominantly native born and white (87 percent); only 11.5 percent were foreign born and white, and only 1.5 percent were from minorities (predominantly black).[35] Such figures, however, masked the ethnic composition of the labor force. While the proportion of foreign-born women working declined, second-generation ethnic women likely predominated in the labor force, as they had at the turn of the century.[36]

Among white women, there was a dramatic increase of married women working both in number and as a proportion of the female labor force. In 1920, married women formed only a tiny fraction of women working (only about 8 percent). There was substantial difference in labor force participation between black and white women; almost one in three black married women worked. Combining marriage with wage work for white women remained an anomaly. Black women historically had shown a greater propensity to work while married. This pattern persisted, but the gap between white and black women began to narrow in the depression decade. By the 1930s, the percent of married white women working had almost doubled at 15 percent.[37] Both locally and nationally, the rate of married black women's participation in the labor force declined during the period from 1920 to 1940. While the magnitude of this change was small, disproportionate unemployment among blacks and the decline of the domestic service sector played a role in altering the pattern of married women's work.[38]

In the early years of the economic crisis, many young women simply could not find work. Neither the migrating Girl, her brother, nor her city-

Table 1.4 Labor Force Participation by Sex, Minneapolis, 1910–1940

Year	Men	Women	Percent Female	N
1910	87.5	31.2	24.2	143,412
1920	88.1	31.7	26.8	174,076
1930	84.8	34.2	30.4	211,799
1940	78.6	34.1	32.9	222,955

Source: U.S. Bureau of the Census, *16th Census, 1940*, vol. 3, pt. 3, *The Labor Force*, table 2, 689.

born peer could expect to find a job easily. By the end of the decade, there were fewer young women working. Lingering unemployment, extended school, and postponed entry into the work force meant that the median age of women workers increased during the period from 1920 to 1940. Overall, women's labor force participation peaked early at age twenty-five with nearly 70 percent of all women in that age group working (see figure 1.3).

The increase in the participation of women in the labor force occurred in the years immediately following marriage, from ages twenty-five to thirty-five. This new pattern suggests that women workers experienced an important shift in life cycle patterns. Older generations of working women had dropped out of the labor force on marriage. During the 1930s, the number and proportion of women working after marriage gradually increased with education, opportunities in the clerical sector, changes in consumption, and men's unemployment.[39]

Despite shifting patterns of women's work, significant differences in the work trajectories of men and women remained. During most of the twentieth century, men expected to work for wages throughout their lives, and the proportion of men working exceeded 90 percent for almost every age group.[40] Only after age sixty did men's labor force participation drop, and better than one in every two men worked until they were seventy years old. Significantly, men's work careers were influenced more by the economic crisis of the 1930s than women's. Whether through unemployment or the increased benefits of the welfare state, men gradually withdrew from the labor force after age sixty. By 1940, the labor force rate had declined for men of every age. (See figure 1.4.)

Shifts in the composition of the labor force and in the timing of work changed the work histories of men and women in another fundamental way. While the length of men's work life began to shorten with longer

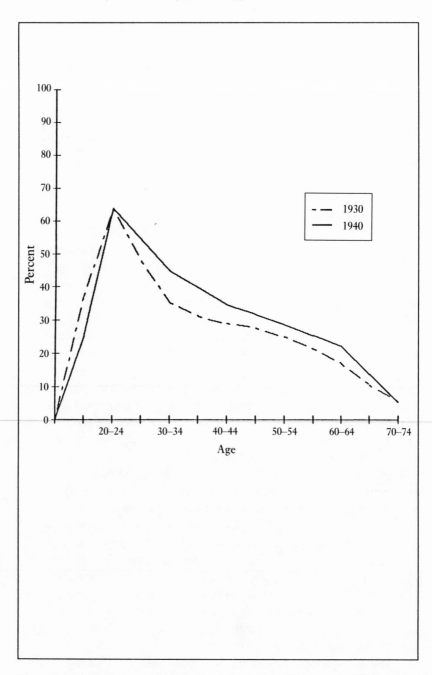

Figure 1.3 Labor Force Participation by Age, Women, Minneapolis, 1930 and 1940

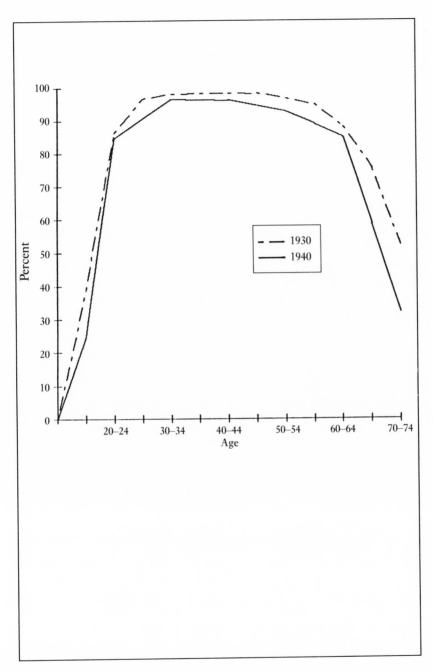

Figure 1.4 Labor Force Participation by Age, Men, Minneapolis, 1930 and 1940

periods of compulsory education and declining labor force participation in later years, women's gradually began to increase.[41] Between 1910 and 1950, with improvements in pension laws, workers' compensation, and wages, men's work lives were shortened by nearly four years. In contrast, women's work careers were extended by four and a half years. (See table 1.5.) The growing assumption of wage work in the years after marriage led to this corresponding growth in women's work lives. As Claudia Goldin has argued, no woman could predict her own labor force experience based on her mother's. Social proscriptions of married women working may not have changed prior to World War II, but women were choosing or were forced to choose wage work.[42]

Arriving in the city at age eighteen or twenty, the "Girl" of Le Sueur's story entered a life significantly different from her mother's—both in her circumstances and in her expectations. The urban community where she would live was diverse in ethnic and racial terms; its class experience was more homogeneous. Whereas an earlier generation of women migrants might have expected that wage work would be a temporary experience with marriage and children following at a rapid pace, the depression generation could predict no certain future. What is more, whatever their expectations, women would spend more years working than their mothers.

Gender and Industry in a Changing Economy

In Le Sueur's novel, the Girl goes to the city and becomes a barmaid at an ethnic club called the German Village. Until it closes, she works at her job with other women, earning wages and tips that enable her to survive through the early years of the depression. Her experience, while not incompatible with our knowledge of women's work in the 1930s, represents only one of many paths which women took to work in the city. A woman might be a sewing machine operative, a sales clerk, an assembler of batteries; she might even wind up on the WPA. Given changes in the local economy, she was also likely to be a secretary or a social worker.[43]

In the years between 1910 and 1940, there were significant changes in the kinds of work men and women did. For women, the most important structural shift was the decline in domestic service and growth in clerical occupations.[44] At a time when the absolute number of women employed in manufacturing remained relatively stable, the number and proportion of women working in clerical occupations increased by nearly 150 percent (see table 1.6). Similarly, while men increased their dominance of indus-

Table 1.5 Mean Years in Work Force by Sex, Age 14–65, Synthetic Cohort,
Minneapolis, 1920–1950

Year	Men	Women
1920	45.4	14.8
1930	44.7	16.8
1940	42.7	17.7
1950	41.2	19.3

Source: U.S. Bureau of the Census, *16th Census, 1940*, vol. 3, pt. 3, *The Labor Force*, table 2, 689; *17th Census, 1950*, vol. 2, *Characteristics of the Population*, pt. 23, *Minnesota*, table 76, 202–3.

trial jobs in both absolute and relative terms, the importance of women as part of the industrial labor force declined and continued to do so through the 1930s.[45]

The economic crisis of the 1930s intensified the trend toward white collar employment among men and women even as women increased as a proportion of the labor force (from 30.4 percent in 1930 to 32.9 percent in 1940).[46] Significantly, working men were employed in increasing numbers in the clerical and sales sector. As part of the proliferation of sales and clerical jobs, men worked increasingly in trade, even in a barren market. For nearly eight thousand men, white collar work was a remarkable sign of hope in the midst of a sluggish and stagnant economy.

The decreasing importance of manufacturing, both as a consequence of the unemployment crisis and as part of a longer trend, and the growth of the clerical sector transformed the world in which men and women sought work, acted in the workplace, and eventually organized unions. Not all of these changes were incorporated into the vision of the labor movement; indeed, the most significant change—the growth of white collar employment in trade and clerical occupations—remained curiously marginal to the drive to organize the unorganized, whether men or women.

Gender and Life Cycle in the Economic Crisis

The interwar years witnessed abrupt reversals in the fortunes and lives of working people. Migrant and resident, female and male, black and white, they needed to address economic crises and political changes that were not confined in time to the depression decade but rather characterized the

Table 1.6 Manufacturing and Clerical Employment by Sex, Minneapolis, 1910–1930[a]

	Manufacturing Employment				
	1910	1920		1930	
	Number	Number	Change (in %)[b]	Number	Change (in %)[b]
Male	45,250	51,282	+13.3	54,826	+6.9
Female	8,000	8,953	+11.9	8,822	−1.5
Total	53,250	60,235	+13.1	63,648	+5.4

	Clerical[c] Employment				
	1910	1920		1930	
	Number	Number	Change (in %)[b]	Number	Change (in %)[b]
Male	28,692	40,813	+29.7	49,666	+21.7
Female	10,361	21,458	+107.1	27,761	+29.4
Total	39,053	62,271	+59.4	77,427	+24.3

Source: U.S. Bureau of the Census, *13th Census, 1910*, vol. 4, *Occupational Statistics*, table 3, 166–79; *14th Census, 1920*, vol. 4, *Occupations*, table 2, 1144–47; *15th Census, 1930*, vol. 4, *Occupations by States*, table 3, 828.

[a]Figures for 1940 are excluded due to incomparability.

[b]From ten years earlier.

[c]Includes trade and communications clerical workers.

period as a whole. Agricultural depression followed the settlement of the war in Europe in 1918, bringing with it mass migration into the city from the countryside and urban unrest. Beginning in 1920 and lasting through the winter of 1921–22, there was high urban unemployment as well. While the clerical sector expanded throughout the decade, workers in manufacturing, food products, the metal trades, and knitting filled the ranks of the unemployed.[47] Further, the changing economic base of the city as it moved from an industrial to a commercial and service economy brought larger than usual numbers of the unemployed men into the Gateway

District. Veterans of World War I competed with younger men for the jobs in the manufacturing sector. In addition, an open shop campaign in Minneapolis depressed wages and undermined worker bargaining.[48]

The magnitude of the 1930s depression spread the uncertainty beyond the bounds of the Gateway. Wage-earning families and salaried workers alike needed to supplement wages, cut expenditures, and stretch their resources. As John Modell has argued, families' adaptations to the economic crisis fit our image of nineteenth-century defensive strategies, thus differing from the accumulative approach of contemporary families. These strategies involved the entrance of wives and children into the labor force, migration or desertion of children and spouses, conservative consumption patterns, and reliance on the state. They also deeply affected fertility and family decisions in ways which would reshape family life, individual life cycles, and the importance of women's work.[49]

In the face of the "unparalleled catastrophe," as novelist Thomas Bell described the Great Depression, families had to change their expectations. Men and women chose to postpone marriage and children. In Hennepin County, for instance, the number of people marrying dropped consistently from the year 1929 through 1932 and stayed low through 1935, increasing only in 1936.[50] Those who married later also had fewer children. There was a significant drop in the number of births in Minneapolis in the years from 1927 to 1936. Perhaps the steepest decline was in the year 1933, a drop which reflected decisions men and women made in the worst year of the depression. In that year the birth rate, which had been declining since 1927, dropped from 16.6 to 15.1 births per thousand population. Nationally, the birth rate was also on the decline (from 17.5 to 16.7), as contraception and/or abstinence were common responses to the economic crisis.[51]

Inevitably, women having fewer children changed the structure of family life and the meaning and significance of women's work. They could work longer, a necessity for many families with an unemployed head of household. Due to high youth unemployment during the decade, women also might need to replace the income of children who formerly were regular wage earners in a multiple-earner household.

Short-term changes in patterns of family formation and dissolution ultimately changed the composition of households within which men and women lived. Divorce, desertion, and male mortality played a significant role in the increasing number of women and children dependent on the resources of a woman wage earner or the state.[52] Dramatically, the number of female-headed households in Minneapolis increased over the course of the decade by 64 percent (from 17,433 to 28,600). Where women headed one in six households in 1930 (14.9 percent), a decade later they headed almost one in five (19.5 percent). While many cities during the depression witnessed the increase in female-headed households, it was particularly true in Minneapolis. Women in Philadelphia headed the same proportion of households in 1940 as Minneapolis women did; but the rate of change was slower, only 22.6 percent compared to Minneapolis's 30.9 percent. Similarly, female-headed households increased in Cleveland, Chicago, and South Bend—but not at the same magnitude.[53]

The reorientation of family life toward defensive strategies was only one of the major changes in women's lives during the depression decade. Even for working men and women who managed to avoid the breadlines and retain their jobs, the depression brought other consequences. As several historians have argued, the persistence of sex typing in the workplace meant that men, who dominated the work force in the crisis areas of manufacturing and construction, were much more likely to be unemployed than women. At the height of the crisis in Minneapolis, nearly 25 percent of men were unemployed. In 1940, 10 percent of women workers were unemployed, but 12.6 percent of working men were unemployed.[54]

Women's wage and income contributions were of increased importance in the defensive family economy of the 1930s. Among both white-collar and low-skilled blue-collar families, married women were contributing to maintaining the family standard of living in the face of male unemployment and underemployment. Among Minneapolis–St. Paul families from the public use sample of the census, one in four women married to an unemployed man worked; and one in six worked overall. Among the wage-earning class, the married woman least likely to contribute to family income was a woman married to a skilled blue-collar worker. (See table 1.7.)

The practice whereby married women contributed wages to the family economy was not new in the twentieth century, but the frequency of its occurrence and its importance to the family income shifted. While children had been major contributors to the family budget in the nineteenth century, reduced availability of work for youth, higher levels of compulsory education, and social prohibitions against child labor contributed to the decline of children's contributions in the twentieth century. Moreover, political and economic factors in the depression decade worked to con-

Table 1.7 Married Women's Labor Force Participation by Husband's
Occupation, Minneapolis–St. Paul, 1940

Husband's Occupation	Percent Homemakers	Percent Working Wives	N
Unemployed	75.0	25.0	140
Semiskilled Workers	80.7	19.3	378
Clerical-Sales	82.2	17.8	309
Professional-Managerial	84.7	15.3	314
Laborers	87.0	13.0	131
Craftsmen, Foremen	89.3	10.7	337
Total	83.6	16.4	1,609

Source: U.S. Bureau of the Census, Public Use Sample, Minneapolis–St. Paul,
1940.

strain youth employment. Thus, the importance of women's income increased for families struggling with the consequences of economic disaster.[55]

Married women's wages were not their only contribution to meeting
family needs. Their contributions also came in other forms familiar to the
working class. Careful consumption, balancing of income and expenditure, production of goods for family use—sewing clothes instead of buying
them off the rack; tending gardens; canning food; laundry, child care, and
other services—these were among the expectations for the wife's role; they
became even more important under the threat of unemployment, poverty,
and hunger. In addition, women resorted to ways of producing income
that were also familiar to the working class but abandoned in more prosperous times: taking in boarders and selling marginal goods.

Family budgets reveal some of the strategies employed by families in the
crisis years of the 1930s. While the frequency of extended families does
not seem to have dramatically increased among wage earners' families,
many adult children resided with parents. Families also relied on debt and
credit to maintain a decent standard of living, and they sent more of their
members out to work. While there is no comparable information for the
1920s, the data underscore the impact of the depression on wage-earning
and salaried workers.

In over one-third of households analyzed by the U.S. Bureau of Labor
Statistics in Minneapolis and St. Paul (n = 494), family expenditures ex-

ceeded income. Four in ten families (about 40 percent of the sample population) had expenditures in excess of 10 percent of their income. Deficits ranged from a paltry sixty-one cents to over a thousand dollars for a single year. These families were principally involved in buying durable goods like automobiles or furniture, and they may have relied on savings as well as credit. Their experience was not the norm, as the majority of families either stayed within their income or had fractional deficits. But the gap between expenditure and income was a major aspect of the family economy of the 1930s.

Deficits were met in any number of ways. Life insurance policies were cashed in; family members and friends lent money; savings accounts were closed.[56] Another source of income was taking in boarders and lodgers. Of the 494 wage-earning family households in the Bureau of Labor Statistics study, eighty-eight (20 percent or one in five) reported rent from boarders. Of the 119 boarders in the sample, thirty-seven (31.1 percent) were known to be related to the family. Most of the kin boarders were unmarried adult children in their twenties; they paid a set rent to the family for lodging, and their income was separate from that of the economic family. While these figures indicate that boarding was not a strategy employed by a majority of wage-earning households, the income earned from it could help a family to survive during the crisis. The mean income earned from boarding and lodging rent was $101, which represented from 4 to 25 percent of a family's income. While this was not a sum sufficient to replace a wage earner, it represented on average nearly 7 percent of the income of a family that took in boarders. In an economy where family expenditures overran income by an average of 8 percent, the income from lodging could keep a family from serious debt.[57]

In the context of marginal family economies, male unemployment, and uncertainty, labor organizing can be seen as yet another family strategy for defense and survival. The Great Depression underlined the vulnerability of working-class families to economic uncertainty and crisis. Given this, it is not surprising to find that job security—through seniority rules and union contracts—was one of the major demands of workers in the newly formed unions of the CIO. Further, the anger, militancy, and persistence of labor organizing throughout the decade undoubtedly were linked to the same causes. Unemployed men did lose status in families, among their mates, and in society at large; and women who continued to work were blamed for men's condition. Working women felt impinged upon by the conditions of their employment; young men and women who wanted to marry and have children felt burdened by the lack of work and income that would make it possible. As a result, the family took on tremendous but ambiguous meaning in the labor movement of the 1930s. For single men wage earners, for unemployed men, for former harvest hands and mine workers, for veterans of the war and of the IWW—male solidarity in the workplace, on the picket line, and in the political party was the form of adaptation to the depression that seemed most likely to defend men's interests. For working and family women and for married men of different backgrounds, community organization, a broad-based labor movement, and political activism were also forms of adaptation rooted in family solidarity. Between men's and women's forms of activism, the future of the labor movement would be made.

Le Sueur's Girl has served as an illustration of women in the urban working class of the twentieth century. Her life as depicted in the novel represents the lives of women in this historical epoch. Migration, work in the new service and clerical jobs, poverty, relief, and the solace and pain of personal relations under conditions of economic and social crisis—all sketched the outlines of the possibilities and probabilities for working women. Still, the narrative of the Girl's coming of age and into her power as a mother would not be complete without an analysis of these conditions as the basis of collective action.

In Minneapolis, a city with a diverse urban economy, nearly one-third of all women worked. While men were laid off from jobs in the heavy industries most affected by the crisis of the 1930s, women who were employed in clerical and service jobs worked steadily, if in poorer working conditions, throughout the decade. Between 1920 and 1940 there were also significant changes in the length and timing of women's working lives.

In the lives of working people, these larger trends were only a backdrop to a more personal drama. Discharged from jobs, one-third of all men and women workers nationally sought new jobs or some kind of relief allowance until they found a job. For many, the experience of being unemployed left serious psychological scars.[58] But at the time, men and women simply looked for ways to survive the crisis.

The labor movement needed to adapt to a new constituency as more women entered the labor market. Its inability to do so was in part due to the nature of the 1930s crisis. In this period, families assumed their central role as a buffer against short wages and no work. While many families did not have to resort to taking in boarders, adult children stayed in the household and contributed toward the family income. Short-lived as these strategies were, one result of the Great Depression was that the family's importance as an aspect of the economy and as metaphor was reinforced. The uncertainty of employment led to both a material and a sentimental dependence on family ties and on the psychological compensation of family authority.

As this chapter has shown, the Girl of Le Sueur's story only represented one facet of working-class experience during the interwar period. The lives of unattached women, like those of migrant working men, gave substance and form to the fiction and politics of the depression-era Left;[59] what was equally compelling is the extent to which economic crisis brought the family to center stage.

In the context of the 1930s, when job security, seniority, and family became predominant concerns, the labor movement would build from its community base and transform the workplace. But it could only do so by tapping the time and resources of its workers—both men and women. It was here that gender differences in life patterns and socialization came into play. Because men and women evolved different social networks, organizational and affective loyalties, and social roles, they would have to develop the labor movement as a community which integrated these different aspects. The strain of the Great Depression on the family, an institution in which men and women shared equally, had long-range consequences for the ability of workers to create an egalitarian labor movement.

Two

Gender, Politics, and the Labor Movement, 1914–1934

The fight of the telephone workers for a decent living will go to a finish which will make necessary marshalling all of labor's forces in this desperate struggle.
—*Labor Review*, 1918

It is the women of the farmers and the women of the city workers who feel most severely the agricultural depression that has brought tragedy to thousands of homes. We want the women of the city and the women of farm communities to appreciate that we all prosper or suffer together.
—Susie Stageberg, 1928

On November 15 of 1918, the citizens of Minneapolis and St. Paul were greeted with a headline that read, "Hello Girls Toot Horns to Inform Phoneless Twin Cities of Strike." The photograph beneath the caption was one of carnival. The New Woman dressed in flapper clothes and cloche hat, engaged in joyous revelry, was walking off the job. A parade of 1200 strikers marched through the streets of the Twin Cities, using horns, rattlers, automobile sounders, and "everything else that would make a noise." They convened at strike headquarters in the Non-Partisan League campaign office. As a newspaper reported, "There was no suggestion of disorder"; the strikers did not even picket telephone exchanges.[1]

In November of 1918, Myrtle Cain, a telephone operative from the Northeast neighborhood, led the women of local 89(A) of the International Brotherhood of Electrical Workers on strike against the telephone company. Backed by the city's labor union, the Working People's Non-Partisan League, and other progressive organizations, Cain and her fellow workers protested the artificial ceiling on wages that had existed while prices soared under wartime conditions. While factory workers faced the postwar period with ambivalence, telephone workers saw the end of the war as an opportunity to voice long-suppressed grievances.

What were the community and workplace bases for worker militancy in Minneapolis during the progressive era? How did women workers, long disaffected from the mainstream labor movement, fare in the wartime expansion of labor and the interwar period? The end of World War I, the political struggles of the Farmer-Labor movement, and the economic crisis of the 1930s all played a role in shaping the response of labor unions to the militancy of women and men workers in a period of decline and rebirth.

Hello Girls on Strike

The telephone strike began with a spirit of carnival and celebration as the flapper-militants gave public voice to long-held grievances. Parading through the center of cities, blocking traffic, and obstructing telephone company business, the striking operators and electrical workers showed their anger at the firm's wartime opportunism. The primary cause of the workers' protest was economic; wage increases did not match the escalating cost of living during the war. While management pleaded for a rate hike to cover increased costs, it also sought to acquire a monopoly over state communications.[2]

During the war, the United States Post Office under Postmaster General Burleson had control over telephone and telegraph companies. Designed to keep military communications unencumbered, the arrangement served telephone companies by restricting both wage increases and protests. But the end of the war did not return the companies to private control; rather, the federal government intervened not only in the local strike but in the national wave of telephone strikes in 1919.[3] In the Twin Cities' case, Burleson intervened immediately by sending a telegram that stated that "strikes are not permissible in government service." He formally requested the attorney general to prosecute any employee or striker who interfered with the operation of telephone lines. Interference also meant the refusal of workers to return to their posts.[4] During the next week, company officials submitted a petition for a rate increase and visited workers in their homes, and the number of strikers declined. The telephone company also threatened prosecution of striking workers and withheld their Liberty Bonds, exercising its economic power to force an end to the protest.[5]

Even in the face of these threats, striking women operators and repairmen were a visible and active presence at local telephone exchanges. Daily the strikers marched through the streets in rainy November weather. They sang on the picket line. There were reports of a woman militant carrying a riding whip "just for display purposes." She must have presented an intimidating obstacle to loyal company workers.[6] Strikers cut telephone lines, jeered replacement workers at exchanges, and played hide-and-seek with operators trying to sneak into work. Taxicabs bringing workers to the telephone company were stopped in the street while pickets addressed returning workers.[7] One night, a group of pickets broke into the main Minneapolis exchange through a window in the women's room. They cut the building's wiring and closed the heating vents. It soon filled with smoke. These activities led to the arrest of fourteen strikers and sympathizers, including Helen Sullivan, an active picketer, and two boys from the community who were identified as part of the crowd at the telephone exchange.[8]

The strikers engaged in a kind of labor protest that crossed the boundaries between workplace and community. Despite the havoc caused on the telephone exchanges and the stoppage of phone service, the strikers had a tremendous amount of community support. On one occasion, when police threatened to carry off a woman picket from the line, the crowd rescued her. Parades of strikers were cheered, and the head of the Northeast Neighborhood House arranged for meetings with the women.[9] While local newspapers carried editorials decrying the actions of the strikers and attributing militancy to bolshevik influences, there were also letters from "Hello Girls Friend" and "Central Park" which gave public expression to the discontent of loyal and patriotic operators. Another letter protested the use of society girls who "kindly volunteered as strikebreakers to try and deprive the working girl of what was not even a living wage." The author urged a little housecleaning at home to "curtail the power of the money autocrats who permit their daughters to 'scab' on the working girl."[10]

While the phone companies formerly had praised the patriotic efforts of operators as "the front ranks of our national 'army of women,'" they hoped to drive a wedge between the strikers and the community. Ads which depicted the woman operator as the vital hub of war communications were used to undermine support for the strike. In one instance, the operator's very fingers were seen as "forg[ing] a chain of conversation from shipping board to shipyard, Quartermaster General to supply depot." While the operator had stuck by her post, the "increasing complexity of military, business, and civil life" worked smoothly. Glorifying the operator who remained at work, the company wrote, "Hers is patriotism applied. She is performing her part with enthusiasm and fidelity."[11] Implicit in the company's argument was that the failure of women to perform their part, as exemplified by their strike against the military machine, was a failure of patriotism.

After twelve weeks, the telephone strike ended in a stalemate on February 8, 1919. Although the company agreed to an arbitration award for higher wages premised on a rate increase, the government intervened and blocked settlement. Eventually, those strikers who could returned to work.[12] The militancy of the telephone operators had surprised the labor establishment even as it confounded government efforts to curtail the growth of unions. Using their own symbols of solidarity—tooting horns and waving rattlers, singing and posturing on the picket line—these new union women had woven together the strands of community in their struggle.

The Community of Labor

The telephone workers' militancy was rooted in a community-based labor movement. A coalition of progressive organizations from the Non-Partisan League to the mainstream trade union movement supported the strike, using political platforms and newspapers to advocate wage increases and its political clout to open up the arbitration process. More important, however, the strike expressed the connections between workplace and community in who it involved and how.

As a stronghold of socialist and labor politics, Minneapolis created an atmosphere conducive to labor organizing. The city was home to numerous socialist clubs and a strong radical press, including *New Times* and the Norwegian-language paper, *Gaa Paa* (meaning "forward").[13] The immigrant population of Minneapolis—including substantial numbers of Norwegian, Swedish, and Finnish workers—were inheritors of the social democratic legacy. They enthusiastically joined the Socialist party and drastically altered the composition of its membership.[14] Organized into foreign-language federations, they formed an active socialist-labor culture with German singing groups, Scandinavian orchestras, and Finnish cooperative guilds. Latvian, Bulgarian, and Macedonian workers formed their own clubs. Much of this activity was not organized by the party but served to promote a connection between community, workplace, and political concerns.[15]

Women's activism was an important aspect of socialist culture. Finnish women in the cooperative movement, ethnic women in the foreign language locals, and native-born American women in socialist clubs and those of its populist counterpart, the Non-Partisan League, contributed to the party's institutional growth.[16] Further, in the face of a growing suffrage movement and under pressure from women members, the Party established a Women's National Executive Committee in 1910. Local women's committees soon followed, further supporting the growth of women's membership. Women soon represented nearly one in four (24 percent) Socialist party members locally and held one of ten leadership positions.[17]

After the turn of the century, women socialists were increasingly involved in the politics of equality. Unlike their predecessors, they enlarged women's terrain in the party to include both general party issues and specific women's demands. Women like Anna Maley, former head of the Women's National Committee and manager of socialist-machinist Thomas Van Lear's successful mayoral campaign in 1916, quickly rose from the ranks. They proved that women were invested in the party on grounds broader than class. Instead, they could pursue a two-fold agenda of women's rights and class struggle.[18] Like women in the rural Non-Partisan League, women in the Socialist party played an important role in extending the program of labor and the Left beyond electoral and trade union politics. Their educational and social activities created an alternative socialist culture that gave meaning to its formal political program. In redefining politics by lobbying for the inclusion of birth control, relief, temperance, and suffrage on the socialist agenda, women broadened the party's constituent base.[19]

As community organizations, ethnic associations, consumer cooperatives, and local political alliances proliferated, the ranks of labor kept growing. The IWW, a powerful force on the Iron Range in northern Minnesota and in the western wheat fields, set up an office in Minneapolis; and it began to recruit workers in the cities' industries.[20] Local AFL unions boasted phenomenal increases in membership. By 1916, there were over sixteen thousand trade unionists in the city. After the tumultuous labor conflicts of the war years, union members numbered nearly thirty thousand, as better than one in five workingmen belonged to trade unions.[21]

The greatest gains in membership proportionally were among women workers. In 1916, the state labor department recorded only 232 women in trade unions; four years later, they numbered almost 1,600. As in other cities, more women went on strike than joined unions, but garment makers (workingmen's clothing), musicians, railway clerks, and waitresses were among the new unionists. Women workers also joined new locals for the coach cleaners (although in separate white and black locals), broom makers, retail clerks, public service employees, glove workers, clothing workers, furriers, press assistants, and typographers.[22]

The power of community-union connections percolated through the labor conflicts of the period. In 1916, Thomas Van Lear, a machinist, was elected the city's first Socialist mayor. The election of a Socialist mayor and the new alliance of workers and farmers in the Non-Partisan League suggested the extent to which the labor movement, broadly defined, had become a powerful force. The selection of a Socialist as chief of police seemed to promise labor the control of the streets and perhaps industry itself. The wartime labor shortage further underwrote the new and aggressive power of unions.[23]

World War I provided the context in which the labor alliance became fragmented and eventually suppressed. Elected on the basis of its progressive platform, the Republican state government responded to growing public opposition to the war by the passage of a sedition act and the use of the criminal syndicalism laws. In addition, the government created the Minnesota Commission of Public Safety. As part of the offensive against labor unions and the Left, these new weapons were employed in the ensuing battles over ideological and political ground. Because the IWW and the Socialist party opposed the United States' entry into the war, they became a visible focus for commission activity. Conflict also heightened ethnic and racial tensions among workers.[24]

Through war propaganda, strikes against employers could be defined as unpatriotic. When in the course of a strike, workers interfered with transportation, communication, or the production of war materiel, they could be charged with sedition. Opposition to conscription provided an additional justification for those seeking to break up the alliance of labor and political activists. None of these developments were unique to Minnesota, but they occurred much earlier than comparable events nationally. The level of class conflict in Minneapolis thus gave urgency to the employers' argument that labor unions were undermining the city's economy.

Despite the campaign of the Minneapolis business community against unions, recruitment continued.[25] Sensing an opportunity in the wartime prosperity, the Minneapolis Trades and Labor Assembly funded a drive to organize textile workers. The union had soon recruited over one hundred members from the antiunion Northwest Knitting Company. When the war ended in November 1918, however, there were two developments: first, an influenza epidemic provided the excuse for a ban on public gatherings; second, the end of the war brought an end to government contracts and a severe cutback in the labor force of the mills. As Lynn Thompson, a labor organizer, later reported, "The work is slack and this seemed to put the fear in the members, and it is going to be a hard case to keep this organization a going."[26]

The Aftermath of World War I

As the strike of 1918 demonstrated, the telephone operators drew from the strength of the laboring community, refusing to heed the signs of increased state hostility. They were something new on the labor scene: class-conscious women who—on the basis of their wage-earning role— demanded support from the labor movement. They represented a social movement that had come of age in its acceptance of women's work and militancy.[27] Their leader, Myrtle Cain, was a symbol of what this new women's militancy could do for the labor movement. She drew upon the connections between gender and class to work in the Working People's Non-Partisan League, the WTUL, the Woman's party, and labor unions, thus fostering progressive coalitional politics.[28]

The militancy of the telephone operators opened up possibilities for a new relationship between women workers and the labor movement. Both in absolute terms and as a proportion of women working, clerical workers doubled their numbers between 1910 and 1920. Of over ten thousand new women clerical workers in Minneapolis, about two thousand were telephone operators. They represented change in women's work—the feminization of the white collar sector and the growing acceptance of work as a normal stage in a woman's life course.[29] The hello girls were new women; their work symbolized what was modern in American life. Like clerical workers in general, telephone operators had a romantic and even a sexual image. They talked intimately with customers on the phone; they joined in social and political activities with male co-workers; they crossed the boundaries between traditional women's work and the new work of serving the public.[30]

The highly sexualized character of the telephone workers' protest— with its images of women in carnival, carrying riding whips, and physically assaulting pickets—mirrored the image of the secretary; it was not, how- ever, compatible with labor's politics of the family wage. After the strike ended, there was little attempt made to capitalize on its gains, either by more vigorous recruiting at the company or by a more generalized union campaign for women workers.[31] When women workers did organize, they organized as they had historically—without the support and sometimes in the face of hostility from male unionists. The memory of the labor movement also proved porous. The 1918 strike faded fast, as did the coalition which supported the extraordinary activism and militancy of women on the picket line.[32] The inability of the labor movement to capitalize on these changes, to accept both the public work and the public sexuality of women, was a portent of things to come. Instead, it found a new voice in the masculine politics of unionism.

Like their brother workers, women benefited from the upsurge in labor activity before and after the war. The telephone strike was a dramatic instance of this activism and community support. Further, woman unionists established a Minneapolis committee of the WTUL as an institutional base to make inroads among teachers, retail clerks, and fur workers. Led by Amy Bjork, women workers organized a Household Helpers' Union with the support of the league. Waitresses under the guidance of May Rhodes and international organizer Mary Dempsey began organizing in 1915 and renewed their efforts with league encouragement. The league also promoted a scholarship for a school for women workers and supported the minimum wage law.[33]

The political clout of organized employers, however, constrained union growth and began to constrict even long-existing union locals. While organizing among women workers continued, the defensive posturing of male-dominated local labor establishment meant fewer resources and considerably less tolerance. For the waitresses who had been active since 1915, lack of union support manifested itself in concrete ways. The Trades and Labor Assembly gave insufficient attention to recruitment of women unionists, and male unionists did not adhere to union solidarity. As the waitresses reported, "The lack of support by the union members is discouraging and union men even the ones that holler the loudest we find them eating in places where there are no union waitresses."[34]

Women active in the waitress alliance found little solidarity among their union brothers, but they were not the only ones to experience the failure of unions to find a common ground. Economic and political crisis constrained labor's ability to act in the 1920s. Culminating in the nation-wide Palmer raids of 1919, antiradicalism had a deleterious effect on the labor movement generally. Worker organizations were dismantled or seemed to

disintegrate of their own accord.[35] In Minneapolis proper, union membership reached a high in 1920; but the open shop campaigns of the
Citizens' Alliance (an employers' association) undermined both the ability
and the will of workers to resist employer offensives. Faced with the
political victories of the Citizens' Alliance and a polarized constituency,
the working-class movement was in disarray. The Non-Partisan League
coalition began to crumble as new divisions arose between its populist
base and new left-wing members; the Socialist party suffered a similar
challenge as the foreign language coalitions finally broke from the nativist
leadership and moved into the new Communist party.[36]

Two other developments helped to weaken the labor movement's position: the decline of the Minneapolis economy in the face of the postwar
depression and labor's new emphasis on political tactics. An important
factor in the suppression of organization was the effort of the Citizens'
Alliance to refuse aid to the unemployed. Denying that any crisis existed,
the alliance opposed the registration of the unemployed, the creation of
public works jobs, and the extension of relief to the homeless.[37] While the
trade union council spent between three and four thousand dollars in
relief to its members, the city council debated the level of appropriations,
whether and how much wages should be paid for relief work, and whether
there ought to be residence qualifications for assistance. The political
controversy over relief blocked attempts at relieving the situation.[38]

Another significant problem during the decade of the 1920s was the
shift in labor's strategy from one which linked the politics of work to the
community to one which separated the two. Essentially, unionists abandoned workplace tactics for political and consumer struggles. The focus of
these struggles was the Farmer-Labor party and consumer boycotts,
union label organizations, and consumer-producer cooperatives.[39] The
coupling of such strategies with a broadly based unionism and a strong
labor press was part of the unified strategy long advocated by labor radicals. Yet the emphasis on credit unions, home loans, boycotts, and cooperatives, which had been empowering before the war, only served to ossify
the labor movement in the 1920s. Trade unions built a labor temple,
organized a building and loan association, and started a cooperative
creamery, but labor's reach stopped there.[40]

The politics of consumption were an important aspect of community-
based unionism, but what marked the labor movement's consumerist
strategies was the extent to which workplace categories defined consumer
and community struggle. In the case of the milk drivers' strike of 1919,

workers established the Franklin Creamery to create a workplace free from the control of the Citizens' Alliance. It worked because of the allegiance of working people. But as a cooperative, it was defined primarily as a means of controlling production. Skilled workers organized community strategy around workplace demands. Campaigns constructed "at the point of consumption"—that is, boycotts, union label buying, and cooperatives—were constrained by contradictory claims to be for all workers and in defense of the craft-based trade unions.[41]

At the same time labor leaders tried to distance themselves from their radical roots. Organizations which before World War I had served to connect the struggle over wages and hours to issues of community survival and collective identity were now labeled as subversive. This included the Finnish-led cooperative movement, ethnic associations, and the political groups. Women's activism faced similar disavowal as the trade union movement turned toward other concerns.[42]

Labor's third-party allegiance was focused elsewhere. Former mayor Thomas Van Lear and William Mahoney, a printer and editor of the St. Paul–based *Minnesota Union Advocate*, played a prominent role in the formation of the Working People's Non-Partisan League, which worked in coalition with the rural league. These groups had supported a broadly based Farmer-Labor program of government ownership of utilities, regulation of transportation, and legal sanctions for labor.[43] Between 1918 and 1924, however, the league shifted gears in order to conduct a solid electoral campaign on the newly formed Farmer-Labor party ticket. While the electoral successes of the Farmer-Labor party in the early period were attributable almost solely to its rural constituency, it was urban trade unionists who initiated the third-party campaigns.[44]

In emphasizing political struggle, Minneapolis labor separated two of the three strands of labor's strength. The consequences for the movement were enormous. During the decade, labor membership declined precipitously. From a high of twenty-seven thousand members in 1920, the number of unionized workers dropped to fourteen thousand in 1928 and seven thousand in 1933.[45] With the exception of the milk drivers' victory, unions faced a long series of defeats. Garment, hosiery, and cap workers went on strike periodically throughout the decade; all of the strikes were lost. Women workers involved in such actions did not have sufficient support either from the labor movement or in the community.[46]

Individual women did find the means to continue their activism. In 1923, Myrtle Cain's district in northeast Minneapolis elected her to the state legislature. Her working-class constituents earlier had supported Van Lear for mayor and continued to vote for Farmer-Labor candidates. Where before the war they had participated in struggles to build strong unions and extend the terrain of the labor movement, they now found expression in the political arena. In voting for Cain, Northeast neighborhood residents proved that class and gender concerns were inextricably linked. They had not only elected a woman but also chosen a vocal member of the National Woman's party. Like Marian Le Sueur and Bertha Moller, local women activists, Cain asked "equal rights and no favor" for women. She picketed the White House for woman suffrage during the war, one of only eleven Minnesota women who was a Silent Sentinel. As "the flapper legislator," Cain demonstrated her commitment by working for the passage of laws that would give illegitimate children rights, restrict the Ku Klux Klan, and establish equal rights for women at the state level. Only the equal rights bill failed. After one term, Cain lost her seat, but her activism did not end with her electoral career. Like many women of her generation, she continued to work on the labor front in a political role.[47]

Cain's shift to the political arena was a sign of the change in working-class organization, a change that had begun with the dissolution of a strong community-based labor movement after the war. This loss had severe consequences for the welfare of men and women workers. As historian Frank Stricker has argued, the decade of the 1920s saw a deterioration in the real wages and levels of employment for industrial workers and in their standard of living.[48] Labor's inability to respond to this decline was due to its weakness on both economic and political levels. Labor watched employers further encroach on workers' control of the labor process even as they endured wage losses. Corporate welfare and paternalism softened the immediate impact, but over the long term they did nothing to forestall economic crisis.[49]

There was one further consequence. The decades between the vibrant laboring culture of 1914 and the rise of union activism in 1934 gave birth to a kind of amnesia about how one built an inclusive labor movement. The union movement—which had responded to the telephone workers' protest, fought the state on issues of free speech and women's suffrage, and tried to develop an alternative culture of schools, newspapers, theaters, and music—suffered in the aftermath of World War I. Far from integrating women and men on an equal basis, the unions which developed in the crisis years of the 1930s put such gendered issues on the back burner. The language of class, gendered in equality in 1914, assumed a more intensely masculine tone in the Great Depression.

The Great Depression in Minneapolis

On the heels of labor's political defeat, the "diseases of our economic system," as Charles Walker put it, visited the city of Minneapolis with a vengeance. While national newspapers and novelists celebrated the decade's prosperity, writers and political activists of the farm belt understood the underlying desperation of farmers and workers in the 1920s. Popular culture played on Babe Ruth, the automobile, and bathtub gin; the culture of Farmer-Labor politics pursued the McNary-Haugen farm bill, unemployment insurance, and attacked the monopoly of the chain banks over credit.

The illusion of prosperity ended not as the single crash of the markets in stocks and bonds or the closing of the banks but with what must have seemed like the inexorably slow collapse of the economy.[50] Minneapolis had its richest market in the agricultural and mining regions of Minnesota, the Dakotas, and Iowa. The failure of farms and banks led to the failure of many other firms, and rural crisis fueled the deteriorating urban conditions.

While the diverse economy of the Twin Cities kept the unemployment rate well below that of single-industry cities like Detroit, Toledo, or Lawrence,[51] the crisis affected every sector of the economy. As the producer of farm equipment, workingmen's clothing, and other consumer goods, the manufacturing sector in Minneapolis was hit by the agricultural crisis. Unemployment was already high compared to national levels. Employment rose only 1 percent between 1926 and 1929 while the labor force grew 6 percent. Alarmed by the economic portents, unions sponsored conferences and meetings on unemployment as early as 1928.[52] In depressed industries like garments and construction, employers began laying off workers before October of 1929.

Between 1929 and 1933, the number of factories had decreased by nearly one quarter. Workers produced less than 50 percent of the goods they had in 1929. The closing of factories was only one sign of the crisis. In a city where over five thousand men earned a living by transporting goods to market, economic crisis might be more accurately reflected in the closing of wholesale and retail firms. In both these areas, there were significant losses in the early 1930s. In wholesaling, nearly 25 percent of businesses closed or moved, and there was a drop of nearly 40 percent in the value of goods sold. Retailing also declined, a trend revealed by the decline in profits alone. From 1929 to 1933, the value of goods sold dropped nearly 45 percent.[53]

It is difficult to know how many men and women were unemployed during the Great Depression; statistics for the decade are unreliable.[54] Nationally, at least one in three workers was unemployed in 1932. Within each city, however, unemployment took a different shape, and the regional economy varied in its effect on industries. In the unemployment census of 1930, 9.2 percent of working men and 4.5 percent of working women in Minneapolis were either unemployed and seeking work or temporarily laid off their jobs.[55] Underemployment accounted for another 5 percent. Compiled before the depth of the crisis, the census already gave some indication of its severity.

In the decade of the 1920s, when the city was relatively insulated from the effects of rural depression, the relief department opened an average of 214 cases annually. By 1930, however, the number of cases jumped to a yearly average of over 4,500.[56] At the depth of the depression in 1932, when the level of unemployment reached its peak, private agencies were compelled by financial exigencies to transfer their cases to the city's Division of Public Relief. During that year alone, over 10,000 cases were opened by city relief officials. Using 1928 as a base, we can see the effects of the economic crisis in the expanding number of individuals on public relief.[57] Before the transfer, the number of cases opened annually had grown six-fold. After 1932, the caseload continued to remain high, reflecting both an increase in public responsibility for providing assistance to the poor and the continuing need for individual relief.[58]

There were dramatic shifts in the clientele for relief agencies. Before the crisis of the 1930s, recipients of assistance in the city had primarily been widowed mothers, the aged and infirm, and migrant male laborers. As the decade progressed, recipients of relief became a more diverse population, including young as well as old, married couples and nuclear families as well as single men.[59] In 1933, 12.1 percent of men and women (or 56,329 from 18,697 households) were receiving some aid. Of these households, 56.5 percent were male-headed family units; 14.9 percent were families headed by women. Only 28.5 percent of the families were single-person families, with the majority being single men (24.1 percent of the relief population).[60] The large number of single-male households on relief was due in part to the role of Minneapolis as a center for the region's casual labor market. As a highly mobile and unstable population, the men of the Gateway were a visual reminder of the social impact of economic crisis. Single men crowded into city shelters and flophouses and filled Salvation Army halls and the Union City Mission during the early years of the depression.[61]

Figures of profits and losses, business failures, and even unemployment rates fail to capture the experience of the Great Depression in human terms. Working men and women and their families experienced economic crisis in both material and psychological ways. Business failures meant the loss of jobs and often of a sense of self-worth. Workers experienced the depression through hunger, illness, and even death. Changes in the expectation of life, of marriage, and of family demonstrated the seriousness of a crisis which amounted to more than a simple downturn in the business cycle. It had a profound and devastating impact on people's lives.

At the Northeast Neighborhood House, the head social worker wrote detailed monthly reports on the impact of the depression. Because the house served the functions of welfare agency, employment bureau, and community center, the supervisor was able to record the steady worsening of conditions in the neighborhood, where Slavic, Polish, and Italian immigrants lived. In October of 1929, he had already noticed increasing joblessness as the employment bureau was deluged with women clients and the nursery school population began to decline. Over 30 percent of male heads of household in a neighborhood survey were unemployed. "The sudden laying off of men was . . . without a doubt the real cause of the unusually large increase of women seeking work."[62]

One such family was the Krovak family, who lived in the Northeast neighborhood of Minneapolis. Mr. Krovak had been a blacksmith in Czechoslovakia; in the United States he worked irregularly in the iron-molding industry. The Krovaks had thirteen children, of whom nine were living in 1929. Their four oldest children contributed to the family income. At twenty-eight, Maria, the oldest, worked for the telephone company; John, her younger brother, joined the navy. The depression ended the family's hopes that the younger children would finish school: Viola gave up high school and went to work; Robert as well. Already destitute by November of 1929, Mrs. Krovak went to the settlement house to ask for some fuel and some assistance. "We are on the rocks," she said. They had spent their savings and lacked money for the children's clothing or her husband's shoes.[63]

By January of 1930, the situation had become worse. Of over three hundred women applying for work, settlement workers could place only seventy. "The women come in day after day and leave discouraged because we have to tell them we have no calls for them," the head worker reported. "When conditions are such it seems almost ironical for a woman to come here from Chicago or an Indian Reservation expecting and hoping to get work." Regularly employed men, accustomed to supporting themselves, were out of work; and some women became the sole support of families. Commented the head worker, "My weak pen cannot draw the picture that unemployment has caused and which presents itself to us in the course of our work."[64]

For families confronted with unemployment, frustration could lead to family violence or dissolution. Families which had been stable and prosperous in the 1920s found themselves faced with decisions to pawn belongings, surrender life insurance policies, and leave bills unpaid. Finally, the family might lose its home. "Along this time in the march of events," a settlement worker sadly concluded, "the mother is generally working or looking for work and the family is living on a semi-starvation diet." In some instances, a man discouraged by his inability to find work would begin to abuse his wife or children. The intervention of outside agencies, such as the settlement house or a church (like the Russian Orthodox Society of Saints Peter and Paul) was the only resource many families had to answer the crisis.[65]

Working women across the city faced the crisis with a sense that they were losing ground. Teachers and clerical workers did day work in homes; factory workers were laid off from one factory only to search futilely for a job in another. One woman wrote, "I worked in a factory until six years ago, and things began to change. Girls were let out little by little, only a few were able to hang on, working a few days a week. I tried every place then, all the factories."[66] Another worker, calling herself Jane, wrote to a newspaper that she had "never been any good at housework" and had learned machine work in her father's shop. During World War I, Jane had been a tool checker for the Great Northern Railroad, saving enough money for business college. "Now," she wrote, "I got domestic work."[67]

In 1934, there were an estimated seven thousand women unemployed, and more were expected as women graduated from school or were released from seasonal work.[68] Where these women found sustenance was, as Meridel Le Sueur writes, "one of the great mysteries of the city." Women did not stand in breadlines in the Gateway District, and there were no safe places for women to sleep. Le Sueur continues, "There are no flophouses for women as there are for men, where a bed can be had for a quarter or less. You don't see women lying on the floor at the mission in the free flops. They obviously don't sleep in the jungle or under newspapers in the park. There is no law against their being in these places but the fact is they rarely are."[69] It was much more likely, Le Sueur added with irony, that women, isolated from their own gender, would turn to men for help or starve in private.

There was a certain irony in women's invisibility on the urban stage. For decades, social reformers had worried about the number of young women in large cities. They established boarding homes, social organizations, and reform societies for the protection of the working girl. In the wake of women's suffrage victory, however, the woman worker was no longer an issue of concern. It was the boy tramp, the male citizen out of work, the older male transient who elicited the most concern. Policymakers pondered if young men denied job opportunities would regain their desire to work. The impact of unemployment on men's emotional stability and family authority became another focus of inquiry. Finally, groups of unemployed men in the cities added to fears of strikes and revolution. Concern for the material and moral well-being of young unemployed women was lacking in one of the most severe depressions in the history of the United States.[70]

In many ways, concern for women as victims of the economic crisis was mediated by family status. The worthy poor had always been cared for, if inadequately. Female heads of households were presumed to be provided for by mothers' pensions; older women, mental cases, and victims of domestic discord were assigned to the Special Service Bureau of the Family Welfare Association; and married women found aid through their husbands and the public relief department. Public and private agencies largely denied the existence of single women among the unemployed for, they believed, "Many women were being served in their families."[71]

In the fall of 1930, however, the mayor of Minneapolis found it necessary to open the city jail as a shelter for unemployed women workers. Women from social service agencies met with the mayor's committee on public welfare to discuss the condition of women on relief. They found the mayor's plan inadequate to meet the needs of women, particularly young single women.[72] The Women's Occupational Bureau, an employment counseling service, raised funds for a new facility by participating in a national theater benefit. Aid from the community chest, the mayor's theater fund, and labor unions provided the original capital to support the endeavor. On January 20, 1932, the Seventh Street Club for Girls opened as a shelter to provide temporary housing, food, and counseling for women in the city.[73]

The sheer volume of women who attempted to find employment through the Women's Occupational Bureau and the Seventh Street Club is testimony to women's need. Over ten thousand women sought counseling through the bureau's offices in 1932 and 1933. The club had 788 cases in 1932 and served 1581 women and girls in its first two years of existence, an average of 50 a day. While the club's facilities could only partially meet the needs of unemployed women, it provided its clients with shelter and food in exchange for work in offices or private homes. In addition, women received gifts of clothing or bus fare to aid them in looking for regular employment.[74]

Many women clients of the Seventh Street Club felt that the help which they received came at too great a cost. Identifying herself as Leah, a woman wrote to *United Action* with her story. "I was sent," she wrote, "from the Occupational Bureau to the Travelers' Aid, to the Great Northern Depot, a matter of many blocks." Before she was through she had visited the courthouse and the girls' club and had been interviewed by five different social workers: "Then began my slavery between the relief and the homes they sent me to. I myself would like nothing better than in broad daylight to heave bricks of patent dynamite into the windows of bureaus and agencies that are supposed to be established for the benefit of unemployed girls."[75] Hostility toward "the virgin women who dispense charity"[76] was scored with underlying sexual conflict. It was rumored that the same women who gave you your subsistence might also force you to be sterilized. Interviewers' notes from case files suggest that, among some social workers, suspicion and hostility toward single women who sought charity was common. Marital status—especially of those women living apart from families—became a marker and a divider under depression conditions and scarce resources.[77]

The Politics of Unemployment

The instability of the Minneapolis economy and the exhaustion of private resources in the face of economic crisis undermined the efforts of individual women and men to survive the depression. By 1932, the funds of private agencies were depleted, and these agencies could no longer meet a substantial part of the relief burden.[78] In 1934, the Seventh Street Club closed its doors to working women; a year later the Organized Unemployed, another self-help agency employing women on sewing projects, was disbanded by the federal agency which had provided its funds. Dislocation effectively blocked further private efforts.[79]

The inadequacy of relief programs was demonstrated by the government's lack of response to the agricultural and industrial crisis. Direct relief for farm and urban families came from local welfare boards that were unable to meet the crisis. State unemployment levels rose from 8.2 percent in 1930 to 23.4 percent in less than three years. By 1932, over 12 percent of the population was on the city relief rolls in Minneapolis. The Family Welfare Association, a major source of private relief, had to transfer the majority of its cases to the Board of Public Welfare. The escalating crisis left the local government dependent on bond issues to meet the costs of emergency assistance.[80]

Despite expanding federal support, eligibility rules, distribution of funds, and decisions to participate in welfare programs were made within the local arena. In Minneapolis, this process became politicized because welfare was an arena of conflict between local labor unions and the Citizens' Alliance. As the city council and the relief board disputed both the acceptance and distribution of federal and state monies, Farmer-Labor ward clubs formed oversight committees on welfare practices and expenditures. When local alliances of businessmen pressured the Public Welfare Board to deny relief to striking workers, Farmer-Labor committees took on advocacy roles.[81]

Unemployed workers organized to address their need for subsistence, housing, and community. Along with them, labor unions and political organizations lobbied, protested, and fought for relief. As they did in cities nationwide, Communist party organizers helped develop the Unemployed Councils and block clubs to fight evictions and protest relief cutbacks. By 1930, an Unemployed Council in the Gateway District enrolled nearly four hundred members; other, family-based neighborhoods organized block committees.[82] These were particularly productive. On the south side, in a traditionally Swedish and Norwegian enclave, an active council was set up; in the northeast, Poles and Slavs organized another council; and on the north side, the Finnish, Jewish, and black communities organized separate relief groups.[83]

Organizing around ethnic, racial, and familial identities, the Unemployed Councils sought an answer to the economic crisis among those workers who were marginalized in their own communities and outside the trade union movement. The councils also provided a new arena for women's activism. Writer Meridel Le Sueur tells a story about a group of women and children in Gateway Park. Gathered in front of an expensive grocery store by the Nicollet Hotel, the women "floated across the street" and pressed up against the windows. "The windows seemed to break" as the women entered the store. Inside they began to take things from the shelves. As Le Sueur said, it could easily have turned to disorder as women grabbed the food. Instead, the women made a list of everything they took, telling the store owner that they would pay for it. In one part of the store, a black woman filled her arms with bacon. Then, rather than leaving for home, she cried out, "Who has the most children here?" She distributed the meat in order of need.[84]

As the *Hunger Fighter*, the newspaper of the Unemployed Councils, recorded in every issue, the transient population sporadically protested in the public space of Bridge Square and the market areas; but it was the women of the councils who fought patiently on a daily basis to stop evictions and win better welfare provisions. They provided basic support for a working-class movement that built labor unions in the midst of the crisis.

Significantly, organizers in the unemployed movement were attracted by the possibilities of radical politics among the transient population. Actively recruiting among men in the flophouses, shelters, and breadlines, council members hoped to transform the migrants into a disciplined unit, capable of confronting city hall and the relief department. At a time when block committees dominated the action in the Unemployed Councils, the Minneapolis *Hunger Fighter* depicted a typical meeting at the Union City Mission. "Mostly young, husky and hard-faced," a dozen men from the Unemployed Councils entered the mission. Gathering the unemployed, they began the meeting. Into the doorway came thugs, the paid and deputized flunkies of the Citizens' Alliance. Strutting like villains in a Hollywood Western and carrying blackjacks, they shouted at the leader of the unemployed, "Get down, you damned Red!" The council boys quickly made short work of the bullies. Triumphant in the fight and in organizing the unemployed, they emerged from the building. As the writer exuberantly concluded, "The boys in the hole are all afire, you can hear them singing, 'Hold the Fort' for three blocks."[85]

This romantic image of male struggle pervaded Communist party efforts. Street fighting was transformed from its brawling character to a political statement. New gangs of men, on the Right and the Left, began to battle it out. The Unemployed Councils, and later the General Drivers' local 574, developed their own guard units to mirror the deputized units of the employers' association. But unlike the Communist party in Weimar Germany, it was unable to keep its units intact. While unemployed workers continued to participate in community-level strikes, their organizations could maintain only a fluctuating membership. Only the regularization of work relief under the WPA created the preconditions for the development of project locals.[86]

In *Poor People's Movements*, Frances Fox Piven and Richard Cloward argue that the mobility and spontaneity of the early movements of the unemployed was essential in pressuring the state to meet the needs of the poor. Like many other students of social movements, they share the belief that social movements are born out of alienation, discontent, and disorganization. This underlying assumption, along with its disdain for the local, the "traditional," and the settled, skews our perceptions of how change occurs. In the past decade social historians have helped to sever the connection between transiency and discontent.[87]

The task of the unemployed movement of the 1930s was not so much organizing the unsettled as allowing the settled to organize. Unemployed Councils were rooted in specific neighborhoods and communities, creating a base for political organization in both social and electoral forms. Indeed, the attraction of the Communist party to organizing single, unemployed men undermined the more successful block clubs by diverting time and resources to the transient population. Eventually, the party and other organizers turned their backs on the relief population altogether, preferring the workplace focus of the Workers' Alliance and the labor movement.

Community Activism Reborn

When Myrtle Cain led the telephone workers on strike, she had the support of a working-class movement that had its base in community, workplace, and polling place. On the surface, it was a similar coalition that backed her when she emerged as the spokeswoman in local Farmer-Labor relief politics in the 1930s; but the similarity was deceptive. In the years before World War I, the labor movement was an arena for discussion and debate, one which invited and encouraged the activism of both women and men, workers and family members. Its rhetoric spoke of "marshalling all of labor's forces"[88]; its practice was that of heterodoxy, of pluralism, which could encompass both the familialism of older populist politics and the new unionism, the activism of new women as well as new men. Labor began to develop visions which accepted implicitly a new sexual politics for the working class. Tooting horns and waving flags, it announced its vitality and promise.

World War I, political repression, organized employers' offensives, and the labor movement's own defensive posturing helped to weaken this promise. The economic crisis which followed only further undermined the possibility of a labor movement for which gender as well as class were grounds for activism. Instead, as a crisis in wage earning and hence in men's social role, the depression emphasized the masculine character of protest for the working class. Far from embracing the popular feminism of the telephone strikers, the labor movement became polarized between masculinist visions of the unemployed movement and familial Farmer-Labor politics. This polarity made room for women only in auxiliary roles.

Like other women in the Farmer-Labor movement, Myrtle Cain seems to have found the transition from striker to Farmer-Laborite an easy one. As she shifted her attention from organizing women as workers to recruiting women as family members and voters, Cain abandoned the picket sign for the accoutrements of office. In this path, she was joined by other peers. Perhaps her way was smoothed by the relative quiescence of the labor movement of the 1920s; perhaps its masculinism impeded her progress. Advocacy of the family and the family wage probably appeared less a contradiction than a continuation of her role in a working-class movement. Despite her activism in the Woman's party, Cain never acquiesced to the notion that women and men might have contradictory and conflicting interests, and she adapted to her new role without protest.

The working-class movement of the 1930s did not acknowledge differences among its adherents either. Building on a base in the community, proclaiming the unified interests of all workers, the labor movement had no memory of its qualitatively different configuration in the prewar period—neither the diversity of its agenda and constituency nor the importance of gender issues to its program.[89] It lacked a specific vision of alternative forms. In fact, it was the image of the worker as male, of the single transient, that kept the labor movement from reconstructing its past and future in the light of its prewar successes. This amnesia, more than the employers' offensive itself, kept the working-class movement from rebuilding for over a decade. When it did rebuild under conditions of economic crisis, it had only a partial memory of what had gone before. Assembling the building blocks of community, workplace, and political organization, the Left responded to the crisis of unemployment; but as we shall see in the next chapter, it left its past behind.

Three

___

Gender, Language, and the Meaning of Solidarity, 1929–1945

Few on either side gauged the long term effects of the rank-and-file victory. But wider and wider circles of men and women in Minneapolis who had no connection with the craft of driving a truck were to feel the impulse of the drivers' strike and to act on it.
—Charles Rumford Walker, 1937

In his account of the Minneapolis truckers' strike of 1934, Charles Walker described it as a pivotal moment—the "dynamo of change" which powered the transformation of a single city from an open shop paradise to a union town. The motive force behind the strike, Teamsters' local 574, spread unionism in "wider and wider circles" to a working class previously immobilized by economic crisis and political despair. The language, images, and symbols of unity generated by the strike portrayed strong men shouldering responsibilities for the entire working class. These above all caught Walker's imagination and the imagination of his readers.[1] (See illustration 3.1.)

Reading Walker's first articles in *Survey Graphic*, Marian Le Sueur had a different reaction. She objected to Walker's presentation of the truckers' union as solely or even principally responsible for the momentous changes in the city. "I have lived in the stress of labor battles for a good many years," she wrote, "and I have seen battles won and battles lost—but I have never seen a way of life given to the people of a whole city by the winning of a single battle."[2] Walker's narrative distorted the nature of that struggle by showing only one aspect of it: the workplace. Further, he focused on the coalescing image of the worker as male and thus ignored the role of women in setting the course for working-class politics.

Accounts of labor history have generally assumed that solidarity is the same for everybody, that all workers have the same relationship to companies, unions, and fellow workers. Division, disagreement, and difference evaporate before their unified narrative.[3] What is clear from the varying

First Annual

LABOR PROGRESS OUTDOOR EXPOSITION

Nicollet at 29th Street

SAT., JULY 27 to SUN., AUG. 4, 1935

Souvenir Program

"LABOR PROGRESSES BY STRUGGLE"

3.1 This program cover from an art exposition sponsored by General Drivers' local 574 in 1935 is an example of the flourishing labor union culture; it also demonstrates the masculinism of labor representations in the depression decade. *Labor Progress Outdoor Exposition*, 1935 (Courtesy of Minnesota Historical Society)

accounts of Walker and Le Sueur, however, is that the languages of labor
in the Great Depression were (and always had been) plural: the masculine
solidarity of workplace conflict and street struggle; the cross-class militancy of women's strikes; the familialism of the labor Left that expanded
the boundaries of labor's concern out into the neighborhood, the community, and the state house.

In its art forms and symbols, labor culture offered a richly diverse legacy
to its many heirs. Both Le Sueur's community and Walker's workplace
found a language in which to express their solidarity. Among these varied
voices, however, there was disagreement on issues of who was the legitimate heir, who possessed the authentic language, and who shaped the
future. How the culture of unionism expressed and constructed solidarity
for men and women workers in a decade of unemployment crucially
determined who would be organized and who would lead. Given the
silence which followed the telephone workers' strike of 1918, would the
militant actions of women during a decade of labor organization pass
unseen, forgotten by those who controlled the language and the memory
of solidarity?

The younger generation of labor history scholars would agree with
Charles Walker; for them, the pivotal force, the "dynamo of change" in the
Minneapolis labor movement, was General Drivers' local 574. Union
campaigns equally large in scope escaped notice. What is more, stories of
Farmer-Labor activism in the politics of relief and employment have been
lost or less frequently told, subordinated instead to the narrative of the
party's electoral rise and fall. For these reasons, labor historians have
made the history of the truckers' union coterminous with the history of the
Minneapolis labor movement. While highlighting a critical moment for
the city's working class, this perspective rendered other aspects of the local
labor movement, particularly the participation of women, invisible.

This chapter focuses on the redefinition and gendering of the American
labor movement and the nature of solidarity during the 1930s. Employing
labor newspapers as its principal source, it reconstructs ideas of gender,
history, and solidarity which pervaded the labor movement during the
depression decade. Conscious of their role in history, militant labor unions
viewed their actions through a highly refined lens and recorded them in
essay, iconography,[4] and ritual. They forged a web of symbols which
romanticized violence, rooted solidarity in metaphors of struggle, and
constructed work and the worker as male. In the midst of a community-
based labor movement, the gendering of solidarity as a masculine trait had
serious implications for women in the labor movement.

The "Dynamo of Change"

The enveloping crisis of the Great Depression destroyed the hopes of many union organizers that the labor movement could be revived after the severe losses of the 1920s.[5] Organizing among the unemployed appeared as one sign of hope. When industry began to recover in 1934, workers in three cities staged major strikes. In San Francisco, the longshoremen struck the shipping industry; in Toledo, workers at the Auto-Lite plant walked out; and in Minneapolis, truck drivers halted city traffic. In each case, labor disputes in a particular industry escalated to the level of the general strike; and in each case, the workers were faced with a major citywide organization of employers ready to stop the strike at any cost.[6]

In Minneapolis, this militant unionism had its principal source in the union, General Drivers' local 574. It had survived the 1920s as a small craft union, but this was to change rapidly. Through the efforts of two militant unionists, Vincent Dunne and Carl Skoglund, the union began organizing coal yard drivers in 1933. In February of the following year, over six hundred drivers struck the yards, and a union election gave General Drivers' 574 their first victory. Over the next two months, three thousand drivers from other industries joined the union. The 574's success at organization led it to press for a collective bargaining agreement with employers. When the arbitration effort failed in May, the truck drivers went on strike.[7]

At this stage, the community became mobilized through the drivers' activism. A strike committee of one hundred met to discuss decisions and plans; organizers set up telephones, a strike kitchen, and a hospital, and the pickets gathered for duty. Another aspect was the establishment of a woman's auxiliary to recruit support from the wives and families of drivers. Under the leadership of Marvel Scholl and Clara Holmes, the auxiliary was organized during the May strike. Skoglund and other union leaders hoped that the auxiliary would undercut the "nagging wife syndrome," language which revealed implicit fears that women could not or would not hold the line against employers. The auxiliary proved otherwise. Auxiliary members and their community allies served the strike in several capacities: cooking and serving in the commissary, raising funds, distributing the *Organizer*, and intervening with the relief board.[8]

When in May employers refused recognition to the truckers' union, negotiations ended in a stalemate. By July, the union once again controlled truck traffic in the city. This time, however, the Citizens' Alliance, a

Minneapolis employers' association, forced a confrontation between police and pickets. On July 21, 1934, the police force circled a truck of
roving pickets in the market area of Minneapolis and opened fire at point-
blank range, killing two and wounding over fifty. In rage and grief, over
twenty thousand workers attended a mass funeral for the first victim,
Henry Ness.[9] The death of strikers brought in the active interference of
the state government and the National Guard. Despite pressure to concede, General Drivers' 574 won a union contract with the majority of
trucking firms in Minneapolis.[10]

Mobilizing drivers in the Minneapolis truckers' strike of 1934, the 574
was a "dynamo of change"; its victory marked the revival of the labor
movement in the city. As a community-based labor organization, the 574
experimented with democratic forms of organization, invented the cruising picket as a form of workers' control, and encouraged the growth of
women's involvement through its auxiliary.[11] The use of a strike daily, the
Organizer (the newspaper of General Drivers' local 574), promoted local
communication and solidarity, and its circulation soared to ten thousand a
few days after the 574 began publication.[12] The union bolstered community support by organizing among the unemployed, by protesting and
organizing on relief issues, and by relying on community institutions.
Finally, workers from different occupations, political activists, labor organizers, and family members became invested in the strike, a fact which
stimulated the organization of all city workers.

Symbols in the Web

Like many labor unions in the 1930s, Minneapolis General Drivers' 574
envisioned the labor movement as a war, a violent battle against harsh and
oppressive employers, who had all the weapons of state and economy on
their side. This was in part realistic. The Minneapolis police and National
Guard units were visible enemies who wielded not only billy clubs and
rifles but also the legitimacy of the state. But what the labor movement of
the 1930s had, which its predecessors did not have, was a romantic and
heroic perception of violence.

Beginning with the mass strikes of 1934, the romanticization of violence
in the labor press occurred gradually throughout the decade.[13] In Minneapolis, members of the 574 did not hesitate to rough up a few scabs or stop
truck traffic in the city with roving pickets. Initially the physical struggle

was limited to fists and clubs. Bloody Friday, however, caused many strikers to take to the picket line armed. As Farrell Dobbs wrote, "After the shooting, many who had escaped injury dropped from sight briefly, only to return soon armed with various kinds of weapons. They now had shotguns, deer rifles, revolvers, hunting knives, and various souvenirs from World War I, which the veterans among them had brought back from France. Having bested the cops club-against-club, the strikers were now prepared to face them gun-against-gun."[14] Even though the leaders of the union acted swiftly to disarm the pickets, violence escalated throughout the strike. "Local 574's incomparable soldiers" went to battle barehanded, "instructed to defend themselves against any attack."[15]

As the violence escalated, so did the rhetoric and imagery of violence. Reports in the *Organizer* talked increasingly of busting heads and working over scabs. Cartoonists in the newspaper used violent imagery to depict labor's struggle. Labor, a young brawny man, faces off time and again against the round, effeminate and corrupt image of capital with its accompanying thugs.[16] Labor is itself solid, unyielding, almost as if the figure were made of concrete rather than flesh. Its face is almost obliterated in cartoons, portraying the masses of workers in the same solid gray mass behind its leader—the unyielding 574.[17] (See illustration 3.2.)

In the metaphor of struggle, the very size and violence of labor was predicated on the unnatural conditions of its birth. Cartoons like "He Goes On Fighting" and "Seeing Red" revealed the angry, uncontrollable quality in the creation of a working class. Monstrous labor was defiant, willing to strike back, unwounded by the tiny forces of state and police. Like Gulliver, it would set itself free from the Lilliputian forces of capital; like Frankenstein, the worker would eventually turn to devour his creator.[18] (See illustration 3.3.)

There were other narratives of struggle. Sport metaphors were particularly prevalent in labor newspapers across the board (see illustration 3.4). The figure of labor was presented as boxer or soldier, gladiator for truth, fighter against injustice, and protector of the weak.[19] In one cartoon, "Just Men—That's All" face off against capital at the bargaining table. "Capital—Big Shot" sweats at the sight of united labor; the "Prostitute Press" (a corpulent woman) twirls its beads; and the effeminate "Goofy Bainbridge" (the mayor) follows in capital's trail.[20] (See illustration 3.5.)

Military metaphors dominated reports in the labor press. In one article, a writer claimed that "if it [took] all summer," the truckers must defeat the Citizens' Alliance. Recalling how General Grant dogged the Confed-

He Goes on Fighting!

3.2 Representations of labor unions and workers in the 1930s became both more masculine and more massive. General Drivers' local 574 here confronts Capital, Cop, and Thug with sheer numbers. *Organizer*, August 2, 1934 (Courtesy of Minnesota Historical Society)

erate army, the writer argued that the labor movement must win "not by slick maneuvering, not by over-subtle cleverness, not by fine tricks" but through "bull-headed persistence." He wrote that truckers "regard this fight as a battle in a great war—the war between predatory Capital and exploited Labor."[21] In another issue, an editorial drew parallels between the Boston Tea Party and the struggle of the drivers as "blows against injustice."[22] In both cases, the writers asked if contemporary workers were worthy of their forefathers as warriors and as men.

If the solidarity of the trenches served as one set of metaphors, symbols of men's coming of age also functioned to represent the maturation of class solidarity. Charging that political leadership was "trying to keep labor in short pants," Len De Caux of *CIO News* once wrote: "Those who think labor looks cute in swaddling clothes or a Little Lord Fauntleroy suit but who fear its coming of age have no real answer to these questions." Labor was no "mama's boy"; it was "shooting up rapidly into full manhood."[23] In contrast, unorganized workers were caricatured as weak, immature, and fearful; they were depicted as younger brothers, children, and street brats.[24] In one cartoon, the Citizens' Alliance figure, dressed in the traditional hat and tails of the capital figure, pushes a vulnerable-looking "Minneapolis worker" over a cliff into the open shop abyss. In another

Gulliver Awakes!

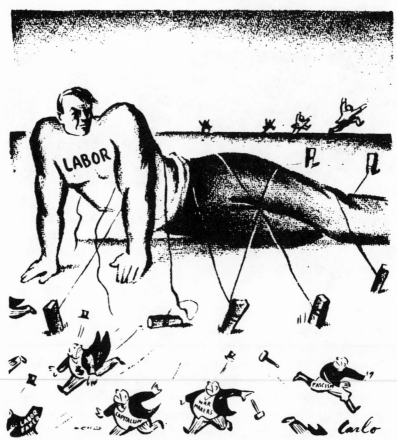

3.3 Labor culture relied on metaphors from literary and popular culture, using familiar forms to convey new political messages. Here, the awakened form of labor forces Lilliputian employers to scatter. *Northwest Organizer*, May 26, 1939 (Courtesy of Minnesota Historical Society)

scenario, a muscularly adult local 574 is attacked by small boys, who represent competing locals. Finally, an artist has labor inviting huddled and fearful nonunion workers (called "boys") out of the rain and into the house of union protection.[25] (See illustrations 3.6 and 3.7.)

What is noticeably absent from these cartoons is any representation of the worker (and especially the union worker) as female. Under the circumstances, this might be understandable. We can hardly imagine a

Safe at Home Plate   (BY BAER)

Courtesy Labor.

3.4 The *Labor Review* differed significantly in style from the *Northwest Organizer*.
Contrast this picture of victory with the violent, masculine representations with
which we began the chapter. Apart from the use of sport metaphor, the artist
uses few of the same conventions, relying instead on an earlier, populist style.
John Baer, formerly of the Non-Partisan League and cartoonist for *Labor*,
penned this one. *Labor Review*, September 14, 1934 (Courtesy of *Labor Review*
and Minnesota Historical Society)

And the Fight Has Just Begun!

3.5 This cartoon owes something to period comic strips as well as gendered norms of political behavior in the characters of the cowardly cop, the Prostitute Press, and the gangster-employer. "Toodles" is identified as "Goofy Bainbridge," the mayor of Minneapolis. "Just Men" represent the aloof and virtuous individuals of both Western and detective fiction. *Organizer*, July 26, 1934 (Courtesy of Minnesota Historical Society)

trucker identifying with a female clerical worker. But the strike created a new image of labor. From then on, even when the *Organizer* included articles about the struggles of other unions, representations of the worker and the union were male. One of the most revealing cartoons responded to the national textile strike of 1934, in which women had played a prominent role. "The Secondary Defense" portrays the textile worker as a football player who has just tackled capital, cop, and thug. He runs toward three other team members—Union Recognition Board, Stretchout Board, and Hours and Wages Board—with the intent to score.[26] (See illustration 3.8.)

Secular Saints: The Worker as Martyr

The crucial themes in the art and narrative of the labor movement were the celebration of collective struggles, heroic sacrifices, and brotherly bonds which transcended individual lives. They resonated with another

Look, Pal, Communists!

3.6 The nonunion worker as Charlie Chaplin. Again we see familiar stereotypes of employer corruption and deceit and worker innocence, immaturity, and lack of manhood as he is duped into the Open Shop abyss. *Organizer*, August 13, 1934 (Courtesy of Minnesota Historical Society)

important community ritual: the mass funeral which—along with mass trials and collective celebrations—served as public affirmations of class solidarity in the 1930s. In the case of the 574, the death of two of its members in the 1934 strike became a central aspect of the group's mythic identity.

An active unionist and an unemployed worker, Henry Ness and John Belor symbolized the two components of labor's struggle in the 1930s.[27] From the day of the incident through the 1930s, their deaths were recalled at numerous union anniversaries and events. On Bloody Friday, these working-class sons had been shot like "animals in a trap." Marching alongside their union brothers, "They [had been] shot in the back by base cowards. But oh, these lions of men, these heroes of the working class. They do not falter for an instant. Not for a second do they hesitate. . . . Their stout hearts beating with a magnificent courage they face the enemy unflinchingly and seek to stop the scab truck out to rob them, to rob their

"Come on in out of the rain, boys!"

3.7 The Big Brother in the doorway of the House of Union Protection offers to protect the weaker, more effeminate nonunion workers in a world before Orwell. *Organizer*, August 25, 1934 (Courtesy of Minnesota Historical Society)

wives and children of the miserable crusts of bread which are their lot."[28] Writers for the 574's *Organizer* emphasized the courage and martyrdom of the men, and they openly vowed to avenge the murders. They proclaimed, "The Blood of its Heroes will only nourish the roots of the 574 and make it a mighty oak."[29]

Funeral orations captured the central elements of the myth. The speakers were eloquent in expressing their sorrow over the death of a union brother; the story they told about Ness focused on family—he had a wife and four children. More important, brother Ness "was a son of a working

The Secondary Defense

3.8 This cartoon explicitly uses masculine sport metaphor to define solidarity. The irony of the cartoon is that a significant portion of the textile workers on strike were female. *Organizer*, September 26, 1934 (Courtesy of Minnesota Historical Society)

class family and in his life you could see the life of almost every worker born and raised under the worst possible conditions." These characteristics he shared with many others on strike. His service in the army in France and membership in the Veterans for Foreign Wars had a central place in the oration. A fighter for freedom and democracy, Ness had not met with justice or peace at home. For these reasons, he joined the ranks of labor. In striking, Henry Ness "understood well that he was giving his life for the cause of labor and was ready to sacrifice all for the working class."[30]

For these reasons, Ness became the central figure in the myth, and the anniversary of his death was a key ceremony in reaffirming union identity and collective will. It was before his grave that labor mourned. The news report a few days after Ness died gave details of his life and quoted his last words, "Tell the boys not to fail me now," words emblazoned on banners at union meetings nearly two years afterwards. On the anniversary of his death, two thousand workers demonstrated in a testimonial to the two men killed.[31]

The martyrdom of Bloody Friday contrasted with another incident in the strike. Early in May 1934, a group of pickets who responded to a dispatcher's call were ambushed and beaten in Tribune Alley. The union later discovered that the dispatcher was working for the employers' association. Among the wounded were five women. After this incident, women were not allowed to picket, and injured women remained anonymous in the strike history.[32] Although the Tribune Alley incident stirred some sympathy for the strikers, women's participation, even their sacrifice, was made prosaic by the deception involved. Compared to the heroic and cataclysmic martyrdom of Bloody Friday, Tribune Alley was business as usual: capital once again tricked and wounded the workers. Moreover, pictures of the injured women were used to show "what police and gunmen of the Citizens' Alliance do to workers when they ask for a living wage," promoting the image of victimization rather than martyrdom.[33]

The importance of heroic martyrdom to the labor movement was understandable in a culture which relied on religious themes and overtones even in wartime. Alluding to Christ, one writer described Ness as the man who "[gave] his life so that others might live." This messianic image, complete with the manly sacrifice of the crucifixion, echoed language used during World War I.[34] Vulnerable to violence, powerless in the depth of the depression, unionists' sense of embattled manhood resonated in the description of those victimized as "animals in a trap." The loss of work and of the ability to fight back took away the traditional symbols of their masculinity.

Important as well is the emphasis in leftist and labor rhetoric on the notion of a class war. As one labor poet put it in the *Organizer*,

> The Gods of Fate do so decree
> That man must fight to win
> That classes rise and classes fall
> Amid the battles' din.[35]

The enemy (in this case, the employing class) was portrayed as criminal, savage, and grotesque. Corpulent and bald, his body suggested waste, impotence, and emasculation. Given to cowardice and unnatural cruelty, the enemy employer used diabolic means to achieve his ends. The worker, on the other hand, possessed the saintly qualities of heroism and self-sacrifice, which made it possible to portray the employer not only as nonhuman but as a Christ killer.[36]

This treatment was not unique to Minneapolis. Psychologist Sam Keen found that similar metaphors of enmity and opposition characterize national and class propaganda.[37] Reading reports of the San Francisco general strike, the Chicago Memorial Day massacre, or the steel strikes of the late 1930s, we can find numerous examples of the use of hagiography to illuminate workers' sacrifice and to build solidarity. Further, most of these themes mirror the representations in political propaganda. In the language of militant labor, the enemy class is reprehensible; it lacks humanity; the only way to stop it is war.[38]

Moreover, the powerful connection between sexual ambiguity and employer corruption underlined corruption as feminine. Artists portrayed big business and its toadies as emasculated and effeminate; by the end of the decade, they were also increasingly represented as female. In "Spring Planting," the corpulent female figure of industry leaps through a field planting seeds of hysteria, sacrifice, long hours, and wage fixing.[39] Serial cartoons like "The Upper Crust" and "The Upper Clawses" portrayed effete males and callous, aggressive females in a biting critique of bourgeois capitalism.[40] For labor unions and the Left, there was undoubtedly something subversive about the number of women continuing to take and hold jobs in a time of high male unemployment. It was no wonder that "The Only Friend That Labor Has!" was the working man in the mirror.[41] (See illustrations 3.9 and 3.10.)

An Army without Banners

The emergence of the Popular Front in the mid-1930s marked a departure in labor and Left representation of women and solidarity. While proletarian art and literature celebrated a virtual cult of masculinity and romanticization of violence, the new politics of the Popular Front tried to reestablish the centrality of American labor traditions on the Left.[42] Female representations which valorized motherhood and women's supportive role resurfaced in the labor press. These icons of militant motherhood coexisted with images of female victimization.[43]

As symbols of how the home might be politicized, the auxiliary woman in cartoons was not "pretty"; she was stout, motherly, and imbued with a crusading spirit. Her political role as mother and consumer, however, did not come naturally; she needed to be educated into union consciousness. Like the woman in "Let's Put Shingles On Our Own Homes!" she vowed to her union husband not to destroy their shelter by buying foreign-made goods or nonunion products. Once politicized through her motherhood (and her consumerism), the auxiliarist would become a crusader for the union cause. She demanded union-label goods. She marched to the

CHALLENGE TO PUBLIC WELFARE

3.9 The caption reads, "The economic royalists who insist that a judge is in the prime of life in the seventies are the same who throw their own workers on the scrap heap at 40!" alluding to the court crisis of 1937. More to the point, the cartoon expresses the explicit gender antagonisms built into the depression as youth and women workers were perceived as being in competition with older men. *Minnesota Leader*, March 6, 1937 (Courtesy of Minnesota Historical Society)

The Only Friend Labor Has!

3.10 The use of the universal male in labor representation sometimes went to extremes. After a decade of collective representations, the worker figure is strangely isolated in this 1939 cartoon, embodying both the rugged individualist and Narcissus. Note that the mirror enlarges the size of the worker. *Northwest Organizer*, August 31, 1939 (Courtesy of Minnesota Historical Society)

drums in the "Spirit of '36" (a familiar union theme), and she rushed the war bonds ramparts as a modern Molly Pitcher once the United States had gone to war.[44] Like the Republican mother before her, the woman fighter of the Popular Front wielded buying power, not a club; she fought for her family, not herself.[45] (See illustrations 3.11–3.13.)

In "Jenny and Her Neighbors," a serial published in *United Action*, the female hero is a fighter, involved both in the class war and in the domestic

Let's Put Shingles On Our Own Homes!

3.11 Labor consumer politics here defends and protects the American worker's home even as the woman consumer pledges not to undermine it by buying foreign goods and nonunion products. In the republican order, woman was to use her domestic role to support the labor movement. *Labor Review*, September 1, 1939 (Courtesy of *Labor Review* and Minnesota Historical Society)

arena. Jenny's militancy extends her sphere far beyond the domestic. Despite her own desires to keep her house immaculate and spend all her time with her child, Rosamund, Jenny scrimps on the household chores so she can walk the picket line.[46] In one installment, Jenny returns home from nursing a woman who, threatened with the loss of relief payments, has induced an abortion. While blaming poverty for the woman's state,

3.12 This cartoon depicts Republican womanhood in the 1930s. Here women's auxiliaries celebrate the labor union spirit with farmers and labor unions. *Labor Review*, July 3, 1936 (Courtesy of *Labor Review* and Minnesota Historical Society)

Jenny yearns for a future when women will not have to make desperate choices. Contrasted with the Christmas holiday, the woman's story is stark, for it is then—the author reminds the reader—that workers celebrate the birth of "one of the first great teachers of the brotherhood of man" to Joseph, "a poor worker," and Mary, "just a woman of the people."[47] Rewriting the story of Christianity as a parable of worker and wife, the

THE NEW CRUSADER

3.13 Consumer politics, union solidarity, and the might of organized womanhood support the labor movement. The woman worker is nowhere to be seen. *Labor Review,* August 30, 1940 (Courtesy of *Labor Review* and Minnesota Historical Society)

author, Esther Bilyeu, lays claim to motherhood as the basis for women's participation in the workers' movement. "Jenny and Her Neighbors" is a retelling of the class struggle from the kitchen table. While men were battling employers in the streets, "Millions of working class women all over the world [were] putting up the same desperate battle against dirt and cold, hunger and pain . . . with bare hands, with primitive weapons, against terribly unfair odds—and always alone . . . a vast army of silent stubborn fighters . . . an army without banners." Here the class struggle was a war not only against employers but also against filth and disease.[48]

It was in this maternal army that women became most visible in the literature and iconography of the Left. Writing of the 574 auxiliary, authors attributed tremendous power to the wives, mothers, and sisters of workers and asked their support.[49] In doing so, they relied on a language of maternity and republicanism: "You too must realize that, in this struggle for a decent living, for the right to educate your children and give them a fair chance to continue to live peacefully after you have passed on, you must take your place beside your husband. His struggle is your struggle. His wages are your livelihood. Stand shoulder to shoulder with him and fight."[50] This call to action, like much of the literature of labor and the Left in the 1930s, relied on the expected supportive and familial role of women and invested them in the struggle through their children and husbands. The designation of women as domestic soldiers mirrored the popular culture of the 1930s, where there was a clear separation between the fight for labor in the streets and the fight against illness in the home. Most significantly, the women who battled in the household were "always alone." Only the victory of the working class would unite women.

The image of women as solitary warriors contrasted starkly with the public solidarity of men. For while there was ample evidence of women's militancy in labor's history, the silence of union culture in relaying this history suppressed this evidence. In the Elizabethton strike of 1929, for example, the strikers as "disorderly women" manipulated stereotypes of women's passivity and weakness to intimidate National Guardsmen and to frustrate the court system. One of the consequences, however, was that their actions were displaced in the event's history.[51] The metaphors of struggle, even political struggle, are the metaphors of war and battle; and in the class culture of the labor movement, war was not portrayed as female.

If passive images of womanhood contradicted the experience of women on the Left, they also drew upon a tradition of populist and Farmer-Labor iconography. Labor unions and the Farmer-Labor party agreed that the political party and the state were fundamentally gendered arenas in which men and women held different and oppositional roles. Far from denying sexual difference, women like Marian Le Sueur and Susie Stageberg used it to promote the equal claims of women in the polity. While Le Sueur may have objected to the unitary depiction of labor in Walker's Minneapolis stories, she shared assumptions with his representational tradition and those of the labor movement and American political culture. Among these were the presumption that women were more nurturant than men and that they would not "play politics with suffering" or—as Stageberg wrote— "disqualif[y] themselves as protectors of the human family" through a propensity for violence. The militant mother of the auxiliary, the consumer's league, and the Farmer-Labor relief committee comfortably fit within a familial context of solidarity; it contradicted only the notion of solidarity as exclusively masculine.[52]

In the rhetoric and iconography of both the labor and the Farmer-Labor movements, moreover, there was a reliance on female symbols for hunger, deprivation, and victimization, much as in Tribune Alley women had represented working-class victims. "The Eternal Nightmare" was labor's version of the Great Depression. In this narrative, women and children were helpless pawns of capitalism. While the hags of unemployment, low wages, and hunger hovered, workers' families were in constant danger. Fathers vainly tried to protect weeping women and children. "In the Richest Country in the World," economic crisis threatened to blot out the sun. Labor argued that it was men's job to protect woman and child from the darkness. America needed to awaken to the grasping hand of hunger even as men sheltered powerless women. Finally, women facing the ravages of unemployment and poverty had little choice between the red light district and the river. From the perspective of the Left, the paternal state had to intervene to save single women from their fate. In all of these visual parables, female figures represent the victims of poverty, economic crisis, and war; men, on the other hand, could provide the only ray of hope in a darkening world.[53] (See illustrations 3.14 and 3.15.)

The reliance of the labor movement on familial metaphors had a similar function. The 574, like other labor unions, relied on the language of family as the symbol of solidarity and bonding. The labor brotherhoods celebrated their common bond by the use of the kinship term in formal and informal discourse, symbolizing an equality among men. The use of this metaphor, however, had connotations for the labor movement that went beyond the maternal and nurturing sense of family in communitarian ideology.

Like families based on kinship, the family of labor had a hierarchy, even as it symbolized equality among men. Union men saw themselves as big brothers and the nonunionized as dependents. The labor tradition held that union members were brothers but also heads of families, and families remained subordinate to the struggle. But where brothers were everywhere in evidence in the labor press of the 1930s, sisters were invisible. Even when union papers recognized women's membership in the family of

THE ETERNAL NIGHTMARE.

3.14 The hags of bad conditions, insecurity, and low wages in their feminizing guise threaten the American worker's family. Father-worker protects the weeping woman and child victims. *Northwest Organizer*, March 11, 1937 (Courtesy of Minnesota Historical Society)

SURE . . . SHE HAS HER CHOICE

3.15 Published in response to relief cutbacks in 1937, this cartoon depicts a classic dilemma in reform thought: the supposed choice of women between the evils of prostitution and a respectable death, with little alternative. Representing women as victimized through the loss of virtue was a constant theme in old Left traditions which did not reflect new sexual mores. *Minnesota Leader*, October 16, 1937 (Courtesy of Minnesota Historical Society)

labor and supported their struggles, they did not view women as equal. For them, women held the same protected status as children and nonunionized workers. Even working women remained outside the arenas of men's shopfloors, streets, and union halls, where the class struggle made all workers brothers. (See illustration 3.16.)

"What do you say, Brother?   Are you going to help me?"

3.16 Brotherhood has been a persistent theme both in working-class movements and in a language expressive of labor solidarity. Here the 574 tries to free its more conservative and unliberated trade union brother. *Organizer*, August 21, 1934 (Courtesy of Minnesota Historical Society)

Roots of Labor's Iconography

The imagery of work and workers which was pervasive in the labor movement in Minneapolis had its origins in older traditions of the Left. Historians have examined these traditions by analyzing the transformation of iconography in socialist art and propaganda from the mid-nineteenth century through the First World War.[54] While this literature focuses on European movements, the language and ideology of the labor movement have been shared among cultures; and the transfer of visual symbolism and allegory among Western movements has been fairly substantial. From the ideology of working-class republicanism in the eighteenth century to the emergence and spread of Marxism in the twentieth, the Left in the United States and Europe have in common a legacy of political symbolism and language.

Nineteenth-century images of labor cast a strong connection between worker and craft, identifying them by tools, costume, and pose. While artists took artisans rather than laborers as their principal subject, no trade became the norm.[55] The popularity of republican ideology among American workers would suggest that craft identification also dominated labor art and language in the United States. This reliance on craft and individuality was in sharp contrast with the portrayal of women in period iconography. In the first place, the few images of women working were formulaic

representations of women in female trades. The republican tradition focused instead on the depiction of women as maternal and "natural," that is
beyond the particular and individual character of history.[56]

In the early nineteenth century, the most common representations of
women which appeared in the visual art of the Left were idealized and
allegorical symbols of the great virtues—Faith, Truth, Liberty, Nation, and
People. It was these idealized female virtues which dominated the iconographic tradition of the socialist movement. According to Eric Hobsbawm,
women's centrality was due primarily to the important role women played
in preindustrial society as peasant wives and as workers in cottage industry.
He argues that both in work and social protest, women were seen as an
integral part of movements for social change. As women's productive labor
became less central to the family, however, the representation of work
changed as well. Labor iconography obscured or ignored female work and
focused instead on the urban tradesman and later on the proletarianized
worker.[57]

By the twentieth century, the style and content of labor iconography
began to change. While skilled workers continued to dominate the trade
union movement and socialist politics, the central use of the proletarian
worker in illustrations reflected an ideology of labor which claimed to be
inclusive and which posited that unskilled workers were the most militant.
In the United States, iconographic changes were first seen in the literature
of the IWW. Identifying itself as a union of all workers, its core imagery
was that of brute strength, nominally in the service of capital but with the
power and will to break free from its chains.

The language and iconography of the Wobblies reflected their belief
that working "stiffs"—lumberjacks, miners, harvest workers—were the
working class in America and the key to eventual revolution. This image of
the Wobblies contrasted with their diverse constituency, which included
domestic workers and—above all—textile workers. The influx of workers
into the IWW during the Lawrence and Paterson strikes, where the majority of strikers were women and children, was not reflected in its self-
image and visual art. The question we need to ask is not whether this
image reflected reality, but rather, why this particular image of the worker
began to dominate leftist art and literature in both Europe and the United
States when it did.[58]

Any explanation which attributes these changes solely to ideology is
inherently flawed. While political theory played a central role in determining the style and subject of socialist art, this particular kind of art—the use
of generalized symbols and figures in illustration, cartoon, or commentary

for the purpose of propaganda—relied for its popularity and effectiveness on emotional appeal. At the same time female figures in socialist art were transformed from idealized depictions of the great virtues to particular representations of poverty and victimization, the images of men as workers became more abstract, more physical, and more universalized.[59]

The parallels between the depiction of male workers as brute strength in workers' art and the middle-class rhetoric of masculinity also are manifest. As white collar workers were less able to control their work and less involved in its physical aspects, they responded with a rhetoric which emphasized the need for "the strenuous life." At the same time, skilled workers as a group were losing their battle for control of production. Union after union collapsed as corporations deskilled work, fired skilled workers, or forced them to work longer and harder for lower wages. The number of trades in which it was possible to be "one's own man" or "a man's man" declined. There was no pride in being the fastest on the production line. New forms of workers' control had to rely on soldiering and sabotage.[60]

In addition, the sheer number of unskilled and semiskilled industrial workers dwarfed the membership of organized trade unions. While many of the new workers had physical strength and numerical superiority, their own tenuous hold on employment meant that they were difficult to organize. What is more, these new industrial workers came from ethnic and religious backgrounds that were different from those of the skilled workers with whom they competed for jobs. Paradoxically, it was the very "brutishness" of industrial workers that became a part of their image not only in the journals and posters of the IWW, but also of the trade unionist AFL. It was the image of working-class strength in the context of their unnatural oppression that was visualized and celebrated by the iconography of the Left.

The Impact on Women's Unions

Labor iconography reinforced the identification of women with motherhood and the home by the silence with which it approached women workers. As women's bodies were connected to fertility and barrenness, plenty and hunger, their inclusion into the masculine world of the worker as created in political cartoons would have signified changes in women's status beyond the labor movement. Contrarily, outside the role of nurturer and victim, women had very little place in the visions of men who represented labor solidarity through art, even in union cultures where they formed the vast majority of members. By the end of the 1930s, the total number of women in unionized garment and textile industries in Minneapolis was almost equal to that of men in General Drivers' 574, and they constituted three in four members of the unions. But garment union journals paid little attention to the fact that the majority of readers were women. In *Justice*, the newspaper of the International Ladies' Garment Workers' Union (ILGWU), prose and illustration were similar to those found in the labor press generally.

In the political cartoons which appeared in *Justice*, workers were represented overwhelmingly by male figures. In "A Pair of Cloak Runners Come Home," the New York cloak makers score vital runs with their "union power" bat; in "Will He Cross It This Year?" a man with the shield of union labor crosses the bridge to 1936.[61] In another cartoon, a muscular man, representing the union, dams a river of runaway shops.[62] Notably, men in these cartoons also represented the union legacy. In one cartoon, the powerful image of the Triangle Shirtwaist fire was used to evoke solidarity with the garment workers' historic struggle. An older male cutter describes the tragedy of the fire, where 146 women died, to a young woman in the shop, making no reference to the gender or identity of the victims. The workers' graves are unmarked; the mourners outside the cemetery are male. Absent from this scenario is the uprising of twenty thousand women workers, whose strike was the historical impetus for the ILGWU.[63]

When women did appear, they often served as witnesses to the drama of male action. "On the Eve of the Knitted Garment Strike" depicts men threatening cheating employers with "the union, our strength" while women reach for a basket of food. Another cartoon shows a working man laying down planks of union contracts even as a woman looks on in the background.[64] In 1936, "Jane Higgins, Worker," a comic strip, was first published in *Justice*. In the first installment, women pickets at a factory watch as men fight company thugs. In subsequent episodes, a male organizer confronts sweatshop owners, cops, and strikebreakers. The identity of the union worker was so firmly defined as male that cartoonists primarily focused on working men. The title of the strip seemed irrelevant to its subject.[65]

Justice occasionally published cartoons in which abstract ideas like "the union spirit" were represented by female figures. Like the symbol of liberty, the characters were highly idealized. In one cartoon, the female

ILGWU figure leaps hurdles alongside the graceful "French Dressmakers' Union." "The Spirit of the ILGWU" holds a torch before a male
worker at the beginning of the New Year in 1935. Another cartoon portrays the union spirit welcoming cotton and rayon workers to the house of
the ILGWU with the promise that "There is Room for Us All Under This
Roof."[66]

By the end of the decade, as the United States prepared for its entry
into the second international conflict of the century, and under the influence of the Popular Front, women reemerged from their representational
silence—not as workers, but as wives. Even at a time when women were
joining labor unions in hundreds of thousands, they continued to be
portrayed as secondary players in the dramatic struggle for freedom. On
the union front, as well as in the workplace and in mass media, women's
motivations and actions were dressed in the rhetoric and imagery of
motherhood and nurturance. Compared to the silence of the early 1930s
and in light of the masculinization of work and solidarity during the
decade, this auxiliary role, however small in comparison with their work,
was still better than complete exclusion.[67] Finally, the symbolic trio of
worker-soldier-wife took precedence over representations of the woman
worker during the war years.

The woman worker in *Justice* cartoons was working either in anticipa-
tion of marriage or children, and garment union cartoonists worried
whether women were undermining male solidarity. In an episode of "Needles and Pins," a union official is told his wife is on the phone. She wants
to know, the messenger says, "why [he] doesn't marry the Union."[68]
Another cartoon in the same series has two women whispering about
another garment worker. Contrary to her expectations, they insist, marriage won't keep her from the shop.[69] In these scenes, there was very little
recognition of women who viewed work or the union movement as a
permanent career path. That the editor of *Justice* found it necessary to
develop a column called "On Women" suggests just how peripheral the
ILGWU leadership thought its own women members to be.

The Spirit of 1934

The history of the labor movement of the 1930s illustrates the growth and
transformation of labor's culture as it threw off communitarian images of
the nineteenth century and invested in a much more instrumental, imper-

sonal, and masculine vision of labor. Art and language followed ideology in assigning the public arena, and more specifically the union hall, to men, downplaying the importance and work of women in building solidarity. While pragmatic politics may have dictated this, the continued representation of the worker as male depended on the extent to which labor's version of its history clouded and obscured women's participation. It repressed or distorted the history of Farmer-Labor struggles. As elsewhere, the role of women in strikes was omitted in histories which emphasized street battles and neglected the strike kitchen, which romanticized violence and erased the memory of pacifist protest.

The rapidity with which labor unions wrote their own history in newspapers and books suggests that they understood its importance in maintaining the bonds of brotherhood. Union newspapers like the *Northwest Organizer* and the *Labor Review* ran serial columns on labor history and recalled their own history with anniversary reprints of strike reports, photographs, and cartoons.[70] Like exchanging war stories, the retelling of the great strike brought men together in celebration of their common experiences. What they understood less well was the extent to which it circumscribed the organization and participation of women who did not fit the model of the male industrial worker.

The representation of workers in the labor movement of the 1930s was a continuation and transformation of earlier forms. The almost total neglect of the woman worker in cartoon and illustration in the labor newspapers of the early 1930s suggests that the masculinization of labor iconography, underway since the late nineteenth century, intensified under the strain of economic crisis. Even as men and women vied to describe and inscribe the class struggle in their own voice, they had to come to terms with this crisis as it was daily deployed in the language of politics and mass culture and captured in the figure of "the forgotten man."[71] While men could no longer be certain that skill, strength, or ability would guarantee them a job, they needed visual reassurance of their identity as workers and as men. The constant image of the worker, dwarfing capitalism and war, hunger and death, was that reassurance. It was the mask behind which the uncertain victory of the working class might become a reality.

Finally, while class as a unifying metaphor is constantly disrupted and undermined by other social solidarities, it has proved remarkably resilient among those labeled "other" by the labor movement. As the labor movement constructed the brotherhood of labor as male and defined solidarity as masculine, it also constructed the enemy as feminized and subversion as female. Yet working women in the 1930s organized into the labor unions which labeled them outsiders, auxiliaries, and subversives. It may be that the images and texts of the labor movement, which coded and expressed class conflict in gendered terms, were subverted by working women's own perception that they, too, were included in the notions of solidarity. As one linguist has argued, male language—and, by extension, masculine symbols—are read as masculine only by men; women read them as universals.[72] The icons and martyrs of labor's public expression, however, remained male. The univocal representation of union identity and solidarity would shape the subsequent relationship of women to labor unions. In emphasizing the commonality of experience for workers even as it represented them in increasingly unitary and male terms, the labor movement failed to deal adequately with gender division and inequality among workers, and its failure undermined the basis of inclusive working-class solidarity.

Four

Women and the Revival of Unionism, 1933–1936

The Strutwear Knitting Works had a sudden and lively strike ten days ago—still on. It is so hard to get the straight of the various conditions. The employers tell the newspapers their story. . . . Stories of the workers are different.
—Oscar Hawkins, 1935

There was unity at last in the labor movement, labor seeing its struggles not as isolated conflicts but as part of a great forward thrust. Each victory was a victory for all.
—Mary Heaton Vorse, 1938

In August of 1935, the Strutwear Hosiery Company dismissed eight working men from its employ on alleged grounds of incompetence; most knew it was for union activism. After months of covert recruiting and over two decades of antiunion practice by the firm, local unionists were not surprised by the firings. It was the cost of organizing in Minneapolis, a town only recently beginning to loosen open shop conditions in the wake of the truckers' victory. A strike would be a greater risk; perhaps all 150 union knitters would be fired as a result. Only two years before, skilled workingmen had lost their jobs in the Robitshek-Schneider strike. The question at Strutwear was how the employees would react. Up to that point, the only workers who had been approached were the men in the knitting room. Would the over eight hundred women and youth employees support the strike? Would the unorganized production workers hold the line?

Only a year before, the strength of the General Drivers' local 574 had reshaped the language and culture of unionism, embedding the ideal of solidarity in a masculine terrain. With one in four knitters willing to return to work, the gender of solidarity was in some doubt. Not only Strutwear workers but those women workers in the garment trade and in clerical work confronted the silence of labor. In the absence of an all-inclusive union culture, working women expressed solidarity on the picket line, in relief protests, and in cultural programs. But how the labor movement would incorporate women through the community-based tactics of unions and political organizations remained an open question.

This chapter seeks to explore the community and workplace bases of the labor movement in its growth years of the mid-1930s. Concerned both with the process by which working men and women created a community-based movement, it explores union organizing campaigns and the Farmer-Labor movement. Fundamentally, the paths to organization in both union and party were gendered in their origins. Power and authority were distributed and male and female militancy sanctioned within the broad outlines of gender ideology. While industrial organization constrained moves toward integration of the labor force and of labor institutions, dynamics internal to the specific history and culture of unions would profoundly limit the possibilities for change.

"NRA Babies" and the Garment Trade

The success of the Farmer-Labor party and the dramatic victory of the General Drivers' 574 altered the goal of the local labor movement from single-industry organizing to a broad-based campaign to "make Minneapolis a union town" (see illustration 4.1). Spreading the union gospel to the mass of unorganized workers, rank-and-file unionists hoped to change the relationship between workers and employers and to begin to control the conditions of their labor. The mobilization of women workers in nonunion sectors was an important key to the overall success of the union campaign, and one of its principal targets was the garment trade.

The garment industry employed nearly five thousand workers in Minneapolis, over 75 percent of whom were female. Women held a disproportionate number of unskilled and semiskilled jobs in the trade, as they did nationally. The industry was subject to seasonal and fluctuating employment, and this irregularity was intensified by the economic crisis. These factors undermined attempts at organization during most of the early twentieth century. But from the shop campaigns of the ILGWU to the strike origins of the hosiery workers' union and the orchestrated negotiations of the textile union, workers unionized and eventually proceeded along the path of bureaucratization.

Beginning with its revival in the early 1930s, the ILGWU was an important voice of community-based unionism and a central arena for women's labor activism in Minneapolis. In contrast to the male-dominated leadership in New York and Philadelphia, women presided over the local board during the 1930s. The reasons for their predominance were rooted

The Old Spirit Returns (By Baer)

Courtesy Labor

4.1 "The Gospel of Unity and Unionism" rang clear throughout the decade. By 1933, it was clear that a massive response to unemployment and depressed wages was in the offing. The labor movement relied on communal and religious themes to rally workers to its cause. *Labor Review*, September 1, 1933 (Courtesy of *Labor Review* and Minnesota Historical Society)

in the relatively late evolution of the garment trade in the city. It was only in the 1920s that cotton and silk dress companies had flourished in the city. (See map 4.1 for the distribution of garment shops.) In addition, the regional labor market was unique in that the skilled positions of cutter and presser were predominantly female.[1]

Despite the belief that women had sporadic work careers and early

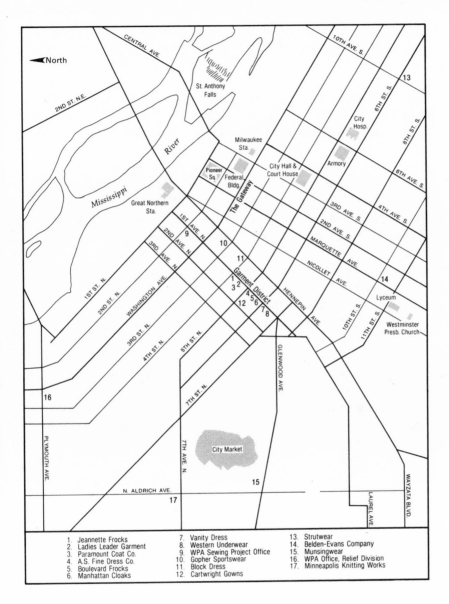

North

CENTRAL AVE.

2ND ST. N.E.

St. Anthony
Falls

River

Mississippi

Milwaukee
Sta.

Great Northern
Sta.

Pioneer
Sq.

Federal
Bldg.

The Gateway

City Hall &
Court House

Armory

Milwaukee Sta.

10TH AVE. S.

City
Hosp.

6TH ST. S.

8TH ST. S.

13

6TH AVE S.

3RD AVE. S.

2ND AVE. S.

MARQUETTE AVE.

NICOLLET AVE.

4TH AVE. S.

1ST AVE. N.

2ND AVE. N.

3RD AVE. N.

1ST ST. N.

2ND ST. N.

WASHINGTON AVE.

3RD ST. N.

4TH ST. N.

5TH ST. N.

7TH ST. N.

9

10

11

Garment District

1 2
3
4 5 6 7
8
12

HENNEPIN AVE.

10TH ST. S.

11TH ST. S.

14

Lyceum

Westminster
Presb. Church

16

PLYMOUTH AVE.

7TH AVE. N.

City Market

GLENWOOD AVE.

15

N. ALDRICH AVE.

17

LAUREL AVE.

WAYZATA BLVD.

1.	Jeannette Frocks	7.	Vanity Dress	13.	Strutwear
2.	Ladies Leader Garment	8.	Western Underwear	14.	Belden-Evans Company
3.	Paramount Coat Co.	9.	WPA Sewing Project Office	15.	Munsingwear
4.	A.S. Fine Dress Co.	10.	Gopher Sportswear	16.	WPA Office, Relief Division
5.	Boulevard Frocks	11.	Block Dress	17.	Minneapolis Knitting Works
6.	Manhattan Cloaks	12.	Cartwright Gowns		

4.1 Minneapolis Garment District Businesses (map by Cartography Lab,
University of Minnesota)

retirement trajectories, a small minority of women in the labor force were essentially lifers. Moreover, there was an increasing number of women who worked after marriage or who were the sole support for families. Seasonal, fluctuating employment in the industry was one option for these women; moreover, the garment trade itself relied on skills sex-typed as female, the sewing skills that every woman was supposed to possess in abundance. For these reasons the trade employed a large number of older women who were widowed or divorced, the sole support for families. "It [was] really hard to live on your own. I didn't. I lived with my family," Loretta DuFour, a young woman when she entered the industry, recalled. "Not too many [of the garment workers] had husbands, and you could always pick them out. They were better dressed than the rest of us."[2] Among married women, the depression undermined faith in the security of a husband's wage. What these garment workers shared in common was a perception of themselves as permanent, if sporadic, wage earners who had life careers in the industry.

Economic crisis framed the lives of women garment workers. The trade had always been unstable, seasonal, and low paying; and over 65 percent of workers in the clothing and textile industries were unemployed in the early years of the depression.[3] "You were lucky," said one worker, "to work four days a week. Wages were small, and you worked long hours." The rates in the industry were reduced to a minimum. As one worker said, "I was working on the machine. The operators were making very little. In fact, just thirty-five cents a dress. . . . Well, believe me, you worked hard to make eight dresses a day, so you know we didn't make much money."[4]

Piecework encouraged competition among workers in response to the new demands and strains on the family economy. As one woman explained, "Some people could make a living and others couldn't. And [the employers] always tried to put the price of the garment on the fastest operators." Moreover, piecework was "a constant back-breaking job." In these sweatshop conditions, women rarely sat up or took time away from their machines (see illustration 4.2). Predictably, the fastest workers were often not the best dressmakers. Some working women even tried to smuggle work home in order to increase their daily production. Other workers had to keep a watchful eye on their workmates to prevent such practices from lowering the piece rate.[5]

When the National Industrial Recovery Act (NIRA) was passed in 1933, however, things began to change. As in the trucking industry, the passage of the NIRA provided the first opportunity to change the condi-

ONE OF THE "TEN PER CENT!"   (By Baer)

Courtesy Labor

4.2 The use of populist style pits the corrupt boss against innocent labor, as depicted by working women in sweatshop conditions; political cartoons rarely depicted another aspect of the situation, female labor solidarity. The cartoon responds to the sweatshop conditions that the National Recovery Administration rules were to control. *Labor Review*, June 30, 1933 (Courtesy of *Labor Review* and Minnesota Historical Society)

tions of work in the garment industry. The National Recovery Administration (NRA) blue eagle served as a symbol of government concern for working families. In local parades, it buoyed hopes for economic recovery.[6] Under its sanction, women workers began to organize in the small but growing cotton and silk dress industry. As Marguerite Belton, an early member of the ILGWU, remembered: "Actually . . . the manufacturers knew they were up against it because there were quite a few dress shops at that time, and we all banded together."[7] In the dress shops of St. Paul, a group of shop workers asked the state labor federation for aid in unionizing the industry. They wrote to David Dubinsky, president of the ILGWU, to request an organizer and admission to the union in 1934. Soon after they set up the first garment workers' local in St. Paul.[8]

In the fall of 1934, Dubinsky appointed Sander Genis of the Amalgamated Clothing Workers (ACW) to organize part time for the ILGWU. Genis had firsthand experience organizing in the open shop city of Minneapolis. An immigrant from Russia, Genis had worked in the coat trade before the First World War and helped to establish the first local of the Amalgamated in St. Paul. The ethnic origins of many of the industry's workers in Scandinavia and eastern Europe meant that they shared a heritage of social democracy and an interest in socialism. As a Socialist, Genis was able to work with political activists and draw on labor and social contacts in the community. His leadership in the 1929 strike of garment workers in the city proved his familiarity with the terrain of antiunion employers, deferential workers, and hostile courts.[9]

When Sander Genis set out to "preach the gospel of unity and unionism" to the garment workers of Minneapolis,[10] he hired Myrtle Harris to assist him. As "a good loyal union person," Harris had been shop steward and financial secretary of United Garment Workers' local 27 for ten years. With members of the Ladies' Auxiliary, she staffed the commissary during the truckers' strike of 1934; and her contacts among truckers' wives, many of whom were garment workers, helped to root the ILGWU in the antiunion sweatshops of the women's clothing industry.[11]

From their base in St. Paul dress shops, garment workers organized their peers in Minneapolis. In the mornings, Harris waited outside dress shops as they opened and took her place by the door as the women left work. She contacted others by making calls and visiting them in their homes. While Genis worked the office end, Harris and other women who volunteered were responsible for face-to-face contact, the routine process of recruiting workers on the shop floor and in the community. Acutely aware of the obstacles facing the union drive, especially the threat of employer retaliation, they worked to subvert employer sabotage and build worker confidence.[12]

Genis initiated his campaign by trying to enforce NRA industrial codes to organize garment shops. Through correspondence and meetings, Genis hoped to convince workers to join the union by citing NRA code violations. Handbills and letters sent out to dress workers "had a very good effect on the shops where we had an organization started and some people in the union." In a large cotton dress shop, however, it "had the opposite effect. . . . The firm said it voluntarily complied." Genis complained that workers tended to see the government as the savior while union officials had to face worker resentment of dues.[13]

Despite the ambiguity of its provisions, the NRA became a powerful tool in the hands of labor organizers. They sought out women who would be willing to testify that their shops violated the code's standards for minimum wages and maximum hours. Code enforcement soon took a central, symbolic place in union circulars and pamphlets.[14] Women's depositions demonstrated the importance of labor unions in adjusting wage and working conditions to the code standard. Their testimony revealed that women, like men, were subject to intimidation by employers and threatened with dismissal if they protested code violations. One worker, Jenise Storelie, had worked for seven years at Block Dress as an experienced operator but never made the minimum for her job. She claimed that "to [her] knowledge there [was] only one girl in the shop who gets the minimum, [and she was] supposed to be the third fastest girl in the shop." Storelie had not complained, however, for "fear of being discharged."[15]

Sarah Presant, later a union shop steward, also testified about employer violations of the code. An operator employed for three years, she knew that most of her co-workers still earned below the minimum. Despite working forty or more hours per week, most of the operators only earned between fourteen and seventeen dollars a week, barely half the code standard.[16] During one season, Presant earned the minimum wage only by working more than regulation hours. Her willingness to protest quickly brought threats of dismissal: "About three weeks ago, the employer told me to mind my own business . . . implying that if I will not discontinue my activity in the union, I will lose my job."[17]

The slow pace of organization suggests that the NRA-based campaign was not widespread enough to bring workers into the union. Employers in the cotton dress industry resisted the code authority and applied for exemptions. When these proved unattainable, employers moved shops to Minneapolis where the effort to organize dress shops was still in its early stages. Genis argued that the ILGWU would "only succeed by getting these firms individually." After the shops were signed, it might be possible to have a market agreement for all city shops. Until that time, unionists had to develop a new set of tactics. They needed to find ways to recruit and mobilize women in the garment industry who were beyond the reach or focus of the federal labor mediators.[18]

Women and Union Activism

The efforts of women as rank-and-file organizers demonstrated their commitment to the union movement and their sense of responsibility toward the laboring community. As worker-organizers, they often put in ten, twelve, and fourteen-hour days, combining work, labor organizing, and commitment to family. For union pioneer Marguerite Belton, organizing had to be fit in between work and raising her daughter: "I spent many, many nights over in Minneapolis organizing. I'd get home eleven or twelve o'clock at night and get up the next morning for work." Loretta DuFour, another worker active in the union, spent many of her evenings calling on workers.[19]

In an anonymous strike diary of the period, one woman organizer wrote of the difficulties and boredom involved in the job. As head of a union picket squad, the diary's author was in daily contact with police, workers on the floor, pickets, and internal informers. She became acquainted with Joe, one of the nonstriking workers in the shop. Using him as a source, the union diarist was able to keep track of strike effectiveness and company reaction, but the relationship had a cost. The diarist recorded that Joe "belittled me as a cutter, the picket line as a whole, but said I was a good girl." However, Joe argued, he could "replace any person [the organizer pulled] out of the shop in one half hour." Such resistance prolonged union action, added to the organizer's sense of frustration, and increased doubts of union success.[20]

One of the recent findings of labor historians of women has been the extent to which union activity is predicated upon freedom from the responsibilities of marriage and family. Women unionists were for the most part single, divorced, or widowed. If they had familial responsibilities, they focused on the care of children or siblings, but work took precedence over family for most organizers. Union activity could be seen as both necessary to their familial commitment and central to their worker identity.[21]

The organizer's brief diary suggests just how costly this involvement was. A strike that lasted over six weeks required that unionists spend long days on the picket line, bolster co-workers, and sacrifice personal resources for the long-term success of the protest. Calling on workers meant going to nightclubs, attending weddings, and meeting them in their homes. Employers could threaten physical retaliation or dismissal; one worker became upset "about the possibilities of the withdrawal of the picket line as she [had] more to lose and [was] a legitimate striker."

Policemen could and did say that an organizer would "be in jail before [she] left town." The union diarist recorded these events in everyday language, suggesting their ordinariness.[22] Both the risks and the boredom of organizing took a toll on workers. For this reason, union campaigns in the 1930s had to be highly personalized efforts that relied on social networks, educational programs, and conversion experiences that empowered women workers, whom many assumed were bound to the home, to become militant public activists.

The extent of women's union involvement is hard to judge. During strenuous organizing campaigns, unionists devoted long days to calling and visiting workers. Levels of participation varied from person to person. A list of union officers and activists compiled from newspaper and archival sources included the names of 250 men and women activists. Only about 60 of these were officers. Women's careers as unionists included a few years of service as treasurer or secretary of a local. In addition, an officer served on the Twin Cities Joint Board of the ILGWU and might possibly be a delegate to the city Central Labor Union. Serving on a committee for negotiation or oversight of contracts was another routine appointment. In contrast, men organizers had a clearer path to mobility within the union structure. Many were hired from the local arena to work for the national union.

Labor union women did not record the time they spent in union activities. Locals met at least once or twice a month, and classes and clubs met weekly; a woman might have sporadic attendance at either. She also might serve as an officer in several capacities at the same time. What does seem most significant, though, is the extent to which unionism had its own subculture. It was rare that election to a union office was not accompanied by involvement in other aspects of the union—ranging from ILGWU summer school to political work. Inevitably, there were a few women for whom involvement in a labor union became a career. Marguerite Belton became instructor for garment operators through union contacts. Mae Counrod, who was president of a local in Minneapolis, went to manage a local in Vandalia, Missouri, and later returned to work in a Minneapolis garment shop. Leah Schneider, an education secretary for the Twin Cities Joint Board, was promoted to organizer of garment shops in California.

Developing social and educational programs was essential to methods of community organization in the ILGWU. Its initial drives in Minneapolis involved the organization of dress shops with as few as twenty-five workers. The size of garment shops and their ability to flee union constraints by relocating, employer paternalism, and the isolation and poverty of garment workers all contributed to uneven union success. Less than a year after workers organized the first ILGWU locals, the Twin Cities Joint Board hired an educational director. Aided by the Minneapolis Labor School, the union organized classes in parliamentary law, public speaking, labor history, and labor journalism.[23] Later, a dance troupe, glee club, and dramatics program developed.[24]

The union's educational program was designed to develop skills in a broad base of the membership. Giving workers communication skills, knowledge of their history, and familiarity with union procedure was one way to overcome the split between organizer and organized. While the enrollment figures are sketchy, ranging from thirty to one hundred students per term, evidence suggests women were the target audience. The union was over 75 percent female, and news reports listed women who attended the classes. Rarely if ever were men mentioned. In a similar way, the curriculum between 1935 and 1938 was ostensibly gender-neutral; but in seeking to give members, women prominent among them, skills in public speaking, parliamentary procedure, and organizing, it laid the basis for a broader distribution of leadership and activism among the rank and file. Many women workers lacked skills of speaking and debate; classes such as these made it possible for women workers to participate in these union activities.[25]

Betty Hoff, a teacher in the labor school, expressed the connections between education and organization in the ILGWU: "The union is more than just an organization to protect your job and working conditions. Your union provides an educational and recreational life."[26] The Twin Cities Joint Board began publishing the *Twin City Guardian*, a newsletter that ran its first issue in 1937. The members felt strongly that the *Guardian* ought to "express the opinions and conditions prevailing in [their] own industry before anything else."[27] Union newsletters, workers' theater, and programs which expressed the value of unionism for workers both individually and collectively were vital to the success of union community building.

Farmer-Labor Women's Activism

As women in the garment industry were establishing their first Minneapolis locals, state and local Farmer-Labor activists faced the problem of creating the political conditions conducive to labor organization. Coordinating its efforts to ameliorate the economic crisis with those of unions, community groups, and other political parties, the Farmer-Labor party distributed resources to the unemployed, advocated consumer demands, and launched a program of alternative education and culture. Its adherents sought to unite the disparate and diverse interests of working men and women into a Popular Front against those who had, as Marian Le Sueur said, "played politics with human suffering."[28]

The economic crisis in Minnesota's rural and urban regions provided the basis for new Farmer-Labor organizing and political initiatives. As the successor to the insurgent populism of the Non-Partisan League, the Farmer-Labor party had tried to elect candidates to office through the 1920s. Under the leadership of Floyd B. Olson, the party captured the state House in 1930. Winning the governor's office, however, did not translate into adoption of the Farmer-Labor program. The legislature responded with some emergency relief measures during Olson's first term of office (1931 to 1933), but it was not until the federal government began channeling funds through the Federal Emergency Relief Agency (FERA) that local relief efforts expanded to meet the problem. The abolition of labor injunctions, passage of a moratorium on farm mortgages, institution of significant tax reform, and development of a constituency among the unemployed accounted for many Farmer-Labor legislative victories, but its broader program failed before the organized opposition of the Republican party, which retained control of the Senate. Monies for existing programs were often held hostage by the hostile state legislature, while bills which complied with federal programs for relief funds were used as bargaining tools to restrict other Farmer-Labor initiatives.[29]

Women's substantial representation as members, activists, and public officials in the Farmer-Labor party gave them a voice in shaping social policy. Their role as party activists dated back to the Non-Partisan League, in which women were visible not only at picnics and fund-raisers but as league organizers, educators, and candidates.[30] One of the first women elected to the state legislature in 1922 (the first year women were eligible for legislative office) was league member and labor organizer Myrtle Cain. Now Farmer-Labor women ran as candidates for office; several served on state school and library boards, and two were elected to the state legislature in the late 1920s and early 1930s. Women were even more numerous as appointed officials (and as recipients of party patronage) under the Farmer-Labor governorships of Olson and Benson.[31]

During the 1930s, women Farmer-Laborites shifted the focus of their organization toward a role in the political sphere. As the Farmer-Labor political organization grew stronger in the cities, the Federation of Farmer-Labor Women's Clubs (also known as the Farmer-Labor Women's Federation) became an avenue for party office and political activism. In 1932, Farmer-Labor women in Minneapolis formed their own local club separate from the ward clubs. Organizers and officers from the three main cities in the state—Minneapolis, St. Paul, and Duluth—dominated the Women's Federation.[32] With the predominance of urban women in the organization, there was increasing emphasis on party concerns, political education, and social welfare policies. Ultimately, the Farmer-Labor women engaged at a local level in struggles for relief.[33]

Support of the Minneapolis welfare board by the Hennepin County Farmer-Labor Association and the local Farmer-Labor Women's Club helped to balance the opposition to relief by the local employers' association. The city council divided along party lines as Farmer-Labor and Republican council members fought over relief policy. Even after the election of a Farmer-Labor mayor in 1935, the Board of Public Welfare remained a political battleground. The city's relief funding was dependent on bond issues, so Republican council members were able to use the bonds as a lever to force Farmer-Labor delegates off the welfare board. Employer organizations and conservatives on the city council also used the threat of a business tax strike as a weapon against Farmer-Labor initiatives.[34]

The Hennepin County Farmer-Labor Women's Club acted both independently and in alliance with other labor and relief groups to investigate abuses in the welfare system and to force the welfare board to respond to local needs. In 1935, the Hennepin County group placed one of its members, Myrtle Cain, on a committee to investigate practices of the Minneapolis Board of Public Welfare. After it had investigated over fifteen hundred cases, the committee concluded that the city relief system should eliminate its casework approach to relief, relying instead on categories of need. Further, the investigating committee found that welfare workers refused to disburse rent payments unless relief clients asked for them at the office, that there were wide discrepancies in budgets, and that case-loads were inordinately heavy. The number of cases assigned to a single social worker had increased from 30 to 175 in the years between 1930 and 1935.[35] To keep informed on welfare board activities, the Hennepin County Farmer-Labor Women's Club established an oversight committee—the Labor Committee for Relief—headed by club members Marian Le Sueur, Myrtle Cain, Hilda Humphner, Myrtle Hillerman, and Eva Baltuff.[36]

As an advocate of women's needs in the political arena, the Hennepin County Farmer-Labor Women's Club came to play a vital part in shaping the politics of relief. Its members became involved in the struggles over relief eligibility and acted as advocates on the Board of Public Welfare. Selma Seestrom, one of its more visible members, was instrumental in fighting for supplementary aid for relief workers. The Hennepin County group also played a role in developing and promoting public support for state relief measures.[37]

While the Farmer-Labor Women's Club included women wage earners and government workers, the majority of its members were married women whose central public commitment was the movement. This perspective inspired them to organize the Women's League against the High Cost of Living in 1935. As a political tool, the league served to add to the agenda of the Farmer-Labor government an awareness of consumer and family concerns. Its first action was to meet in the Minneapolis mayor's office and call a citywide meeting of over forty women's groups, including women's auxiliaries, fraternal organizations, church and neighborhood groups, parent-teacher associations, unions, and political clubs.[38]

Setting the stage for the conference, Farmer-Laborite Selma Seestrom argued that "it was the great hardships which Minneapolis housewives had in making both ends meet that forced a group of them to get together to do something about the high cost of living."[39] Their struggle was one in which producers and consumers would be united; the wages of the factory and office were spent in grocery stores and clothing shops. The league's goal was to stop losing through the market what workers won on the picket line. When the burden of the crisis fell equally on workers and their families, political action had to be balanced between the claims of workplace and community.[40]

With maintenance of a decent standard of living as its primary goal, the league aimed to reduce the costs of food staples, utilities, taxes, and rent. In these efforts, it formed a political alliance with the Farm Holiday Association. The focus of their joint activism was the midwestern food processing industry, which made profits off both the farmer and the customer. Skeptical of the New Deal's farm program, the league attacked the food industry and its monopolistic practices; further, it accused the Roosevelt administration of forcing "the common people [to] bear the burden of relief, instead of taxing the high incomes of the monopolies."[41] Populist anger, which had engendered the Farmer-Labor movement in the early 1930s, empowered and mobilized league women. As chair Hulda Lundquist declared, "The organizations they represented were ready to go to any length to obtain an immediate reduction in the cost of table commodities, even if it involved strike action."[42]

The Women's League against the High Cost of Living began by petitioning the meat-packing industry for voluntary price reductions. It sought a 25-percent drop in the cost of meat. When firms failed to comply, the league staged a five-day meat strike in the city.[43] The issue was framed in terms of familial need. Petitioning the government, league officers wrote, "The meager subsistence of the Unemployed who were unable to buy meat for themselves and their families even once a week" boded ill for their children, whose lives and health were endangered. League member Marian Le Sueur added, "They say that all these 'isms' are breaking up the home but the only 'ism' I know of that is doing that is 'capitalism.'" It was capitalism, in the specific form of the meat-packing and food industry, that underfed the children and ruined homes. Sparked by this rhetoric, league members and housewives picketed supermarkets to urge other consumers to join the protest.[44]

The Minneapolis League against the High Cost of Living was not the only organization of this kind. Joined by leagues in Detroit, New York, Washington, D.C., and Chicago, it formed a national coalition of housewives and political activists. By far the most successful league was in Detroit, where over five hundred women served on local committees and thousands of women upheld the boycott. Mary Zuk of Hamtramck, who led the Detroit meat strike, was later elected mayor of her town. In Minneapolis, the meat strike had minimal results, but it created an institutional base for Farmer-Labor women. They continued to protest prices through meatless Thursdays, legislative lobbying, consumer education, and investigation. In these campaigns they were joined by consumer guilds, cooperatives, and labor unions, as well as by the organized Farmer-Labor party.[45]

The locus of women's activism in all these activities was the Hennepin County Farmer-Labor Women's Club, but it was fed from the various streams of union and community work of the women involved. The Unitarian Society was one such source. Marian Le Sueur and others were regular members; they fused religious and political meanings in their work. This same group of women had links to social work in the settlement houses; to clerical organizing through local 17661 of the Secretaries, Bookkeepers, and Tax Accountants; and to cultural work through the Minneapolis Theater Union. Many also had membership in leftist political organizations, including the Socialist party, the Minnesota Communist party, and the Communist League, a Trotskyist organization.[46]

Complementing the intervention of the Farmer-Labor women, women's union auxiliaries pressured government officials to provide relief for strikers' families. Wives and daughters of carpenters, painters, iron workers, streetcar conductors, printers, and machinists formed auxiliaries during the decade. Perhaps the most visible of these groups was the Ladies' Auxiliary of General Drivers' 574. Led by Marvel Scholl and Clara Holmes, its three hundred women members worked in the commissary, distributed strike newspapers, staffed a hospital, and raised funds. They also used their organization to demand relief for strikers during the strike. Carrying signs and children, auxiliary members occupied part of city hall while their leaders negotiated to meet with the mayor. The women left a petition at city hall on behalf of destitute workers and their families. After the strike, Scholl, Holmes, and leaders from the Minneapolis Central Council of Workers focused on raising the relief budget in alliance with the Farmer-Labor party and other groups.[47]

Scholl's concern for the welfare of families on relief extended to the arena of child custody hearings. Women on mother's aid, that is single women with children, were subject to the scrutiny of the court on issues of morality and fitness of the mother. In these situations, the only buffer between women on relief and the hostility of private charities like the Child Protective Association was the intervention of outsiders. Marvel Scholl and others who had been involved in the General Drivers' struggle worked with women on mothers' pensions in custody cases. When the Child Protection Association challenged the fitness of the mother in court, members of a new organization, the Federal Workers' Section (FWS) of General Drivers' 574, often volunteered to take temporary custody of the child. While assuming a nominal role as foster parents, Marvel Scholl and her husband, Farrell Dobbs, returned the children to the custody of their mothers. At one time, they were foster parents to fourteen children. When the mother was ill or could not support her children, Scholl helped to find union families with whom the children could stay.[48] The objective in these cases was to protect the family unit. Despite an iconography that emphasized the lone figure of labor doing battle with fists or hammers against a powerful business foe, the underlying metaphor of the labor movement in the language of strikers was the family. It was the common ground linking politics and labor.

The extent to which labor could support relief for women and children outside the sphere of work demonstrated the power of that metaphor. Through the media of the Farmer-Labor movement, the Women's League against the High Cost of Living, and relief workers' organizations, women brought previously marginal families into the labor movement. They incorporated issues of unemployment and general welfare into the agenda of unionism, integrating the isolated relief population into working-class politics and broadening the awareness of union members to include community concerns.

The web of community-labor relations also extended to the creation of a labor stage during these years. Members of various unions, including the ILGWU and General Drivers' local 574, formed their own drama groups during the decade. The centerpiece of this cultural activity was the Minneapolis Theatre Union, which was formed in 1935. Members of the Farmer-Labor Women's Club were centrally involved in its creation, including Selma Seestrom, Emily Bortnick, Madge Hawkins, and Mercedes Nelson. In addition, others active in the Communist party helped to found the Theater Union. Over the next few years, the union worked to integrate the strands of community, labor, and political activism in what one historian has called a popular front of culture. Its dramatic program, performed in front of diverse audiences, gave lessons in the meaning of community and class solidarity, respect for difference, and pacifism. In such productions as *Sailors of Cattaro*, *Our Generation*, *Peace on Earth*, *To the Day I Die*, *Waiting for Lefty*, and *Bury the Dead*, workers' theater revived the sense of community through presentations of shared experience and values.[49]

Gender and Strategy in Craft Unionism

The Strutwear Strike of 1935–36 dramatically illustrated the permeability of the boundaries between shop floor and community. For many workers and activists, the Strutwear campaign represented a coming of age for the Minneapolis labor movement as the forces of community were both vital and visible in the struggle. The culture of solidarity created by the strike promoted interunion cooperation, the coalition of political and workplace organizations, and the support of community and social activists. In this context, the community of union workers struggled with the legacy of narrow craft unionism and its privileging of male craft workers over women and young male workers on the production line. In doing so, it organized the unorganized by recruiting workers formerly excluded.[50]

When workers at the Strutwear Hosiery plant walked out in August of 1935, they challenged one of the most viciously antiunion firms in the city; but they were ill prepared for the exigencies of a strike. Supported by the American Federation of Hosiery Workers, the union of knitters had organized only skilled male workers in the industry.[51] The majority of the plant labor force—580 women workers engaged in seaming, looping, mating, and mending socks—were not members of the local; neither were the nearly one hundred "boys" who worked production line jobs as toppers.[52]

Strutwear had been active since World War I in antiunion activities. In 1927 it locked out a small union of knitters; and in the aftermath of the strike, the firm forced workers to sign a yellow-dog contract. Under the NRA, Strutwear management established a company union to undermine organizing efforts at the plant. Peter Fagerhaugh, a leader of the striking knitters, recalled, "A hundred men in my department were told to come downstairs for a meeting. We were told to form a union." If the men did not cooperate, they were forced to leave the firm.[53] Strutwear demanded that only skilled workers create the company union. Like the hosiery union they sought to combat, Strutwear managers thought the domain of their union should be restricted to men knitters and should not include production workers.

In the summer of 1935, a group of knitters visited a unionized plant in Milwaukee. On their return, they held a series of mass meetings among their co-workers, where they advertised the higher pay and better working conditions of the union plant.[54] Three-fourths of the two hundred male knitters joined the new union, local 38 of the American Federation of Full-Fashioned Hosiery Workers. But following disputes over union recognition, managers dismissed eight workers for union activity. The leaders called a strike.[55]

On the first day, production workers chose to honor the strike by failing to show up for work or refusing to cross the picket line. The knitters who called the strike made no provision for the participation of the operatives, but recruiting them was essential to the success of the union. In an earlier strike, failure to organize the operatives had caused the union's defeat, as it had in the Robitshek-Schneider garment strike in 1933.[56] A profile of Strutwear workers showed why. Strutwear had a labor force divided largely along gender and skill lines, with only the intermediary job category of topper opened to both men and women. Moreover, skill lines masked inequality among workers. Knitters started at a wage nearly double that of production-line workers. While even an experienced woman on the line could only get a few dollars above the NRA code minimum, knitters earned twice as much on average as women and as men training as toppers. Also, the company had a practice of hiring learners below the minimum and firing them at the end of training.[57] Knitters were not only a minority, but they were also comparatively privileged and distant from their peers on the production line.

A strike which began with the grievances of skilled workers eventually had to address the generally poor pay and working conditions of both men and women operatives. After the shop committee called the strike, it began to contact production-line workers; most knew about the strike from co-workers or public rumor. On the day of the strike, the divisions in the labor force seemed to make little difference. Women and young men workers held the line. Knowing that they needed the support of all departments, leaders urged operatives to attend union meetings and actively sought their participation.[58]

The union went beyond the shop door into the community and neighborhoods where workers lived. When the company tried to open the plant on the fourth day, three thousand workers and union supporters formed a massive picket line by the end of the day. Police clubbed several on the picket line, driving them from the pavement. Afterward, strikers followed the fifty knitters who had stayed with the company from the factory to a department store, where the police hoped they would be lost in the crowd. Pickets confronted disloyal workers in the aisles of the department store; some followed scabs home. In contrast to the men knitters, women who had returned to work were approached by strikers in the store and asked only to come to the union meeting.[59]

In the bitter cold of a Minneapolis winter, men and women strikers could rely only on relief payments and the meager strike fund. Flora, a Strutwear worker, told of the hardships involved: "I wish to say how bad we are. I have no clothes. I have to sit here. I can't get work to do, and we can't keep any food to eat and they tell us they ain't going to give us nothing and relief is going to quit besides."[60] Few workers had adequate protection against the wind and snow. As a writer for the *Northwest Organizer* noted, "The young girl that led the march of the pickets around the Strutwear plant Friday was short on clothes. But she had what it takes. Courage!"[61] Farmer-Laborite Oscar Hawkins seconded the motion. Reporting on the Strutwear walkout, Hawkins said that a knitter confessed to having endured "the tough conditions of eight years and would long ago have quit but for his family. . . . But he said now they are courageous and out of 200 machine men all but 39 have joined the union."[62]

Young working men and women gathered at strike headquarters, talking, playing cards, and waiting to walk the picket line. One writer noted that there "never had been a group of boys and girls [he] took more pride in working with and [leading] than this group of young people." Mothers and children also were part of the picketing crowd. In one instance, a woman picket on crutches challenged scabs on the picket line. Rumors had it that she was the widow of a trade unionist "driven to his grave" by blacklisting.[63]

The labor protest at Strutwear built upon layers of meaning within the working-class community. As the funerals of workers had become massive demonstrations of commitment, unity, and mourning, so too other rituals were staged to express protest and solidarity. A funeral for the company union became one such ritual. On the fifth day of the strike, union leaders organized a large picket line. At midday, hundreds of workers from the plant and the community formed a funeral procession for the company union. Circling the plant several times, they carried a casket aloft. Pickets later held rites in a vacant lot across from the factory. Evoking the ties between family, community, and workplace, they buried the old union and made way for the new.[64]

Hosiery workers shared common experiences and values through their community. Although Scandinavian and eastern European workers predominated, the labor force came from diverse ethnic groups. The plant itself was located near the Cedar-Riverside and Seward neighborhoods, strongholds of Swedish and other Scandinavian workers. Union meetings took place at Dania Hall, South Side Auditorium, and Eagles Hall, landmarks in the heart of these neighborhoods. Further, family connections between different unions rooted the union struggle in the social relations of the working community.[65]

Relief became a major battleground for conflict with the Citizens' Alliance. The employers' association exerted continual pressure on the relief department to restrict eligibility and to reduce allotments. In the spring of 1936, before the strike at Strutwear ended, the alliance lobbied for stopping welfare payments to all striking workers. In response, the welfare board rewrote regulations to restrict the number of single men and women eligible for assignment to the WPA.[66]

Backed by the Minnesota State Industrial Commission, the city welfare board denied hundreds of women already on relief their allowances. The women were forced to accept domestic jobs (as maids or servants in private homes) that paid one to three dollars per week. Workers picketed the WPA office to demand "that no relief client, man, woman, single, married or homeless be required to accept work unless at union wages." Miscellaneous Workers' local 665, a union which supported the Strutwear workers throughout the strike, demanded that women relief clients receive a minimum wage of eight dollars a week. Defining the root problem as women's unemployment, the Hennepin County Farmer-Labor Women's Club protested the new regulations.[67]

A committee of the Hennepin County Farmer-Labor Women's Club—including welfare board member Selma Seestrom and federation members Jessaline Scott (wife of an alderman and a former union activist), Marian Le Sueur, and Myrtle Harris (the labor organizer), among others—found that the welfare board "ha[d] made an organized effort to force single girls who are on relief to accept jobs as domestics in homes at starvation wages, resulting in forcing these girls to accept employment at substandard wages and possibly forcing them into prostitution."[68] While the women's committee was "heartily in favor of seeing that these girls are employed," they condemned the practice of forcing women to work at low wages. Further, the committee found, most single women on relief were not qualified for domestic service. The relief cuts were eventually restored.[69]

Stopping relief was not the only tactic of the company. In the first few months of the strike, Strutwear contracted work out to another large knitting plant in town. Some workers began to pick up night work at the plant until union leaders reacted by threatening to picket Munsingwear Company as well. Given the limited resources of the union, this threat could not be carried out. Subcontracting could not, however, undermine the strike's success. The powerful Citizens' Alliance, of which both Strutwear and Munsingwear were members, forced the relief board to restrict aid, but cooperation did not necessarily extend beyond the political arena. In fact, in the ensuing months, the company management relied increasingly on court actions.[70]

Over the eight months of the strike, the labor community in Minneapolis supported the Strutwear workers. Its members organized dances for strikers, staffed a strike commissary, and donated to the strike fund. In the course of the strike, workers at the plant were joined by members of a broad range of labor and political organizations. Emphasizing labor unity, organizations of the unemployed, the Hotel and Restaurant Workers, and the ACW would come to walk the picket line. At one time, nearly a thousand workers could be called upon to support the strike. The Women's League against the High Cost of Living organized a boycott of Strutwear goods, and the Farm Holiday Association sent in trucks of food for the strikers from rural communities.[71]

In addition, General Drivers' 574 provided essential services in blocking the removal of company equipment and goods from the Strutwear plant in December of 1935. The Strutwear management filed a replevin action in federal court, applying for the release of company goods allegedly promised to a company in St. Joseph, Missouri. The company's action was intended to undermine the strike, but the drivers double-parked their trucks by the factory entrance, obstructing removal of the goods by U.S. marshals, and threatened to strike any firm which helped haul the goods. While the goods were eventually moved, the delay strengthened the strikers' morale.[72]

When the truckers stopped the company goods from leaving the plant, the violence began to escalate. In the days surrounding the event, three workers were arrested, and several strikers were injured. At this time, Governor Olson called in the National Guard to prevent the company from opening the plant and to lower the risk that police would be involved in another fatal shooting, such as that which had recently occurred at Ornamental Iron.[73] Following this action, Strutwear Company and its supporters in the business community brought suit against Governor Olson, Mayor Lattimer of Minneapolis, and the Hosiery Workers' Union for obstructing trade and ignoring a court injunction. While the case momentarily stopped picketing, eventually the union returned to the picket line.[74]

For women workers at the plant, the success of the prolonged strike marked a turning point. Craft unionism, a strategy that marginalized and excluded both men and women operatives and sanctioned the poor conditions of their labor, was at least temporarily in retreat. In April of 1936, Strutwear management agreed to most of the strikers' demands, and the strike was won.[75] The eight-month protest had created an opportunity for the union to enlarge and broaden its scope. At the conclusion of the strike, membership had grown to more than seven hundred, including nearly five hundred women. The Hosiery Workers' Union, which had long excluded them as members, now rushed to recruit women to its ranks and sought to provide them with the benefits and protection of membership. By the end of the following year, Strutwear workers signed for a closed shop. New contracts brought both higher wages and the hope for greater occupational mobility within the plant.[76]

Wider and Wider Circles of Organization

The labor militancy expressed in the dramatic strikes of 1934 and 1935 brought with it the organization of groups of working men and women who were new to the labor movement. Not only were ethnic and black workers organized for the first time in large numbers, but workers in the hard-to-organize categories of white collar and service jobs also joined in the general will to make Minneapolis a union town. The organization of clerical workers, however, followed a different path of development than did industrial unionism. In Minneapolis as elsewhere, nearly 40 percent of all women wage earners worked in the clerical sector; and those who did work were remarkably homogeneous in background and training. Employers demanded a native proficiency in English. Moreover, in Minneapolis, almost all clerical workers were white, of Scandinavian or German heritage, and educated in public schools.[77] Further, the sex-segregated nature of clerical work and its stratification along gender lines promoted gender-specific organization. These characteristics made the clerical sector a fruitful and necessary ground for the organization of working-class women.

Labor leaders and activists, however, believed that the organization of clerical workers was problematic because of white collar workers' ambiguous and contradictory place in the class structure. For this reason, the AFL and later the CIO did not target them for organizational drives in the way that steel or textiles were targeted. Indeed, little time or money was spent in recruiting clerical workers into the existent AFL union of Stenographers, Bookkeepers, and Tax Accountants (SBTA) at the national level. In mass production industries, clerical workers from office staff to shipping clerks were organized into the industrial unions. Other clerical workers established locals of the SBTA; the State, Local, and Municipal Employees (later American Federation of State, County, and Municipal Employees); and the United Office and Professional Workers Association of the CIO.[78]

Workers organized the SBTA local 17661 in Minneapolis in 1923. It consisted of only a handful of secretarial workers, most of whom worked in union offices. With the decline of the labor movement in the open shop atmosphere of the 1920s, the SBTA had a small constituency; and most unions pleaded lack of resources when faced with the demands of their clerical workers.[79] During the depression, however, members of local 17661 became interested in organizing clerical workers on a broader scale. It was clear that organization of clerical workers would take place not through a national campaign but at the community level. In particular, workers from the truckers' union and the cooperatives were instrumental in developing a viable local. Jennie Sammele, who worked in the Franklin Cooperative Creamery, served as union president from 1926 to 1928; Jewell Flaherty, who worked in the office of the Central Labor Union, was elected president of the local and delegate to the Central Labor Union intermittently throughout the 1930s; and Josephine Schroth, an officer of the ILGWU, was a member and officer of local 17661. Finally, the connection between other unions and the SBTA was strengthened by the participation of its members in political work in the Hennepin County Farmer-Labor party.[80]

As part of the drive to build the union, in the fall of 1936 the SBTA hired Florence Strong Huber as its business agent with the intent of building union membership. By December, Huber had signed clerical workers at the Lee Overalls Company to a wage contract with a minimum union scale.[81] Florence Huber came from a family of labor and left activists. Her sister, Claire Strong Broms, organized the housewives' union in St. Paul, and another sister worked with the farmers' union in Iowa. Florence had become active in the local Communist party and had joined the clerical union in the 1920s. Her role in the SBTA formed the basis of activism in the Farmer-Labor movement and in the state government, and she was appointed as a member of the Minimum Wage Commission in 1937.[82]

In that year, Huber focused on negotiating a number of closed shop contracts for clerical workers. Her energetic efforts increased the union's membership from twenty in 1936 to over six hundred in 1938. The demands for most workplaces were the same. Workers asked for a minimum union scale of twenty dollars a week, higher pay for skilled classifications, paid vacation, and seniority rights.[83]

The campaign for organization of clerical workers ran parallel to other efforts in the labor movement. Beginning with a small, highly select group of skilled workers, the office workers' union tried to branch out and capture new members in related fields. Not surprisingly, it looked to areas of strength in the labor movement to build its membership. In targeting firms where management was already familiar with union contracts, it hoped to tap already established networks of activists and to build the base for future organizing efforts. Finally, the office workers' union acted as a bridge between union struggles that would have otherwise remained isolated. As a labor union which recruited union secretaries, it continued to build and promote the union community itself.

The Revival of Unionism and Community

In the fall of 1936, the Farmer-Labor Women's Cavalcade wound its way through Hibbing and Virginia and other small towns in Minnesota on a modern whistle-stop campaign. Having engaged a car with loudspeakers and printed hundreds of pamphlets, its organizers, Hulda Lundquist and Marian Le Sueur, went on the road to spread the Farmer-Labor word. Their message was to the women of the state: children lacked the oranges, milk, and meat that would make them strong; families suffered as farms failed and men could not find work. In their speeches, they gave witness to Farmer-Labor efforts to put an end to the devastating crisis of the depression. Only the reelection of Olson to the governorship and a strong Farmer-Labor legislature would save farmers, laborers, and their families.[84]

Speaker Marian Le Sueur was her own testimony to the power of a social movement that identified itself with labor—the labor of farmers, of industrial workers, and of wives and mothers. The daughter of temperance leader Antoinette Lucy, Le Sueur responded to her unhappy first marriage by taking her children to Oklahoma, where she began a new life. From there, she found her path to Farmer-Laborism by teaching at a people's college in Kansas, supporting the farm movement in the Dakotas, and finally becoming one of the better known speakers in the Minneapolis Farmer-Labor circuit. Le Sueur's trajectory from wife and mother to party activist was not a common one; and yet in her linking of farm and labor politics with those of the consumer and the family, she represented her generation better than most. As daughter Meridel wrote: "With no skill and no training she had to batter everything out of the wilderness of oppression, of being a woman, and was often angered by her unjust helplessness. In all her political struggles, she was never given a political office; like most women she was relegated to the hot dish, the dishwashing, at most the column in the paper and her magnificent oratory."[85]

The words of Meridel Le Sueur about her mother could be applied to any of the thousands of women active in the labor movement of the 1930s. On the basis of their family status, their worker identity, or their social role, women like Marian Le Sueur, organizer Myrtle Harris of the garment workers, and agent Florence Huber of the office workers engaged in struggles to increase relief allowances, raise wages, and better working conditions. They faced the consequences of the Great Depression with a style of labor politics that embraced consumer protest, the union movement, and the political front. Their union activism seemed to spread from one arena to another. Marian Le Sueur, active in the Unitarian Society, became involved in supporting the Minneapolis Theatre Union, worked politically through the Farmer-Labor party, and helped establish the Women's League against the High Cost of Living. This, in turn, led to direct intervention in Minneapolis relief politics, where along with other Farmer-Labor women Le Sueur became an active voice in fighting for relief for strikers.

What was true on an individual level was also true for union strategies. Involvement in diverse union struggles was the ground on which the labor movement of the 1930s was built. Organizers employed a range of strategies and institutional structures and experimented with strike tactics and educational work to recruit members. They learned to draw upon the resources of the working-class community, brought together unemployed workers and union members from other industries, and mobilized the support of radical organizations. Men and women from a broad spectrum of trades and industries contributed to the struggle on the picket line, in the strike kitchen, and in the polling booth; they were crucial to the goal of "making Minneapolis a union town."

Myrtle Cain was a labor organizer and Farmer-Labor activist. *Minneapolis Tribune* (Courtesy of Minneapolis Historical Collection, Minneapolis Public Library)

Images of the unemployed in the 1930s, like those of this protest march in Minneapolis, focused on "the forgotten man." *Minneapolis Star* (Courtesy of Minnesota Historical Society)

This parade of children in support of the National Recovery Administration depicts two standard themes from the 1930s—the familial cast of politics and the patriotic acceptance of New Deal programs. *St. Paul Daily News* (Courtesy of Minnesota Historical Society)

The 1934 truckers' strike, as captured in this photograph taken in Minneapolis on May 21 of that year, took on overtones of heroic violence in street confrontations between police and employers' groups and the striking workers. *St. Paul Daily News* (Courtesy of Minnesota Historical Society)

This photograph of a strikers' soup kitchen suggests the role often delegated to women in the labor movement. Nevertheless, the Ladies' Auxiliary of General Drivers' 574 proved to be crucial to the victory of the truckers. *Minneapolis Star* (Courtesy of Minnesota Historical Society)

The heroic martyrdom of working men like Henry Ness, a former veteran, combined with patriotic symbols, was a major theme in the labor union culture of the 1930s. *Minneapolis Star* (Courtesy of Minnesota Historical Society)

Activist women in the Farmer-Labor party brought about change in the relief system. This is a photograph of the officers of the state Farmer-Labor Women's Organization in 1934 with Susie Stageberg at center. *Minneapolis Star* (Courtesy of Minnesota Historical Society)

The participation of women workers, often neglected in the written sources, surfaces in photographs like this one of pickets and striking workers during the Strutwear Knitting Company strike of 1935. *Minneapolis Star* (Courtesy of Minnesota Historical Society)

Community and union politics were joined in Farmer-Labor directed protests like this one in 1935, when farmers and the unemployed brought their plea for relief to the state capital. *St. Paul Daily News* (Courtesy of Minnesota Historical Society)

Selma Seestrom was a Farmer-Labor activist on the Minneapolis welfare board. *Minneapolis Tribune* (Courtesy of Minneapolis Public Library)

Concern and discontent show in the faces of those protesting the welfare board's dismissal of Seestrom. The presence in the crowd of black men and women testifies to the extent of black activism in the Farmer-Labor movement (including organizations of the unemployed). *Minneapolis Tribune* (Courtesy of Minneapolis Public Library)

This photograph of a Minneapolis sewing project was taken in 1938 before WPA cutbacks under the Woodrum Act. The industrial character of relief work is unmistakable here. *St. Paul Dispatch* (Courtesy of Minnesota Historical Society)

The WPA strike in 1939 was organized in meetings like this one, in which Walter Frank of the Plasterers and Lathers Union addresses the Workers' Alliance. The diversity of the crowd in gender, race, and age contradicts written testimony and that of the courts; far from being a narrow group of men intimidating those working on WPA projects, the strike was a collective protest. *St. Paul Dispatch* (Courtesy of Minnesota Historical Society)

Pickets at the WPA sewing project during the strike of 1939. *St. Paul Dispatch* (Courtesy of Minnesota Historical Society)

Five

The Changing Bases of Labor Solidarity, 1936–1939

A few mistakes like these and all the good girls will leave the union.
—Sander Genis, 1936

It is against my better judgment to fight such a large group of workers and also against my ideals for unionism. After all, we're workers in one shop and most of them my friends. Why should I after preaching the gospel of unity and unionism be one to oppose them now?
—Florence Olson, 1937

In 1938, the executive board of the ILGWU met in Minneapolis. When their train arrived at the station, local members dressed in ethnic costumes greeted officers with union songs. The union president, David Dubinsky, posed for a photograph with a garment worker of Native American descent. Around them were gathered fifty women unionists attired in Scandinavian, Scottish, German, and Slavic costumes. Later, the glee club and dance troupe of the local union entertained the officers with the local review, *Who's Getting Excited*. While officers debated the institutional future of the union, women of the Twin Cities Joint Board celebrated the past of their community and their union in the rituals of song and verse.[1]

The event dramatized common themes in labor history. Rooted in a diverse ethnic and communal heritage, rank-and-file unionists focused on fostering local solidarity. Although they acknowledged their loyalties to the ILGWU, their unionism was a product of ethnic, class, and local solidarities. For national union leaders, however, such loyalties were problematic. Preoccupied with institutional and bureaucratic issues, union officers insulated themselves from the problems and possibilities of community labor organizing.

Between 1936 and 1939, the relationship between community-based unions and their national organizations changed. In essence, the community foundations of labor militancy were not so much destroyed as abandoned in the face of continued unemployment, inter- and intraunion factionalism, federal government initiatives, and conflict between local unions and their national affiliates. These changes were not gender-neutral. The abandoning of community-level, grassroots organization was a central component in the marginalization of women within newly empowered union bureaucracies.

The path between the community-based solidarity of the Strutwear strike and the workplace-oriented labor movement of the 1940s was not preordained; neither was the marginal status of women in a social movement based on class inevitable. What were the processes by which a labor movement respectful of local autonomy, rooted in community-based activism, and imbued with a sense of community as well as workplace solidarity was transformed into the more familiar form of bureaucratic unionism? Why did women become marginalized in the process?

The Decline of Community Unionism

The high tide of community-based unionism in Minneapolis had been reached in the Strutwear strike. Cooperation of the local labor establishment with national unions, political groups, and community activists underscored the importance of local activism for defeating the open shop and organizing the unorganized. In fact, the coalition which had undergirded the labor revival was rapidly disintegrating for ideological, political, and social reasons. The Farmer-Labor party was defeated in mayoral and gubernatorial elections in 1937–38, and the losses split the party. Local right-wing groups formed a guard organization, the Silver Shirts, ostensibly supported by some business interests. Its appearance signaled a local revival of anti-Semitism.[2]

As rivalry between the AFL and the CIO heightened, national unions increasingly began to intervene in the affairs of locals. Two of the most important unions in terms of local labor, General Drivers' 544 (formerly the 574) and the machinist unions (formerly affiliated with the International Association of Machinists, now with the United Electrical, Radio, and Machine Workers of America or UE), began competing with one another. As James Matles, director of UE organization, wrote of his Minneapolis organizers, "They are facing one of the most difficult fights with the entire AFL, led by the Teamsters in Minneapolis. There is actual civil war going on and about fifteen of our members have gone to the hospital as a result of these physical combats."[3] Jurisdictional battles among other unions further undermined the cooperation which was the basis of community unionism. Finally, the National Labor Relations Board's prohibition of sympathy strikes and secondary boycotts defused local union solidarity by denying the legitimacy of these tactics. Whatever the motivation for unified struggle earlier in the decade, the tension among supporting institutions and legal constraints discouraged future efforts.[4]

The consequences for unions—and for their men and women members—were severe. Rank-and-file members of all unions were increasingly isolated from decision making. Women in the garment and textile unions, where the conflict between men and women members and leaders had traditionally been strong, lost the fragile gains of the early 1930s. Sexual inequality in labor leadership reasserted itself as national networks, dominated by men with ties to the union movement, replaced local gender-integrated ones at the local level.[5] General Drivers' 544 was increasingly besieged with directives and interference from the international union. With these losses, the promise of an egalitarian, broadly based union movement faded.[6]

In its initial campaigns in the Twin Cities, ILGWU leadership remained largely local, relying on the skills of union veterans from the Twin Cities. When the national union began to establish its control over the regional affiliates, it replaced Genis with two temporary organizers. These appointments were symbolic of changes in union policies in which the national office asserted control over local officers.[7]

In the spring of 1936, Loretta DuFour and members of the ILGWU were organizing workers at Boulevard Frocks, the fifth largest cotton dress shop in the United States, employing from four hundred to six hundred workers. Originally organizers tried to use NRA code violations as an organizing tactic. Boulevard managers, however, claimed that they voluntarily accepted the code minimum, and this earned them a vote of confidence from the workers.[8] With the abolition of the NRA in 1935, organizers urged workers to turn to the union in order to protect recent wage gains and improving conditions. Only through collective bargaining could workers "retain in this industry the privileges and security established by the NRA."[9]

Despite slow progress at Boulevard, Sander Genis felt that the groundwork had been laid for a generous contract at the firm. At the same time, Genis slowly withdrew from ILGWU activities and concentrated on his own union, the ACW. Conflicts with the union at both the local and national level were at the root of his choice. A man familiar with the local circumstances and supported by the membership, Genis repeatedly asserted the primacy of community concerns. He maintained that cooperation among unions was necessary to unionize the industry and that expelling unemployed workers would only weaken the local union. In most cases, the national office overruled him. At one point, Genis responded angrily to requests for regular dues payments to the union; work in the cities was scarce and many members were unemployed. Jurisdictional battles between the ILGWU and the ACW was yet another cause for discontent.[10]

The business agents who followed Genis were more attuned to the needs of the national office. The first of these, George Glass, wrote to Dubinsky that he had found "a very poor dues-paying institute," and he hoped to set it right.[11] Contract negotiations were similarly mishandled as Glass infuriated the ILGWU organizers by agreeing to a clause making women machine operators responsible for the mistakes made by the predominantly male pressers. This clause unjustly penalized women workers to the advantage of a group of better-paid men. Resentment began to build. As Genis later reported, "A few mistakes like these and all the good girls will leave the union."[12] At the same time that Genis and another business agent continued negotiating with Boulevard Frocks, regional director Meyer Perlstein intervened and eventually took over the contract negotiations himself. In his report to Dubinsky, he wrote that Boulevard Frocks could become "a model union shop in the cotton dress industry naturally if properly handled." He gave no credit to local organizers, nor did he pay attention to local discontent with three successive business agents. Rather, the signing of the union contract, which brought few benefits to the workers at Boulevard Frocks, was portrayed as a victory for the union's efficient bureaucracy.[13]

In the wake of the Strutwear victory, both the garment workers and the local labor establishment thought the agreement with Boulevard Frocks could have been stronger. Both resentment and suspicion surrounded the contract negotiations.[14] Moreover, personal enmity between Perlstein and Genis was a recurring topic of discussion in the labor community. Their animosity opened the door for the ILGWU and the ACW to raid each other's organizations. Union officers at one cloak factory tried to persuade workers to abandon the ACW in hopes of finding organizing jobs with the ILGWU. The cloak makers' actions prompted their dismissal from the shop. At the same time, Genis was accused of targeting shops in an effort to keep them away from Perlstein.[15] Further, serious criticisms of the Boulevard agreement led the truckers' union, General Drivers' local 544, to try to organize those workers who were left out of the contract.[16]

Members whose wives worked at the Boulevard factory provided the basis for organization; the wives' own lack of loyalty to the ILGWU is further evidence of local resentment toward the union. And while unionists fought for the joint board's autonomy by rejecting one organizer, the New York office intervened by appointing Michael Finkelstein; local ILGWU members had wanted one of their own brought in as business agent.[17]

Changes in local union leadership occurred as the local ILGWU geared up for a new organizing drive. The goal was Munsingwear Company, a major hosiery and undergarment firm and, with nearly two thousand workers, one of the city's largest employers. Women operatives were the majority in all departments at the factory except hosiery knitting, cotton lapping, and engineering. They even held the titles of cutter and presser, jobs which were elsewhere restricted to men.[18] Like Strutwear Knitting, Munsingwear had a long history of company paternalism and antiunion activity. Munsingwear officers were prominent members of the Citizens' Alliance, and they had played a role in the Strutwear strike by agreeing to subcontract some work for the company. To fight unions within the company, Munsingwear established a company union under the NRA. Further, its management played a key role in the regional labor board, where some of its officers were able to circumvent independent actions by the company union.[19]

Munsingwear had long been a target of the ILGWU local leadership. After signing Boulevard Frocks to a contract in 1936, organizers began to make contacts with workers at Munsingwear. In November of 1936, Underwear and Lingerie Workers' local 265 received a charter.[20] Sam Schatz was appointed as special organizer; many women were also involved in the Munsingwear drive, including educational director Leah Schneider and rank-and-file members. By March of 1937, officers had been elected, and thirty people signed up with the promise of more. At the ILGWU convention that year, the local reported two hundred members.[21]

On the strength of membership growth, ILGWU director Perlstein sent a letter to the Munsingwear management stating that the "time was ripe for a collective bargaining agreement." "Our union," he continued, "is eager to avoid any interruption of production and cessation of work."[22] Despite Perlstein's optimism, the ILGWU was not successful in its campaign at Munsingwear. It simply could not attract enough members to call for an election. After nine months of organizing, union members had only managed to sign a small fraction of the labor force.

At this time, Munsingwear management began negotiating with the

Textile Workers' Organizing Committee of the CIO (TWOC-CIO). In two mass meetings, the workers voted to sign with the Textile Workers' union and to approve a contract that appears to have gained some wage increases and union recognition for Munsingwear workers.[23] The effort was headed by the new local CIO committee and its regional director, Sander Genis. He played a central role in convincing workers to join the Textile Workers' local 66. The company had been negotiating with TWOC in Chicago, and its reception of union overtures may have encouraged the workers. Distrust of the ILGWU also played a hand in the organization. As was clear from a local labor unity meeting, memories of the Boulevard Frocks contract remained intact.

Despite the ILGWU's advocacy of direct appeal to the workers "without the help of firm, foreladies, or shop facilities," it did not convince the Munsingwear workers. With the signing of the contract, the company union dissolved, and members of the ILGWU were faced with the choice of resigning from the union or, it was alleged, resigning from the company.[24] One ILGWU member, caught between the ILGWU, to which she owed loyalty, and the labor ideal, wrote to president David Dubinsky: "It is against my better judgment to fight such a large group of workers in one shop and most of them my friends. Why should I after preaching the gospel of unity and unionism be one to oppose them now? You understand if it had not been for my utmost pride and joy to belong to such a fine organization as the International [ILGWU] I might also have gone over to the larger group."[25] It was only after a year-long organizing campaign that the company became unionized. The decision of the firm and its employees to choose the CIO Textile Workers' Union was made in the context of labor politics in Minneapolis and in response to the needs of the company and its labor force.

The ILGWU's failure to organize Munsingwear was rooted in trends in labor organization toward a more corporate, industrial unionism that stabilized the labor force and provided a higher standard of living for semiskilled workers. At the same time, the Munsingwear campaign demonstrated the choices workers had between the two models of unionism in the 1930s—the ILGWU, dominated now by nationally appointed officers, or the new CIO union, whose claims were stronger and more immediate because of the participation of a familiar community organizer. While the company union had been outwardly controlled by management, Munsingwear workers trusted its union officers enough to sign with the CIO.

Shifting Relief Politics in a Time of Crisis

Changes in the political economy of relief helped shift the focus of unions from community to workplace. The most significant factor was the creation of the WPA in 1935. It shifted federal payments to the unemployed from direct relief to work relief.[26] This change in program structure altered the relationship of the unemployed to the labor movement and government. Previously outsiders, relief workers could now participate in union politics on the issues of wages, hours, and conditions.

Given the new emphasis on work relief, labor activists recruited the unemployed, project workers, and direct relief clients into organizations modeled after union locals. Among WPA project workers, labor and leftist organizations soon formed project locals. Compared to earlier attempts to organize the unemployed, these groups were relatively stable, with a dues-paying membership and links to parent organizations.[27] The Workers' Alliance, a coalition of unemployed groups, was the most important organization on the state level. In Minneapolis proper, it competed with the 544-sponsored FWS. Although the project locals had no legal sanction for their activities, stewards intervened in the workplace to address grievances or make demands. The FWS and the Workers' Alliance worked to forge cooperation among a broad clientele and a diverse set of communities.[28]

Early in 1936, those at the Vocational High School sewing project formed a local of the FWS. Over five hundred women worked at the Vocational project, making it one of the largest funded by the WPA. They produced garments, bedding, and other commodities for the relief population.[29] Many of the women who worked on the project were themselves former garment union members. Initially, two of the women project workers had called FWS organizers to a meeting. Within two years, two other projects in rural Hennepin County and the suburb of Columbia Heights developed strong locals of the FWS.[30]

Women project workers were centrally involved in protest against poor working conditions. In June of 1936, the women's work project local picketed the office to protest an unauthorized reduction in salary. The women argued that the WPA had cut the wages of seamstress helpers when the project had been transferred from Vocational High School to the New England building. A week later, six women from the sewing project demonstrated in front of the WPA office in Minneapolis. They claimed that officials had sent women and children out to an employment site where conditions were filthy and damp and that WPA charged exorbitant rent for the facilities. They were joined by dozens of women protesting WPA standards. The protest lasted ten days before some of the workers were reassigned to hospital projects.[31]

Throughout 1936, the Workers' Alliance and the FWS exerted pressure to maintain the level of WPA employment. In part, the need for farm labor in rural districts created a seasonal demand for workers that gave government administrators a justification for cutting relief. Urban business interests also wanted to reduce the number of people eligible for relief, both to lower taxes and as a form of labor control. To counteract these forces, the Workers' Alliance staged protests over the consignment of relief clients to camps, reductions in their wages, and other kinds of harassment.[32]

There was one issue that particularly affected relief clients as women—eligibility for work relief among potential Aid for Dependent Children (ADC) recipients. In this respect, the structure of the WPA program reflected the gendered character of public policy in the depression. Like much of the New Deal, it was created with underlying assumptions about the family wage, thus privileging men, especially male heads of household. Reacting to what they believed was widespread public opinion, administrators restricted the proportion of WPA jobs open to women to between 12 and 16 percent. Other obstacles to women's employment on the WPA included rules which prohibited married women and those eligible for ADC allowances, except in extreme circumstances.

These controls and restrictions were designed as "a brake on women's eagerness to be the family breadwinner" and on their alleged desire to work for pin money.[33] Further, mirroring labor-force segregation, the WPA adhered to the traditional sexual division of labor on projects. Nationally, more than one in two women (56 percent) employed by the WPA worked in sewing rooms. While this assignment capitalized on women's learned skills, sewing was defined as unskilled; and experienced garment workers worked alongside displaced homemakers. Moreover, the projects competed with a major sector of unionized employment for women. Whether sewing projects were designed to address unemployment in the garment trades or as a response to more general unemployment among women, administrators relied heavily on them to take up the slack.[34]

Sex discrimination in wages and in eligibility under the WPA was another major issue for relief organizations. The state mother's allowance system (in force until 1937, when the state changed to federal ADC) had allowed twenty dollars for the first child and fifteen for each additional child; no provision was made for the mother's support. Direct relief paid fifty dollars a month to families, and the WPA paid a security wage of sixty dollars a month, which could be supplemented by city funds. Mothers' pensions and federal ADC barred household heads (almost entirely women) from obtaining supplementary support through wage earning.[35]

The shift toward workplace organization in the relief population eventually widened the gap between relief clients and workers and reoriented the agenda of the labor movement from adequate support for all families into a defense of workers' rights. In the long run, the emphasis on the recruitment of WPA workers also had a gendered subtext. The policy questioned women's right to work on relief programs. It isolated relief recipients dependent on the invisible resources of old-age assistance and ADC, a group that was disproportionately female. A further consequence was that labor ties to the community became more attenuated.[36]

"The Depression Will Become As Severe Again"

During the latter half of the 1930s, unemployment levels remained high, despite government efforts to alleviate the problems. Signs of economic recovery were overshadowed by the Roosevelt recession of 1937. More workers were unemployed in August of that year than had been in June; in manufacturing, unemployment increased by 20 percent.[37] As the 1937 unemployment census revealed, one in six men were out of work as were one in eight women (see table 5.1).

Unemployed workers were more likely than not to be young, single, unskilled, and increasingly female.[38] In part, this was a reflection of their status as new workers, for older, more experienced workers usually retained their jobs or found new positions. Government relief workers were also older than average. These factors combined with sex discrimination in government programs meant that there were few jobs at all available to young women.

Workers in the depressed manufacturing sector were at the greatest risk of unemployment. Recovery was sluggish even in consumer goods like processed food, textiles, and garments; and there is some indication that the end of the decade brought another slump in this sector. In the textile and apparel industries, one in five potential workers was totally or partially unemployed, while nearly 10 percent of the labor force (400 of 5000) relied on WPA emergency work for income. This meant that effectively

Table 5.1 Employment Class by Sex, Minneapolis, 1937

	Male	Female	Total
Full Time Unemployed	16,453	7,586	24,039
Emergency Workers	7,946	1,630	9,576
Partially Unemployed	7,708	2,457	10,135
Total Unemployed	24,399	9,216	33,615
Unemployed as Percent of 1940 Labor Force	16.3	12.6	15.1

Source: U.S. Bureau of the Census, *Census of Partial Employment, Unemployment and Occupations, 1937*, vol. 2, table 1, Unemployment Census—Minnesota, 329.

Note: The 1937 census of unemployed workers seriously understated unemployment by nearly a third. Despite this inadequacy, we can estimate that the proportion of unemployed workers in 1937 (as a proportion of the labor force in 1940) was higher than 1930 estimates. Approximately one in six male workers and one in eight women workers were unemployed. The differential by gender, while still strong, narrowed over the depression decade.

one-third of all workers in garment and textile production in Minneapolis were unemployed (1462 of 4500 workers) in 1937.

By 1937, prolonged periods of unemployment began to have an adverse effect on the labor movement. Recently appointed business agent Michael Finkelstein wrote that the ILGWU was "in pretty good shape but we have been hit by the recession and all our people are out of work and have been for the past five weeks." While this meant that dues collections decreased, the most devastating effect was on local unions, where unemployment caused a rapid turnover in the membership.[39]

The caseload for the Minneapolis relief department reached a peak of nearly eighteen thousand cases in 1937.[40] Since the city council had made issuance of new relief bonds contingent on severe cutbacks in eligibility, the department was in financial crisis. Measures included the removal from eligibility of single men under age forty-five and single women under age thirty-five for four months; a reduction in the clothing allowance; the requirement that all resident adult children or relatives contribute to family income; and the exclusion of all workers who either owned a car or could obtain credit.[41] Local agencies in both Minneapolis and St. Paul began to reinvestigate relief clients; and the Ramsey County Welfare Board (St. Paul) announced that the county would close dental clinics for relief clients, reduce allotments, and force clients to dispose of all personal property except homesteads.[42]

The Hennepin County Farmer-Labor Women's Club protested new relief rules that would force "widows and their children . . . to dispose of small personal property," eliminate aid to men and women who owned homes, and take all single men off relief.[43] In particular, the Farmer-Labor Women's Club was disturbed by reports of landlords refusing to rent to relief clients with children, and they demanded an investigation of housing conditions.[44] Supported by the Central Labor Union, the Farmer-Labor women publicly lobbied against the new relief reductions. When a court order forced the city Board of Public Relief to accept the claims of single men but retained its restriction on single women, the Farmer-Labor women responded: "We are amazed at this brazen attempt to force the single women of Minneapolis into resorting to the worst forms of existence. Such an action by the welfare board is but an invitation to increase the white slave traffic, and is so utterly callous and such a vicious attack against the single women of this city that every decent person must rise to protest it."[45] The Minneapolis Labor Committee for Relief (headed by the Farmer-Labor Women's Club officers) was instrumental in pressuring the council both publicly and through state channels to change its policies. After a third threat by the Farmer-Labor state relief administrator to cut state aid, the Minneapolis Board of Public Welfare finally rescinded regulations denying single men under 45 and single women under 35 relief and supplemental aid.[46]

The Workers' Alliance, the FWS, and the Farmer-Labor Women's Club made the low levels of funding available to female-headed households (who comprised almost 15 percent of the relief population) a central issue on their agenda. Due to their interference, Minnesota became one of a small number of states that interpreted the rule flexibly according to need.[47] The issue of women's eligibility for work relief surfaced repeatedly through the 1930s. As with married women's right to work, the rights of working mothers to public jobs brought questions of family security and fairness into play. Women who accepted WPA employment could be seen as usurping male entitlements. The willingness of labor and political organizations to intervene on the behalf of women household heads increased the ability of these organizations to appeal to and recruit women; the availability of WPA work also gave women one means of access to the local labor movement at a time when it was shifting its focus away from broad community concerns.

Bureaucratic Culture and Dissent

Changes in the practices and ideology of local unions followed heightened conflicts in the labor movement, continued high levels of unemployment, and changed political circumstances. In the ILGWU, the business agent and the regional director increasingly set the priorities of the union by controlling union meetings. They were concerned largely with contract supervision and industrywide cooperation with management, while the needs of rank-and-file members as women, as union members, and as workers were downplayed. In the struggle to maintain a regional garment industry against national competition, unions focused on employer demands for wage concessions rather than improving working conditions.[48]

Loretta DuFour, a union veteran, described a meeting where the business agent urged them to concede a portion of their wages before the company went bankrupt. When DuFour refused to comply, the agent asked if she would like to lead the discussion. When DuFour started to walk to the head of the hall, the agent told her to "shut up and sit down." Still, as she recalled, "When the firm went broke, I still had my wages; the others lost theirs. . . . But they wouldn't listen to me. I was just a young snot."[49] In effect, the national union advised the women to accommodate the employer and proved intolerant of individual dissent.[50] Still other workers recalled the weakness of the union in the face of repeated shop closings. While many workers still experienced some improvement in hours and wages in union shops, the union became a prerequisite for employment, not a refuge from the demands of management. Moreover, decisions to strike or stay in the shops were directed by the board, the business agent, and the regional director. Complaints against the nationally appointed business agent, while brought to his attention, were usually dismissed as the work of troublemakers.[51]

At a time when women were the front line for union solidarity, the ILGWU educational program backed away from concerns about building community among workers and union democracy into a more utilitarian form of union education. Union classes increasingly focused on the training of union officials and on time and motion studies. Taking a few classes in union procedure was now required of new union members. In a brief orientation, between thirty and sixty workers were introduced to union structure, procedures, and history. While these classes promised to turn "card carrying workers into real union members," they were a poor substitute for the earlier full-term classes in parliamentary law, labor history, and public speaking. More important, the educational program put new emphasis on training union officers, not members.[52]

In the garment trades, tension between working men, who dominated positions of skill and leadership and the "young, pretty, inexperienced girls" who were "NRA babies" had been palpable throughout the decade. Regional director Perlstein wrote, "The problem of raising the new locals is as difficult as raising children." He argued that workers, especially women, needed to be "nursed carefully." They suffered from "infantile disorders" like gossip and jealousy.[53] Perlstein and other union officials agreed that women workers needed to break their individualistic habits. Only if they were "whipped into shape" could they become "trained and loyal members of our great family, the ILGWU."[54]

The union went to some trouble to explain how women could be brought into the union and how the union hall could be a more conducive atmosphere for women's participation, but it recognized the resentment of men toward the "damned skirts" who dared "invade the sacred halls of masculinity." Bringing women into the union, the ILGWU argued, did not mean that men would be "forced to submit to an atmosphere of rose-tinted femininity."[55] While a woman organizer for the union "might help to overcome the girls' reluctance to join or to go on the picket line," the pamphlet reminded the reader that a "personable man in a predominantly feminine group adds a certain piquancy to the situation."[56]

Classes on time and motion study, piecework, and industrial engineering were set up in conjunction with local employers. Although none of these programs were gender-specific in their design, they were chiefly taught by men and with the object of reinforcing the role of the specialist, officer, and expert in labor relations. In one instance, foreladies, class instructors, and production managers met jointly as a committee to set prices on piecework; they were joined at the meeting by students from the classes in industrial problems and time and motion study. With the purpose of "developing methods of improving relations and eliminating shortcomings that affect earnings and interfere with shop efficiency," students were expected to cooperate and even emulate industrial engineers.[57] Workers like Stefannia Petra, a dressmaker, occasionally were chosen to supervise time and motion study in their own factories and sent off to different cities for training.[58] But because women were disadvantaged in training and education, the new place of union efficiency experts did not escalate women into the national leadership. Finally, during the war, both ILGWU and Minneapolis Labor School classes increasingly incorporated domestic classes into their curriculum.[59]

By the end of the decade, national initiatives had restructured the local joint board. The cutters' local, which had been predominantly female from its inception, now had men as officers, and the same men became part of the leadership of the Twin City Joint Board. In effect, the cutters' local was the men's local. Men were overrepresented on the executive board, relative to their number in the general membership. Moreover, while the staff of the local ILGWU board remained predominately female, decision-making power rested with the male business agent and the regional director, whose ties to the national ILGWU were stronger than any local solidarities.

Finally, the dominance of men within the union movement—the product of union culture, institutional closure, and of the process by which bureaucracies reproduce themselves—had an impact on the local market. Finkelstein kept in constant contact with the national board and the Chicago joint board. Through them he recruited skilled male workers as cutters for local firms. This would not be remarkable, except that Minneapolis was one of the few markets in the country where large numbers of women were employed as cutters.[60] Bringing in men from the national market was one way to establish a sexual division of labor in the workplace and to bring the union more in line with the national ILGWU.

The declining fortunes of the ILGWU at the local level did not immediately affect those of other CIO unions in the city. The continued growth and vitality of the union at Strutwear hosiery is a case in point. In the aftermath of the strike, the hosiery union developed a full cultural program. Unionization also provided many women with upward mobility in the firm. In 1939, for instance, women entered the previously all-male ranks of the knitters, a fact which was important despite its relatively minor place in the union newsletter. Several women also served on the shop committee, even outnumbering men, a ratio that reflected the female dominance in the labor force.[61]

For many women who sought an active role in the union movement, neither union membership nor its benefits were sufficient to fill all of their needs. Their solution was to form auxiliaries in the 1930s, organizations which directed the efforts of working women and workers' wives. As the history of the Minneapolis truckers' auxiliary and the Flint Women's Emergency Brigade demonstrated, women's role in strikes proved crucial.[62] These organizations continued to play a political role in the labor movement by serving as a base of social support and an arena of activism for women workers.

In May of 1938, women workers at Strutwear organized a union auxiliary. They had attended a national hosiery workers' convention where Wanda Pilot, the only woman organizer of the American Federation of Hosiery Workers, suggested auxiliary work as an arena for women's activism. Sixteen women delegates had intended to form a women's division of the union. Because a separate organization was not permitted in the union constitution, they formed an auxiliary. Membership was open to union members and to wives and daughters of members. It focused on social and educational work central to the union.[63]

The coming of the union at Strutwear had reshaped not only the relationship of women to unions in the plant but also the relationship of unionism to workers generally. James Tibbetts, chair of the Strutwear shop committee, wrote an editorial in support of the auxiliary in October 1938. He understood that men in the Strutwear union, as a minority of the labor force, feared that women were going to take over the union. Competition between men and women over jobs could soon follow. Tibbetts argued that "in shops like ours where the majority of members are women, men are always fearful that the women will try to take control of the union. This fear is not justified. . . . Women are usually willing to fill the role that nature put them in, that of being the supposedly weaker sex."[64] The auxiliary could make a vital contribution to the union. Recent studies of the auto industry, he claimed, showed that "a woman on the picket line is worth two men." But in effect, Tibbetts still envisioned the auxiliary's role as supporting the union. He wrote, "When shops are organized and picket lines seem a remote dream, [ladies' auxiliaries] have a different part to play. Their job is to spread the gospel of unionism into channels that otherwise wouldn't be penetrated."[65] Finally, Tibbetts argued that auxiliaries could help women, who lacked a collective spirit and who were traditionally not good union members, to learn unionism. His perception starkly revealed how the solidarity of the women workers who supported the narrowly conceived craft union strike in 1935 had been forgotten.

Both the auxiliary and the women members of the Strutwear union helped to create a union culture. They organized diamondball and bowling leagues with teams from almost every department.[66] They also planned social events to bring together the membership and raise funds for the local. These included a standard fare of dances, annual picnics, and Christmas parties for union children.[67] Finally, the union newspaper, *Strutwear Worker*, enabled union members to keep track of union events and meetings, reported the events of workers' lives from marriages and births to deaths and promotions, and included articles on political events and topics of historical interest, including a series of articles on "The Trade Union Woman."[68] Both men and women unionists increasingly saw the needs of the community—for information, community, and education—as being within the purview of unions.

Despite their numerical superiority, women workers at Strutwear did not participate at all in the union leadership. There were no women officers of the union; women were noticeably absent from the contract negotiating committee.[69] The auxiliary disbanded in 1939. Given the different needs and conditions of men's and women's work at the firm, a difference paralleled in a fairly rigid division of labor along skilled and semiskilled lines, the lack of women's participation in negotiating union contracts seriously undermined their ability to receive equal treatment from the union. It also suggests that, despite women's role in establishing and building the labor union in Strutwear, they continued to be excluded from its leadership. The fate of women workers at Strutwear reveals how women's place in the union—conditioned by its creation during the strike of skilled workers—did not change.

Factionalism in Clerical Unions

Women of the office workers' union, SBTA local 17661, were faced with internal divisions that paralleled those of the labor movement as a whole and contributed to their marginalization within it. During the 1936–37 organizing drive, the union increased its membership from twenty-three to over six hundred.[70] Ideological and personal disputes among the membership, however, led to the firing of the business agent and organizer, Florence Huber. Huber had been engaged in organizing clerical workers two years at the time of her dismissal. Although she had increased the membership dramatically, her political affiliations with members of the Popular Front wing of the Farmer-Labor party and her ambition provoked criticism. More to the point, she openly opposed decisions of the executive board and sought to set her own priorities for the organization. While she had been organizing clerical workers in the packing houses, wholesale businesses, and creameries, she had always enlisted the aid of other unions to which workers in these firms belonged. Huber seemed both too independent and too ungrateful of their aid. Further, Huber recruited Farmer-Labor activists into the union on what the officers thought were false pretenses.[71] When she contravened union rules to complete contract negotiations, union officers had finally had enough. In a tumultuous meeting, they confronted Huber with charges of incompetence, only to find that she had stacked the meeting with her supporters. The executive board immediately dismissed her.[72]

Conflicts between Huber and SBTA 17661 officers had their source in the ideological and political configuration of the local labor movement. Beyond her handling of contracts, Huber was accused of "attack[ing] Teamsters' 544 after relying on them." At the time, the president of the union executive board was Jewell Flaherty, the wife of 544 leader Miles Dunne.[73] The majority of executive board members aligned themselves with Flaherty and the 544; this faction included the women who had held the union together in the 1920s. Of this group, only Jennie Sammele, a former union president, backed Huber. Those who supported Huber were a minority of the board; some of her rank-and-file supporters were members of the Communist party and her own recruits. Backed by Doris Anderson, Communist union members, and others, Huber launched a fight to retain her office and control of the union. Her supporters also included Farmer-Labor activists like Selma Seestrom, who had joined the union through a social work affiliation. Eventually, the mainstream unionists defeated Huber. Their victory was due in large part to fear and distrust of Communist party influence.[74]

After Huber's dismissal, the union hired Rose Seiler as business agent. Originally the Central Labor Union refused to approve Seiler on the grounds that "it was a man's job" to organize. Robert West, a friend of organizer Roy Wier, cautioned him against "the cruder forms of sex prejudice against women as organizers." West reminded Wier of his "high respect for Myrtle Harris," and stated that West "firmly believed that Rose Seiler [was] potentially as good an organizer as Myrtle Harris . . . [although] our first experience with a woman organizer was unfortunate."[75] Finally, West hoped that Seiler would be able to make peace among the factions.

Seiler's appointment was evidence of the changing nature of labor organization. By her own account, Seiler was a political activist who became a labor organizer. Born in northern Minnesota in 1906 of a farming family, Seiler grew up in a female-headed household where education was seen as the only route to social mobility. In her late teens, she entered the University of Minnesota and graduated with a degree in sociology and political science. Seiler spent the next decade of her life working as a social worker and relief administrator in a variety of jobs in both Minnesota and Washington. Starting off as the coordinator of girls' projects at the Northeast Neighborhood House, she also worked at a maternity hospital, the Family Welfare Society, the Children's Bureau, and the state transient commission.[76]

Like other social workers in the period, Seiler was drawn to progressive political action. Both the Northeast Neighborhood House and the Phillis Wheatley House supported political organizations for the unemployed. But, as Seiler later told an interviewer, she "decided [she'd] had it with social work as a means of ameliorating the problems of the human race."[77] As a member of the Farmer-Labor party, she had contact with labor organizers and had taken labor history and economics as a student. At that point, Seiler joined the office workers' union through her friend, Adeline Geehan, a former president; in the fall of 1937, she became the business agent.[78]

Seiler organized for the union with moderate success, recruiting newspaper workers, department store clerks, and creating an industrial contract for creamery workers.[79] In September of 1939, she tried to sign clerical workers of Consolidated Freightways to a union contract. A weeklong strike and the support of the General Drivers' local 544 forced the firm to negotiate. The first strike in the union's history ended in a victory as eight office workers employed by the firm returned to work with a raise of five dollars a week and some benefits.[80]

Increasingly, however, the office workers' union ran into jurisdictional problems in organizing. Clerical workers employed in manufacturing often belonged in production workers' units, and firms did not want to bargain with more than one union.[81] Further, while Seiler negotiated contract renewals, organizing new workers was a decreasing union priority. As a result, the union simply did not grow under Seiler's term as business agent. In 1940 she had been with the union two years, and the membership numbered around six hundred.[82] Moreover, the union became increasingly dominated by male leadership. Under Seiler's tenure as business agent, men were elected to the senior offices of president and vice-president as well as junior offices like trustee, sergeant at arms, and delegate.[83]

Finally, factionalism among members did not evaporate when Huber left as business agent. Continued political conflict within the union led to Seiler's expulsion and the active intervention of the AFL. At the center of the conflict were the Teamsters, whose leadership was expelled during a 1941 struggle. Seiler herself was embroiled in Teamster politics through

Ed Palmquist, who later became her second husband. As both a Farmer-Laborite and a Trotskyist supporter, Seiler was open to attacks by the AFL leadership. Her indictment for conspiracy under the Smith Act undermined her credibility as a union organizer.[84]

The AFL-CIO split also played a part in the struggle. Seiler's expulsion was tied to her attempts to affiliate the office workers with the industrial unions. As she recalled, "Bill Green [the president of the AFL] sent his international representative to oust Rose Seiler. . . . I don't think I was being discriminated against because I was a good organizer. . . . their excuse in ousting me from office was, 'too sympathetic with the CIO,' which was true." The AFL then appointed a new business agent, William Wright, to local 17661 and began investigating its membership.[85]

The expulsion of Seiler was followed by other expulsions, including that of Jewell Flaherty from her position as secretary of the city labor federation. An employee of the Central Labor Union for seventeen years, Flaherty had married Miles Dunne, one of the Teamster leaders. When the General Drivers' leadership tried to leave the AFL in 1941, the federation fought back at both the local and national level. It ordered the local affiliate to fire Flaherty because she had access to confidential information.[86]

Violet Johnson, a friend of Flaherty's and a long-time member of the office workers' union, wrote to the AFL president on her behalf. Johnson argued that Flaherty had personally been involved in exposing and ridding the office workers' union of Communists and had done "all she could to safeguard AFL connections." Moreover, Flaherty was an older woman who had come to the Central Labor Union right out of high school and had spent most of her work life with the labor movement. "Her age and her labor experience" were now liabilities on the labor market. Finally, Johnson pointed out that there were those who believed that Flaherty's marriage was alone grounds for her dismissal. Johnson continued, "From all I have been able to read in your publications, I have never found anything supporting this anti-married woman feeling, but it exists among some prominent local labor people, and so, if you answer this at all, would you please tell me when and why labor has reversed its traditional upholding of woman's right to work, whether married or single?"[87] Finally, she argued that it was undignified for the labor movement to deprive a man, his wife, and family of an income. Despite Johnson's intervention, Flaherty lost her job. As AFL President Green insisted, Flaherty was intimately connected with a rival union.[88]

The use of divisions between the AFL and CIO and the differences among members of the office workers' union had dire consequences for the survival of clerical unionism and the role of women in the labor movement. Ideological differences in particular were among the principal causes for the dismantling of clerical unions in the 1940s and 1950s.[89] But it is important not to let these differences obscure the meaning of other trends in organizing women clericals.

Factionalism between Trotskyists and Stalinists led to the gradual replacement of women union leaders with men as union officers. Three years later the split between the AFL and CIO, combined with accusations of communist influence in the local labor movement, was an opportunity for the international union to reestablish its control over the office workers' local. In both cases, the power of women in the union and local autonomy were connected. Inter- and intraunion conflict underlined the extent to which, for the labor movement, factionalism was a trait contrary to masculine solidarity and thus both characterized as feminine and attributed to women.[90] It does not seem coincidental that the women ousted under union pressure were not adherents so much as sympathizers and intimates of the Left. Ultimately, the survival of a union in a predominantly female occupation required a harmony of interests at the local level if it was to survive the hostility to women unionists in a male-dominated labor movement.

Union Bureaucracy and Women's Labor Activism

The democratic expression of local, ethnic, and class community with which we began this chapter stands in stark contrast to the evidence of union bureaucracy, national control, and factionalism that we have explored. Apart from the loss of diversity, cultural expression, and rank-and-file participation, the transformation of the labor movement away from its community base to a more hierarchical, routinized, and workplace-oriented unionism effectively marginalized the women in its ranks and short-circuited their future recruitment. The fate of white collar unionism was particularly devastating in terms of the long-term prospects for the labor movement and women workers. That it fell victim to ideological conflict and infighting is both ironic and tragic.

When in the late 1930s the industrial unions adopted new policies that emphasized national authority over local autonomy, stability over militancy, they alienated many rank-and-file members who were the heart of the drive to organize the unorganized. Centralization and union support for the war changed the nature of women's role in the labor movement even as unions closed down possibilities for women in the leadership and direction of their own affairs.

In particular, this trend was related to the economic status of most women workers. Employed in unstable, seasonal, or secondary occupations, women workers were faced with cyclical unemployment in garments, light manufacturing, and domestic work. In clerical work, unemployment appears to have increased gradually over the decade of the thirties. Unemployment was not the only source of union instability among clerical workers; local ideological and political divisions made room for national unions to assert control over local ones. In this move, the stenographers' union lost more than local autonomy. As in other unions, conflict discredited women leaders and dismantled local union leadership.

The movement away from community issues, organizations, and control toward a more corporate, workplace-oriented unionism took place in an atmosphere of increasing political antagonism and continued economic crisis. Community-based unions had made possible the rise of labor in Minneapolis, and only divisiveness in the distribution of union power and resources at the local level could undermine their strength. Late in the decade, unionists at both the local and national levels came to believe that highly centralized, bureaucratic, national, and male-led unions could give the locals the stability they needed. This choice altered the nature of unionism and the relationship of women workers to the movement.

Six

Gender, Labor, and the State in the WPA Strike of 1939

These WPA layoffs are causing a lot of misery. . . . it's taking the Wolf away from one door and putting him down in front of another. The way things are going, perhaps there won't be enough wolves to go around, but there will be misery enough for all.
—Puzzled? 1939

The motors spin, the drive shafts hum,
And everywhere a busy whirl.
A working mother's heart is numb.
She sees the growing boy and girl
Without the things she works to give,
Without the things they need to live.
And as she turns, her tears will fall.
And why the sorrow of her way?
A 403 [discharge slip] for Mother's Day.
—*Northwest Organizer*, 1939

Described at once as a quiet woman and a "whole army of wrath," Minnie Kohn lived in Minneapolis all her life. Until the depression came, she was a single working woman, running a beauty shop on the margin. Sometime during the first years of the crisis, Kohn lost the shop and wound up on relief, eventually getting a job at the WPA sewing project in North Minneapolis. She joined the project local organized by the FWS of General Drivers' 544. She never spoke at union meetings; its leaders did not know her. Yet, in the fall of 1939, Kohn was sentenced to the county workhouse for forty-five days, charged with being a ringleader in a major strike. No less than thirty witnesses testified that she had physically assaulted women who dared to cross the picket line.[1]

Her codefendant, Sigrid Asunma, was the sole support of six children. A Finnish immigrant, she had been widowed during the depression. On the WPA project, Asunma now earned almost a living wage of sixty dollars a month, more than what she received from ADC. When threatened with layoffs, Asunma—like many others—militantly policed the picket line. The judge who tried both Asunma and Kohn wondered how women so ladylike could be so vicious. In Asunma's case, he concluded, it must have been her Finnish blood.[2]

Minnie Kohn and Sigrid Asunma were only two of the more than sixty women indicted for their solidarity with the WPA strike. But while the court focused on their verbal and physical abuse of project workers, horrified that they tore the clothing of those women who crossed the picket line, the trial raised fundamental issues about the nature of solidarity, the access of women to work and welfare, and the rights of working men and women to strike. How did labor react to the rights of women under these conditions? How did gender shape the militancy of the WPA strikers and their response to the particular needs of women?

Gender and the State

By the late 1930s, continued high levels of unemployment and conservative reaction to the New Deal had severely constrained the willingness and ability of government agencies to respond to demands for greater levels of relief. Tales of welfare abuse and patronage politics promoted an image of the WPA as a refuge for radicals and slackers; the presence of women as project workers, while less noticeable, was still the object of some dissent. These attitudes also surfaced in sporadic complaints about married women working while the nuclear family remained imperiled by male unemployment.

Government policy and political discourse shaped women's right to work in two arenas: the welfare arena, in which eligibility rules, work and family status, and level of allowance were decided, and the burgeoning arena of the state bureaucracy, which dealt with civil service employment, entitlement programs, and the regulation of work. Although married women's access to work was settled in part by the federal government through clauses in the Economy Act of 1932,[3] local and state governments wrestled with the problem of women and work throughout the decade. In Minnesota, both labor and political groups were engaged in debate over the access of women, particularly married women, to work and to party patronage. Women in the Minnesota state government had weathered early attempts to bar them from employment under the Olson administration with support from the Farmer-Labor party. In the aftermath of the 1937 recession, bills were once again introduced in the state legislature to bar married women from state employment; but they were ultimately unsuccessful.[4]

The Farmer-Labor program in Minnesota promoted a more egalitarian approach to social insurance. In proposals for both federal and state levels, Farmer-Laborites urged the adoption of unemployment insurance for all workers, regardless of work history, sector of employment, or marital status. The proposal included a program of national health insurance and maternity benefits for women workers. Introduced into the U.S. Congress by Farmer-Labor Congressman Ernest Lundeen, unemployment insurance was also a central part of the Farmer-Labor platform. In its refusal to categorize workers by work history or current employment status, the Lundeen-Dunn bill was the broadest proposal for social insurance considered in the 1930s. The inclusion of maternity and health benefits was a serious attempt at ameliorating the effects of childbearing on women's access to federal resources.[5]

The Lundeen bill also attempted to establish a social security administration which would be controlled at the federal level and encompass all forms of economic assistance from unemployment and old age pensions to aid to dependent children grants.[6] Social security then would have provided a means of bridging the division in the welfare state between wage earner and dependent benefits while shifting the emphasis away from questions of morality raised about single mothers on ADC.[7] The New Deal social security program included generous grants to states, but continued local control made eligibility for ADC difficult to attain and set benefits below the subsistence level.

The Farmer-Labor Women's Federation exerted pressure on the party through resolutions and political work to retain women's access to patronage jobs. In a resolution written in 1938, the Hennepin County Farmer-Labor Women's Club complained that many married women were being discriminated against in state employment. Given the commitment of their party to "justice for all, regardless of sex," the Farmer-Labor women resolved that "if a married woman has merited an appointment or position by virtue of her activity in the Farmer-Labor movement, her married state should not bar her from seeking such employment. . . . no married woman already employed should be discharged on the ground of her being married."[8] Specific demands followed the resolutions. In Hennepin County, the Farmer-Labor Women's Club discovered that the Minneapolis Board of Public Welfare began to discriminate against married women in hiring after a group of women employees asked for leaves of absence during pregnancy. At a gathering of over fifty women, the Farmer-Labor women argued that "such attempts to discriminate against minority groups represent the first step in a long chain of steps tending to isolate and defeat minority groups with the final view of embracing a decreased standard of living on the American people."[9] While the protest was aimed at stopping discrimination against married women in particular, it was framed within the language of equality for minority groups, signifying the reluctance of the Farmer-Labor women to base their claims on gender.

Farmer-Labor women activists pursued protective legislation for women who otherwise were vulnerable to seasonal and poorly paid employment in the private sector. In conjunction with union activists, they began to address these problems by promoting legislation to improve the conditions of women's work. Some of the most visible advocates for protective legislation, they were women committed to equality and the welfare of the poor and were often members of the labor movement. The issue of women's working conditions, however, was debated in an atmosphere where the economic rights of married women, indeed the rights of all women, came increasingly under scrutiny, as unemployment remained high during the long decade of the 1930s.

In Minnesota, both labor and political groups debated the question of access of women, particularly married women, to work. Women in the Minnesota state government had weathered early attempts to bar them from employment under the Olson administration with support from the Farmer-Labor party. Similarly, unions addressed the problem in the early years of the depression. In 1930 and 1932, the Minneapolis Central Labor Union argued that barring married women from work would be "exchanging one set of unemployed for another" and "a cloak to confuse the real solution to the problem."[10]

Controversy over women's right to work surfaced again in 1939 when legislators introduced bills to bar married women from state jobs. Popular opinion on the issue was divided between those who believed women worked "to fill the family pocketbook" and those who thought married women should give way so that "our boys and girls could get employment." While an apparent majority of letter writers asked for some kind of restriction, if only in government employment, there were a range of issues and complaints.[11] Single women's right to be on the WPA was challenged. One writer even invoked ministerial authority to condemn married women who worked and argued that "thousands of government positions are filled with politicians' wives and women who have political drags, otherwise 'PETS' of leading politicians are employed." The minister suggested that state government "clean house" of all married women.[12] The right of married women to work continued to be an issue before labor groups as well. After strenuous debate, Minneapolis labor unions eventually adopted a resolution reaffirming women's right to work regardless of marital status. Only the intensive lobbying efforts of a coalition of women's and labor groups helped purge the civil service and state employment bills of discriminatory restraints.[13]

During legislative sessions in 1938 and 1939, labor unions, Farmer-Labor, and women's advocates sponsored legislative measures which indirectly affected conditions of and access to work for women. In 1938, the legislature passed a minimum wage law for women, hoping to revitalize laws which had been invalidated by a Supreme Court decision in 1925.[14] The new wage law was considered vital to the improvement of women's economic condition in the state. Minnesota State Wage Order Number 13 had broad jurisdiction over the wages of women and minors. A court order prohibited the state from applying the law to women working in the needle trades, laundries, restaurants, and telegraph offices, resulting in a virtual suspension of the minimum wage for adult women in industry.[15]

Employers fought the imposition of the minimum wage order. Garment and textile manufacturing firms played a central role in these actions. While they publicly applauded the wage order, all major employers in the industry supported the court challenge to oppose its application.[16] The court ruled that due process had been violated in establishing wage rates; thus the state minimum wage board scheduled hearings to determine separate rates for each industry that filed a complaint.

For the garment industry, the conflict focused on two issues: first, the need for geographically uniform rates and second, employer use of exemptions from provisions of the law for handicapped persons.[17] The state industrial commission felt that each firm should apply for exemptions separately, but the result of the exemption clause was that one firm, under ILGWU contract, issued handicapped permits for 6 percent of its five hundred employees, whom they declared slow or superannuated at age forty. Other firms began dismissing women in the forty- to fifty-year-old age group.[18]

Both state and federal wage laws, while they raised the wages of women, took the issue out of the hands of the union. This reorganization of the labor force and the divorce of unions from responsibility for a minimum wage can only have further disrupted the local union.[19] Minimum wage legislation was considered vital to the improvement of women's economic condition in the state, but the forces arrayed against it prevented the easy passage or implementation of the programs.

Minnesota Minimum Wage Order Number 15 was written to regulate the wages of women and minors in the apparel industry. Its chief provision was the minimum of thirty-five cents an hour, but it was undercut by provisions for apprentices and handicapped workers.[20] The Minimum Wage Advisory Board established a minimum wage for women in 1938 ranging from eleven to fifteen dollars a week. Wage adjustments for the first six months totaled over fifteen thousand dollars. In the garment industry, adjustments amounted to 25 percent of a woman's pay, and 700 of the 4,200 workers in the state received a raise when new increases went into effect in 1940.[21]

Court cases obstructed the board's efforts to enforce either general wage levels or wages by industry.[22] The formal agreement of major industrial groups and unions to set wage scales in 1939 did not lessen the opposition of small businesses, and the wage law continued to be controversial. As late as 1943, a business challenged the law on the grounds that minimum wage laws pertained only to single, self-supporting women. In *Tepel v. Sima*, the defendant argued unsuccessfully that married women were not covered by the law.[23]

Similarly, the Farmer-Labor party supported measures to regulate the hours of women's work. In 1933, the Farmer-Labor House led the way to a 54-hour law restricting women's labor.[24] Efforts in 1937 to further limit women's hours of work repeatedly failed in the state legislature. Opposition forces included not only the Republican majority but the state business and professional women's clubs.[25] Eventual passage of the bills did little to alter the wage and working conditions of women, in part because legislation could do little to ameliorate unemployment for these workers.

The passage of these bills coincided with efforts in the legislature to restrict the number of women eligible for work relief and to bar or restrict married women workers. In a time of unemployment, the regulation of women's work fostered active discrimination against them on behalf of private and public employers, and the passage of national unemployment and labor standards acts which supposedly covered all steadily employed wage earners did little to change these practices. As Judith Baer has argued, protective labor legislation in the late 1930s and 1940s was one of the principal means of justifying discrimination against women.[26]

High levels of unemployment made the effect of government assistance programs on women and their families a central issue in the labor politics of the 1930s. The isolation of women and their economic dependency made the question of their eligibility for relief a controversial topic, particularly when federal policy and local governments concerned with welfare costs promoted the dismissal of women from WPA rolls. That Minnesota, and especially its principal city, Minneapolis, rejected easy solutions to the problem was due in part to the pressure of groups at both the state and local level for high levels of relief and broad categories of eligibility. This concern, however, worked in tandem with moralistic approaches to the welfare system which intervened in the private lives of welfare families over child custody and promoted work relief rather than direct cash grants.

Under the New Deal, social programs assumed that women had a single relationship to the relief system as members of family units. This assumption often made programs providing for single women vulnerable to cutbacks in light of their "marginal" need. Female-headed households faced different forms of discrimination. As potential recipients of mothers' pensions (later ADC), their access to employment and/or better paying work relief was severely limited. Finally, their fitness as mothers became a focal point for criticism of the relief system.[27]

The ideology of the family wage implicit in the New Deal had long been on the agenda of labor progressives and the Left. Early in the depression decade, family welfare had been muted in the masculinist rhetoric of unions and unemployed organizations, but the passage of labor legislation reinvigorated the familialism of the Left. This can be seen in the contrasting way in which men were treated as relief recipients. While New Deal federal programs placed a high premium on finding work for unemployed men through various relief administrations, there was little consideration of the needs of women workers in the design of such programs as the Civil Works Administration, the Emergency Relief Administration, and the WPA. Officials and legislators concerned with families left destitute by the depression assumed that family men should be the principal recipients of such aid.[28] Federal programs did not distinguish between men on the basis of family status, and local programs which attempted to make this distinction failed. Women, whether single or married, did not have the same access to wage work and were presumed not to need or require access to public employment.[29]

The hostility directed at women workers under the strain of continuing economic crisis and the failure of unions and the Left to respond to women's needs on the same basis as men's undermined the sense of solidarity and community which held the labor movement together. At a time of growth in membership and power, labor unions had been generous in their extension of benefits to new sectors; the 1937 recession, infighting, and a decline in political influence restricted the meaning and upped the stakes of solidarity. In the WPA crisis of 1939, this hostility would be moved from the legislative chambers to the streets. Thousands of workers walked off their government jobs, declaring that they were workers, not relief recipients who could be punished by budget cutting. In Minneapolis, women played a central role in this strike as both participants in and symbols of struggle and victimization.

Taking the Wolf from One Door

Congressional and local reaction to the cost of welfare programs put increasing pressure on politicians to trim relief rolls. By 1939, the broad definition of relief eligibility for unemployed men and women, which had been a high priority for both unionists and the Farmer-Labor party, was rapidly losing its appeal. Factionalism and electoral defeat had eroded the effectiveness of Farmer-Labor organizations; the women's coalition dissolved over the issue of Popular Front influence. When Congress passed the Emergency Relief Appropriations Act (the Woodrum Act), a measure which effectively cut WPA programs in half, labor unions and unemployed organizations had to take the lead in protesting the changes. While many Farmer-Labor women participated as union members, the Farmer-Labor Women's Federation, so effective in the crises of 1936 and 1937, no longer played a role in the protests. Consequently, even as relief issues continued to have gendered implications, women no longer had an autonomous organization to voice their concerns. The arena of struggle had shifted.

The Woodrum Act implemented the cuts in relief spending through a revision of eligibility requirements for WPA employment. The act barred new immigrants, old-age pensioners, and workers who could receive ADC or unemployment insurance from WPA work.[30] The overall program cut several millions of dollars in direct relief appropriations to state and local governments. Finally, the bill put pressure on local authorities to provide compensatory relief and heightened competition over federal work relief jobs.

In the early months of 1939, nine hundred women were dismissed from work relief jobs. Among the first local workers affected by the cuts, the women were dismissed under the assumption that they were eligible for ADC. All lost their jobs before intake interviews could determine their eligibility, a step which created personal hardships. The waiting period before a woman and her dependents could receive ADC benefits meant the threat of hunger or debt. If denied eligibility, women had little choice but to accept any available private employment, which usually meant poorly paid day work. Reapplication for WPA employment took several weeks.

Even for women who were granted benefits, ADC paid less than the security wage women were earning on WPA. Because of the pressures to cut work relief, all working mothers were vulnerable.[31] Union leaders and the FWS of 544 intervened on behalf of those dismissed, but only twenty women were reinstated. The vast majority had little option but to apply for relief. WPA officials refused to reinstate any woman who could become eligible if she swore out a warrant against her husband for abandonment or failure to support.[32]

The state ADC system was overloaded because of the recent transfer of women from the local mothers' pension system. The new federal program had only twelve caseworkers in Minneapolis, and the department could handle only sixty new cases each month. At this rate, some of the nine hundred women laid off from WPA would have received their interviews several months after being laid off, by which time some would have become ineligible.[33]

The strains of a decade of depression and political reaction began to show in the struggle against the relief cuts. This time the Farmer-Labor Women's Federation was virtually silent on the issue of women's eligibility for work relief. In 1938, their organization foundered on political rifts; at the same time, their party lost control of both state and local government.[34] Unions tried to address the problem, but they were weakened by the recent passage of a restrictive state labor relations act (nicknamed the "Stassen Slave Labor Act") and the provisions of the Woodrum Act itself, which prohibited interference with WPA workers.[35] Members of project locals had little choice but to lead themselves. With few resources and a constituency that had traditionally been passive, project workers had to plan and execute their own protests, aided only by militant unionists. In 1939 the major organizations involved in this effort were the FWS of General Drivers' local 544 and the Workers' Alliance.

Sewing project workers played a crucial and controversial role in the protests that spring and summer. As women who were the chief support of their families, they were particularly vulnerable to any change in income or support. Among the lowest paid and most marginal of those on WPA projects, women from the sewing projects became the heart of the relief protests. They demonstrated against the Woodrum Act because its cuts were directed at them. A reporter wrote, "The militancy of these women and their earnest desire for work gives lie to all WPA jibes from here on out. These women want to work. Until the depression forced them on relief, they had taken care of their children with no outside help whatsoever." Working for the WPA, these women had attained a certain dignity and security; they now fought to retain their jobs.[36]

The largest sewing project in Minneapolis was on the near north side, at 123 North Second Street. Over a thousand women and a hundred men worked at the project. They produced coats, jackets, dresses, trousers, and other attire—as well as mattresses for direct relief clients and WPA workers. A wide range of women from ages nineteen to sixty worked at the project. They were the principal wage earners for their families—whether widowed, divorced, single, or married to a disabled husband. They represented the growing number of female-headed households in Minneapolis during the decade of the depression.[37]

In the spring of 1939, challenges to relief cutbacks increased as more workers were dismissed or received wage cuts. By April, 1,600 men and women in Hennepin County alone received a 30 percent pay cut, due to a $50-million decrease in state relief appropriations. In May, another 800 workers lost their WPA jobs in Minneapolis, as did 4,400 statewide. The severity of the situation was brought home by the elimination of entire departments and projects.[38]

Project workers planned several demonstrations to protest the cuts. In May, over 1,500 members voted for a one-day holiday protest. Demanding an immediate reinstatement of laid-off workers, a hike in relief budgets, and an enlargement of old-age pensions, they announced a march for June 2. On that day, more than 5,000 workers and their supporters gathered in front of the WPA office.[39] Almost all of the morning shift left their workplaces to participate in this three-mile-long parade of cars and trucks. The vehicles bore signs that read "Bread Not Bullets"; "Keep the Bull in the Stockyards, Stassen, We Want Jobs," and "Maintain Relief Standards or We Fight." At the state capitol, the newly elected governor, Harold Stassen, addressed the workers, assuring them that "no one need go hungry." A month later, the strikers would have cause to remember his words.[40]

Women Pickets and Women Finks

Initial cuts in the WPA provoked strong responses from workers on relief. Appealing to the federal government and to the state, workers asked and sometimes demanded the maintenance of basic relief, using timeworn but powerful metaphors for the risk of hunger and deprivation. An anonymous worker, signed "Puzzled?," wrote the governor about the drastic cuts ahead. Opening with "Your excellency," the author pointed to the increasing fear of WPA workers that they would not be reinstated on work relief. The worker continued: "This 18-month business isn't much good; it's taking the Wolf away from one door and putting him down in front of another. . . . Let us hope that the administration of relief will keep us from starving to death."[41]

In July, the Woodrum Act mandated changes in WPA employment. The hours and wages of all workers would now be uniform. Workers who had been employed for more than eighteen continuous months were fired from their jobs. The state WPA administrator, Linus Glotzbach, announced a reduction in the relief rolls of four thousand people. In effect, this meant that not all those dropped from WPA work would be replaced. Although dismissed workers were eligible again in six months, they would effectively be placed on the bottom of the waiting list. In addition, the bill eliminated skill distinctions in pay, one of the key achievements of the WPA struggle in 1936. While these rules may have had the effect of reducing inequality among relief clients, little or no provision was made for those workers now unemployed.

Returning from the Independence Day holiday on July 5, WPA workers across the country were greeted by notices of layoffs and wage cuts.[42] In Minneapolis, the workers on the state fairgrounds were among the first to respond. Putting down their tools, they boarded cars and drove from one project to another, urging a general strike of the projects. By the second day, nearly all projects in Minneapolis were closed when 8,000 workers joined nearly 125,000 striking relief workers nationally.[43]

The decade-long struggle to ameliorate and control the conditions of work and relief prepared the way for men and women to "strike against the government." A coalition of the Hennepin County Workers' Alliance and the FWS of General Drivers' 544 coordinated the strike. Demonstrating the strength and continuing resonance of workers' bonds, the Building Trades Council and the Central Labor Union pledged their support. Finally, the backbone of the strike was the 500-member strike committee, composed of job and project stewards of the FWS and the Workers' Alliance.[44]

Across the state, workers struck on WPA projects. In St. Paul, five thousand workers walked out July 5th, and in Duluth another fifteen hundred workers closed the projects on the second day of the strike. But when the state administrator Glotzbach threatened all WPA workers with dismissal by invoking the five-day absence suspension rule, many project workers returned. By July 12, Ramsey County and Duluth workers were back on the job, although nearly nine thousand workers remained on strike in Minneapolis.[45]

On the third day of the strike, the mayor ordered police to the north Minneapolis sewing project. Fights broke out between pickets and those who remained on the project. Policemen escorted "several score of women and a few men" out of the workplace, swinging their clubs at the crowd. They injured a few pickets. One of the policemen on duty died of a heart attack later that day, a death which newspaper strike hysteria attributed to the crowd. The project was closed down for three days.[46]

The sewing project was the central arena for confrontation between strikers and the police. As Rosalind, a WPA worker, later told journalist Anna Louise Strong, "Every day for a week, the police brought the women through the lines." Such an escort did not preclude the harassment of those who had chosen to remain on the projects. Max Geldman, the head of the FWS, recalled years later that women workers stood on the picket line militantly protesting the loss of money and security from the WPA cutbacks. Women and men from the sewing project and other unemployed workers called the nonstrikers names. There were accusations of "feminine hair-pulling," and men engaged in fist fights.[47]

As the organizer of "a formidable picket line," Minnie Kohn and her troops created a new tactic. When nonstriking women tried to enter the building, the squad rushed to "virtually tear the clothes off the scabs." As Max Geldman, the head of the FWS recalled, "It was quite a sight. The strike-breakers naked amidst the jeers of the strikers."[48] When the strikers were tried in the months after the strike, the disrobing of women workers, their intimidation and humiliation, was a central focus of the prosecution's case. Exposing the nonstrikers to the verbal abuse of the crowd, Minnie and her sister strikers brought the "rats, finks, and scabs" before the gaze and judgment of the crowd. But by their actions they also contradicted the image of women as victims. As viragoes, they raged across the picket line and violated women who refused the solidarity and community of those on relief.

Up to this point, only sewing and construction projects had been affected. Police brutality at the project brought out white collar workers at technical and professional projects to support their fellow workers.[49] An incident at the University of Minnesota research project soon followed. Philip Slaughter, a nonstriking worker who was a member of the Silver

Shirts, slashed two pickets with a knife. Although they did not retaliate, the incident provided the excuse for further police intervention.[50]

On July 13, WPA officials called women project workers to threaten them with dismissal and loss of relief payments if they remained on strike. On the next day, about a fourth of the workers had returned to the reopened project. The first shift of workers made it into the building with no trouble. But by the afternoon nearly a thousand pickets, WPA strikers and their supporters, had formed a crowd outside the building. Later it became clear that at least twenty-five plainclothes FBI agents were also at the project. As the crowd grew active, a police motorcade came to escort the workers from the building—with motorcycles, cars, and a Black Maria.[51]

When the women remaining on the sewing project emerged, the pickets waved their signs and began shouting. The police escort began firing tear gas into the assembled crowd. "Tear-gas isn't as bad as you think," said Rosalind. "I always thought you just laid down when you got it. But if you don't rub your eyes, you keep right on going." The gas "sizzled" and "popped" in the air. The experienced pickets ducked and ran from the gas. "Then we came back. The police were shooting, so we scattered again." In the confusion, police turned their guns on the strikers.[52]

Seventeen were seriously injured, including two children. Emil Bergstrom, an older unemployed worker, died later that day.[53] Like Henry Ness and John Belor, the victims of the truckers' strike of 1934, Bergstrom became a symbol for the labor movement's continuing struggle. Twenty-five hundred went to his funeral at Crystal Lake cemetery, where Ness and Belor were also buried. One of the union speakers, a man from the painter's union to which Bergstrom had belonged, said, "Emil came of a union family with union ideals. He was there on the picket line for all workers." Another contended that Bergstrom's name would be "added to the golden list of labor's martyrs."[54]

On July 21, WPA workers agreed to a settlement of the strike and a return to work. In effect, the Woodrum Act reductions withstood the protest. Strikers who had been gone more than five days were fired; those rehired were asked to sign affidavits attesting that they had not been engaged in criminal acts. Although the pay cuts remained in force, the workers were guaranteed that none of the strikers would be the targets of reprisals.[55] Most WPA workers returned to their projects as soon as possible.

Central to the language of the strike and to its meaning was the participation of women on both sides of the picket line. At the sewing project where a large number of women worked, violence had broken out with women as both victims and (as Max Geldman later admitted) perpetrators. Letter writers and journalists decried the "disgraceful mob attacks on working women"; they played upon images of women, "some of advanced years with graying hair, some of them with small children to support." It was these women who were endangered by the racketeers, these whom the "state utterly failed."[56] But whose women were the most important; which group had the larger claim to the protection of the police; how was labor to react to the situation?

As Robley Cramer, *Labor Review* editor, argued at a mass meeting, "The authorities have tried to make a great point about the strikers seeking to harm the women WPA workers at the sewing project. The fact is that the labor movement went to help the women workers, not harm them." The irony was that the majority of women had maintained solidarity with the strike by walking the picket line.[57] Yet pickets had directed their hostility at women workers who did not hold the line with the WPA.

The hostility and intensity of the crowd was due to several factors, not the least of which were that the project primarily employed women and that it was in close proximity to a relief office, where unemployed men gathered daily. Cutbacks in funding had disproportionately affected women eligible for ADC, but over a thousand women remained at the sewing project, making it both a logical and visible target for public opposition. The strikers were not identified by their gender, but newspapers called the women who had returned to work "women finks," an epithet which played upon notions of feminine subversion and male solidarity.

The violence at the project and similar attempts of strikers to harass women on other picket lines suggest that hostility directed at those who broke with the labor movement had a gendered message. Called ugly names like "scab" and "strikebreaker," women workers who crossed the picket line were divorced from their community. In a similar fashion, men who broke the rule of solidarity had their manhood questioned. While the right of women at any time to work was questioned, all those who violated labor's unity during a strike were subject not only to verbal intimidation and threats but to a violent response determined by their gender.

In the aftermath of the protest, it was the WPA workers, including women from the sewing project, who had to face the devastating consequences. While those who went on strike were reassigned to work, nearly half the WPA work force was laid off a month later. The sewing project "was almost snowed under in a storm of pink [discharge] slips," as workers lost their eighteen-month eligibility. Those charged with intimidation and conspiracy in a subsequent trial found it difficult to find work or receive aid.[58] American Legion Bearcat Post 504 protested the women's victimization and accused administrators Glotzbach and Stolte of "over-riding the federal civil service laws to strike at the widows and wives of the heroes of the World War."[59]

Solidarity on Trial

The community-based unionism revitalized momentarily by the WPA strike faced its biggest and last challenge when those involved were indicted for conspiracy to intimidate relief clients under Section 28 of the Woodrum Act, a felony according to the terms of the bill.[60] Two months after the settlement, Attorney General Frank Murphy initiated proceedings against those who participated in the WPA strike. The grand jury's findings surprised those who anticipated condemnation of police brutality; not the perpetrators but the victims of the July 14 attack now stood accused—as did the leaders of the FWS, organizers in the local labor movement, and pickets.[61]

Over 160 people were eventually indicted, about one-third of whom were women. As the *Northwest Organizer* wrote, the accused were "a veritable cross-section of the city's population"; they included the rank and file and leaders as diverse as the Central Labor Union's Myrtle Harris and Trotskyists Max Geldman and Ed Palmquist. They were arrested in their homes at night or on the street and brought handcuffed into the station. The bail was set at $10,000 for each of the accused. Labor lawyers for the defendants got the bail reduced to $57,000 total, for which the newly built Labor Temple served as security.[62] The swiftness and brutality of the arrests raised protest from national organizations as a violation of civil liberties. What it came down to for most of the observers was a case of citizens' rights (specifically, the right of a worker to strike against the government) or of relief politics (in particular, the question of whether those living on government allowances provided by the WPA were justified in protesting the conditions of relief).[63]

What followed the indictments and arrests were three trials, in which about one-third of the accused went to court; the rest were dismissed. In the first trial, eight men were accused of instigating a fight at the university WPA project and specifically of provoking the slashing attack of Philip Slaughter, a key witness for the prosecution. In the second trial, five men were charged with assaults at a Wayzata road project; Charles Conners, the only black worker brought to trial, had allegedly engaged in a fistfight when one of the nonstriking workers made a racist remark. In the last trial, twenty-five men and women faced charges of physical and verbal intimidation of WPA workers at the sewing project.[64]

The first trial began in October, less than three months after the strike. An impassioned labor press reminded readers that the eight on trial were "worthy men . . . fathers and the heads of families, men who would not be content to take anything from the government without working."[65] Much of the trial defense was devoted to the familial status of the accused. When they and the next group of men were convicted, however, the prospects began to look bleak for the acquittal of the next ninety defendants, whom the prosecuting attorney hoped to bring to trial together.

On the eve of the third trial, Marvel Scholl wrote a column on their fate. The women coming to trial, she argued, were dedicated to others, wanting a better life for their children. "It might have been easier," Scholl suggested, for the women to obtain ADC as mothers, "but women are no more ready and willing to take something for nothing than are the opposite sex. They clamored for and got jobs, sewing, cleaning, assisting in hospitals, clerical work—anything at which they could work to earn money."[66] As Scholl argued, "If 'conspiracy' is helping your man to a better life; if conspiracy is putting bread into the mouths of hungry children and old people; if conspiracy is giving your all with never a thought for yourself, then they stand convicted. They are real women. They make me proud to be a woman!"[67]

Like Minnie Kohn and Sigrid Asunma, most of the women were project workers over the age of fifty, and many had families dependent on the WPA wage. Accused of "high crimes against the government," they were "ordinary housewives, mothers, and even grandmothers."[68] Even those who were single, like Minnie Kohn, were self-supporting older women. Thus, most of these women neatly fit the image of the crusading mother that was central to women's political claims in labor ideology. Putting the same mothers on trial for demanding dignity and a wage adequate to feed their children could only be defined as injustice.

The trials were full of dramatic rhetoric and fury. The fourth attorney added to the defense team, Tom Davis, was an old populist lawyer who conducted most of the cross-examinations and the summation.[69] In one instance, he brought dictionaries to the court to define the use of words used on the picket lines. In another case, Davis had a defendant repeat in court his original speech to the WPA workers to show that it was not intimidating. Thus were the issues of the strike introduced into the courtroom. Finally, a witness testified that one of the defendants, Margaret Schoenfeld, had sung "Solidarity" on the picket line. He charged that it was a "Communist" song, which he had heard during the Strutwear strike. When Schoenfeld took the stand, she told the astonished jury that she had heard it sung only in union meetings and in a movie, *When Tomorrow Comes*. This last admission—giving the song an air of legitimacy and even homeyness, if not banality—only could be aimed at undermining the red-baiting of the prosecution.[70]

The principal issue in the trial was the extent to which the accused men and women had intimidated or obstructed the women workers of the sewing project, the legal grounds of conspiracy notwithstanding. The struggles that had broken out in the crowd were witnessed by many; the question was who had provoked the fights, whether pickets had harassed the women, and who was at fault. The leaders of the FWS were identified as the major cause, but what of the picketing women? Whether Kohn had indeed ripped clothing from women, sixty-seven women were prepared to testify that they had been intimidated, and thirty were willing to point the finger at Minnie Kohn.[71]

Defense attorney Davis brought up what he considered two pieces of evidence that would mitigate whatever had happened on the picket line. First, he brought witnesses who testified that, prior to the strike, the accused women had charged WPA project officials with corruption in purchasing supplies. Some of the women had been met with threats; others were dismissed. Second, and perhaps more important, Davis argued that it was the petty jealousies of the nonstriking women workers that had created most of the charges. Numerous witnesses who testified were eager to condemn their sister workers. As one labor newspaper wrote, "Guard as they would against the admission, now and again the keen cross-examination of Tom Davis elicited the testimony that pointed to the jealousy and envy seething on the sewing project before the strike."[72] Conflicting evidence, about Kohn in particular, Davis argued, suggested that the witnesses against her were exhibiting no more than "the fury of a woman scorned."[73]

While in the former two trials, and in the defense of men in the third, defense lawyers condemned the accusations of violence as the created and distorted product of labor spies and thugs, accusations against the women were given some credence, if only as proof that the women had been sniping at each other long before the strike. The stereotype of the wrathful, illogical, and childish woman taking revenge on others inspired Davis's closing remarks. Much like the subversive female of the depression's deepest fantasies, the image of the jealous female undermined any positive interpretation of the striking women's actions. In pursuing this line of defense, Davis discredited the motives of the strikers.

The defense strategy failed. All of the women were found guilty; most were given probation. Identified as the "ring-leader," Minnie Kohn received forty-five days in the workhouse. The judge further condemned other leaders as "self-seeking" individuals who talked the defendants into striking. The men received short jail sentences. There was little or no doubt in the minds of the jury that the defendants had indeed intimidated the nonstriking women at the project, and therefore they had broken the law.[74] With the conviction of the twenty-five defendants, the WPA prosecutions were over, the vengeance of the New Deal on its constituents largely spent. As Cramer wrote in January of 1940, even "the judge seems to feel the whole thing has descended to the level of persecution."[75]

The mass trials of 1939 signaled the weakness of the community-based forces of unionism at the end of a decade of depression. The arrest and prosecution of unionists and WPA workers revealed that further union activism would come at a cost—both individually and collectively.[76] The union and political activists targeted by these campaigns were advocates of local autonomy and rank-and-file control. They had refused to adjust to new bureaucratic norms of labor relations or to abandon community struggle. As a consequence, the labor movement lost some of its most articulate local leaders.

Ironically, the unity which emerged from the mass strike and the trials that followed was a unity built on division and disharmony. Incidents at the sewing project were not so much state violence directed against strikers, the outcome of which was likely to provoke a united front among working men and women, as they were illustrations of intraclass conflict. Desperate strikers physically and verbally harassed desperate scabs, women and men who felt they had no choice but to return to work. The existence of agents provocateurs in the protesting crowd did not change that. What is more, the agents of punishment, of coercion, of exposure had been women at once hailed as victims and viragoes. The powerless had been empowered only at the expense of others as powerless as they.

Gender, Solidarity, and Political Activism in the 1930s

The WPA strike of 1939 provides a dramatic example of the strength of the labor movement's vision of moving beyond the workplace. During the early thirties, unions had helped create a movement that addressed the needs of the unemployed for adequate levels of relief, for defenses against eviction, and for connections to a wider community. But, when the federal government established work relief programs in the late 1930s, labor and political organizations broadened their strategy by using shopfloor tactics to control the conditions of public relief jobs. Of necessity, the increasing use of job stewards and grievance procedures in monitoring government work relief altered labor's understanding of the stakes involved in the unemployed movement.

In the welfare arena, job security and seniority rights—the two major accomplishments of labor in the 1930s—took on new meaning. Demanding that the government be the employer of last resort, workers asserted their rights to a place in society, to dignity, and to family security. Further, workers on relief were isolated and dependent on the resources of the state. As relief clients, they ceased to be involved in the labor movement. Only through a working-class politics that addressed issues of social welfare could men and women of the working class be assured of a place in a community defined by work and struggle.[77]

The incorporation of union strategies into the unemployed movement did not initially alter the commitment of labor unions to the needs of the relief population. In their defense of WPA workers, labor articulated a new relationship to unemployed workers, whether men or women. Unions and their allies on the political Left in Minneapolis challenged assumptions which proscribed work for women and limited their access to the welfare state. By the end of the decade, however, severe cutbacks in federal work and direct relief funds made such a position increasingly untenable. In the arena of the labor movement and the state, the Left expressed the tension that had existed all along between its persistent, historical familialism that subordinated women under the rhetoric of the family wage and the single-focus, single-sex solidarity that ignored women's needs or perceived them as threatening.

The gender dynamics of labor conflict in the late 1930s, and their relation to an increasingly bureaucratized and defensive labor movement, came into play in the massive WPA Strike of July of 1939. In response to cutbacks in federal commitment to work relief and continued high levels of unemployment, workers walked out of their WPA jobs with demands for a restoration of wages and an extension of eligibility for thousands of workers whose WPA employment had been terminated.

While women constituted only about 10 percent of workers on local WPA projects, many worked at a sewing project where strike protests became violent. Women project workers unaccustomed to public protest nonetheless led the picket lines. They became both the heroes and the villains of the strike, lionized in the labor press as "mothers" and vilified in court as militants and opportunists. Images of female viragoes and victims filled pages of newspapers, memoirs, and court testimony that fall, but public hostility toward women strikers and nonstrikers suggests the collision between gender-neutral ideals of equality and gendered perceptions of difference. The context for this drama was the rapid consolidation of New Deal labor policy, continued high unemployment, and the crisis of masculinity that valorized struggle but preferred the symbol of female victim or mother to that of the militant woman.

The street and courtroom drama of the 1939 WPA strike has served to bring the problematic relationship of women to the labor movement sharply into focus. The sewing project women, marginalized by poverty and family status, demonstrated the vulnerability of women to political and social crisis. Economically disadvantaged, they depended on the patriarchal (and collective) institutions of state and union for their well-being and identity and experienced demands of solidarity and need as contradictory. Born of both class and gender imperatives, of collective and individual perceptions, women's actions during the strike—whether to hold the line or cross it—were related only in indirect ways to feminism as a political identity; but for those who crossed the line and those who held it, the solidarity of women was an issue of both class and gender; feminism surfaced not as political theory but as political practice.

For women active in the Farmer-Labor party and the labor movement, women's economic and political weaknesses were the limitations within which they too had to live. Farmer-Labor women saw need conflict with commitment, language tear apart and confuse memory and practice, factionalism undermine unity. Lacking an autonomous voice in the labor movement (which they never had) or in their own political party (which they had for a decade but lost), their practice of feminism as class politics faded into a rhetorical emphasis on women as victims.[78]

As we have seen, the use of women as scapegoats and symbols of victimization was woven into the fabric of labor's gender ideology. Both labor and the Left had created female representations of victimization throughout their history; the same symbols were employed historically to call upon the state to ameliorate women's needs, in contradistinction to the more voluntarist stance toward men workers.[79] While this policy shifted in the Great Depression with the promotion of state guarantees for workers in the areas of collective bargaining, unemployment insurance, and old age pensions, the welfare program still embraced sexual difference as the basis of differential—and unequal—treatment. To a great extent, the community of suffering and struggle workers created during the Great Depression was a community founded and foundering on its divisions.

Seven

Working
Women and
Unions during
World War II

P.S. I still am not in favor of women tak-
ing over any part of our organization.
When the employers become women then
I will be in favor of women organizers.
—Buford Eastman, 1941

BETTY UNION SAYS:
The cost of stockings—WOW!
The cost of clothes! WHY, HECK!
If we don't get wage adjustments,
I'm going to look a wreck.
—*Twin City Ordnance Plant UE News*,
1942

The narrative of women's subordination
in the twentieth century has been presented as a story of the decline and
revitalization of the women's movement. Focusing on the fate of feminist
politics, scholars of women's history have characterized the interwar period as quiescent decades in which gender consciousness failed to provide
a spur for meaningful political action. The unprecedented numbers of
women in the labor force during World War II serves as a turning point in
this tale of events, a catalyst for changes in the postwar reconstruction of
gender politics—first through domesticity, only later by revolt.[1]

The actual experiences of working-class women in the labor movement
of the 1930s remind us that the configuration of gender and power in
American society has changed not in one direction but in multiple and
contradictory ways. The relations of men and women, citizens and states,
employers and workers, and blacks and whites were profoundly affected
by economic crisis, social dislocation, and political struggle; and these, in
turn, preconditioned response to the exigencies of war. Gender consciousness surfaced not only in the self-conscious gender politics of the
New Deal[2] but also in the practice of local parties, organizations, and
unions.

The question then must be this: What was the fate of women in the
work force, the state, and the labor movement under the conditions of
depression, war, and postwar reconstruction? Viewing the period as a
whole, we have seen that workers revived the labor movement through the
community-based activism of the early 1930s. Proceeding through local
networks, institutions, and educational and cultural practices, community

unionism was rooted in practices of local autonomy; languages of communalism and mutuality; rituals of unity in picket lines, parades, and funeral marches; and methods of organization. Unions were therefore fundamentally gendered in ways that authorized the participation of women.

Despite high levels of unemployment, women continued to work during the depression. The addition of women's wages to family budgets was essential to the survival of working-class families but problematic for working-class politics. The mere fact of women working did not rupture the connection between masculinity and work; women's persistence in the labor force, however rationalized in individual cases, symbolically violated the social order. Even as women did not replace men in the labor force (due to the resilience of the sexual division of labor), the issue of their right to work repeatedly surfaced in debates over public policy. By the late 1930s, prolonged unemployment and union conflict reestablished bureaucratic, centralized, and workplace-oriented practices of solidarity in the labor movement, the consequence of which was the exclusion of women from union leadership and, to a lesser extent, from union membership.

The impact of World War II on women's status and their relationship to labor unions must be seen in the context of a social movement already distanced from its community and hostile in institutional ways to women workers. The millions of women who joined the labor force during the war ostensibly provided unions with the opportunity to recruit women not just for the duration but as a permanent constituency. Would the labor movement respond to the challenge, or would the masculinism of warfare reinforce the new masculinism of unions? How would the languages of nationalism, patriotism, and class loyalty shape the ways in which working women were recruited into the labor movement?

The Wartime Economy

By 1941, government defense contracts began to stimulate the recovery of the weak Minneapolis economy. Local firms received over $140 million in contracts for the production of items ranging from shells and bullets to biscuits, parachutes, and army underwear.[3] The newly constructed Twin City Ordnance Plant (TCOP) became a major producer of armaments. When it was first opened, it employed over 8,500 workers; by 1944, the TCOP labor force had grown to over 30,000. Honeywell Heating Regulator Company retooled for the production of periscopic sights and firing controls. It received defense orders for over two million dollars; the corresponding increase in work led to its hiring of nearly a thousand men and women (a 50 percent increase) between 1940 and 1941 alone. Other plants like the family-owned Onan and Sons or Minneapolis-Moline grew into national corporations through their production of badly needed machine tools and generators.[4] Men and women who had worked intermittently for years were now recruited for jobs under lucrative contracts. Early in 1941, employment rates reached 1937 levels (the high point of 1930s employment); by June of that year the number had increased by 12 percent. Only six months after the bombing of Pearl Harbor, local defense plants sought over sixteen thousand production workers.[5]

The labor shortage in defense employment was a compelling reason to hire the vast reserve of women and minority workers. TCOP planned to hire women for up to 60 percent of the expanding labor force, and it was among the first companies to develop specific policies for recruiting and hiring them. Although some resisted the trend, many firms—including the almost exclusively male machine shops at Moline and Onan—soon adapted their hiring strategies and workplace conditions for women.[6] By the end of 1942, the regional office of the War Manpower Commission noted that "women constitute the greatest reservoir of manpower and . . . this reservoir has not even been tapped as yet in [the] area."[7]

Despite problems of recruitment, housing, and child care, the local labor shortage prompted the committee to urge employers to hire the logical reserve. The local office of the United States Employment Service (USES) reported that women were being hired for positions "previously filled only by men and, while a large number of employers still prefer[red] to hire men for [the] occupations, they realize[d] that women [had to be] used to satisfy a very considerable part of the demand."[8]

Women's economic position changed substantially over the war years. Between 1940 and 1945, over sixty thousand women entered or reentered the local work force; they increased the number of women workers by 54 percent. Their pattern of wartime employment mirrored the changes in manufacturing and in the labor force as a whole. The majority of them were employed in industry, where thirty-seven thousand women worked in positions once held by men or newly created as part of the war effort. In addition, over twenty-three thousand women found jobs in the sales and trade sector, filling positions held by men who had been either drafted or transferred to more lucrative manufacturing jobs. While in 1945 there were fewer women professionals than in 1940—in both real numbers and as a proportion of the female labor force—the shift of women into defense work and the employment of women as nurses or clerical workers in the armed forces could account for much of the decline. (See tables 7.1 and 7.2.)

Both men and women benefited from the vast increase in defense production. For the first time since the late 1920s, the opening up of manufacturing jobs meant steady, highly paid, skilled work for men. During the depression, they had experienced levels of unemployment of over 20 percent; in manufacturing, the figure was closer to 35 percent. As a result of increasing defense jobs and the draft, men on the home front could choose from a wide range of positions. They left the jobs that had sustained them during the crisis—namely, public relief work, sales, and service—for defense plants producing airplanes, machine parts, and transportation equipment. Forty percent of working men held positions in manufacturing during the war years, a phenomenal increase in an area of high wages and strong unionization.

For women workers, the increase was even more dramatic. Only one in seven (14.8 percent) women workers held industrial jobs in 1940. Most of these women worked intermittently or in the seasonal garment market. With the wartime labor shortage, the number of women in Twin Cities manufacturing firms grew from sixteen thousand to over fifty-three thousand. Women industrial workers grew as a proportion of the female labor force from 15 to over 30 percent. Further, the growth in women's employment fundamentally altered the sex ratio of occupations. In 1945, women represented 34.1 percent of industrial workers, a substantial increase from 1940 (21.7 percent). Women also were a larger part of the labor force as a whole, representing three in ten workers in 1940 (30.9 percent) but almost one in two (46.2 percent) in 1945. (See table 7.2.)

With the War Manpower Commission promoting the reserves of available labor, firms built plants under the assumption that they could employ women. TCOP, for example, had nearly seventeen thousand women employees in 1945. Similar increases in transportation equipment and metal and machinery meant that nearly ten thousand more women worked in these industries than had before the war. Even in the traditionally female-dominated industries like textile and apparel, there was growth. Large defense contracts at Munsingwear and Strutwear created 1,750 new jobs for women.[9] (See table 7.3.)

Industrial expansion offered opportunities for racial and gender inte-

Table 7.1 Changes in Women's Employment by Industry, Twin Cities, 1940–1945

Industry	Women Employed 1940	1945	Net Change 1940–1945	% Change 1940–1945
Agriculture	603	900	297	49.2
Construction	406	400	−6	−1.5
Manufacturing	16,316	53,550	37,234	228.2
Trade	29,032	52,300	23,268	80.1
Services	25,708	19,200	−6,508	−25.3
Trans./Comm.	4,078	7,700	3,622	88.8
Finance	7,597	10,700	3,103	40.8
Professions	20,292	15,350	−4,942	−24.3
Government Work	3,882	6,500	2,618	67.4
Other	2,654	4,000	1,346	50.7
Total	110,563	170,600	60,037	54.3

Source: Calculated from tables in Demand-Supply Supplement, March 1945, Ziegler Field Office Records, Records of the Women's Bureau, RG 86, Box 1395, NA.

gration of the labor force. Despite color bars to employment in the predominantly white cities of Minneapolis and St. Paul, labor shortages and explicit federal policies mandating minority recruitment forced changes in local employment practices. In this sense, the increasing bureaucratization of labor relations had short-term benefits for previously excluded groups. Companies which had refused to hire black women in production jobs employed them as power machine operators and other skilled positions during the war. Munsingwear, which produced parachutes and underwear for the army, hired its first six black women workers in January of 1943; by the end of the year, thirty of their machine operatives were minority workers. Notably, these plants were unionized under the aegis of the CIO, whose policies enforced employer compliance with government regulations.[10]

Minority workers made substantial gains in other unionized jobs during World War II. While some local unions had made direct efforts to recruit black members and to insist on their equal participation before the war,[11] black men and women had been barred from most unionized jobs due to a combination of industrial or union discrimination. Despite federal directives that defense industries must employ minority workers, local compli-

Table 7.2 Employment by Sex and Industry, Twin Cities, 1940 and 1945
(in Percentages)

1940

Industry	Men	Women	Women in Labor Force[b]
Agriculture	6.8	0.5	3.4
Construction	6.6	0.4	2.4
Manufacture	23.8	14.8	21.7
Trade	24.1	26.3	32.7
Services	6.3	23.2	60.8
Trans./Comm.	12.7	3.7	11.5
Finance	5.1	6.9	37.5
Professions	5.8	18.3	58.7
Government	5.8	3.5	21.1
Other	2.4	2.4	30.4
Total[a]	99.4	100.0	30.9
N =	247,282	110,563	357,845

1945

Industry	Men	Women	Women in Labor Force[b]
Agriculture	5.4	0.5	6.4
Construction	5.6	0.2	2.8
Manufacture	42.9	31.4	34.1
Trade	15.9	30.7	57.7
Services	2.8	11.2	73.8
Trans./Comm.	14.4	4.5	18.2
Finance	3.0	6.3	59.6
Professions	3.7	9.0	63.0
Government	5.2	3.8	34.2
Other	1.2	2.3	46.2
Total[a]	100.1	100.0	46.2
N =	241,200	170,600	412,200

Source: Calculated from tables in Demand-Supply Supplement, March 1945, Ziegler Field Office Records, Records of the Women's Bureau, RG 86, Box 1395, NA.

[a]Figures do not always equal 100% due to rounding.

[b]Women as proportion of labor force.

Table 7.3 Changes in Women's Employment in Manufacturing, Twin Cities, April 1940–April 1945

Industry	1940	1945	Net Change
Ordnance	0	16,850	16,850
Food Products	3,404	6,750	3,346
Machinery	895	5,200	4,405
Transportation Equipment	152	5,100	4,948
Printing and Paper	2,796	6,000	3,204
Textiles and Apparel	5,293	7,050	1,757
Iron, Steel	1,004	1,400	396
Lumber, Furniture	359	1,300	941
Clay, Stone, Glass	258	2,100	1,842
Other Manufacturing	2,155	1,750	− 405
Total	16,316	53,550	+ 37,234

Source: Calculated from tables in Demand-Supply Supplement, March 1945, Ziegler Field Office Records, Records of the Women's Bureau, RG 86, Box 1395, NA.

ance required active prosecution of discrimination in industry through cases filed with the Committee on Fair Employment Practices. In the Minneapolis–St. Paul area, the Urban League filed a few cases during the war, from both men and women workers. Most minority workers were able to find work in the defense industry for the duration. As with women workers, the implications of this employment for union activism and for permanent labor force participation were ambiguous during the war and contradictory in its aftermath.[12]

Recruiting Rosie the Riveter

By the late 1930s, the labor movement had to adjust to conditions of peacetime conscription, expanding defense industries, and impending world war. On the one hand, labor unions had far greater resources at their disposal: the dues check-off meant more money in the coffers, and closed shop government contracts lent legitimation to collective bargaining.[13] Greater competition for workers during the war made possible major gains in wages, working conditions, and worker rights.

On the other hand, conditions of employment and union activity under the war emergency constrained union initiatives. The no-strike pledge, War Labor Board regulations, security checks on personnel,[14] and the language of union recruitment all contributed to limiting the scope of unionism. Winning the war on the home front meant employing nationalist rhetoric to undergird union participation; it also dictated a certain dependence on the government, subordination of worker demands to the war effort, and acquiescence to those employers who took advantage of the war emergency. The organization of production and the composition of the labor force were also always at stake. Maintaining the hard-won gains of the depression decade was uppermost on the union agenda, but it required constant vigilance. Labor unions quickly found that wartime prosperity did not lead to greater institutional power.[15]

Another new development was the dramatic increase in women holding union jobs. Although there are no figures for the period before the war, a reasonable estimate of women unionists would probably have been about 20,000 (in manufacturing and service sectors) out of 110,000, or less than 20 percent, in 1940. By 1945, the majority of industrial women workers in the Twin Cities were required to report to work with a union button. This meant effectively an increase of nearly 40,000 local women union members.

More union women did not signal significant change in the attitudes of labor leaders. Initially, unions resisted the entry of women into any occupational category that had been exclusive to men before the war. When it became clear that the labor shortage was too severe to ignore women, unions engaged in campaigns to recruit them. Under these conditions, unions fought for equal pay for equal work, not so much to defend women's political rights as to protect against deskilling and erosion of the pay scale. The use of the equal pay issue, however, may have had an unintended impact on women's attitudes toward work.[16]

Traditions of union paternalism, discriminatory (ostensibly protective) constraints on women's labor, the dynamics of social closure within labor leadership, and anxieties about postwar recession also contributed to the unions' failure to respond to the historic opportunity to organize women workers on a permanent basis.[17] One suspects that, like employers, labor unions believed that the war would be of relatively short duration and that the level of unemployment in 1940 was such that even the dynamic expansion of defense work would not absorb all of the unemployed.

Given the drama of the war and the level of home front patriotism, the emergence of Rosie the Riveter was only a sideshow. The image of the new working woman was subordinated to the more pressing concern over the war effort. It was not only that local, state, and federal authorities staged rallies, parades, and other rituals of patriotic commitment. Unions also supported the war effort. Labor's Volunteers for Victory and Union Victory Girls[18] set war production goals to win another Navy E banner, organized bond rallies and scrap drives, and wrote to the boys on the front—sending candy, knitted socks, and copies of *UVG to GI Joe* with the latest union gossip. A newly formed union told workers to "Sing a Song of Salvage":

> Save your PAPER . . . Save your TIN
> Save your GREASE for Glycerin;
> Each unneeded POT and PAN
> Goes to help us lick Japan.

During the "I am an American Day" parade, unionists demonstrated their commitment to the winning of the war, even at the sacrifice of other goals.[19]

Labor organizers employed the language of patriotism to call workers to the union banner. Fighting an unfair employer was like fighting Hitler; one cartoon claimed, "Japan Smash My Union! I'll Smash Japan!" The revival of American Revolutionary War symbolism was an eye-catching device for recruiting union members. "Brother, I'm In!" evoked the minuteman of a bond poster to show that "Labor Saves to Save America!"; "Modern Molly Pitchers" showed the rush of union auxiliary women to buy their share. (See illustrations 7.1–7.3). Unions evoked patriotism in the recruitment of women to labor's cause; the husbands, sons, and brothers on the front were a good reason for the women at home to join.[20] These cultural developments robbed the influx of women into the labor force of any special significance. Indeed, women workers lacked the sanctions necessary to demand parity in unions or workplaces while union men were fighting overseas. For these reasons, recruiting women into the labor movement sometimes was an attempt to organize manufacturing jobs, not the workers who held them.

During the war, local machine, metal-working, and ordnance plants were the target of the broad-based campaigns of the CIO. The UE was particularly active in the electrical machine industry at such plants as Minneapolis Honeywell and Moline and competed with the AFL over bargaining rights at ordnance plants. During the war, the UE recruited

"Brother• I'm in—every pay day!"

7.1 In the bond and recruiting drives of World War II, Tom Paine emerged to ride again as a figure in both government and union propaganda. The minuteman figure echoes the revival of American symbols that was part of Popular Front culture. *Labor Review*, December 5, 1941 (Courtesy of *Labor Review* and Minnesota Historical Society)

thousands of workers (many of them women). Alongside these efforts, the Central Labor Union in Minneapolis mobilized TCOP ordnance workers (thus organizing the largest manufacturing plant in the area) into an AFL federal union.

Unionization of defense plants required both government contracts and the active intervention of the War Labor Board and the National Labor Relations Board (NLRB). After a decade of conflict at Honeywell, employees only succeeded in organizing the factory under the aegis of the

"To The War Bond Ramparts - - Modern Molly Pitchers"

7.2 This cartoon depicts Republican womanhood and consumerism in support of the war. The revival of American revolutionary symbolism here enhances the bond drive. *Labor Review*, November 19, 1942 (Courtesy of *Labor Review* and Minnesota Historical Society)

7.3 Self-sacrifice and patriotism were bound up in the new wartime construction of labor solidarity. Familial roles also loomed large as republican mothers worked to make arms for soldier husbands and to support labor unions for growing sons. *Minnesota CIO Yearbook*, 1942 (Courtesy of Minnesota Historical Society)

War Labor Board. At TCOP, both employment and the benefits of union membership accrued from the rapid expansion of defense sector employment. Long-term union opponents such as Honeywell, Ford (in St. Paul), and Moline accepted unions as a permanent part of labor-management relations under wartime conditions. What was most striking about these union drives was that, despite roots in local leadership and autonomy, their success was dependent on the process of government labor arbitration.[21] As in other converted defense plants, unionization had an important and lasting impact on employee wages and benefits, but for the most part such gains included women only for the duration of the war.

The example of UE campaigns is instructive. Electrical workers targeted machine shops, foundries, battery plants, and other light electrical plants in the Twin Cities. Capturing stagnant locals of the machinists' union, the International Association of Machinists (IAM), under the leadership of William Mauseth and Harry Mayville, over six thousand workers changed their affiliation to the burgeoning UE-CIO. Using these locals (1139 and 1140) as a base, Mayville, Mauseth, and others hoped to unionize holdouts from the foundry campaign and the large Honeywell plant in the city.[22]

Even during the depths of the depression, Minneapolis Honeywell Heating Regulator Company employed a labor force of 1,500 to 2,000 workers. In World War I, the plant had been converted to produce firing controls and other armaments; during peacetime most of the workers assembled heating controls and thermostats. Numerically the majority, men employees held a wide range of occupations—most highly skilled and specialized—in the tool, punch press, and hand screw rooms. Women were assigned ostensibly lighter work on the assembly line in relay, glass, and coil winding departments. They may have accounted for as many as one in three workers. Both men and women, however, were subject to the vagaries of employment at Honeywell. In the first year of the depression, the firm sent home eight hundred workers in the first of a series of layoffs. With housing starts down and the economy uncertain, the corporation adjusted to fluctuating demand for heating equipment by keeping its work force flexible.[23]

Cutbacks in employment and threats of dismissal were effective methods in preventing the organization of the firm's workers. Although Honeywell informally allowed its tool-and-die makers to belong to an IAM local, it fought plantwide unionization. The company belonged to the powerful Citizens' Alliance, and union organizers accused the firm of collusion in opposing major strikes. Some of its managerial employees had been deputized during the truckers' strike of 1934; the firm had also aided the recruitment of strikebreakers during the Strutwear strike.[24] Moreover, the congressional LaFollette Committee on Labor found that the firm hired the Burns Detective Agency to spy on suspected labor activists. Under pressure from the NRA, Honeywell converted its employee association, the MinnReg Veterans, into a company union. The organization later disrupted UE-CIO campaigns.[25]

Despite Honeywell's resistance, a union organizing drive began in 1933 when men who worked in the tool room reestablished the dormant local 382 of the IAM. Chair of the organization committee of the Tool and Die Makers' Club, William Mauseth applied for work at Honeywell under an assumed name. With the help of Harry Mayville, he recruited members for an independent union. Both Mauseth and Mayville were known members of the Communist party; still, organization occurred not through party lines but along workplace networks. First the basement tool room was organized, then workers in the punch press department. With the dismissal of a number of employees, the union folded. By 1935, however, it was revived under new leadership; in 1939, local 382 went over to the UE.[26]

Among women workers at the plant, labor organization was nonexistent until 1937. In that year, Evelyn Knutson joined the union and began working to organize her co-workers on the relay bench. Reahn Reinhard, the wife of a union organizer earlier discharged from Honeywell, joined the union and helped to organize women in the repair department. As the NLRB reported, "[Reinhard] talked to every girl in her department and to girls in other departments, and succeeded in getting several to join. She wore her union pin in the plant and became one of three auditors for the Union."

Women like Knutson and Reinhard helped spread the organization from skilled men in the basement rooms to the women assembly workers on the upper floors.[27] They were only the first of many women who spurred the organization of Honeywell. By 1941, the union papers regularly featured the activities of women UE members, stewards, and organizers in a now-public display of their unionism. The union publicized the activism of Lillian "Dolly" Fleming, a steward in the glass department; Elsie Hunt, the union financial secretary; Orene Carpenter, a worker on the relay bench; and later Helen Harper, the fighting UE-CIO committee member. Their ideas about organizing were discussed in the union newsletter, and they became visible examples of what union women could be to the hundreds of unorganized women workers on the shopfloor.[28]

As union organizing became more successful, it became more public; and the firm dismissed several workers for union activity, among them Reinhard and Knutson. Unlike their male co-workers, the women were dismissed on the grounds of gender. The company sought to justify the firing not under normal seniority rules but rather on the basis of the women's marital status. According to her foreman, Quarfot, Evelyn Knutson was discharged because she was a married woman. Quarfot testified that Honeywell "was getting a lot of heat from the public" because married women were working at the plant. Although Honeywell had a very precise seniority policy, it lacked uniform rules regarding married women. Even after Knutson's dismissal, the firm retained other married women workers. In defending the firing of a union woman, Quarfot assumed that the rationale would stand in court. The NLRB examiner concluded that Knutson's union activism was the cause of the layoff and ordered that she be reinstated.[29]

In the face of dismissals and impending labor board decisions, the UE continued to organize on the shopfloor and in the community. Competing against the company union and a newly formed AFL federal union, UE local 1145 found it difficult at first to make headway against worker and employer resistance. Despite the rhetorical emphasis on equality in industrial unions, the local AFL union was more effective in attracting women members.[30] Further, Honeywell management maintained an aggressive posture toward labor organization. It forced an early NLRB election in 1941, which gave no union the right to bargain for Honeywell workers. Despite personal, house-to-house organizing and hundreds of recruits, the UE lost the election and at first was resigned to failure. Fighting back with charges of unfair labor practices, however, the UE scheduled a second election in 1942. This time the union won. Under the conditions of the war emergency, Honeywell workers finally certified the UE as its bargaining agent.[31]

Selling the Union

The nature of the organizing campaign at Honeywell reveals the central goals and strategies of the wartime CIO. Long before the formal declaration of war, organizers at Honeywell chose nationalist and patriotic themes for their recruiting drives. They equated the protection of America through defense production with the equally great need to find protection for workers through unions. Workers were urged, "Don't Be a Tory— Fight on the Side for Freedom"; they received "An Appeal to Reason" which told them that the UE would give them "democracy through collective bargaining on the job."[32] Associating unscrupulous employers with tyrants, union leaders asked workers to evaluate employer interference with the question, "Is this democracy—or is this Hitlerism?" As one handbill argued, to have management determining wages and working conditions was "as UnAmerican as to have our home life policies or politics dictated to us."[33]

Second, in trying to bring working women into the UE during the war, the UE relied on a set of equally powerful themes in its membership appeals. Patriotism was one language which the union continued to use throughout the war years. Betty Lou Olson, a new union member, proclaimed that the UE welcomed women and "pledged to stand side by side with [them]—to win this war—and make Honeywell girls a unit our fighting men can point to with pride as leaders in an arsenal of democracy."[34] After its first election defeat, the union was increasingly concerned with broadening its appeal to women workers. It brought in a woman organizer, and others began to approach workers through the Catholic Church, at least one indication of community and presumably women's outreach. What is more, when the union understood how crucial women were to its victory, it changed its message. Nationalism and patriotic fervor still pervaded union rhetoric, but fairness was seen as a theme specifically concerning women.[35]

On October 24, 1941, the *Honeywell UE News* published a cartoon that broadcast the new message (see illustration 7.4). The UE-CIO, a man in dapper clothes and a snap-brim hat offers to a woman Honeywell worker the gift of a dress labeled "union gains." At the window stands a sinister symbol, a masked man representing the AFL federal union. The rapacious and villainous character of the alternative suggests the extent to which underlying themes of solidarity, sexuality, and consumerism merged in the union appeal. In a later editorial, a woman UE member trying to convert her sisters described the AFL campaign as "disruptive," "filthy," "ashamed," and "wrong"; she claimed that women who belonged to the federal union had been "duped into believing that the AFL was sincere in a desire to help us." The language resonates with fears that "home life policies and politics" could be dictated to the worker.[36]

Implicit in these narratives of union competition and victory was the sense that efforts to woo workers into the union relied on the romance and attraction of the labor movement. Organizing was a selling job, not a conversion. In that sense, consumerism—highlighted by the juxtaposition of the masculine union with the feminine worker and the role of the

> # PRICES UP ↑
> U.E. 1145 DEMANDS . . .
> IMMEDIATE 10c WAGE INCREASES!
>
> JOIN 1145 . . . SUPPORT THIS DEMAND!

7.4 Depicting union recruitment as romance, this cartoon shows that by the 1940s, the gender of labor union solidarity had changed. Union and worker became separate and distinct—male and female, active and passive, attractor and attracted. While the worker could now be represented as female because of the increased numbers of women war workers, he or she was placed in a subordinate role. *Honeywell UE News*, October 24, 1941 (Courtesy of UE) worker in receiving, passively, the gains—took on new meaning for union organizers. Labor used what Betty Friedan once called "the sexual sell."[37] Consumer campaigns, union-label advertisements, even cartoons were part and parcel of a new consumerist twist on labor that had begun in the late 1930s. Betty Union despairs of getting a wage adjustment that will enable her to dress well:

> The cost of stockings—WOW!
> The cost of clothes! WHY, HECK!
> If we don't get wage adjustments,
> I'm going to look a wreck.[38]

Women were encouraged to "buy union," not only for reasons of family solidarity but because it made for a better love life. In one ad, "Peggy O'Connor, thrifty and wise, wears union hosiery, has many guys." A muscular CIO figure, dressed like a lifeguard, walks with bathing beauty Wage Increases on his arm while the out-of-shape Tories can only huff and puff. Or John Lady-Killer learns that if he's ever going to win Mary Union-Conscious from the arms of Tom Union-Builder, he had better buy union-label clothes.[39]

The inscription of the Honeywell worker as female, as someone to be wooed and won, to be attracted and seduced, marked a break with the past. This use of female representation for the worker signaled an awareness of the growing numbers and importance of women in the plant work force.[40] It also suggested that reliance on manly workplace solidarity would not win the day. Under the no-strike pledge, loyalty and compliance with the union agenda—not grassroots militance—was the sign of solidarity. Moreover, the new symbols and metaphors indicated a shift in the language of unionism to the language of bureaucratization. In bureaucratic language, the worker was to choose between suitors—in this case, the manly and romantic CIO over the cowardly AFL. Significantly, the new symbols placed worker and union in a hierarchical relationship spoken in the idiom of gender. Where union and worker were identical in the militant union symbolism of the 1930s, here worker and subordinate were depicted as female, union and superior as male.

Unions began to translate the general patriotic sentiment of home front struggle into the specific organizational loyalty of unionism; organizers had to convince workers—especially women workers—that they were both individually entitled to higher compensation (equal pay) and that they required a collective and specific union identity to receive it. In essence, union campaigns speaking to women had to walk a line between patriotic self-sacrifice (embedded in general propaganda about the war) and individual selfishness (assumed in any demand for higher wages). Resonating with patriotism, the equal rights tradition, and gender-specific claims, the equal pay issue bridged the gap.

Equal Pay and Union Solidarity

In selling women on the labor movement, the equal pay demand became a major contribution to the UE campaign. Beyond whatever use it might have had in protecting pay scales and union membership, pay equity also had tremendous symbolic and practical significance for women. Right before the second NLRB election at Honeywell, the issue of equal pay surfaced in the union news sheet. Announcing that UE women at Moline received a higher starting rate than those at Honeywell, the writer urged them to seek the same protection under a union contract. Throughout the last stages of the organizing campaign, equal pay remained an important issue; what is more, the debate over it was carried into the negotiation. Women workers met separately from men workers in discussing the contract; equal pay was a major item on the agenda; and women's role in winning the contract was affirmed publicly.[41]

The crosscutting themes of national identity and patriotism, secular and individual interests, and collective union goals suggest the difficulty in measuring and assessing the impact of the war. Historians have suggested that the pleas for self-sacrifice for the nation, the reminders of men serving in the armed forces, and the constant framing of issues like equal pay for equal work in a familial context undermined whatever emancipatory impact war work had on women.[42] But, as Maureen Honey argued in a recent study, the images of women used in war propaganda campaigns were complex and often contradictory; Rosie the Riveter was both a symbol of the nation at war and a reminder of families in peacetime. Rosie both sought a public role and defended a private one.[43] Viewed in the context of the larger campaign to mobilize the defense production army and women war workers in particular, union propaganda—its language, images, and choice of issues—reflected the same drives for individual sacrifice, collective unity, and public duty. In that sense, union leaders both embraced the participation of women in the labor movement on the basis of equal work and at the same time undermined the meaning of this participation by framing it within the language of national, class, and gender identity.[44]

Because the language of patriotism was malleable, particularly as it affected women, it was possible not only for union forces to use it but also for antiunion firms to bend it to suit their own ends. In 1943, the UE directed its organizers to Onan and Sons, a nonunion firm specializing in electric generators. Targeting the women on the line, union flyers merged the issue of equal pay with familial concern. "Dear Sister," read one handout, "Of vital concern to both women on the job and the men who will return to industry after the war is the question of equal pay for women." To preempt accusations of subversion, one flyer read: "We are your neighbors on the bench, the fellow on the next machine, the girl in the khaki overall. We, together with you, did our part to earn that 'E' pennant. Our husbands, sons, brothers, sisters and relatives are in all branches of the armed forces, just as yours are. We want to assure that they get everything they need for a speedy victory. That's why we are organizing."[45] UE organizers seemed to assume that working women, "as soldiers on the production lines," would fight for the standard of living of their male kin. Called to the banner of "One Nation—One Flag—One Union," the women of Onan had no desire to sign into the UE army.[46] The self-proclaimed 100 percent Americans lost the union election by an almost two to one margin. Attributing the loss to union mistakes, the organizer also admitted that wages at Onan were not significantly lower and that the bonus system had resolved other doubts. What is notable is the extent to which the UE had avoided making pay equity an issue at Onan. Equal pay to help returning soldiers was not the same as equal pay for women. Unlike union organizers at Honeywell, those who tried to organize the Onan plant failed to realize the attraction of the fairness issue for women workers. They relied instead on conservative appeals to family and nation. But the stress on American ideals backfired when the employer was as patriotic as the union.[47]

Telling the Truth

The union victory at Honeywell coupled with well-meaning failures in other defense plants suggests that when unions tried to capitalize on gender ideals, they had—at best—limited and uneven success. Just as the campaign to mobilize women workers in the war effort was subject to the vagaries and resistance of women themselves, labor organizing during the war met with an audience of working women with few reasons to believe labor unions. Union attitudes after the war suggest that the women were right. Before the war, the district president of the UE, Buford Eastman stated, "When the employers become women, then I will be in favor of women organizers."[48] Robert Wishart, the head of the UE drive at Honeywell, had similar reservations. After successfully organizing the plant, in large part because women loyal to the AFL changed sides, Wishart remained more sanguine about recruiting men than women. While employers and unions appeared anxious to recruit women, by 1945 companies were as skeptical about their ability to hire women as they were enthusiastic about hiring male veterans.[49]

Martha Ziegler, a Woman's Bureau field inspector, assessed the situation in the postwar era and found the prospects for women depressing. Many women were unemployed; no one even knew where the thousands who had been employed at the Twin City Ordnance Plant now worked and lived. As thousands of veterans returned to the labor force, unions responded to their needs, not those of the women who were assumed to be their temporary replacements. Ziegler asked George Lawson, president of the Minnesota State Federation of Labor, to predict the future. While hesitating to "tell the truth," Lawson finally replied that "the immediate post-war period would probably be a period of unemployment and difficulties." "He stressed," Ziegler reported, "that this period could be more or less temporary after reconversion has been completed."[50] It was a far cry from asking women to join the army of labor.

Given the messages of a singular and hostile male solidarity that proliferated in the 1930s and the ambiguous celebration of equal pay and participation for women during the war, the extent to which women trusted in the labor movement enough to walk picket lines, risk their jobs, and put their signatures on union cards may seem astonishing. Women union leaders certainly believed, with Minnesota CIO leader Estaire Wurst, that what working women needed was to think as trade unionists.[51] But the willingness of women to join unions was not, as some might suggest, a result of false consciousness of their position in society, resignation to their fate, acceptance of irrevocable and damaging sexual difference, or even, finally, a sign of their own collusion with the patriarchy of state and union. The working women whose history we have followed had limited evidence to bear on the issue, and the evidence was this: unions said that they acted in the interest of workers, and working women saw themselves as workers—as part of the working community or class. At some point, it did not matter that the labor leadership, mostly men of long experience, saw workers as male and women as nonworkers; the word "worker" to a woman holding a job also meant "woman."[52]

Conclusion

Women, Labor, and the State in the Twentieth Century

Between 1915 and 1945, unparalleled catastrophe and change in the form of two major wars and global economic crisis transformed the place of the United States in the world and the lives of its men and women citizens. The perception that 1914 marked the end of an era was widely shared during the period; and in retrospect, it seems suspect only as understatement. Focusing on the labor movement within a specific community in this tumultuous epoch has allowed us to see closely the interplay of class, gender, and—to a lesser extent—race and ethnicity as they shaped configurations of power and the historical experience of men and women.

Within this brief period, wars have dominated the historical discussion as to how and why the lives and status of women changed, and yet the Great Depression precipitated equally important transformations in the realms of family, work, and the state. Economic crisis fundamentally changed both capital and labor. At the beginning of the decade, businesses and unions were organized at the community level. Groups such as the Minneapolis Citizens' Alliance and local Chambers of Commerce held greater sway over conditions of work and the suppression of labor than national organizations like the National Civic Federation. Labor unions were also concentrated into small local units while internationals held their locals in a loose national federation. Economic upheaval and legislation beneficial to large corporations—for example, the National Recovery Administration of the early New Deal—created opportunities for the further concentration of capital even as national unions benefited by the regulation of labor relations under the Wagner Act.[1]

The magnitude of the depression sanctioned government initiatives in the welfare arena. Under the New Deal, federal entitlement programs supplanted community and local-level relief efforts. Particularistic forms of welfare, which emphasized worthiness above need, were augmented by programs of old-age assistance and workers' compensation premised on regular and continuous work histories. The product of these changes was a two-track welfare system, one which—like the system of industrial relations that reinforced the segmentation of the labor market—privileged white male wage earners.[2]

During the early years of the depression, labor unions demonstrated breadth in their commitment to community and workplace action. This commitment presented a unique opportunity for the organization of women workers. Women workers found the renewed community support and strength needed to improve wages and working conditions. In Minneapolis, they formed substantial locals in the predominantly female labor force of the garment and knitting industries. At the same time they participated in the growth of more integrated factories such as those in electrical manufacturing.

Although women organized primarily in the industrial sector, the climate of militancy made it possible for service workers and clerical workers to revive long-dormant unions or to start new ones within the CIO. This was an important step for the long-term prospects of women in the labor movement. If women could organize their co-workers in the clerical field, the conditions and wages of one-third of all women workers could be improved; and women would have a more substantive and autonomous voice in the labor movement. The issues of local autonomy and women's autonomy were linked.

Union politics did not exist in a vacuum. The labor movement which moved quickly to capitalize on the opportunities of the 1930s also needed to respond to unemployment and mass suffering. Allied with the local Farmer-Labor movement, workers sought to change the political landscape for unionism. At one level, this political activism directly involved the control of the state and local government, which had been used to undermine the success of striking workers through arrest, injunction, or refusal of relief. At another level, it expressed the desire of workers that the labor movement be more than an economic force. Union members and their leadership shared a vision of a country in which education, jobs, and home ownership would be more widely distributed. In this effort, the Farmer-Labor movement played an important role in expressing the will of unionists to take their movement outside the workplace.

By the late 1930s, prolonged unemployment and preparations for war increasingly threatened community-based and locally led unions. Developments in the economy and the state underwrote the shift of labor from its community base to the more bureaucratic, workplace-oriented and corporate unionism that we are familiar with today. Moreover, despite increasing numbers of women members, most unions failed to incorporate women in the leadership. While there was a rhetorical commitment to democratic unionism and the expansion of women's political role, the historical experience of most women workers was that things did not significantly change. Most labor unions retained an almost exclusively male leadership; the Farmer-Labor movement's fortunes after 1936 put limits on redistributive politics; and except at the shop and community levels, women lost the little access they had to channels of policy and power.[3]

Still, it is important to remember that the labor movement in the 1930s was in a period of transition in which the outcomes were not known. The possibilities for the full integration of women workers into a democratic labor movement were greater then, if only because the movement was focused in communities and drew upon the local autonomy of unions as a base from which to grow. Women were central to this effort as both workers and wives largely because of the attention of workers and their unions to what might be described as the reproductive sphere and the intersection of family and community with workplace concerns.

That women workers did not achieve a position of equality in the labor movement is due to the extent of the economic, social, and psychological crisis of the Great Depression. Because the 1930s represented a crisis in men's ability to earn wages, and hence to fulfill their socially ascribed role, it was as well a crisis of masculinity.[4] Given society's ambivalence toward gender equality, the competition among men and women was acted out politically and economically in the labor movement.

Further, this competition was expressed in the realm of government. The New Deal administration did not accept the role of employer of last resort but tried to ameliorate the suffering of workers through the creation of programs like the WPA. The issue for the federal government, and for other policymakers who wanted to restrict the employment of women in the depression, was the unemployment of men. In all the debate about married women's right to work, there had never been any question about the marital status of men or whether single men should sacrifice their own jobs to married ones.

Even as the depression gave real and material importance to women's work—in the home, the workplace, and the labor movement, there was a need to deny its importance. Women were almost entirely absent from the labor press of the 1930s. When their participation is recorded, it is in roll-call style. The officers of auxiliaries and social committees were named, but their activities were not described, and women's voices were seldom heard. The need for rituals of subordination (titles, the claims of family) increased in the midst of working women's growing autonomy and importance.[5]

The long-range impact of women's wartime experience is more difficult to evaluate; but the shift away from community-based unions, the suppression of local autonomy by national unions, and the collapse of separate organizations for women within the union movement meant continued marginality for women workers. During the war years, women joined labor unions in greater numbers than ever before, earned union wages, and were socialized into labor unions. This experience and their subsequent exclusion from union jobs during reconversion shaped women's response to wage work and union membership. The failure of unions to integrate women into the local labor movements during the 1930s led to their continued marginality in and exclusion from that movement.

The dramatic increase in women's employment in unionized sectors of the economy during the war, particularly in well-paid defense work, provided labor leaders with a unique opportunity to recruit a loyal following among women, which might have been retained even as women shifted back into traditional employment during the postwar reconversion. Women joined labor unions during the war, but in large part this was caused by the closed-shop contracts of many defense firms. The dues check-off provided the labor movement with a continuously high level of membership at the same time it proved an obstacle to continued efforts at revitalizing union membership through education. Further, the language within which women were recruited into unions was curiously ambiguous, stressing patriotic and class loyalty as compelling substitutes for women's solidarity in the labor movement. Even during the war years, unions maintained their identity as masculine institutions.

In the best case, women from the United Automobile Workers created a woman's department to voice their concerns,[6] but even this kind of development could not halt the deterioration of women's position after the war. Although temporary, women's experience in unionized jobs might have carried with it the motivation to organize female-dominated sectors of the economy, but for a number of reasons, women emerged from the war experience more unionized but less active in unions.

While contemporary feminist politics have supported a revival of women's concerns through organizations such as the Coalition for Labor Union Women, the simultaneous decline of the labor movement's fortunes suggests limits to its use as an advocate of women's interests. Too absorbed in the struggle for their own survival, labor leaders have advocated instead an increasingly defensive trade unionist posture in the political and economic arenas. This is clearly the wrong direction if working women are to have a voice in labor politics.

Despite these dismal prospects, the idea of the labor movement and its possibilities for change still engages the attention and hopes of the unorganized. Recent polls suggest that two-thirds of women and minority workers would join a union if there was one available. While this may be an optimistic reading of the evidence, workers in the secondary and largely unorganized industries of service, light manufacturing, and clerical work endow the labor movement with a trust no political party can muster in the arena of work. The empowering ideology of the labor movement, with its strong themes of solidarity among workers, can still be a force of change for women in society.

As a crisis of wage earning and gender, the Great Depression reoriented the expectations of men and women, restructuring opportunity and formalizing discrimination on the basis of gender even as it witnessed the dynamic growth of unionism among all workers. This suggests that the Great Depression needs to be reintegrated into our understanding of history. In the formulation of a new social history of the twentieth century, still in its infancy, it will be necessary to see the economic crisis of the 1930s not as an aberration in American progress and growth but as a period which fundamentally altered the relationships between man and woman, labor and capital, citizen and state. The origins of our contemporary experience lie not only in the periodic wars and conquests of our history but in our response to civil crisis as well.

Appendix

Social and
Economic Data
on Minneapolis

Table A.1 Population, Minneapolis, 1880–1950

Year	Population	Increase	Growth Rate (%)
1880	46,887	33,821	259
1890	164,738	117,851	251
1900	202,718	37,980	23
1910	301,408	98,690	49
1920	380,582	79,174	26
1930	464,370	83,774	22
1940	492,370	28,014	6
1950	521,718	29,348	6

Source: U.S. Bureau of the Census, *17th Census, 1950*, vol. 1, *Number of Inhabitants*, table 4, 23–11.

Table A.2 Population by Nativity and Race, Minneapolis, 1910–1940
(in Percentages)

Nativity/Race	1910	1920	1930	1940
Native White	30.1	35.0	41.9	47.2[a]
Native with Foreign Parents	33.1	40.8	39.6	36.0[a]
Foreign Born	36.2	23.1	17.4	15.1[a]
Other[b]	0.6	1.1	1.1	1.7[a]
Total[c]	100.0	99.0	100.0	100.0
N =	301,408	380,582	464,370	492,370

Source: U.S. Bureau of the Census, *13th Census, 1910*, vol. 2, *Reports by States*, table 2, 1014; *14th Census, 1920*, vol. 2, *General Report*, table 17, 67; *16th Census, 1940*, vol. 2, pt. 4, *Characteristics of the Population*, table B-36, 173.

[a]Estimates from Minneapolis–St. Paul 1940 census public use sample with the effect of giving higher black and foreign born population estimates. Aggregate census data gives foreign-born population of Minneapolis at 13% and the minority population at 1.1%.

[b]90% black.

[c]Figures do not total 100% due to rounding.

Table A.3 Rural and Urban Population, Minnesota, 1880–1920

Year	Rural	% Increase	Urban	% Increase
1880	632,853	—	147,920	—
1890	867,234	37.0	443,049	199.5
1900	1,153,294	33.0	598,100	35.0
1910	1,225,414	6.3	850,294	42.2
1920	1,335,532	9.0	1,051,593	23.7

Source: U.S. Bureau of the Census, *Farm Population of the United States, 1920*, table 77, 180.

Table A.4 National Origin of Foreign-Born Whites, Minneapolis, 1930

Country of Origin	Number	Percent
Great Britain	3,880	4.8
Canada	6,731	8.3
Germany	7,549	9.3
Eastern Europe	13,431	16.6
Norway	15,492	19.2
Sweden	24,866	30.8
Other Countries	8,885	11.0
All Foreign-Born Whites	80,834	100.0

Source: U.S. Bureau of the Census, *15th Census, 1930,* vol. 3, pt. 1, *Reports by States*, table 12, 1204.

Table A.5 Ethnicity of Native Whites of Foreign Parentage, Minneapolis, 1930

Country of Parents' Birth	Number	Percent
Great Britain	8,679	4.7
Ireland	10,512	5.7
Canada	15,397	8.4
Eastern Europe	21,281	11.6
Germany	33,299	18.1
Norway	33,917	18.4
Sweden	45,597	24.7
Other Countries	15,529	8.4
All Native-Born Whites of Foreign Parentage	183,941	100.0

Source: U.S. Bureau of the Census, *15th Census, 1930,* vol. 3, pt. 1, *Reports by States*, table 19, 1222.

Table A.6 Birthplace by Sex, Minneapolis–St. Paul, 1940 (in Percentages)

Birthplace	Male	Female	Total
Minnesota	64.8	66.8	65.9
Midwest	16.1	17.2	16.6
Other U.S.	4.8	4.7	4.8
Northern Europe	9.2	7.5	8.4
Other[a]	3.6	2.4	3.1
Total	100.0	100.0	100.0
N =	3393	3683	7076

Source: U.S. Bureau of the Census, Public Use Sample, 1940.

[a]Mostly from southern and eastern Europe.

Table A.7 Relationship to Head of Household, In-Migrants, Minneapolis, 1935–1940 (in Percentages)

Relation	Men	Women
Head of Household	48.4	8.9
Related to Head	30.2	61.3
Not Relative of Head	12.6	21.4
Not in Private Household	8.8	8.4
Total	100.0	100.0
N =	23,217	30,656

Source: U.S. Bureau of the Census, *Internal Migration, 1935–1940*, table 26, 247.

Table A.8 Labor Force Participation by Sex and Age, Minneapolis, 1930–1940 (in Percentages)

	Men		Women	
Age	1930	1940	1930	1940
14–19	32.4	24.9	31.3	24.8
20–24	86.3	84.6	63.9	63.9
25–34	97.4	96.4	41.5	44.7
35–44	98.2	96.2	30.2	34.5
45–54	97.5	92.6	26.6	28.8
55–64	91.8	84.9	19.3	22.1
Over 65	55.6	31.9	6.9	5.2
Overall	84.8	78.6	34.1	34.2
N =	147,387	149,679	64,412	73,276

Source: U.S. Bureau of the Census, *16th Census, 1940*, vol. 3, pt. 3, *The Labor Force*, table 6, 693.

Table A.9 Female Labor Force Participation (Age 15 and over) by Nativity, Race, and Marital Status, Minneapolis, 1930 (in Percentages)

	Single	Married	Wid./Div.	Total
Native White	69.5	15.7	43.1	38.5
(N = 56,334)				
Foreign Born	76.2	9.7	22.5	20.3
(N = 7,415)				
Black	58.3	27.1	60.5	39.1
(N = 618)				
Overall	69.9	14.4	36.0	34.1
(N = 64,356)[a]				

Source: U.S. Bureau of the Census, *15th Census, 1930*, vol. 4, *Occupations by States*, table 15, 851.

[a]Includes twenty-six working women of other races.

Table A.10 Employment by Industry and Sex, Minneapolis, 1930 and 1940
(in Percentages)

Industry	1930 Male	1930 Female	% Female[a]
Manufacturing	37.2	13.7	13.9
Transportation	12.5	2.8	9.0
Trade	23.1	11.4	17.8
Professional	6.5	14.9	50.2
Service	6.0	28.2	67.1
Clerical	10.6	28.8	54.4
Other Occupations[b]	4.2	—	—
All Occupations[c]	100.1	99.8	30.4
N =	147,491	64,437	211,928

Industry	1940 Male	1940 Female	% Female[a]
Manufacturing	26.2	9.8	16.4
Transportation	13.0	3.3	6.2
Trade	34.3	23.0	26.2
Professional	7.0	14.4	51.6
Service	6.2	28.1	70.3
Clerical	8.9	19.7	53.6
Other Occupations[b]	4.4	1.5	n/a
All Occupations[c]	100.0	99.8	34.3
N =	122,480	63,906	186,385

Source: U.S. Bureau of the Census, *15th Census, 1930*, vol. 4, *Occupations by States*, table 3, 828; and *16th Census, 1940*, vol. 3, pt. 3, *The Labor Force*, table 20, 769–70.

[a]That is, proportion of jobs in each industry occupied by female workers.

[b]Two-thirds of men in protective service (e.g., police).

[c]Figures do not equal 100% due to rounding.

Table A.11 Women in Selected Industries by Marital Status, Minneapolis, 1930

Occupation	% Single	% Married	% Wid./Div.	N
Agriculture	39.1	39.1	21.7	23
Manufacturing	54.7	29.8	15.5	8,818
Communication	76.6	16.4	7.0	1,824
Sales	51.2	32.5	16.1	7,355
Public Service	40.2	33.8	26.0	77
Professional	75.8	16.9	7.3	9,606
Service	52.4	26.0	21.6	18,121
Clerical	78.6	16.1	5.3	18,575
All Occupations	64.3	22.8	12.9	64,393

Source: U.S. Bureau of the Census, *15th Census, 1930*, vol. 4, *Occupations by States*, table 18, 753–54.

Table A.12 Manufacturing, Wholesaling, and Retailing, Minneapolis, 1929–1937

Year	Manufacturing		Wholesaling		Retailing	
	Plants	Product[a]	Estabs.	Sales[a]	Estabs.	Sales[a]
1929	1219	361.1	1316	846.4	6028	303.3
1933	923	170.8	991	515.8	6122	168.6
1935	1007	223.5	1123	626.1	6446	220.8
1937	1038	270.5	1123	750.0	6446	265.0

Source: U.S. WPA, *Industry in Minnesota* (Minneapolis, 1940), 79.

[a]Figures in millions of dollars.

Table A.13 Relief Cases Opened by Year, Minneapolis, 1928–1935

Year	Number	Index[a]
1928	394	100
1929	407	103
1930	969	246
1931	2,507	636
1932[b]	10,182	2,584
1933	7,421	1,883
1934	6,835	1,735
1935	5,405	1,372

Source: Segner, *Minneapolis Unemployed*, vol. 2, 131–33.

[a]1928 = 100.

[b]1932 figures reflect transfer of private cases.

Notes

Abbreviations

CAM Records	Citzens' Alliance of Minneapolis Records
CLUM Records	Central Labor Union of Minneapolis Records
MHS	Minnesota Historical Society
NA	National Archives
NLRB	U.S. National Labor Relations Board
RG	Record Group
SWHA	Social Welfare History Archives
UE Records	United Electrical, Radio and Machine Workers of America Records
USES Records	U.S. Employment Service Records
WMC Records	War Manpower Commission Records

Preface

1. Moody and Kessler-Harris, *Perspectives on American Labor History*.
2. Beard, *A Short History of the American Labor Movement*, 9.
3. White, *Tropics of Discourse*.

Introduction

1. Vorse, *Labor's New Millions*, 234.
2. Kempton, *Part of Our Time*, 211–32.
3. Walker, *American City*, 239. On Charles Walker, see *National Cyclopedia of American Biography* (Clifton, N.J.: James T. White, 1980), 59:405–6. According to Irving Bernstein, it was Walker who had the idea to establish the Theatre Union in 1933. His experience, however, did not alter Walker's critical stance toward working-class culture. The Theatre Union was formed by intellectuals and professionals who wrote plays for workers. In its work, the union reflected the attitudes of writers like Walker who believed that the working class could only be a force for

change if it was led by an educated and enlightened vanguard. See Bernstein, *A Caring Society*, 220–21.

4. Walker, *American City*, 240.

5. Ibid., 239.

6. Vorse, *Labor's New Millions*, 234.

7. Commenting on the strength of the workers' movement in Italy in 1919, Mary Heaton Vorse listed the five aspects of a mature labor movement: (1) strong unions, (2) a strong political movement, (3) powerful cooperatives of production and consumption, (4) a strong labor press, and (5) workers' education (Vorse, *Footnote to Folly*, 199ff.). In many respects, the labor movement of the 1930s was developing along these lines in the United States when the recession of 1938 and the preparations for war began.

8. Vorse, *Labor's New Millions*, 404.

9. Ibid., 234.

10. Kempton, *Part of Our Time*, 216.

11. See Vorse, *Footnote to Folly*, for a full account of her life and her perspective on the labor movement. Vorse exemplifies the politics of nurturance celebrated in Elshtain, "Antigone's Daughters," 46–59. Vorse concludes her autobiography with the statement that the entire book, and hence her entire life, has been about children—a statement demonstrated by her commitment to children's war relief and the peace movement and by her insistence on the labor movement's familial base. This statement was also true of her personal experience. According to Dorothy Day, Vorse "never felt free of the need to support her children and even her children's children" (Gould and Green, "Mary Heaton Vorse," 712–14). See also Vorse, *Rebel Pen*, esp. introduction.

12. See Parkin, *Marxism and Class Theory*, 45–115, on social closure.

13. Manuel Castells first raised the issue of social reproduction as the basis of urban politics—but in a way that seems to divorce the struggle from its labor component. See his *The Urban Question*. A recent application is Mark-Lawson et al., "Gender and Local Politics."

14. Blewett, *Men, Women and Work*, 44–67; Stansell, "The Origins of the Sweatshop," 78–103. On family recruitment, see Hareven, *Family Time, Industrial Time*, 85–119. For family status and militancy, see Louise Tilly, "Paths of Proletarianization," and Hanagan, "Proletarian Families and Social Protest."

15. Rudé, *The Crowd in History*; Thompson, "Eighteenth Century English Society" and "The Moral Economy of the English Crowd"; Louise Tilly, "The Food Riot"; Kerber, *Women of the Republic*, 34–67; Countryman, *A People in Revolution*, 37–45, 182–83; Harding, *There Is a River*, 12–13, 32–33, 65–72, and passim. The most stunning example of women's participation is Harriet Tubman, who brought whole families and communities out of slavery.

16. See Stansell, *City of Women*, 55–62. While the boundaries of the home and street were permeable in the emerging industrial metropolis, it seems reasonable

to suppose that quarrels which—in a less formal political system—constituted a political arena for men and women of the popular classes increasingly became defined as private and thus outside the reach of the state, except at those times when they resurfaced through court battles.

17. I use the term "sentimental patriarchy" to distinguish family forms which seemed to bridge the gap between the patriarchal family of early modern Europe and modern, companionate families.

18. On trade unions, see Stansell, *City of Women*, 130–54. For comparative developments, see Scott, "Men and Women in the Parisian Garment Trades"; and Barbara Taylor, " 'The Men Are as Bad as Their Masters.' "

19. Henry, *Trade Union Woman*; Dublin, *Women at Work*, 86–131; Stansell, *City of Women*, 130–54. The language of republicanism could be a malleable tool for black and ethnic protest as well. See Harding, *There Is a River*; Evans and Boyte, *Free Spaces*, 26–68; Eric Foner, "Class, Ethnicity and Radicalism in the Gilded Age"; Wilentz, "Against Exceptionalism"; and Krause, "Labor Republicanism and 'Za Chlebom.' "

20. Montgomery, *Beyond Equality*, 135–96; Philip Foner, *Women and the American Labor Movement*, vol. 1, 122–40.

21. Norman Ware, *The Labor Movement*; Grob, *Workers and Utopia*, 44–57; Michael Gordon, "The Labor Boycott"; Fink, *Workingmen's Democracy*, esp. 18–37; Oestreicher, *Solidarity and Fragmentation*, 109, 116–17, 129, 214, 223–28.

22. Philip Foner, *Women and the American Labor Movement*, vol. 1, 185–212; Levine, "Labor's True Woman."

23. Turbin, "And We Are Nothing But Women"; Levine, " 'Honor Each Noble Maid' "; Elizabeth Faue, "Women, Work and Protest in a Minneapolis Garment Factory"; Kealey and Palmer, *'Dreaming of What Might Be'*, 316–26.

24. On the decline of the Knights, see Rachleff, *Black Labor in the South*, 157–91; and Fink, *Workingmen's Democracy*, esp. 219–30, and "The New Labor History." On immigrants, see Gutman, *Work, Culture, and Society*, esp. 32–66; Bodnar, *The Transplanted*, 1–34; Deutsch, *No Separate Refuge*, 87–126; and Asher and Stephenson, *Labor Divided*. For the artisanal tradition among these immigrants, see Donna Gabaccia, "Neither Padrone Slaves nor Primitive Rebels."

25. Montgomery, *Workers' Control in America*, 9–32, and *The Fall of the House of Labor*; Brecher, Lombardi, and Stackhouse, comps., *Brass Valley*; Bodnar, *Immigration and Industrialization*.

26. See also Cumbler, *Working Class Community in Industrial America*, 165–94; Gordon, Edwards, and Reich, *Segmented Work, Divided Workers*, esp. 140–44, 150–57; and James Barrett, *Work and Community in the Jungle*, 188–239.

27. Warner, *Streetcar Suburbs* and *The Private City*; Cumbler, *Working Class Community in Industrial America*; Rosenzweig, *Eight Hours for What We Will*.

28. Rosenzweig, *Eight Hours for What We Will*; Couvares, "The Triumph of Commerce"; Erenberg, *Steppin' Out*; Peiss, *Cheap Amusements*.

29. See Kessler-Harris, "Women, Work and the Social Order" and "Problems of Coalition Building"; Baron, "Questions of Gender."

30. On the earlier period, see Prude, *The Coming of the Industrial Order*, 144–50; and Dublin, *Women at Work*, 23–57, and "Rural-Urban Migrants in Industrial New England." On more recent trends, see Meyerowitz, *Women Adrift*, 8–19, and chapter 1 of this book.

31. Louise Tilly, "Paths of Proletarianization"; Stansell, "The Origins of the Sweatshop"; Cooper, *Once a Cigar-Maker*, 218–46; Benson, "The Clerking Sisterhood."

32. See Frank, "Housewives, Socialists, and the Politics of Food"; and Kaplan, "Female Consciousness and Collective Action." In exploring the constraints of the model of separate spheres, Alice Kessler-Harris conflates community and neighborhood with family and argues that historians stretched the model of politicized domesticity to include working-class and black women. See her "Gender Ideology in Historical Reconstruction." I would argue that working-class women's community activism was not politicized domesticity; its origins, expressions, and spaces were historically distinct.

33. See Higham, *Strangers in the Land*, 36–37, 46–52, 70–72, 305–6; Lane, *Solidarity or Survival?*, esp. 95–208; Philip Foner, *Organized Labor and the Black Worker*, 64–102; Kessler-Harris, "Where are the Organized Women Workers?"

34. The ideal of the skilled worker was inscribed not only in masculine but in racial and ethnic terms; see Hewitt, " 'The Voice of Virile Labor.' " On Gompers's attitudes toward the state, see Laurie, *Artisans into Workers*, 176–210. On the family wage, see Martha May, "Bread before Roses"; Barrett and McIntosh, "The Family Wage."

35. See Eva Valesh, "Women and Labor" and "Wage Working Women"; Kessler-Harris, "Where are the Organized Women Workers?" and "Problems of Coalition-Building"; Milkman, "Organizing the Sexual Division of Labor," 114–25.

36. See Robin Miller Jacoby, "The Women's Trade Union League and American Feminism" and "The Women's Trade Union League School for Women Organizers"; Dye, *As Equals and as Sisters*; MacLean, *The Culture of Resistance*; Hyman, "Labor Organizing and Female Institution-Building"; Karen Mason, "Feeling the Pinch"; Cott, *The Grounding of Modern Feminism*, 23–24, 88–89, 122–29; and Norwood, *Labor's Flaming Youth*, 92–109, 136–47, 228–32.

37. Dubofsky, *We Shall Be All*, 57–87.

38. Ibid.; Conlin, ed., *At the Point of Production*; Ebner, "The Passaic Strike of 1912 and the Two IWW's."

39. Jameson, "Imperfect Unions"; Schofield, "Rebel Girls and Union Maids."

40. This is certainly the image embraced by most historians of the IWW. See Salerno's summary in *Red November, Black November*, 8–17, 28–30. The source for this myth lies within IWW imagery itself. For example, Flynn describes migratory workers thus: "They were strong and hardy, tanned and weather-beaten by sum-

mer suns and winter snows. They regarded the city workers as stay-at-home softies—'scissor-bills.' They referred to a wife as 'the ball and chain' " (*The Rebel Girl*, 103). Contrast this with her depiction of the Lawrence and Iron Range strikes as family and community-based struggles (127–43, 207–16). Also see Kornbluh, *Rebel Voices*; and Zurier, *Art for the Masses*.

41. Blee, "The Impact of Family Settlement Patterns"; Tax, *The Rising of the Women*, 241–76; Cameron, "Bread and Roses Revisited"; Flynn, *The Rebel Girl*, 127–73; Golin, "Defeat Becomes Disaster."

42. Murray, *Red Scare*; Preston, *Aliens and Dissenters*; Brody, *Labor in Crisis*; Painter, *Standing at Armageddon*, 344–80. On the textile strike, see Hall, "Disorderly Women," a wonderful example of the community-based unionism discussed here. Unfortunately, Elizabethton, Gastonia, and other textile struggles could not survive the onslaught of state action, political fragmentation, and economic crisis that could have made them the model for a revitalized labor movement.

43. For an overview of events in the 1930s, see Galenson, *The CIO Challenge to the A.F.L.*; Preis, *Labor's Giant Step*; Irving Bernstein, *The Turbulent Years*; Brecher, *Strike!*, 144–220; Milton, *The Politics of U.S. Labor*, and—of course—Vorse's perceptive narrative, *Labor's New Millions*, which is one of the few studies to envision the militancy of the 1930s as a community-based social movement. On specific struggles: for those in Minneapolis, see Walker, *American City*; Dobbs, *Teamster Rebellion*; and Tselos, "The Labor Movement in Minneapolis." For San Francisco, see Bruce Nelson, *Workers on the Waterfront*; and Quin, *The Big Strike*. For Toledo, see Korth and Beegle, *"I Remember Like Today."* See also Gerstle, *Working Class Americanism*, 95–259, on textile workers in Woonsocket.

44. Milkman, "Women's Work and the Economic Crisis"; Kessler-Harris, *Out to Work*, 250–72.

45. For women's activism, see Vorse, *Labor's New Millions*; Philip Foner, *Women and the American Labor Movement*, 278–335; Lasky, " 'Where I was a Person' "; Strom, "Challenging 'Woman's Place' " and "We're No Kitty Foyles"; and Milkman, *Gender at Work*, 27–48, among others.

46. Elizabeth Faue, "Women, Family, and Politics"; Valelly, *Radicalism in the States*. See Mark-Lawson, Savage, and Warde, "Gender and Local Politics," for an exposition of this in Britain. While the British experience was shaped by the active presence of the Labour Party (with many local variations), it was remarkably similar to U.S. developments, especially in Minnesota.

47. Dixler, "The Woman Question," 187–95.

48. Annamarie Faue, " 'A Victory for One Is a Victory for All' "; Lasky, " 'Where I Was a Person.' "

49. Ulman, *The Rise of the National Union*; Aronowitz, *False Promises*, 172–83, 251–62; Milton, *The Politics of U.S. Labor*, 113–38; Davis, *Prisoners of the American Dream*, 52–101. On electoral patterns among the working class, see Oestreicher, "Urban Working Class Political Behavior."

50. Tomlins, *The State and the Unions*; Sanford Jacoby, *Employing Bureaucracy*, 207–39; Hall, Korstad, Leloudis, "Cotton Mill People."

51. Leuchtenburg, *Franklin D. Roosevelt and the New Deal*; Milton, *The Politics of U.S. Labor.*

52. Tomlins, *The State and the Unions*; Lubove, *The Struggle for Social Security*; Barbara Nelson, "Gender, Race, and Class Origins"; Elizabeth Faue, "Women, Family, and Politics."

53. Lichtenstein, *Labor's War at Home*; Tomlins, *The State and the Unions*, 103–281; Davis, *Prisoners of the American Dream*, 52–101.

54. See Scharf, *To Work and To Wed*; and Susan Ware, *Holding Their Own*, among others.

55. See chapter 3. For literary parallels, see Dixler, "The Woman Question"; Rabinowitz, "Female Subjectivity."

56. Milkman, "Organizing the Sexual Division of Labor," 125–33.

57. On the public/private split, see Pateman, "Feminist Critiques of the Public/Private Dichotomy"; for the historicity and gender-specific nature of class, see Scott, *Gender and the Politics of History*, esp. 53–90.

58. An example of a system of thought recognizing the centrality of symbolic and biological reproduction would be the utopian socialism of the Owenites and Saint-Simonians. For critiques of orthodox Marxism and its inheritance, see Nicholson, *Gender and History*; Michele Barrett, "Marxist-Feminism and the Work of Karl Marx"; Balbus, *Marxism and Domination*; Hearn, *The Gender of Oppression*; and Benhabib and Cornell, eds., *Feminism as Critique*, esp. 16–56.

59. Briggs, "The Language of 'Class' "; Sewell, *Work and Revolution in France.*

60. Evans and Boyte discuss this with special reference to the concept of "community" in *Free Spaces*, 182–87. Social theory which relies on a separation between traditional and communal, modern and individuated in the classic formulation of Gesellschaft-Gemeinschaft expresses a suspicion of and contempt for the local. It also reflects a Victorian separation between the private and public, a division that has proved problematic for the study of women.

61. Katznelson, *City Trenches.*

62. Wright, *Class Structure and Income Determination*, 3–18; Thompson, *The Making of the English Working Class*, esp. preface and 711–832; Montgomery, *The Fall of the House of Labor*, 139–40; Gerstle, *Working Class Americanism*, 102. Scott has a particularly acute analysis of Thompson's perception of the public, rational, and masculine character of class; see her *Gender and the Politics of History*, 68–92.

63. Louise Tilly, "Paths of Proletarianization."

64. Barbara Taylor, *Eve and the New Jerusalem*; Scott, "Men and Women in the Parisian Garment Trades"; Benenson, "Victorian Sexual Ideology."

65. Buhle, *Women and American Socialism*, 246–87; Linda Gordon, *Woman's Body, Woman's Right*, 186–245.

66. Certainly this is the argument put forth in such classic texts as Engels's *The Origin of Family, Private Property and the State* and Bebel's *Woman and Socialism*.

67. For women on the Left, see Shaffer, "Women and the Communist Party"; Dixler, "The Woman Question."

68. Friedlander, *The Emergence of a UAW Local*; Hareven, *Family Time, Industrial Time*; Bodnar, *Immigration and Industrialization*.

69. On the political context, see Chrislock, *The Progressive Era in Minnesota*; Gieske, *Minnesota Farmer Laborism*; Haynes, *Dubious Alliance*; Valelly, *Radicalism in the States*.

70. My argument here has been aided by Nell Irvin Painter.

Chapter 1

1. For an analysis of *The Girl*, see Rabinowitz, "Maternity as History."

2. For some of the original worker narratives, see Meridel Le Sueur, *Worker Writers*, 38ff.

3. Walker, *American City*, xv.

4. Meyerowitz, *Women Adrift*, 8–19; Weiner, "Our Sisters' Keepers." Certainly, recent studies of immigration suggest that the city held tremendous allure for the young. See Peiss, *Cheap Amusements*; Ewen, *Immigrant Women in the Land of the Dollars*; and Erenberg, *Steppin' Out*.

5. Interviews with Hjordes Hedlund, May 29, 1985; Marguerite Belton, May 20, 1985; and Elizabeth Banghart, August 8, 1985. Weiner, *From Working Girl to Working Mother*, 20–27, discusses attributes of working women who migrated to the large cities in the early twentieth century, particularly the large number who boarded away from home. Nationally in 1900, Minneapolis was second only to St. Paul in the proportion of women boarding, with 31 percent boarding away from home, including servants.

6. On migration, see Weber, *The Growth of Cities*; Modell, "Mobility and Industrialization"; Roberta Miller, *City and Hinterland*; Dublin, "Rural-Urban Migrants in Industrial New England."

7. Hartsough, *The Twin Cities as a Metropolitan Market*; Minnesota Federal Writers' Project, *Minneapolis: The Story of a City*, 72–94; U.S. WPA, *Industry in Minnesota*, 72–82; Stipanovich, *City of Lakes*, 59–116; Weiner, "Our Sisters' Keepers."

8. Of course, this had not always been true. On women migrants, see U.S. Bureau of Labor Statistics, *Working Women in Large Cities*, 112–15; U.S. Bureau of the Census, *12th Census*; Weiner, "Our Sisters' Keepers"; Meyerowitz, *Women Adrift*.

9. See appendix table A.3.

10. While there are no accurate measures of individual migration in the U.S. Census before 1940, net migration rates can be calculated from published aggregate census figures for Minneapolis. I used the method for net migration described in Lee et al., *Methodological Considerations and Reference Tables*, 15–16, 19.

Migration for a decade can be calculated from population figures and census survival tables using the formula

$$M = P(x + 10) - sP(x) \text{ for each specified age group}$$

where M = net migration rate, $P(t)$ = population at specified time, and s = survival rate. Sources for population statistics are U.S. Bureau of the Census, *14th Census*, vol. 2, table 16, 330; and *16th Census*, vol. 2, pt. 4, table B-35, 172.

Thornthwaite estimated growth in Hennepin County from migration alone at 57,246. See Thornthwaite, *Internal Migration*, table 2, 29–30. On migration nationally, see Taeuber and Taeuber, *The Changing Population of the United States*, 107.

11. Zimmerman, "The Migration to Towns and Cities," 450–55. On the lack of employment for women on farms, see U.S. Bureau of the Census, *Farm Population*, 169–71. For the changing place of women in the farm economy, see Bush, " 'He Isn't So Cranky As He Used to Be' "; Elbert, "Amber Waves of Grain."

12. U.S. Bureau of the Census, *16th Census, 1940, Internal Migration*, table 19, 359–60. Among women migrating, 22.5 percent originated from noncontiguous states; 28.5 percent of the men did, suggesting that men migrate from slightly greater distances.

13. See Theodore Radzilowki's introduction to Minnesota Federal Writers' Project, *Bohemian Flats*, xv–xvi.

14. See appendix table A.7.

15. Schedules 7, 37, 60, 63, 68, 77, "Tentative Schedules for Minneapolis Unattached Women Seeking Relief for Self Alone," Records of the Women's Bureau, Record Group 86 (hereafter RG 86), Box 305, National Archives (hereafter NA), Washington, D.C.

16. See appendix table A.6.

17. Zimmerman, "The Migration to Towns and Cities," 454.

18. Minnesota Federal Writers' Project, *WPA Guide to Minnesota*, 167–73.

19. "Report on Women Wage Earners in Minneapolis, Survey, 1919," vol. 1, 35, YWCA of Minneapolis Records, Box 10, Social Welfare History Archives (hereafter SWHA), University of Minnesota, Minneapolis, Minnesota.

20. Schmid, *Social Saga of Two Cities*, 129. For a complete discussion of the districts and working women, see "Report on Women Wage Earners in Minneapolis, Survey, 1919," vol. 1, 35, YWCA of Minneapolis Records, Box 10, SWHA.

21. Minnesota Federal Writers' Project, *Bohemian Flats*.

22. On ethnic concentrations, see Schmid, *Social Saga of Two Cities*, 136–38, 141–50; Minneapolis City Planning Commission, *A Survey of Housing Conditions*. For the Jewish community, see Gordon, *Jews in Transition*; on the Russian community, see Simirenko, *Pilgrims, Colonists, and Frontiersmen*. On the Northeast Settlement House, see Bolin, "Heating Up the Melting Pot."

23. Carpenter, *Immigrants and Their Children, 1920*, table 175, 407–9; see ap-

pendix table A.2 for nativity figures for 1930. Also see Schmid, *Social Saga of Two Cities*, 131; Kohler and Anderson, *A Social Survey of 20,000 Families*.

24. See appendix table A.2.

25. Stipanovich, *City of Lakes*, 203–58. See Gjerde, *From Peasants to Bourgeoisie*, for a discussion of the migration of Norwegians to the region. Joy Lintelman's dissertation, " 'More Freedom, Better Pay,' " on Swedish women immigrants to Minneapolis promises to shed light on the important aspects of women migrants as domestic servants.

26. See appendix A.4 and A.5; Schmid, *Social Saga of Two Cities*, 150–53.

27. "Report on Women Wage Earners in Minneapolis, Survey, 1919," vol. 1, 9, YWCA of Minneapolis Records, Box 10, SWHA.

28. Several firms, including Munsingwear, conducted their own Americanization programs as did several settlement houses. See Bolin, "Heating Up the Melting Pot." On ethnic history within Minneapolis, see the separate chapters on Finns, Norwegians, Germans, Swedes, etc., in Holmquist, ed., *They Chose Minnesota*.

29. Albert Gordon, *Jews in Transition*, 6–24; Schmid, *Social Saga of Two Cities*, 150–53; "Labor Lyceum is Dedicated," *Northwest Organizer*, November 11, 1939.

30. Schmid, *Social Saga of Two Cities*, 172–88; Harris, *The Negro Population in Minneapolis*. See Karger, "Phillis Wheatley House"; Ruth Griffith, "The Problem of the Colored Girl," "Report on Women Wage Earners in Minneapolis, Survey, 1919," vol. 2, YWCA of Minneapolis Records, Box 10, SWHA.

31. Taeuber and Taeuber, *The Changing Population of the United States*, 160–64, discuss differentials between median age at marriage nationally and in the "great cities." Over the period from 1920 to 1940, the gap between national and local median ages at marriage appears to have narrowed:

Year	Men		Women	
	Minneapolis	National	Minneapolis	National
1920	27.8	24.6	24.6	21.6
1930	25.4	24.3	24.0	21.2
1940	25.3	24.3	23.9	21.3

32. Goldin, "Changing Economic Role of Women," argues that each cohort in the twentieth century has experienced increased female labor force participation, particularly after marriage, and that time-specific factors have shaped women's new work trajectory.

33. Oppenheimer argues that it was in the post–World War II period that married women worked in greater proportions, but others have set the timing earlier; see Oppenheimer, *The Female Labor Force*; and Goldin, "Changing Economic Role of Women."

34. There are methodological problems in calculating changes in labor force participation from 1930 to 1940. The Bureau of the Census changed its measure of employment from "gainful worker" to "labor force participation." The former term, used in the census until 1940, was calculated for all individuals who worked at some point during a particular year, a definition which captured the seasonal and intermittent work careers of men and women. In 1940, a member of the labor force was a person who was either employed or seeking work during a particular week in 1940. The implications for estimating female labor force participation should be clear. Women were more likely to have seasonal or discontinuous work experiences, and the shift in census definition led to an undercounting of women workers that has been a chronic problem for women's historians. See Edwards, *Comparative Labor Statistics*; and Conk, "Accuracy, Efficiency, and Bias."

35. See appendix table A.9.

36. Hill, *Women in Gainful Occupations*, 271–74, on women's occupational statistics by nativity and race. King and Ruggles, "American Immigration, Fertility, and Race Suicide," discusses the high rates of labor force participation of second-generation women. Preliminary analysis of the 1940 public use sample of the census for Minneapolis and St. Paul suggests that men and women of foreign parentage continued to have high labor force participation.

37. See appendix table A.9.

38. Goldin, "Female Labor Force Participation"; Blackwelder, *Women of the Great Depression*, 60–74; Helmbold, "Beyond the Family Economy" and "Downward Occupational Mobility."

39. See Goldin, "Changing Economic Role of Women"; Wandersee, *Women's Work and Family Values*.

40. Thomas Taylor, "The Transition to Adulthood in Comparative Perspective," argues that in the late nineteenth century American men had younger median ages for entering work than German men. This also was true for women. By 1920, this pattern had changed.

41. While there are few existent data on women's work careers in this period, we can use age-specific rates for 1930 and 1940. This method was adapted from one used to calculate mean years married. In order to find some measure of the mean years worked by women over the life span, it is necessary to create a synthetic cohort from the aggregate census data. This assumes that one women's behavior over the life span would simulate that of women in each age group. We then use age-specific labor force participation rates to estimate years worked. Percentage rates are translated into decimals and multiplied by the number of years within an age group.

42. Goldin, "Changing Economic Role of Women."

43. Based on interviews with Marguerite Belton, Elizabeth Banghart, Gertrude Larson, and Rose Seiler Palmquist.

44. Rotella, *From Home to Office*.

45. U.S. Bureau of the Census, *13th Census, 1910*, vol. 4, *Occupational Statistics*, table 3, 166–79; *14th Census, 1920*, vol. 4, *Occupations*, table 2, 1144–47; *15th Census, 1930*, vol. 4, *Occupations by States*, table 3, 828.

46. See appendix tables A.10–11 for occupational statistics. Due to the recurring methodological problems presented by changing occupational definitions, our evaluation must be tenuous. The shift from skill to status categories in census definitions makes documenting white collar shifts particularly difficult.

47. See chapter 2.

48. Klein, *The Burden of Unemployment*, 120, 180; Tselos, "The Labor Movement in Minneapolis," 5–14; U.S. Bureau of Labor Statistics, *Unemployment in the United States*.

49. Modell, "Changing Risks, Changing Adaptions" and "Public Griefs and Personal Problems." Of course, there is also a vast literature on the depression itself, including Wandersee, *Women's Work and Family Values*.

50. U.S. WPA, Minnesota, *Divorce Records Study*.

51. U.S. Bureau of the Census, *Births, Stillbirths, and Infant Mortality*, table 1, and *Vital Statistics of the United States*; Coale and Zelnik, *New Estimates of Fertility and Population*, 23.

52. On divorce, see U.S. WPA, Minnesota, *Divorce Records Study*. Elaine Tyler May, *Great Expectations* and "The Pressure to Provide." The Congress created Aid for Dependent Children (ADC) as part of the Social Security Act in 1935; it was finally implemented in Minnesota in 1937.

53. U.S. Bureau of the Census, *15th Census, 1930*, vol. 6, table 13, 679; *16th Census. Population and Housing*, table 47, 202; Helmbold, "Beyond the Family Economy," table 1, 651.

54. U.S. Bureau of the Census, *16th Census, 1940*, vol. 2, pt. 4, *Characteristics of the Population*, table B-41, 176. Milkman, "Women's Work and the Economic Crisis"; Kessler-Harris, *Out to Work*, 250–72; Wandersee, *Women's Work and Family Values*. See Blackwelder, *Women of the Depression*, 75–89, on the role of occupational segregation in maintaining women's employment. For an historical overview, see Gordon, Edwards, and Reich, *Segmented Work, Divided Workers*, 176–82.

55. See Modell, "Patterns of Consumption"; Zelizer, *Pricing the Priceless Child*, 73–112; Elder, *Children of the Great Depression*.

56. This is based on the Bureau of Labor Statistics interviewer notes on budget forms.

57. The source for these are "Family Disbursements of Wage-Earners and Salaried Workers, Minneapolis-St. Paul," Records of the Bureau of Labor Statistics, RG 257, NA. I coded family members, their characteristics, and overall income and expenditures for five hundred schedules from Minneapolis and St. Paul. For boarders in the nineteenth century, see Modell and Hareven, "Urbanization and the Malleable Household."

58. Elder, *Children of the Great Depression.*

59. The proliferation of proletarian novels focused on the single, transient male, is explored in Rabinowitz, "Female Subjectivity." See also Edward Dahlberg, *Bottom Dogs* (1930); Jack Conroy, *The Disinherited* (1933); and Nelson Algren, *Somebody in Boots* (1935); in addition to Meridel Le Sueur's *The Girl.* For a contrast, see Thomas Bell, *Out of This Furnace* (1941); and Josephine Herbst, *Rope of Gold* (1939).

Chapter 2

1. "Phone Employees Strike," *Minneapolis Journal,* November 15, 1918; "Hire New Girls, Burleson Order," *Pioneer Press,* November 16, 1918; "Hello Girls Toot Horns to Inform Phoneless Twin Cities of Strike," *Pioneer Press,* November 16, 1918.

2. "Phone Demands Mean Rate Rise," *Pioneer Press,* November 17, 1918; I. G. Scott, "Girls Tie Up Twin City Telephone Service," *New Times,* November 1918; "Coercion Fails to Stop Striking Telephone Girls," *Minneapolis Labor Review* (hereafter *Labor Review*), November 22, 1918. On the national strike, see Norwood, *Labor's Flaming Youth,* 156–215.

3. Greenwald, *Women, War and Work,* 185–232.

4. "Bars Phone Strike," *Pioneer Press,* November 15, 1918; Postmaster General Albert Burleson to Attorney General T. W. Gregory, telegram, File 53325, Records of the Post Office Department, Record Group 28 (hereafter RG 28), Box 128, NA.

5. "Phone Rate Plea Ready for Filing," *Minneapolis Journal,* November 19, 1918; "Tentative Rate Charge Offer," *Pioneer Press,* November 21, 1918.

6. "Phone Demands Mean Rate Rise," *Pioneer Press,* November 17, 1918; "Minneapolis Strikers Hold Demonstrations," *Pioneer Press,* November 17, 1918; "Phone Rate Hearing Set For November 26," *Minneapolis Journal,* November 17, 1918; "Jeered by Strikers," *Pioneer Press,* November 18, 1918; I. G. Scott, "Girls Tie Up Twin City Telephone Service," *New Times,* November 1918; "Coercion Fails to Stop Striking Telephone Girls," *Labor Review,* November 22, 1918.

7. "Jeered by Strikers," *Pioneer Press,* November 18, 1918.

8. "Minneapolis Strikers Hold Demonstrations," *Pioneer Press,* November 17, 1918; W. J. Merles, Inspector, to Inspector in Charge, St. Paul, December 9, 1918; Attorney General Gregory to Postmaster General Burleson, December 16, 1918 —both in File 53325, Records of the Post Office Department, RG 28, Box 128, NA; Alfred Jacques, U.S. attorney, to Attorney General Gregory, December 4, 1918, Classified File 16–111, Records of the Department of Justice, RG 60, NA.

9. "Meeting Strike Demand Unlikely," *Pioneer Press,* November 23, 1918; "Phone Rate Hearing Set for November 26," *Minneapolis Journal,* November 17, 1918.

10. Editorials: Hello Girls Friend, "Holding Liberty Bonds"; Anna V. Brennan, "Ready with Snowballs"; Central Park, " 'Stick to Scripture' Pastor Scored for Interfering with Strike"—all in *Pioneer Press*, November 20, 1918; "Thinks 'Buds' in Error: Only Seeking New Fad, Says Defender of Phone Girls," *Pioneer Press*, November 23, 1918.

11. *Non-Partisan League* (Fargo), December 23, 1918, citation courtesy of Helene O'Brien.

12. See Norwood, *Labor's Flaming Youth*, 164–66.

13. On the history of Norwegian radicalism in Minnesota, see Qualey and Gjerde, "The Norwegians," pp. 232ff.; on *Gaa Paa*, see Granhus, "Scandinavian-American Socialist Newspapers."

14. In 1912, 21 percent of local members were foreign born, a number that would increase over time; the Socialist party nationally was only 10 percent foreign born in 1912; by 1919, on the eve of its breakup into left and right wing coalitions, 53 percent of party members were foreign born. See Leidenberger, "Reformers and Revolutionists," 42–45. This figure shows that immigrants were slightly underrepresented even in the local party, as 28.5 percent of the population was foreign born.

15. Ibid., 45–46.

16. Buhle, *Women and American Socialism*, 302–4. Starr, "Fighting for the Future," details the rural women's contribution to the Non-Partisan League.

17. Buhle, *Women and American Socialism*, 160; Leidenberger, "Reformers and Revolutionists," 53–54.

18. Buhle, *Women and American Socialism*, 153–61, 288–317; Leidenberger, "Reformers and Revolutionists," 51–57.

19. See discussion of Claire Strong-Broms in Leidenberger, "Reformers and Revolutionists," 63–69; and the oral history of Sylvie Tygeson, in Gluck, *From Parlor to Prison*, pp. 42–54.

20. Millikan, "World War I in Minneapolis"; Flynn, *The Rebel Girl*, 201, on Agricultural Workers' Organization in Minneapolis.

21. Minnesota Department of Labor and Industries, *Biennial Report*, 15th–17th.

22. Ibid. See also Kessler-Harris, "Where Are the Organized Women Workers?"

23. Leidenberger, "Reformers and Revolutionists"; Nord, "Socialism in One City"; Millikan, "World War I in Minneapolis," 11; Chrislock, *The Progressive Era in Minnesota*, 114–15.

24. Millikan, "World War I in Minneapolis" and "Defenders of Business."

25. Millikan, "Defenders of Business" and "World War I in Minneapolis," 20–22; Chrislock, *The Progressive Era in Minnesota*, 157–60.

26. Thompson, six-month review letter (1919?), Minneapolis Trades and Labor Assembly file, Central Labor Union of Minneapolis Records (hereafter CLUM Records), Box 30, Minnesota Historical Society (hereafter MHS), St. Paul, Minnesota.

27. Strike summary in Minnesota Department of Labor and Industries, *Biennial Report*, 17th, 135–36. For a comparable case in 1929, see Hall, "Disorderly Women."

28. "Brief Career of Minneapolis Committee Filled with Accomplishment." Pruitt, "'WOMEN UNITE!'" traces the roots of modern feminist politics to Myrtle Cain, among others.

29. On clerical workers generally, see Srole, "'A Position That God Has Not Particularly Assigned to Men'"; and Gabler, *The American Telegrapher*.

30. On the sexualized image of clerical workers, see Judith Smith, "The 'New Woman' Knows How to Type"; and Kwolek-Folland, "The Business of Gender," 96–135, 189–95.

31. When telephone workers did organize—as they did on a national scale in the 1930s—they did so through the route of the company union. See Schacht, "Toward Industrial Unionism."

32. In a series of articles on Minneapolis labor history, Carlos Hudson of the *Northwest Organizer* made no mention of the strike, although he did devote one column to the streetcar strike of a year earlier.

33. On the ferment among women workers and the WTUL's connections, see "Twin Cities Progress toward League Organization"; and "Brief Career of Minneapolis Committee Filled with Accomplishment."

34. Minnesota Department of Labor and Industries, *Biennial Report*, 16th (1917–18), 164; "We the Waitresses of Local #593," signed Florence Johnson and Lydia Smith, to the Minneapolis Trades and Labor Assembly (1918?). This was a problem even before the war. See Mae Rhodes, secretary, Minneapolis Waitresses Alliance, to officers and members, Minneapolis Trades and Labor Assembly, September 7, 1917. Both letters are in CLUM Records, Box 11, MHS.

35. Murray, *Red Scare*, and Preston, *Aliens and Dissenters*, give a national account of the Palmer raids.

36. Leidenberger, "Reformers and Revolutionists"; Weinstein, *The Decline of Socialism in America*, 290–323; Montgomery, "The Farmer Labor Party."

37. Klein, *The Burden of Unemployment*, 120, 180, 236.

38. Ibid., 44–46, 236.

39. *Labor Review*, 1919–1929.

40. U.S. Bureau of Labor Statistics, *Beneficial Activities of American Trade Unions*, 135.

41. "Franklin Cooperative Creamery and Its Activities"; U.S. Bureau of Labor Statistics, *Beneficial Activities of American Trade Unions*, 135. See also Frank, "'The Labor Woman Fights at the Point of Consumption'" for an account of the role of women in consumerist struggles.

42. Jensen, "All the Pink Sisters"; Cott, *The Grounding of Modern Feminism*, 243–67.

43. Leidenberger, "Reformers and Revolutionists"; Nord, "Socialism in One City"; Youngdale, *Populism: A Psychohistorical Approach*, 155–86.

44. Valelly, "State-Level Radicalism and the Nationalization of American Politics," 67ff.

45. Minnesota Department of Labor and Industries, *Biennial Report*, 17th; Tselos, "The Labor Movement in Minneapolis," 32, 76.

46. The strikes are recorded in "The Citizens' Alliance of Minneapolis: Law and Order and the Open Shop," Correspondence and Miscellaneous Papers file, Citizens' Alliance of Minneapolis Records (hereafter CAM Records), MHS.

47. Buell, *The Minnesota State Legislature of 1923*, 8–9, 30–33; Foster, *Who's Who among Minnesota Women*, 44; Cain, "Resume of Experience," January 13, 1949, in Myrtle Cain Papers, MHS. On Cain's political career, see Fraser and Holbert, "Women in the Minnesota Legislature"; and Pruitt, "'WOMEN UNITE!'" On the women's movement in the decade after suffrage, see Cott, *The Grounding of Modern Feminism*.

48. Stricker, "Affluence for Whom?"

49. Lizabeth Cohen, "Learning to Live in the Welfare State," 214–98, discusses the extension of corporate welfare work in the 1920s and its inability to meet workers' needs in the face of economic crisis. See also Sanford Jacoby, *Employing Bureaucracy*, 167–206.

50. For the impact on Minneapolis, see Rosheim, *The Other Minneapolis*, 113ff.

51. See Irving Bernstein, *The Lean Years*, 254–59, 316–17, on unemployment. Thirty to forty percent of men in the Toledo labor force were unemployed. In Detroit, it was over 60 percent in the early years of the depression, and in Lawrence, Lowell, and other New England textile towns, the figure was almost 70 percent.

52. See Tselos, "The Labor Movement in Minneapolis," 8, on employment levels. The emergence of unemployment insurance as a major demand in the Farmer-Labor party of Minnesota are covered in Mayer, *The Political Career of Floyd B. Olson*, and nationally in Keyssar, *Out of Work*, 211–16, 292–98. See also "Unemployment to be Topic of Gathering," *Labor Review*, January 27, 1928; "Unemployment Conference Hits Alleged Misleading Reports of Job Conditions," *Labor Review*, February 24, 1928; "Public Works Start Asked to Make Jobs," *Labor Review*, March 16, 1928; and "Workers Tell of Machinery Replacing Men," *Labor Review*, April 6, 1928.

53. Vaile, *The Impact of the Depression*; appendix table A.12.

54. Milkman, "Women's Work and the Economic Crisis." See also Lebergott, "Labor Force, Employment, and Unemployment."

55. U.S. Bureau of the Census, *15th Census, 1930, Unemployment*, vol. 1, table 3, 534.

56. Segner, *Minneapolis Unemployed*, vol. 2, 131–33.

57. See appendix table A.13.

58. Segner, *Minneapolis Unemployed*, vol. 2, 131–33; see appendix table A.13.

59. Segner, *Minneapolis Unemployed*, vol. 2, 131–33.

60. Palmer and Wood, *Urban Workers on Relief*, pt. 2, tables 1–4, 70–76. This

study may have undercounted those on relief and/or unemployed workers. The tables of the study do not total correctly, and the base population for each city varies.

61. Koch, "The Development of Public Welfare Relief Programs in Minnesota," 14; Segner, *Minneapolis Unemployed*, vol. 2.

62. Head Worker's Report, October 1929, Northeast Neighborhood House Papers, Box 6, MHS.

63. Krovak Family file, Unemployment Survey, November 1929, First National Federation of Settlements, Helen Hall Papers, SWHA. The files were taken from a survey conducted by the federation, the results of which were published in National Federation of Settlements and Neighborhood Centers, *Case Studies of Unemployment*, 284–87.

64. Head Worker Reports, January and February 1930, Northeast Neighborhood House Records, Box 6, MHS.

65. Head Worker Reports, February and March 1930, Northeast Neighborhood House Papers, Box 6, MHS. On the work of settlement houses, see Trolander, *The Settlement House*; on the Society of Saints Peter and Paul, see Simirenko, *Pilgrims, Colonists, and Frontiersmen*, 41–42.

66. Meridel Le Sueur, "Twin City Slave Market," *United Action*, September 2, 1935, quoting letters sent to the newspaper.

67. Ibid.

68. Mary Elizabeth Pidgeon, director of research, to Agnes Peterson, Women's Bureau, "Memorandum as to Material Available on the Unemployment of Women," 1932, Survey Material Relating to Bulletin #139, Records of the Women's Bureau, RG 86, Box 308, NA. These figures are estimated from a number of private sources. There were no figures available for unemployment by sex at the time.

69. Meridel Le Sueur, *Ripening*, 140–41.

70. Weiner, *From Working Girl to Working Mother*, and Meyerowitz, *Women Adrift*, argue that it is a change in the perception of women's vulnerability. Women, now the equal of men, at least at the level of suffrage rights, no longer needed protection. I suggest it may be something more than that. The level of unemployment was severe enough to challenge standard perceptions of a masculinity defined by the ability to be a "breadwinner." Even the language here seems suggestive, as if money were sustenance. See Filene, *Him/Her/Self*, on masculine ideology.

71. "Memo on the Special Service Bureau of the Family Welfare Association," 1934, Survey Materials Relating to Bulletin #139, Records of the Women's Bureau, RG 86, Box 308, NA; City Program Form, Minneapolis Division of Public Relief, Survey Materials Relating to Bulletin #139, Records of the Women's Bureau, RG 86, Box 309, NA.

72. "Memo Re History Proceeding the Seventh Street Club," City Program file; "Memo on the Care of Single Women," Special Service Bureau of the Family

Welfare Association of Minneapolis file—both in Records of the Women's Bureau, RG 86, Box 308, NA.

73. "Seventh Street Club for Girls," pamphlet (Minneapolis, 1933), Women's Occupational Bureau, City Program file, Survey Materials Relating to Bulletin #139, Records of the Women's Bureau, RG 86, Box 308, NA.

74. Katherine Woodruff, director of the Women's Occupational Bureau, to Agnes Peterson, Women's Bureau, Department of Labor, telegram, 1934, Correspondence Relating to Bulletin #139, Records of the Women's Bureau, RG 86, Box 13, NA.

75. "Twin City Slave Market," *United Action*, September 16, 1935.

76. Meridel Le Sueur, *Ripening*, 140–41.

77. Meridel Le Sueur, "Sequel to Love," 36–38; interviewers' notes, "Tentative Schedules for St. Paul Unattached Women Seeking Relief for Self Alone," Records of the Women's Bureau, RG 86, Box 305, NA.

78. Koch, "Politics and Relief in Minneapolis," 155.

79. On the organized unemployed, see Tselos, "Self-Help and Sauerkraut."

80. Douglas, *Social Security in the United States*, 41; U.S. Federal Emergency Relief Administration, *Unemployment Relief Census*; Segner, *Minneapolis Unemployed*, vol. 2; Koch, "Politics and Relief in Minneapolis."

81. Koch, "Politics and Relief in Minneapolis"; Elizabeth Faue, "Women, Family and Politics." Chapters 4 through 6 give a more detailed description of these attempts.

82. Leab, "'United We Eat,'" 313.

83. See issues of the Unemployment Council of Minneapolis, *Hunger Fighter*, CAM Records (microfilm, roll 20), MHS. On neighborhood organizing, see Klehr, *The Heyday of American Communism*, 49–68; Alice Lynd and Staughton Lynd, *Rank and File*, 9–33.

84. Meridel Le Sueur, interview with the author.

85. Unemployment Council of Minneapolis, *Hunger Fighter* 1:17 (June 9, 1933) CAM Records (microfilm, roll 20), MHS.

86. Seymour, *When Clients Organize*, 9–10; Rosenhaft, *Beating the Fascists?* gives a parallel from the Weimar period in Berlin.

87. Piven and Cloward, *Poor People's Movements*. For a critique of Piven and Cloward, see Evans and Boyte, *Free Spaces*, 14–17.

88. "Phone Companies Continue Fight for Poverty Pay," *Labor Review*, December 6, 1918.

89. While this may be an issue of some dispute, the prewar Left did engage in the politics of birth control, family, and woman suffrage, as we have seen. The splintering of interests and groups is a major point in Linda Gordon's *Woman's Body, Woman's Right*, 186–245; see also Buhle, *Women and American Socialism*, 246–87.

Chapter 3

1. Walker, *American City*, 245. See also program, Labor Progress Outdoor Exposition (July 27–August 4, 1935), *Labor Progresses by Struggle*, in Minnesota Historical Society Library, Labor and Laboring Classes, Folder 2. The exposition was in memoriam to Henry Ness and John Belor; see later in this chapter.

2. Marian Le Sueur quoted in Victor Weybright, managing editor, to Charles R. Walker, August 12, 1936, Helen Hall Papers, Box 43, SWHA. See also Walker, "A Militant Trade Union," "Minneapolis: Jim Hill's Empire," and "Minneapolis: City of Tensions." The articles formed the basis of his *American City*.

3. There have been instances in which the labor movement has been cognizant and celebratory of difference. During the Lawrence strike of 1912, for example, the IWW set up a strike committee that included both men and women from all ethnic groups working in the mills.

4. Erwin Panofsky defined the concerns of iconography as three—factual meaning, secondary or conventional meaning, and intrinsic meaning. Here we are most concerned in defining artistic conventions and in exploring their intrinsic meaning. See Panofsky, *Meaning in the Visual Arts*.

5. Irving Bernstein, *The Lean Years*, 83–142.

6. Irving Bernstein, *The Turbulent Years*; Brecher, *Strike!*, 150–68.

7. Walker, *American City*, 91, 97–128; Tselos, "The Labor Movement in Minneapolis," 210–30.

8. Dobbs, *Teamster Rebellion*, 68–69; Meridel Le Sueur, "I Was Marching"; and Lasky, " 'Where I Was a Person.' "

9. Walker, *American City*, 155–83; Dobbs, *Teamster Rebellion*, 124–43; Tselos, "The Labor Movement in Minneapolis," 230–42. Numbers for the funeral range from twenty thousand to fifty thousand. Formal marchers were joined on the streets by onlookers and at the cemetery by other workers.

10. Walker, *American City*, 207–21.

11. Lasky, " 'Where I Was a Person.' " Cruising pickets were mobile strikers who traveled from one site of strike action to another, a tactical innovation vital to the success of any transportation walkout.

12. Brecher, *Strike!*, 165.

13. See Irving Bernstein, *The Turbulent Years*, 217–317; Brecher, *Strike!*, 150–76; Milton, *The Politics of U.S. Labor*, 38–68, among others, for coverage of the strikes.

14. Dobbs, *Teamster Rebellion*, 136. See also Walker, *American City*, 113–28, 155–83; Tselos, "The Minneapolis Labor Movement," 241–46.

15. Dobbs, *Teamster Rebellion*, 136–37.

16. "He Goes on Fighting," *Organizer*, August 2, 1934.

17. See, for example, "He Goes On Fighting," *Organizer*, August 2, 1934; "These 40,000 Can't Be Stopped," *Organizer*, August 7, 1934; "All Right—Still Out," *Organizer*, September 9, 1934.

18. See, for example, "He Goes On Fighting," *Organizer*, August 2, 1934; "These 40,000 Can't Be Stopped," *Organizer*, August 7, 1934; "He Packs a Wallop!" *Organizer*, August 22, 1934; "All Right—Still Out," *Organizer*, September 9, 1934; "Seeing Red," in Burck, *Hunger and Revolt*, 65; Gropper, *New Masses* cover (May 1933), reprinted in Fitzgerald, *Art and Politics*, 282. In his editorial, "The Politics of Human Misery," Len De Caux uses the metaphor: "One horror movie the Congressmen should not have missed. That is Frankenstein. For by voting to starve and oppress the unemployed, they are themselves creating a monster of misery which will eventually turn on its creators." *CIO News*, January 23, 1939.

19. "He Packs a Wallop!" *Organizer*, August 22, 1934; "The Lightweight Champion Meets Them All—The Bigger They Are the Harder They Fall," *Organizer*, August 23, 1934; "Somebody Get Lewis a Sponge," *Northwest Organizer*, November 6, 1935; "The Gladiator," *Northwest Organizer*, September 3, 1936.

20. "And the Fight Has Just Begun," *Organizer*, July 26, 1934.

21. "If It Takes All Summer," *Organizer*, July 29, 1934.

22. "Truck Strike—U.S. History Parallel," *Labor Review*, July 27, 1934, reprinted in *Organizer*, July 29, 1934.

23. Len De Caux, "Trying to Keep Labor in Short Pants," *CIO News*, March 12, 1938.

24. "Quit Your Kidding," *Northwest Organizer*, January 29, 1936; "Come on in out of the Rain, Boys," *Organizer*, August 25, 1934. Gulliver and the Lilliputians was another favorite metaphor along these lines; see "10,000 Votes for Progress," *Northwest Organizer*, October 23, 1935; "Gulliver Awakens," *Northwest Organizer*, May 26, 1939; "Little Men, What Next?" *CIO News*, January 8, 1940, among others.

25. "Look Pal, Communists," *Organizer*, August 13, 1934; "What Do You Say, Brother? Are You Going to Help Me?" *Organizer*, August 21, 1934; "The Workers' Choice," *Organizer*, August 24, 1934; "Quit Your Kidding," *Northwest Organizer*, January 29, 1936; "Come on in out of the Rain, Boys," *Organizer*, August 25, 1934.

26. "The Secondary Defense," *Organizer*, September 26, 1934.

27. "40,000 Attend Ness Funeral," *Organizer*, July 25, 1934; "John Belor Dead," *Organizer*, August 1, 1934.

28. "15,000 Workers at Mass Meeting Condemn Johannes Massacre," *Organizer*, July 21, 1934; "The Fight Has Just Begun," *Organizer*, July 23, 1934.

29. "15,000 Workers at Mass Meeting Condemn Johannes Massacre," *Organizer*, July 21, 1934; "The Fight Has Just Begun," *Organizer*, July 23, 1934.

30. Reports from the Burns detective agency, published in U.S. Congress, Senate, *Report: Violations of Free Speech and the Rights of Labor*, vol. 15-A, 5664–68. The reports seem to support other newspaper accounts of the death, funeral, and union reaction.

31. For descriptions of the funeral, see "40,000 Attend Ness Funeral," *Orga-*

nizer, July 25, 1934; "100,000 in Tribute to Ness Protest Johannes Butchery, *Labor Review*, July 27, 1934. For remembrances of the 574 martyrs, Ness and Belor, see "At the Grave of Our Martyr," *Organizer*, July 24, 1934; "Workers Honor Ness and Belor," *Northwest Organizer*, July 24, 1935; "Ness-Belor Memorial Saturday," *Northwest Organizer*, July 15, 1936; "General Drivers' Heroes," *Northwest Organizer*, July 22, 1936; "Do You Remember?" *Northwest Organizer*, June 3, 1937; "1000s Pay Tribute to Ness and Belor Saturday," *Northwest Organizer*, July 16, 1937. The photograph, "Bill Brown Tells Meyer Lewis," (*Northwest Organizer*, November 13, 1935) has a banner emblazoned with "Don't Fail Me Now, Boys!" in the background.

32. Dobbs, *Teamster Rebellion*, 79–80; Lasky, " 'Where I Was a Person,' " 187–88.

33. General Drivers' and Helpers' Union, local 574, "Working Men and Women of Minneapolis Support This Strike," handbill, May 1934, quoted in Lasky, " 'Where I Was a Person,' " 188.

34. "40,000 Attend Ness Funeral," *Organizer*, July 25, 1934; "100,000 in Tribute to Ness Protest Johannes Butchery," *Labor Review*, July 27, 1934. Fussell, *The Great War and Modern Memory*, 118–19, discusses the use of Christ and the crucifixion in the language produced by the war. There are resonances between the mutual suffering and sacrifice of the strikers and those of soldiers in World War I.

35. "The Sharp Shooter," *Organizer*, July 16, 1934.

36. "The Fight Is Not Over," *Northwest Organizer*, March 25, 1936.

37. Keen, *Faces of the Enemy*.

38. Along with Meridel Le Sueur's "I Was Marching," see Tillie (Lerner) Olsen's powerful account of the San Francisco strike, "The Strike."

39. "Spring Planting," *Midwest Labor*, March 29, 1941.

40. These were syndicated or reprinted in a number of papers, including *CIO News*, *Midwest Labor*, and *Labor Review*.

41. "The Only Friend That Labor Has!" *Northwest Organizer*, August 31, 1939.

42. See Gary Gerstle, "The Politics of Patriotism," and *Working-Class Americanism*, 153–87; Isserman, *Which Side Were You On?*

43. For an analysis of these themes in leftist literature, see Dixler, "The Woman Question"; Rabinowitz, "Female Subjectivity in Women's Revolutionary Novels."

44. The cartoons were the work of John Baer, a former Non-Partisan League cartoonist; they were also reprints from *Labor*, the journal of the railroad brotherhoods, where there was a tradition of auxiliary activity. See "Let's Put Shingles on Our Own Homes!" *Labor Review*, Labor Day Annual, September 1, 1939; "The New Crusader," *Labor Review*, Annual Labor Day Review, August 30, 1940; "To the War Bonds Ramparts—Modern Molly Pitchers," *Labor Review*, November 11, 1942. See also chapter 6.

45. Rabinowitz argues that "By valorizing women's maternity as the mechanism by which women responded politically, the Party was subscribing again to a regressive notion of gender.... The ideology of the Popular Front tempered [the

masculinism of the Left] somewhat by sentimentalizing motherhood as a natural well of political understanding, but the implications for women were identical." "Female Subjectivity in Women's Revolutionary Novels," 72. See also Dixler, "The Woman Question," 187–95. On republican motherhood, see Kerber, *Women of the Republic*, 265–88; and Bonnie Smith, *Changing Lives*, 103–7.

46. In "Women and the Communist Party," Robert Shaffer emphasizes the strain on women of the dual role they played in the movement, especially the contradictions between the rhetoric of the Left on the woman question and the subordination of women's concerns to the party's struggles.

47. "No Room at the Inn," *United Action*, December 13, 1935.

48. "A Lick and A Promise," *United Action*, May 1, 1936; "An Army without Banners," *United Action*, March 6, 1936.

49. "Ladies' Auxiliary Gives Benefit Dance," *Organizer*, June 25, 1934.

50. "Women Don't Forget Your Own Organization," *Organizer*, July 2, 1934.

51. Hall, "Disorderly Women."

52. Marian Le Sueur, "Woodshed for Some Solons, Says Woman Speaker," *Farmer Labor Leader*, April 15, 1933; Stageberg, "As a Woman Sees It," *Minnesota Leader*, March 12, 1938; Elizabeth Faue, "Women, Family, and Politics."

53. "The Eternal Nightmare," *Northwest Organizer*, March 11, 1937; "In the Richest Country in the World," *Minnesota Leader*, September 18, 1937; "Awaken, America!" *Labor Review*, November 18, 1932; "Sure . . . She Has Her Choice," *Minnesota Leader*, October 16, 1937. "What Every Worker Should Know," *Northwest Organizer*, May 5, 1940, is an example of woman as war victim.

54. Agulhon, *Marianne into Battle*; Hobsbawm, "Man and Woman in Socialist Iconography"; Scott, "Women and Men in the Parisian Garment Trades"; Hunt, *Politics, Culture and Class in the French Revolution*, among others.

55. Hobsbawm, "Man and Woman in Socialist Iconography"; Sewell, "Visions of Labor."

56. See Bonnie Smith, *Changing Lives*.

57. Hobsbawm, "Man and Woman in Socialist Iconography."

58. For an analysis of the different constituencies of the IWW, see Ebner, "The Passaic Strike of 1912"; Golin, "Defeat Becomes Disaster." Ann Schofield has an interesting analysis of the image of women based on fiction, not iconography, in "Rebel Girls and Union Maids." On the Lawrence strike, see Cameron, "Bread and Roses Revisited."

59. Barbara Taylor, *Eve and the New Jerusalem*; Benenson, "Victorian Sexual Ideology"; Scott, "Men and Women in the Parisian Garment Trades."

60. Montgomery, *Workers' Control in America*, 9–32, and Davis, "The Stop Watch and the Wooden Shoe," discuss the changes in technology that cost skilled workers control at the workplace.

61. "A Pair of Cloak Runners Come Home," *Justice*, July 15, 1935; "Will He Cross It This Year?" *Justice*, January 1, 1936.

62. "Union Ready to Dam 'Runaway' Flow," *Justice*, December 1, 1935.

63. "These 146 Workers Did Not Die in Vain," *Justice*, April 1, 1936. For an account of the uprising, see Tax, *The Rising of the Women*, 205–40; Dye, *As Equals and As Sisters*; and Seller, "The Uprising of the 20,000," 254–79.

64. "On the Eve of the Knitted Garment Strike," *Justice*, August 25, 1934; "105,000 Dress Workers Speak in One Mighty Voice," *Justice*, February 1, 1936.

65. "Jane Higgins, Worker," *Justice*, March 1, 1936; and following issues.

66. "French Needle Workers Win 40-Hour Week," *Justice*, July 15, 1936; "As Congress Gets Under Way," *Justice*, January 15, 1935; "225,000 Workers Are Calling You," *Justice*, December 15, 1935.

67. Honey, *Creating Rosie the Riveter*; Milkman, "American Women and Industrial Unionism during World War II," 168–81; Sandra Gilbert, " 'This Is My Rifle, This Is My Gun.' "

68. "Needles and Pins," *Justice*, April 15, 1940.

69. "Needles and Pins," *Justice*, June 15, 1941.

70. For example, "The Fight of the 574," *Organizer*, August 22–23, 1934; "The Courage to Organize and Fight," *Northwest Organizer*, November 13, 1935; "Labor Observers Look at Local 574," *Northwest Organizer*, November 20, 1935; "Leaving Olson's Resort," *Northwest Organizer*, April 22, 1936; "Do You Remember?" *Northwest Organizer*, June 3, 1937; "The Great Strike of July–August 1934," *Northwest Organizer*, July 14, 1938; "544 Members Rally with '1934' Spirit," *Northwest Organizer*, May 18, 1939.

71. Perrot, "The New Eve and the Old Adam," 58–60.

72. Martyna, "What Does 'He' Mean?"

Chapter 4

1. "New Dress Pacts Discussed by Twin Cities," *Justice*, February 15, 1938; "Acute Labor Shortage in Three Markets," *Justice*, June 15, 1939.

2. The women I interviewed spoke of the age and unattached family status of the women in garment shops. Many of the union women were widowed as well, and some of their daughters worked in the industry. See Loretta DuFour, interview, June 20, 1985; Elizabeth Banghart, interview, August 8, 1985; Grace Neff, interview, July 17, 1985.

3. Vaile, *The Impact of the Depression*, 57; Tselos, "The Labor Movement in Minneapolis," 63–64.

4. Hjordes Hedlund, phone interview, May 29, 1985; Marguerite Belton, interview, May 20, 1985.

5. Loretta DuFour, interview, June 20, 1985; Marguerite Belton, interview, May 20, 1985. Myrtle Harris, in her interview with James Dooley, July 9, 1975, said that the piecework in the garment industry was there to stay because the women liked it. The women I interviewed expressed a strong dislike for the practice. See also

Michael Finkelstein, manager Twin City Joint Board, to David Dubinsky, July 26, 1937, Dubinsky Papers, Box 75, Folder 4A, ILGWU Collection, Cornell University, Ithaca, New York. On piecework, see Lamphere, "Fighting the Piece Rate System."

6. See photograph of NRA parades in Minneapolis. Also, note "Boulevard Frocks Employees Docked for Time Devoted to NRA Parade," *Labor Review*, September 29, 1933.

7. Marguerite Belton, interview, May 20, 1985.

8. Ibid.; George Lawson to David Dubinsky, March 28, 1934, Dubinsky Papers, Box 75, Folder 5B, ILGWU Collection, Cornell University; "The Union in the Twin Cities," *Justice*, May 1, 1937.

9. Sander Genis, interview with Martin Duffy, March 16, 1977; Dubinsky to Genis, April 19, 1935, Dubinsky papers, Box 75, Folder 5A, ILGWU Collection, Cornell University; Sander Genis, interview, June 17, 1985.

10. Sander Genis, interview with James Dooley, November 6, 1974; "Flashes from North, West and South," *Justice*, February 1, 1935.

11. Genis to Dubinsky, August 15, 1935, Box 75, Folder 5A, Dubinsky Papers, ILGWU Collection, Cornell University, © ILGWU; Myrtle Harris, interview with James Dooley, July 9, 1975.

12. Myrtle Harris, interview with James Dooley, July 9, 1975.

13. Genis to Meyer Perlstein, December 10, 1934, Dubinsky papers, Box 75, Folder 5B; Genis to Dubinsky, March 7, 1935, and Genis to Dubinsky, January 30, 1935, Dubinsky Papers, Box 75, Folder 5A—all in ILGWU Collection, Cornell University, © ILGWU.

14. Affidavits of Jenise Storelie, Sarah Presant, and ten others, October 27, 1934; "To the Workers in the Ladies' Garment Industry," pamphlet, 1934—all in Dubinsky papers, Box 75, Folder 5B, ILGWU Collection, Cornell University.

15. Affidavit, Jenise Storelie, October 27, 1934, Dubinsky papers, Box 75, Folder 5B, ILGWU Collection, Cornell University, © ILGWU.

16. Ibid.

17. Affidavit, Sarah Presant, October 27, 1934, Dubinsky Papers, Box 75, Folder 5B, ILGWU Collection, Cornell University, © ILGWU.

18. George Lawson, secretary, Minnesota State Federation of Labor, to Dubinsky, March 28, 1934, Box 75, Folder 5B; "Session here April 5—NRA Review Board Member to Hear Plea for Code Exemption"; clippings—"NRA Review Advisory Board Exemption Silk Dress Code," and "Dress Industry Here Promised Early Hearing"—dated March 14, [1934], Box 75, Folder 5B; Genis to Perlstein, n.d., letter, Box 75, Folder 5B; Genis to Dubinsky, December 28, 1934—all in Dubinsky papers, Box 75, Folder 5A, ILGWU Collection, Cornell University.

19. Marguerite Belton, interview, May 20, 1985; Loretta DuFour, interview, June 20, 1985.

20. The diary was published as an example of worker's writing in Meridel Le Sueur, *Worker Writers*, 44–47, copy in the possession of MHS library. The outlines of the strike match those of the fragmented historical record. The strike, which the local ILGWU conducted at the Manhattan Cloak company in St. Cloud, occurred in 1936.

21. Marguerite Belton, interview, May 20, 1985; Loretta DuFour, interview, June 20, 1985. Walkowitz, "Working Class Women in the Gilded Age"; Turbin, "And We Are Nothing But Women" and "Reconceptualizing Family, Work and Labor Organizing"; Schatz, *The Electrical Workers*, 89–92. Cobble, "Sisters in the Craft," has some detailed data on leaders from the Hotel and Restaurant Workers' Union.

22. Meridel Le Sueur, *Worker Writers*.

23. The Minneapolis Labor School was started in 1934 through the Central Labor Union of Minneapolis. During the better part of the decade, the school benefited from WPA workers' education project instructors, among them writer Meridel Le Sueur. In 1941, after the WPA stopped funding the program, local AFL affiliates continued their support. Minneapolis Union Education Center, *Workers' Education*; "Labor School Records Four Years of Achievement," *Labor Review*, September 21, 1938; and press release, March 3, 1941, Press file, CLUM Records, MHS.

24. "Dorothy Rock Gets ILGWU Appointment," *Labor Review*, November 29, 1935; "Amalgamated and ILGW Progress," *Labor Review*, December 27, 1935; "From Far and Near," *Justice*, January 1, 1936; Dorothy Rock, "Flashes from the Field," *Justice*, February 16, 1936; "ILGW Opens Worker Classes," *Labor Review*, November 6, 1936; "News and Views," *Justice*, December 1, 1936. On the educational department's history, see Wong, "From Soul to Strawberries."

25. See ILGWU, *Handbook of Trade Union Methods* and *How to Conduct a Union Meeting*.

26. Betty Hoff, "Education and Recreation," *Twin City Guardian* (hereafter cited as *Guardian*), 1:9 (1937), © ILGWU.

27. See Harry Rufer to Leah Schneider, March 11, 1937, Chicago Joint Board of the ILGWU Records, Box 13, Folder 3, ILGWU Collection, Cornell University, © ILGWU. Copy of the *Guardian* in Dubinsky Papers, Box 75, Folder 4A, ILGWU Collection, Cornell University, © ILGWU.

28. Marian Le Sueur, quoted in " 'Woodshed' for Some Solons Says Woman Speaker," *Farmer Labor Leader*, April 15, 1933.

29. Mayer, *The Political Career of Floyd B. Olson*; Gieske, *Minnesota Farmer Laborism*; Valelly, "State-Level Radicalism and the Nationalization of American Politics."

30. Starr, "Fighting for a Future."

31. For example, Violet Johnson became tax commissioner; Laura Naplin, a former state senator, became inspector of hotels and restaurants; Marian Le Sueur

served first on a board for utilities and natural resources and later, on a temporary basis, on the state board of education; Mercedes Nelson served as a permanent education board commissioner; and Florence Huber served on the minimum wage advisory committee.

32. Minnesota Farmer-Labor Women's Clubs, *Report of the Sixth State Convention, March 28, 1932*; Farmer-Labor Women's Federation, *Farmer-Labor Women's Federation Annual*, Stageberg Papers, Box 1, MHS.

33. Faue, "Women, Family, and Politics."

34. Koch, "The Development of Public Welfare Relief Programs," 254–95.

35. Ibid., 255.

36. "Complaints Board Probes 1500 Cases of Relief," *Minnesota Leader*, December 21, 1935; "Mayor Bows to Labor in Aid Revolt," *Minnesota Leader*, January 11, 1936.

37. Koch, "Politics and Relief in Minneapolis."

38. "High Cost of Living Meeting," *Labor Review*, September 20, 1935; "Minneapolis Housewives Organize against the High Cost of Living," *United Action*, October 1, 1935. The *Farmer-Labor Women's Federation Annual, 1935–1936* gives a list of these organizations.

39. "Conference Against Living Costs Held," *Labor Review*, October 4, 1935.

40. "We, the people who work for a living, are the consumers as well as the producers. It has been quite natural for us to organize into trade unions and associations as producers. We have been mainly concerned with how much money we can get. But, will high money wages alone purchase any abundant living if as individual consumers we lose as poor buyers across the counter the gains made by our collective bargaining with industry?" Women's League against the High Cost of Living, statement from conference in 1940, quoted in Sorenson, *The Consumer Movement*, 121.

41. Mrs. Charles Lundquist, chair, and Bertha Marshall, secretary, Women's League against the High Cost of Living, to Governor Floyd B. Olson, October 9, 1935, in Floyd B. Olson, Governor, Administrative Records, Executive Letters, MHS. On Farm Holiday Association activism, see Nielsen, "Who Were Those Farmer Radicals?"

42. Lundquist to Olson, October 9, 1935, in Floyd B. Olson, Governor, Administrative Records, Executive Letters, MHS.

43. Governor Olson to Mrs. Charles Lundquist, October 14, 1935, Olson Executive Letters, MHS; "Women's League Calls Meat Strike," *Minneapolis Journal*, October 15, 1935; "Five Day Meat Strike," *United Action*, October 15, 1935; "Five Day Meat Strike Starts," *United Action*, October 18, 1935; "Mass Meeting Protests High Living Costs," *Labor Review*, October 18, 1935.

44. "Five Day Meat Strike Starts," *United Action*, October 18, 1935.

45. Sorenson, *The Consumer Movement*, 119–20; Dixler, "The Woman Question," 137–43.

46. On some of these connections, see Rose Seiler Palmquist, interview with Mary Ellen Frank, June 1, 1977; Hyman, "Political Theatre."

47. Dobbs, *Teamster Rebellion*, 90–105; Lasky, " 'Where I Was a Person,' " 189–91.

48. Dobbs, *Teamster Power*, 78–86.

49. Hyman, "Political Theatre." Notices of Minneapolis Theatre Union and Labor Players' productions in *Labor Review*, January 13, 1935; April 26, 1935; May 17, 1935; September 25, 1935; November 8, 1935; February 21, 1936; October 23, 1936; and April 16, 1937, among others. See also Melosh, "Peace on Demand."

50. Fantasia, *Cultures of Solidarity*.

51. "Strike Ranks Growing Fast at Strutwear," *Northwest Organizer*, August 21, 1935.

52. Newspaper reports estimated as many as 900 women workers of a labor force of 1200; company figures put the estimate at 581 of approximately 845 production workers. See "Code Minima and Strutwear Company Averages," October 17, 1935, CAM Records, undated and 1903–1953 (microfilm, roll 20), MHS. This document was compiled by the company defending itself against the charge of sweatshop conditions, and it probably misrepresents or overestimates the wages paid.

53. "McKeown Given Ovation," *Labor Review*, December 13, 1935; "Police, Troops Plan to Open Strutwear," *United Action*, December 13, 1935; "Organizer Shows Up Strutwear Company As Union Smasher," *United Action*, March 27, 1936.

54. "Swanson Booed by Strikers," *Labor Review*, September 25, 1935.

55. Roy Weir, organizer, Central Labor Union, to Emil Reeves, secretary, American Federation of Hosiery Workers, August 7, 1931; Weir to Alfred Hoffman, secretary, Hosiery Workers local, Milwaukee, April 20, 1934; Weir to Emil Reeves, July 26, 1934—all in Hosiery Workers' file, CLUM Records, MHS. Complaint form 136, Strutwear, June 7, 1935, Hosiery and Lingerie Code, Records of the Eleventh Regional Labor Board, Records of the National Labor Relations Board, RG 25, Box 388, NA.

56. Tselos, "The Labor Movement in Minneapolis," 186–88.

57. "Code Minima and Strutwear Company Averages," October 17, 1935, CAM Records, undated and 1903–1953 (microfilm, roll 20); Oscar Hawkins to Dear Folks, August 29, 1935, Oscar and Madge Hawkins Papers, Box 4—both in MHS.

58. "Organizer Shows up Strutwear Company as Union Smasher," *United Action*, March 27, 1936.

59. "Strike Ranks Growing Fast at Strutwear," *Northwest Organizer*, August 21, 1935; "Knitters Practically All Members of Union," *Labor Review*, August 23, 1935; Dobbs, *Teamster Power*, 91–93.

60. Letter from Flora, quoted in Meridel Le Sueur, "Twin City Slave Market," *United Action*, September 16, 1935.

61. "Young Courage," *Northwest Organizer*, December 4, 1935.

62. Hawkins to Dear Folks, August 29, 1935, Oscar and Madge Hawkins Papers, Box 4, MHS.

63. "CLU Calls for Strike Support," *United Action*, January 17, 1936; "Big Throng Cheers Strutwear Workers," *Labor Review*, December 13, 1935; "Strutwear Assails Cripple," *Labor Review*, March 20, 1936. See also testimony of Isador Katz, general counsel for the hosiery workers, in U.S. Senate, *Report: Violations of Free Speech*, vol. 1, 223–24.

64. "Strike Ranks Growing Fast at Strutwear," *Northwest Organizer*, August 21, 1935; "Strutwear Mills Stay Closed Two Weeks," *United Action*, September 2, 1935.

65. The ethnicity of the workers is from a listing of workers active in the union from 1935 to 1941, derived from labor newspapers and the *Strutwear Worker*, the local's newsletter. In the most visible case of family connection, "Miller Strike Enters 9th Week," *Strutwear Worker* 2 (March 1941), mentions the role of Ole Fagerhaugh of the Miscellaneous Workers' local 665, the brother of strike leader, Peter Fagerhaugh.

66. "WPA, Unemployed and Relief Groups Forge Unity," *United Action*, February 14, 1936.

67. "Welfare Board Cuts Hundreds Off Relief," *United Action*, June 5, 1936; "Union Fights $5 Minimum for Housemaids," *United Action*, June 26, 1936.

68. "Hennepin County Farmer Labor Raps Mill City Relief Authority," *Minnesota Leader*, July 4, 1936.

69. Ibid.; "Aid Pledged to Strikers by Farmer-Labor Meet," *Labor Review*, March 13, 1936.

70. "Strutwear Trickery Probed," *Labor Review*, September 27, 1935; "Strutwear Bosses Try to Crush Strike; Munsingwear Reported Doing Scab Work," *United Action*, October 1, 1935.

71. "Enthusiasm at Strutwear Is Victory Sign," *Labor Review*, September 20, 1935; "Strutwear Blocks Arbitration," *Labor Review*, October 11, 1935; "CLU Prepares to Picket Strutwear," *Labor Review*, November 15, 1935; "Prepare to Mass Picket at Strutwear," *Labor Review*, November 22, 1935; "Employers Attempt Strutwear Opening," *Northwest Organizer*, November 20, 1935; "Strutwear Situation Stirs CLU," *United Action*, February 14, 1936; "Union Officials Tell Strutwear Facts," *Labor Review*, August 30, 1935; "Police, Troops to Open Strutwear," *United Action*, December 13, 1935; "Strikers Will Take Decision of Mayor's Group," *Labor Review*, December 13, 1935; "Strutwear Strikers Get Three Tons of Food," *Northwest Organizer*, November 13, 1935; "Congress May Probe Strutwear," *Labor Review*, December 20, 1935. For the role of the Communists in the strike, see Ross, "Labor Radicalism in the 1930s."

72. Dobbs, *Teamster Power*, 103–5; "Federal Courts Act in Strike," *Northwest Organizer*, December 4, 1935; "Strutwear Strikers Fight Federal Court Battle," *Northwest Organizer*, December 25, 1935; "Strutwear Strike Mass Meet Monday Night at Eagles Hall," *Labor Review*, December 6, 1935.

73. "National Guard Called to Strutwear," *United Action*, December 28, 1935; Tselos, "The Labor Movement in Minneapolis," 341–43.

74. "Employers Launch War on Workers," *Minnesota Leader*, January 11, 1936; "Strutwear Injunction," *Northwest Organizer*, February 26, 1936; "Citizens Alliance in New Fight," *Minnesota Leader*, February 29, 1936; "Strutwear Calendar," *United Action*, March 6, 1936.

75. "Strutwear Plant Reopens," *Northwest Organizer*, April 8, 1936; "Hosiery Union Moves into Strutwear As Strike Ends," *United Action*, April 10, 1935; "Details Strutwear Settlement," *Labor Review*, April 10, 1936.

76. "Strutwear Not Strutting Like It Used To," *Labor Review*, August 30, 1935; "Bosses Try to Smash Strutwear Strike," *United Action*, September 12, 1935; "750 Strutwear Employees Sign for Closed Shop," *Northwest Organizer*, May 6, 1937; "Hosiery Workers Sign Strutwear," *Labor Review*, May 7, 1937; "Strike Record," in Local Strikes file, CAM Records, MHS.

77. Elmer, *A Study of Women in Clerical and Secretarial Work*.

78. For interesting work on CIO clerical unions in the 1930s, see Strom, "Challenging 'Woman's Place'" and "We're No Kitty Foyles"; and Feldberg, "'Union Fever.'"

79. This was true even of the relatively prosperous 574. In one issue, Mickey Dunne accused the SBTA of "making severe demands" on the General Drivers' Union. See his poem in "Keeping Step with the 544," *Northwest Organizer*, December 24, 1936.

80. Several of the members of the office workers' union were active in the Hennepin County (Minneapolis) Farmer-Labor Women's Club, including Violet Johnson, Ruth Shaw, and Selma Seestrom. See Elizabeth Faue, "Women, Family, and Politics."

81. "Civil Service Appointment Hit by CLU," *Labor Review*, January 27, 1928; "Shipstead Is Endorsed by Central Body," *Labor Review*, February 17, 1928; "Central Labor Union Brands Dayton Store Unfair," *Labor Review*, April 27, 1928; "Stenos' Union Will Have an Organizer," *Northwest Organizer*, October 8, 1936; "Stenos' Union Is Out for Members," *Northwest Organizer*, October 15, 1936; "Florence Huber Organizing Stenos," *Labor Review*, October 16, 1936; "Office Workers Sign H. D. Lee Company," *Labor Review*, December 4, 1936; "Stenos' Union Signs Contract with Lee Overalls," *Northwest Organizer*, December 10, 1936.

82. "10 Named to State Board Which Will Set Minimum Pay," *Minnesota Leader*, April 26, 1937; Wilbur Broms, interview, September 26, 1985.

83. "Office Union and Rothschild Store Sign," *Labor Review*, February 26,

1937; "Daily Star Workers Join Typists' Union," *Northwest Organizer*, March 11, 1937; "Stenos, Franklin Sign Closed Shop," *Northwest Organizer*, April 15, 1937; "Franklin-Chippewa Sign with Stenos," *Labor Review*, April 16, 1937; "Office Workers Sign Star-Hamilton Company," *Labor Review*, June 11, 1937; "Office Workers' Union Signs Gas Company," *Northwest Organizer*, August 12, 1937; "Stenos Get Closed Shop with Mill City Gas Company," *Minnesota Leader*, August 14, 1937. "Stenos Get Closed Shop with Mill City Gas Company" (*Minnesota Leader*, August 14, 1937) notes the increase in union membership to 450; and "Stenos' Resolution Referred to CLU Executive Board" (*Northwest Organizer*, October 21, 1937) mentions its increase to over 500. In "Membership of Local SBTA #17661," the figure cited is 600 (Office Workers' Union file, CLUM Records, MHS).

84. "Farmer Labor Women's Cavalcade to Get Out Vote," *Minnesota Leader*, September 5, 1936; "On Tour for Women's Votes," *Minnesota Leader*, September 12, 1936; "Two Farmer Labor Women Tour State, Win Votes for Cause," *Minnesota Leader*, September 26, 1936; "Cavalcade of Farmer Labor Women Spurs Drive in 9th District," *Minnesota Leader*, October 3, 1936.

85. Meridel Le Sueur, *Crusaders*, 71.

Chapter 5

1. "Twin Cities ILGWU Locals Hail GEB Arrival," "Gallery of Nations Greets GEB in Minneapolis," *Justice*, June 1, 1938; "ILGWU Given Greeting That Is Unique," *Labor Review*, May 27, 1938.

2. See Tselos, "The Labor Movement in Minneapolis," 413–17, 470–76; Valelly, *Radicalism in the States*, 139–56. On the Silver Shirts, see Albert Gordon, *Jews in Transition*, 50–52; Tselos, "The Labor Movement in Minneapolis," 457. It is worth noting that one of the central reasons for the Farmer-Labor defeat in 1938 was party factionalism, some of which was expressed in an antisemitic campaign.

3. James Matles to Larry D. Kimmel, vice president, District 11, UERMWA, October 8, 1937, FF 105, United Electrical, Radio and Machine Workers of American Records (hereafter UE Records), University of Pittsburgh Libraries, Pittsburgh, Pennsylvania. See also Tselos, "The Labor Movement in Minneapolis," 418ff., esp. 431–37; "CIO Says Gangs Rule Minneapolis," *New York Times*, November 22, 1937; "Asks Federal Aid in Twin Cities Case," *New York Times*, November 25, 1937.

4. Tomlins, *The State and the Unions*, 103–96.

5. Wellman and Leighton, "Networks, Neighborhoods, and Communities," discuss the creation of communities through different network structures.

6. See Dobbs, *Teamster Politics*.

7. For example, Michael Finkelstein to David Dubinsky, November 30, 1938; Dubinsky to Finkelstein, December 3, 1938—both in Dubinsky papers, Box 16, Folder 2A, ILGWU Collection, Cornell University.

8. Sander Genis to Dubinsky, December 12, 1934, Dubinsky Papers, Box 75, Folder 5B, ILGWU Collection, Cornell University.

9. "Attention Boulevard Frocks Workers," leaflet, enclosed in letter, Meyer Perlstein to Dubinsky, April 4, 1936, Dubinsky Papers, Box 75, Folder 4B, ILGWU Collection, Cornell University, © ILGWU.

10. Genis to Perlstein, February 13, 1936, Dubinsky papers, Box 75, Folder 4B, ILGWU Collection, Cornell University.

11. George Glass, St. Louis Joint Board, to Dubinsky, May 9, 1936, re Twin Cities, Dubinsky Papers, Box 75, Folder 4B, ILGWU Collection, Cornell University, © ILGWU.

12. Genis to Perlstein, March 4, 1936, Dubinsky papers, Box 75, Folder 4B, ILGWU Collection, Cornell University, © ILGWU.

13. Perlstein to Dubinsky, telegram, April 17, 1936; and Genis to Dubinsky, April 29, 1936—both in Dubinsky papers, Box 75, Folder 4B, ILGWU Collection, Cornell University.

14. Perlstein to Dubinsky, telegram, April 17, 1936; Genis to Dubinsky, April 29, 1936; Genis to Morris Bialis (April 1936?)—all in Dubinsky papers, Box 75, Folder 4B, ILGWU Collection, Cornell University. On signing, see "A Company Group Becomes a Real Union," *Justice*, July 15, 1936; "350 Join Union in Boulevard Shop," *United Action*, May 1, 1936; "Boulevard Frocks Signs With Union," *Labor Review*, May 1, 1936; and "Boulevard Frocks, Minneapolis Shop Signs Union Pact," *Justice*, May 1, 1936.

15. On the Harris shop dispute, see Finkelstein to Dubinsky, September 18, 1936; Genis to Dubinsky, n.d.; Harry Rufer to Dubinsky, June 24, 1936—all in Dubinsky papers, Box 75, Folder 4B, ILGWU Collection, Cornell University. On the rivalry between Genis and Perlstein, see "Stenographic Report of the Special Meeting of the Unity Committee of the Central Labor Union on Friday, May 7, 1937, re Munsingwear," Garment Workers folder, CLUM Records, Box 24, MHS.

16. Meyer Lewis, AFL, to Dubinsky, March 16, 1937; Finkelstein to Dubinsky, March 30, 1937; Dubinsky to Finkelstein, April 2, 1937; Finkelstein to Dubinsky, April 8, 1937—all in Dubinsky papers, Box 75, Folder 4A, ILGWU Collection, Cornell University.

17. On several occasions, workers sent letters to Dubinsky asking that Finkelstein be replaced. Finkelstein always responded that the workers were "troublemakers," but persistent complaints would suggest there was some basis for the discontent.

18. "Two of City's Industries to Give 600 Jobs," *Minneapolis Times*, January 1, 1932.

19. Munsingwear Corporation, *Program of the Employment Relationship Between*

Management and Employees of the Munsingwear Corporation (Minneapolis, 1935), in Industrial Relations folder, CAM Records, MHS; Tselos, "The Labor Movement in Minneapolis," 183, 189.

20. "Stenographic Report of the Special Meeting of the Unity Committee of the Central Labor Union on Friday, May 7, 1937, re Munsingwear," Garment Workers folder, CLUM Records, Box 24, MHS.

21. Leah Schneider to Rufer, March 3, 1937, Chicago Joint Board of the ILGWU Records, Box 13, Folder 3, ILGWU Collection, Cornell University; ILGWU, *Report of the Proceedings of the 23rd Convention*, 215.

22. Perlstein to Munsingwear Corporation, April 24, 1937, Dubinsky Papers, Box 169, Folder 1B, ILGWU Collection, Cornell University, © ILGWU.

23. Contract and contact card, dated May 21, 1937, photocopy, courtesy of Keir Jorgenson, Research Director, Amalgamated Clothing and Textile Workers Union, personal correspondence with author, February 28, 1989.

24. Perlstein to Dubinsky, April 27, 1937; Charles H. Green to Dubinsky, June 16, 1937—both in Dubinsky Papers, Box 169, Folder 1B, ILGWU Collection, Cornell University; "1000 Affiliate to TWOC in Vote at Munsingwear," *Northwest Organizer*, May 6, 1937; "Stenographic Report of the Special Meeting of the Unity Committee of the Central Labor Union on Friday, May 7, 1937, re Munsingwear," Garment Workers folder, CLUM Records, Box 24, MHS.

25. Florence Olson to Dubinsky, July 3, 1937, Dubinsky papers, Box 169, Folder 1B, ILGWU Collection, Cornell University, © ILGWU.

26. Schwartz, *The Civil Works Administration*, 252–59.

27. Seymour, *When Clients Organize*, 9–10.

28. Koch, "The Development of Public Welfare Relief Programs"; Dobbs, *Teamster Power*; "27 Jobless Groups Join in Conference" *Minnesota Leader*, February 1, 1936; "State Workers Alliance Sets Up Shop," *Minneapolis Star*, March 23, 1936; "Meetings Arranged by Workers Alliance of Hennepin County," *Minneapolis Tribune*, August 23, 1936; "Sewing Project Workers," flyer, CIOU Local 6, CIO file, CLUM Records, Box 7, MHS.

29. "Company Union Holds Sway on Vocational High Project," *Northwest Organizer*, February 26, 1936.

30. "FWS Organizers Meet Saturday," *Northwest Organizer*, March 4, 1937; "FWS Women For Present Work Week," *Northwest Organizer*, September 1, 1938; "250 Attend FWS Sewing Project Meeting," *Northwest Organizer*, October 27, 1938.

31. "Women Continue Picket line at WPA Office," *United Action*, June 26, 1936; U.S. WPA, Minnesota, Division of Women's and Professional Projects, *Monthly Newsletter*, September 1936, 11–12, in the MHS Library; "WPA Accused of Intimidation by Project Workers," *Minnesota Leader*, July 4, 1936; "Rival Groups Ask Aid Boost," *Minneapolis Star*, August 16, 1937. See also "Resolution," August 17, 1937, local 6, Workers' Alliance, to Governor Benson; Grant Dunne, FWS 544, and Karl Skoglund, Independent Truck Owners' local 544, to federal, state

and district WPA administrations and the president of the U.S., July 22, 1937; Petition against Union City Mission, 1937, among others—all in Elmer Benson, Governor, Administrative Records, Executive Letters, WPA general 1937 file, MHS.

32. Harold O. Bean, secretary, Workers' Alliance to Floyd B. Olson, May 2, 1936; Bean to Olson, May 17, 1936; "To all members of the State Committee of the Workers' Alliance of Minnesota (June? 1936); "A Call to Action!" (handbill, June 1936)—all in Floyd B. Olson, Administrative Records, Executive Letters, Workers' Alliance file, MHS. See also Chester A. Watson, president, Workers' Alliance of Minnesota, to Governor Benson, Administrative Records, Executive Letters, WPA general 1937 file, MHS.

33. Howard, *Works Progress Administration*, 278–85.

34. Susan Ware, *Holding Their Own*, 40.

35. Howard, *Works Progress Administration*, 428.

36. Seymour, *When Clients Organize*, 9–10; Montgomery and Schatz, "Facing Layoffs," 146.

37. Tselos, "The Labor Movement in Minneapolis," 449–50.

38. U.S. Office of the Administration of the Census, *Census of Partial Employment, 1937*, table 2, Unemployment Census—Minnesota, 331.

39. Finkelstein to Rufer, December 17, 1937, Chicago Joint Board of the ILGWU Papers, Box 13, Folder 3, ILGWU Collection, Cornell University, © ILGWU.

40. Segner, *Minneapolis Unemployed*; Koch, "The Development of Public Welfare Relief Programs," 255–56.

41. Koch, "The Development of Public Welfare Relief Programs," 278–80.

42. "Needy Forced from Relief in Twin Cities," *Minnesota Leader*, July 24, 1937.

43. "Welfare Board Is Called Dictatorial," *Minnesota Leader*, August 7, 1937.

44. "Farmer Labor Women Plan Study of Relief," *Minneapolis Tribune*, September 7, 1937; "Farmer Labor Women Score Leach Relief Policy," *Minnesota Leader*, September 11, 1937; "Criticize City Welfare Board Policy," *Minnesota Leader*, September 18, 1937.

45. "Group Hits Board for Relief Order," *Minneapolis Journal*, September 15, 1937.

46. "Criticize City Welfare Board Policy," *Minnesota Leader*, September 18, 1937; "Mill City Board Lifts Ban on Single Persons," *Minnesota Leader*, October 30, 1937.

47. Weiner, *From Working Girl to Working Mother*, 128–32; Koch, "The Development of Public Welfare Relief Programs," 9–11, 418–23; Minnesota State Council of Social Work, *A Study of Mother's Pensions in Minnesota*.

48. This was certainly the case with the Cartwright Dress, with which the ILGWU negotiated a work-sharing agreement between its shops in Minneapolis and Cleveland. The company went broke.

49. Loretta DuFour, interview, June 20, 1985.

50. Ibid.

51. Members of shop to David Dubinsky, May 25, 1939; Perlstein to Dubinsky, June 10, 1939; Finkelstein to Dubinsky, June 6, 1939—all in Complaints file, Dubinsky Papers, Box 20, Folder 2G, ILGWU Collection, Cornell University. The Finkelstein letter is a lengthy denial of accusations made by members, whom he assumed were working in the Jane Arden shop, which was on strike.

52. "Twin Cities to Study Earnings," *Justice*, November 1, 1937; "St. Louis, Kansas City, and Twin Cities Stage Union Classes in Service," *Justice*, February 1, 1939; "Starting Right," *Justice*, September 1, 1939; "Minneapolis and Kansas City to Start Time Study Classes," *Justice*, November 15, 1939; "Compulsory Training," *Justice*, May 1, 1940; "Arrange Training Institutes for Shop Chairmen, Officers," *Justice*, September 15, 1940; "They Learn about the ILGWU and Pass It On," *Justice*, February 15, 1943.

53. Meyer Perlstein, "The Human Side," *Justice*, July 1, 1938.

54. Finkelstein to Dubinsky, September 2, 1936, Dubinsky papers, Box 75, Folder 4B, ILGWU Collection, Cornell University, © ILGWU. Kessler-Harris makes similar points about earlier factional battles in the ILGWU in which women bore the brunt of the attacks. Factionalism, as the expression of private grievances and disagreements, was defined in many unionists' minds as a feminine characteristic. See her "Problems of Coalition-Building."

55. ILGWU, *Handbook of Trade Union Methods*, 25–26.

56. Ibid., 26.

57. "Industry Meetings Set for All Trades in Several Cities," *Justice*, December 1, 1939.

58. "Boulevard Frocks Worker Off to Kansas City for Training," *Justice*, February 1, 1940.

59. "Educational Activities," *Justice*, April 1, 1942; Clippings file, Minneapolis Labor School, CLUM Records, Box 30, MHS.

60. Examples of hiring inquiries: Finkelstein to Morris Bialis, Chicago Joint Board, March 25, 1940, and Finkelstein to Bialis, May 26, 1941, in Chicago Joint Board of the ILGWU Records, Box 13, Folder 3, ILGWU Collection, Cornell University. See "New Dress Pacts Discussed by Twin Cities," *Justice*, February 15, 1938, on the prevalence of women cutters.

61. "Shop Committee," *Strutwear Worker*, 1:16, October 1938.

62. Some reports on the Emergency Brigade are reprinted in Vorse, *Rebel Pen*, 175–200.

63. In October 1938, its membership was reported as fifty; its officers were President Marian Carlson, Vice President Laura Mitchell, Secretary Phyllis Mize, Treasurer Hazel Falldin, Trustees Vera Palmquist (probably the wife of Ed Palmquist, the head of FWS 544), Dorothy Hill, and Hazel Cummings. "Women's Auxiliary," *Strutwear Worker*, 1:16, October 1938. Kessler-Harris has argued that women unionists had different goals for unions than men; in effect, women sought "community, idealism, and spirit" while male trade union leaders wanted "unity,

discipline, faithfulness." See her "Problems of Coalition-Building," 129.

64. "Women's Auxiliary," *Strutwear Worker*, 1:16, October 1938.

65. "Ladies' Auxiliary," *Strutwear Worker*, 1:17, November 1938.

66. "Trade Union Sports Council Conference Held," *Strutwear Worker*, 1:15, April 1938, mentions a committee that included Alrose Andryski of the Hosiery Workers' Union. See also "Girls' Diamondball Teams," *Strutwear Worker*, 1:15, April 1938; "Girls' Bowling Averages," *Strutwear Worker*, 1:17, November 1938.

67. "Scenes from Branch 38's 3rd Annual Picnic," *Strutwear Worker*, 1:16, October 1938; "Join the Ladies' Auxiliary," *Strutwear Worker*, 1:18, December 1938.

68. "The Trade Union Woman," *Strutwear Worker*, 1:19, February 1939.

69. "Officers Nominated by Branch #38 Saturday," *Strutwear Worker*, 1:17, November 1938; "Branch 38 Votes to Extend Contract," *Strutwear Worker*, 1:20, April 1939; "Final Results of Election," *Strutwear Worker*, 2:2, January 1941. During the 1935–36 strike, a woman, Dorothy Trombley was secretary of the union and was important enough to be named in the injunction suit against the local.

70. This figure was part of the dispute in 1938. According to the *Northwest Organizer* the union actually had over six hundred.

71. Violet Johnson, Executive Board 17661, to Meyer Lewis, AFL, November 24, 1937, Allen N. and Violet J. Sollie Papers, MHS.

72. Johnson to Lewis, November 24, 1937, Allen N. and Violet J. Sollie Papers, MHS.

73. "To the membership of SBTA 17661," from President Jewell Flaherty, Vice President Crescentia Brown, et al., mimeographed letter, n.d. (1938), Office Workers' Union file, CLUM Records, Box 33, MHS.

74. "Membership of Local SBTA #17661," mimeographed letter, proposed Florence Huber as business agent and Doris Anderson as president of the union (Office Workers' Union file, CLUM Records, Box 33, MHS). See also Robert B. West to Roy Wier, May 24, 1938, Office Workers' Union file, CLUM Records, Box 33, MHS; the testimony of Violet Johnson in the Dies Committee hearings, U.S. Congress, House, Special Committee, *Hearings, Investigation of UnAmerican Propaganda Activities* (October 17, 1938), 1417–20.

75. West to Wier, May 24, 1938, Office Workers' Union file, CLUM Records, Box 33, MHS.

76. Rose Seiler Palmquist, interview with Mary Ellen Frank, June 1, 1977, 5–9.

77. Quoted in ibid., 9. On the settlement house and church activism, see ibid., 32–33; Karger, "The Phillis Wheatley House"; and Trolander, *The Settlement House*.

78. "Stenotes," *Labor Review*, July 5, 1940, cites January 1938 as the date; her interview gives the fall of 1937, about the time when Huber was dismissed. See Rose Seiler Palmquist, interview with Mary Ellen Frank, June 1, 1977, 32–33.

79. "Kachelmacher, CLU Name for Civil Service," *Labor Review*, January 13,

1939; "CLU Plans Fight on Various Bills," *Labor Review*, March 10, 1939; "CLU Gives Eide Fine Reception," *Labor Review*, April 14, 1939; "Office Workers Sign Rothschild Store," *Labor Review*, June 16, 1939; "Stenos Now Known as Office Workers," *Labor Review*, November 17, 1939; "Young America Signs Office Workers Pact," *Labor Review*, November 24, 1939; Rose Seiler Palmquist, interview with Mary Ellen Frank, June 1, 1977, 10.

80. "Office Workers Strike at Freightways; Company Has Refused to Sign Union Pact," *Labor Review*, September 22, 1939; "Freightways Strike Brings Union Victory," *Labor Review*, September 29, 1939; Rose Seiler Palmquist, interview with Mary Ellen Frank, June 1, 1977, 12.

81. The problem is discussed in "Stenotes," *Labor Review*, July 5 and July 19, 1940.

82. "Stenotes," *Labor Review*, July 5, 1940.

83. "Stenographers Elect Renner and Seiler," *Labor Review*, January 13, 1939; "Odean-Seiler Named by Office Workers," *Labor Review*, January 12, 1940.

84. Rose Seiler Palmquist, interview with Mary Ellen Frank, June 1, 1977, 10–12. See also chapter 6.

85. Rose Seiler Palmquist, interview with Mary Ellen Frank, June 1, 1977, 12; William Green, AFL president, to George Lawson, secretary of the Minnesota State Federation of Labor, June 23, 1941; William F. Wright, organizer, to William Green, July 2, 1941; Green to Wright, July 9, 1941; Violet Johnson, member of 17661, to Green, August 16, 1941—all in American Federation of Labor Records, Minnesota files, Series 11C, Boxes 35–39 (microfilm 568, reel 1), State Historical Society of Wisconsin. See also "Brothers and Sisters of Local 17661" (1941?), mimeographed letter, Labor Handbills Collection, MHS.

86. Green to Lawson, June 23, 1941; Wright to Green, July 2, 1941; Green to Wright, July 9, 1941—all in AFL Records, Minnesota files, Series 11C, Boxes 35–39 (microfilm 568, reel 1), State Historical Society of Wisconsin.

87. Johnson to Green, August 16, 1941, American Federation of Labor Records, Minnesota files, Series 11C, Boxes 35–39 (microfilm 568, reel 1), State Historical Society of Wisconsin.

88. Ibid.; Green to Johnson, August 22, 1941, Allen N. and Violet J. Sollie Papers, MHS.

89. Strom, "We're No Kitty Foyles."

90. See Kessler-Harris, "Problems of Coalition-Building," for a thoughtful discussion of the subject.

Chapter 6

1. "The Last Word," *Northwest Organizer*, December 7, 1939; "13 Women Strikers Get Probation, One Receives 45 Days," *Northwest Organizer*, February 15, 1940; "13 WPA Women Get Suspended Sentences," *Labor Review*, February 16,

1940; Max Geldman, quoted in Dobbs, *Teamster Politics*, 232–33.

2. "13 Women Strikers Get Probation," *Northwest Organizer*, February 15, 1940; "13 WPA Women Get Suspended Sentences," *Labor Review*, February 16, 1940.

3. Scharf, *To Work and To Wed*; Scimé, "Section 213 of the 1932 Economy Act."

4. Florence Burton, superintendent, Division of Women and Children, Minnesota Industrial Commission, to Mary Anderson, Director, January 29, 1937, Correspondence, Minnesota Industrial Commission, Records of the Women's Bureau, RG 86, Box 1290, NA.

5. Olson, *A Primer on Unemployment Insurance*; Van Kleeck, "Security for Americans," 121–24; Douglas, *Social Security in the United States*, 74–83. For Farmer-Labor women's support of the bill, see Stageberg, "As a Woman Sees It," Stageberg papers; and Farmer-Labor Women's Federation, *A Call to the Women of Minnesota*, Arthur and Marian Le Sueur Papers, Box 4—both in MHS.

6. Douglas, *Social Security in the United States*, 69–83; Van Kleeck, "Security for Americans," 121–24.

7. Lubove, *The Struggle for Social Security*, 91–112.

8. Handwritten resolution by the Farmer-Labor Women's Club Committee on Women's Organization, dated 1938, Oscar and Madge Hawkins papers, Farmer Labor Women's Club folder, MHS. For a general discussion of marriage bars to employment, see Goldin, *Understanding the Gender Gap*, 160–79.

9. "Hennepin Women Against Proposal of Relief Board," *Minnesota Leader*, April 9, 1938.

10. Central Labor Union of Minneapolis, quoted in Tselos, "The Labor Movement in Minneapolis," 97.

11. For example, Olivia Johnson, state legislative chairman, Business and Professional Women's Federation, to Senator B. G. Novak, April 5, 1939; "62 Years" to Governor Harold Stassen, January 1, 1939; Tillie Sheehan to Stassen, July 27, 1939; Pastor W. H. Murk, Temple Baptist Church, to Stassen, July 31, 1939—all in Protests against Married Women Working, 1939 Session, Harold Stassen, Governor, Administrative Records, Executive Letters, MHS. Many letters favoring such a ban also make the connection between women working and immorality.

12. Murk to Stassen, July 31, 1939, Stassen Executive Letters, MHS.

13. "CLU Upholds the Right of Married Women," *Labor Review*, November 10, 1939; Burton to Anderson, January 29, 1937, Correspondence, Minnesota Industrial Commission, Records of the Women's Bureau, RG 86, Box 1290, NA; Johnson to Novak, April 5, 1939, Protests against Married Women Working, 1939 Session, Harold Stassen, Governor, Administrative Records, Executive Letters, MHS.

14. The case was *Adkins v. Children's Hospital* (1925), 761 U.S. 525. Minnesota, Minimum Wage Commission, *Biennial Report*; Dietrickson, "The Minimum Wage Situation in Minnesota." On the national scene, see Chafe, *The American Woman*, 79–82; Baer, *The Chains of Protection*, 92–99.

15. United States District Court, District of Minnesota, 4th Division, "In Equity #3014 and #3015," August 27, 1938, *Western Union Telegraph Co. v. Industrial Commission of Minnesota, et al.*; *Yerka v. Williams*, Brief, Division of Legislation and Standards, Material Relating to Court Decisions, Records of the Women's Bureau, RG 86, Box 1476; Florence Burton to Louise Stitt, June 20, 1939, Records of the Women's Bureau, RG 86, Box 1290—all in NA.

16. List of firms included Martin Bros., Northbilt Mfg., Robitschek-Schneider, United Garment Mfg., Strutwear Knitting, Munsingwear, Minneapolis Knitting Works, Winget Kickernick, Boulevard Frocks, among others. See *Yerka v. Williams*, Brief, 4, Division of Legislation and Standards, Material Relating to Court Decisions, Records of the Women's Bureau, RG 86, Box 1476, NA. Florence Burton wrote that the larger firms, under CIO contract, pressed for a higher minimum. See letter, Burton to Louise Stitt, February 2, 1939, Records of the Women's Bureau, RG 86, Box 1290, NA.

17. Burton to Anderson, September 9, 1938, Records of the Women's Bureau, RG 86, Box 1290, NA.

18. Ibid.

19. Seven hundred local garment workers received raises under the Fair Labor Standards Act. See *Labor Review*, August 2, 1940.

20. Burton to Anderson, March 10, 1939; *Western Union Telegraph Co. v. Industrial Commission of Minnesota*—both in Records of the Women's Bureau, RG 86, Box 1476, NA; Burton to Louise Stitt, director, Minimum Wage Division, February 2, 1939, Records of the Women's Bureau, RG 86, Box 1290, NA.

21. "Underpaid Non-Union Women Get Raises," *Labor Review*, August 2, 1940.

22. "New Floor to Wages for Women Set in State," *Minnesota Leader*, April 30, 1938; "Women Workers Get $15,000 in Wage Correction," *Minnesota Leader*, June 11, 1938; "Minimum Wage Law in Minnesota in Effect July 1," *Justice*, July 15, 1938. See also Advisory Board to Mr. J. D. Williams, chairman, Minnesota Industrial Commission, February 14, 1938, Box 1488; Burton to Anderson, March 10, 1939, Box 1476; Summary, from *Federal Supplement*, vol. 24, 370, *Western Union Telegraph Co. v. Industrial Commission of Minnesota*, Box 1476—all in Records of the Women's Bureau, RG 86, NA.

23. Appellant's brief, No. 203, Municipal Court, Ramsey County, Caroline S. Tepel, appellant, v. William Sima, December 31, 1942, Records of the Women's Bureau, RG 86, Box 1476, NA.

24. "Minnesota's 54-Hour Law for Women in Certain Industries," *Farmer Labor Leader*, August 15, 1933; "Farmer Labor Element in the 1933 Legislature Brought Many Reforms," *Farmer Labor Leader*, September 3, 1933.

25. Burton to Anderson, January 29, 1937, Records of the Women's Bureau, RG 86, Box 1290, NA.

26. Baer, *The Chains of Protection*, 66–67; Keyssar, *Out of Work*.

27. Elizabeth Faue, "Women, Work, and Community," 219–21, 228–31.

28. Schwartz, *The Civil Works Administration*.

29. This thesis is implicit in Scharf, *To Work and To Wed*; Susan Ware, *Beyond Suffrage*; Elizabeth Faue, "Women, Family, and Politics."

30. "WPA Layoffs Bring Thunderous Protest," *Labor Review*, December 9, 1938; "Workers and Families Bid to Protest," *Labor Review*, December 30, 1938; "Congress Relief Cut Serious Threat to Children-Invalids," *Labor Review*, January 20, 1939; *Northwest Organizer*, December 7, 1938; "FWS Backs Women in Fight on ADC," *Northwest Organizer*, February 9, 1939. This contradicts previous policy which gave women a choice. See Karl A. Lundberg, deputy administrator, State Relief Agency, to Governor Elmer Benson, February 28, 1938, in Elmer Benson, Governor, Administrative Records, Executive Letters, 1932–1938, MHS.

31. "FWS Backs Women in Fight on ADC," *Northwest Organizer*, February 9, 1939.

32. "WPA Moves to Cut All Persons Eligible for ADC," *Northwest Organizer*, February 2, 1939; "FWS Backs Women in Fight on ADC," *Northwest Organizer*, February 9, 1939.

33. "WPA Moves to Cut All Persons Eligible for ADC," *Northwest Organizer*, February 2, 1939.

34. Hennepin County Farmer-Labor Women's Club, Minutebook (1939–40), MHS; Elizabeth Faue, "Women, Family, and Politics."

35. On the Stassen Labor Relations law, see Strong, *My Native Land*, 190ff; Tselos, "The Labor Movement in Minneapolis," 479–85.

36. Strong, *My Native Land*, 190ff; "On WPA Projects," *Northwest Organizer*, March 9, 1939.

37. "14 Face Count of Conspiracy and Disorder," clipping, n.d., WPA Strike file, Douglas Alan Bruce Papers, MHS.

38. "On WPA Projects," *Northwest Organizer*, April 13, 1939; "FWS Plans Action against Relief Cuts; New WPA Cut of 900,000 Jobs Looms," *Northwest Organizer*, May 4, 1939.

39. Estimates of the crowd go as high as ten thousand. "Stassen Gives WPA Marchers Run Around," *Labor Review*, June 9, 1939; "Trade Unions Will Fight WPA Cuts until Congress Acts to Amend Vicious Law," *Labor Review*, July 14, 1939; Dobbs, *Teamster Politics*, 203–5.

40. "FWS Mass Meeting Friday to Prepare for Demonstration," *Northwest Organizer*, May 11, 1939; "1500 Unemployed Vote Holiday Demonstration Against Policy Cuts," *Northwest Organizer*, May 18, 1939; "On WPA Projects," *Northwest Organizer*, June 8, 1939; "WPA Project Holiday, June 2," *Labor Review*, May 26, 1939; "Stassen Gives WPA Marchers Run Around," *Labor Review*, June 9, 1939; "Trade Unions Will Fight WPA Cuts until Congress Acts to Amend Vicious Law," *Labor Review*, July 14, 1939; Dobbs, *Teamster Politics*, 203–5.

41. "Puzzled?" to Stassen, postcard, August 10, 1939, WPA Strike, Minneapo-

lis, first of three files, Harold Stassen, Governor, Administrative Records, MHS. This metaphor was frequently used in cartooning. See John Baer's cartoon, "The Most Effective Weapon," *Labor Review*, September 28, 1934. See also "Keeping the Wolf From the Door," *CIO News*, November 28, 1938; and "Shooting with Both Barrels," *CIO News*, October 28, 1940, among others.

42. See "125 Unions Vote to Defend WPA Victims," *Northwest Organizer*, August 31, 1939, on the role of the cuts in stimulating the strike.

43. Erickson, "WPA Strike and Trials of 1939"; "WPA Strikers in Twin Cities," *Northwest Organizer*, July 13, 1939.

44. Erickson states strongly that the strike was spontaneous without considering his own evidence to the contrary. At the time of the strike, certain project locals of the FWS and the Workers' Alliance were over three years old. See his "WPA Strike and Trials of 1939."

45. "WPA Strikers in Twin Cities," *Northwest Organizer*, July 13, 1939.

46. Erickson, "WPA Strike and Trials of 1939," 205–6; "WPA Strikers in Minneapolis," *Northwest Organizer*, July 13, 1939.

47. Geldman, quoted in Dobbs, *Teamster Politics*, 210–11; "23 Assaults Charged in WPA Trial," clipping, n.d., Douglas Alan Bruce Papers, MHS; "Davis Brings New Sensation to WPA Trial," *Labor Review*, November 3, 1939; Dwight Macdonald, "WPA Cuts—or Jail."

48. Dobbs, *Teamster Politics*, 232. A consideration of strike hysteria might be important here. In hearings on the Strutwear injunction in 1935, a woman testified that women strikers had threatened to tear nonstrikers' clothing; see "Both Sides in Strutwear Suit Score at Trial," March 13, 1936, Strutwear Strike Clippings file, CAM Records (microfilm, reel 20), MHS.

49. Erickson, "WPA Strike and Trials of 1939," 202.

50. Ibid., 205–6; Dobbs, *Teamster Politics*, 224. On the Silver Shirts, see Dobbs, *Teamster Politics*, 140–45.

51. Strong, *My Native Land*, 195–96; "WPA Projects Closed as Strikers Press Demands," *Northwest Organizer*, July 20, 1939; "FBI's Role in WPA Strike Bared by Cop's Testimony," *Northwest Organizer*, November 9, 1939; Erickson, "WPA Strike and Trials of 1939," 209.

52. Quoted in Strong, *My Native Land*, 185.

53. "WPA Projects Closed as Strikers Press Demands," *Northwest Organizer*, July 20, 1939; Erickson, "WPA Strike and Trials of 1939"; Strong, *My Native Land*, 195–96.

54. "Thousands Hear Tributes to Emil Bergstrom," *Labor Review*, July 21, 1939; "On the Minnesota WPA Picket Line," *Northwest Organizer*, July 20, 1939.

55. "Strike Settlement Ratified; Unions to Fight Frameups," *Northwest Organizer*, July 27, 1939; transcript of WPA meeting, July 19, 1939, WPA Strike, Minneapolis, second of three files, in Harold Stassen, Governor, Administrative Records, MHS.

56. W. H. Frederick, Minneapolis, to J. A. Callahan, editor, *Daily Free Press*, Mankato, July 28, 1939, WPA Strike, Minneapolis, first of three files, Harold Stassen, Governor, Administrative Records, MHS.

57. "125 Unions Vote to Defend WPA Victims," *Northwest Organizer*, August 31, 1939.

58. "On WPA Projects," *Northwest Organizer*, August 10, 1939; "On WPA Projects," *Northwest Organizer*, August 17, 1939; "Bosses Use Black List Against WPA Strikers," *Northwest Organizer*, November 23, 1939; Erickson, "WPA Strike and Trials of 1939."

59. "CLU Unions to Defend WPA Victims," *Labor Review*, August 25, 1939. This emphasis on the claims of veterans' widows underlines the importance of service during World War I as legitimizing strikers' demands; here its usage is similar to arguments for military widows' pensions. See Kärin Hausen, "The German Nation's Obligations," 126–40.

60. "Labor Unites to Defend WPA Strikers," *Northwest Organizer*, August 24, 1939.

61. Erickson, "WPA Strike and Trials of 1939."

62. "CLU Calls Unions to Defend WPA Victims," *Labor Review*, August 25, 1939; "Not Guilty is Plea of All WPA Victims," *Labor Review*, September 29, 1939; Strong, *My Native Land*, 186–87; Dobbs, *Teamster Politics*, 217–21.

63. Macdonald, "WPA Cuts—or Jail"; "Minneapolis WPA Trials Have Become National Scandal," *Minnesota Leader*, October 1939; "Those Minnesota Trials," *New Republic*, November 8, 1939; "Mass Trials in Minnesota," *New Republic*, February 19, 1940; "The WPA Strike," *Newsweek*, July 24, 1939; Raymond Moley, "Diluted Insurrection," *Newsweek*, July 24, 1939; "Mutiny on the Bounty," *Time*, July 17, 1939.

64. Erickson, "WPA Strike and Trials of 1939"; Dobbs, *Teamster Politics*, 223–25.

65. "WPA Princes Join Drive to Jail WPA Men," *Labor Review*, October 6, 1939; see also "Some Heroic WPA Defendants and Families—They Sacrifice for You," *Labor Review*, October 27, 1939.

66. Marvel Scholl, "One Woman to Another," *Northwest Organizer*, October 26, 1939.

67. Ibid. The full text of this column is quoted in Dobbs, *Teamster Politics*, 226–27.

68. "The Last Word," *Northwest Organizer*, September 21, 1939.

69. See Erickson, "WPA Strike and Trials of 1939," 210, where Davis's history as state legislator and Farmer-Labor candidate for attorney general is briefly described; see also Dobbs, *Teamster Politics*, 221.

70. "Two Dictionaries Used as WPA Trial Witnesses," n.d., and "WPA Defendant Repeats Speech Made to Workers," n.d.—both clippings in WPA Strike file, Douglas Alan Bruce Papers, MHS; "Police Who Should Be on Duty Kept in

Court by WPA Prosecution," *Labor Review*, November 10, 1939; "Cops Say Song is Red," *Northwest Organizer*, November 9, 1939; "WPA Prosecution Looms as Threat to Trial by Jury," *Labor Review*, December 1, 1939.

71. "23 Assaults Charged in WPA Trial," n.d., clipping, Bruce Papers, WPA Strike file, MHS.

72. "WPA Prosecution Shot Through With Bitter Hate," *Labor Review*, November 17, 1939.

73. "Davis Brings New Sensation to WPA Trial," *Labor Review*, November 3, 1939; "WPA Prosecution Shot Through with Bitter Hate; Desperation of Prosecutor Disclosed," *Labor Review*, November 17, 1939; "WPA Prosecution Looms as Threat to Trial by Jury," *Labor Review*, December 1, 1939; "State Labor Gives Defense Fine Support," *Labor Review*, December 8, 1939.

74. "13 Women Strikers Get Probation, One Receives 45 Days," *Northwest Organizer*, February 15, 1940.

75. R. D. Cramer to President Roosevelt, January 10, 1940, Robley Dungleson Cramer Papers, Box 1, 1940 Correspondence file, MHS.

76. See chapter 5.

77. Seymour argues that the creation of federal programs for old-age assistance, unemployment insurance, and ADC had the impact of forcing a decline in the membership of the Workers' Alliance by making "invisible resources" available to relief clients (*When Clients Organize*, 9–10). See also Piven and Cloward, *Poor People's Movements*.

78. Elizabeth Faue, "Women, Family, and Politics."

79. See Kessler-Harris, "Rose Schneiderman and the Limits of Trade Unionism," among others.

Chapter 7

1. Chafe, *The American Woman*, was the opening volley in the debate. See reactions, modifications, and rebuttals in Rupp, *Mobilizing Women for War*; Anderson, *Wartime Women*; Susan Hartmann, *The Home Front and Beyond*; Campbell, *Women at War with America*; Honey, *Creating Rosie the Riveter*; among others. There is also a substantial journal literature. The best work on the war's impact on working women is that of sociologist Ruth Milkman. In addition to her excellent essays, see her book, *Gender at Work*.

2. Susan Ware, *Beyond Suffrage*.

3. Federal Housing Administration, Division of Research and Statistics, "Report on the Current Housing Situation in Minneapolis–St. Paul, Minnesota," Minneapolis–St. Paul Background Information file, Box 202; and United States Employment Service, "List of Defense Plants from Labor Market Developments, Twin Cities Area," January 1943, 7–19, Minneapolis–St. Paul file, Box 201—both

in Records of the United States Employment Service (hereafter USES Records), RG 183, NA.

4. Federal Housing Administration, Division of Research and Statistics, "Report on the Current Housing Situation in Minneapolis–St. Paul, Minnesota," 21, Minneapolis–St. Paul Background Information file, USES Records, RG 183, Box 202, NA; for Onan and Sons and Moline fortunes, see the local UE papers.

5. "Problem Areas, Minneapolis-St. Paul," September 6, 1941; and "Labor Market Survey of the Employment Situation in the Minneapolis and St. Paul Area," January 9, 1942—both in Minneapolis–St. Paul Background Information file, USES Records, RG 183, Box 202, NA.

6. On employer resistance, see "Labor Supply and Demand in Minnesota," April 8, 1942, Minneapolis–St. Paul Background Information file, Box 202; and "Labor Market Development Report, Minneapolis-St. Paul Area," August 1943, Minneapolis–St. Paul Background Information file, Box 201—both in USES Records, RG 183, NA. On employer policies toward women workers, see "Labor Market Development Report, Minneapolis–St. Paul Area," January 1943, USES Records, RG 183, Box 201. The report outlines employer requirements—e.g., at the ordnance plant, women had to be under forty-five years old and have no infant children; at O. B. McClintock, women were to have good "character, eyesight, personal habits, education and personality"; at Onan and Sons, women were to be "alert and active and between 18 and 45."

7. Federal Security Board, Bureau of Employment Security, Reports and Analysis Division, Region VIII, "Status of Major War Projects," June 24, 1942, USES Records, RG 183, Box 202, NA; War Manpower Commission, Twin Cities Area, Minutes of the Meeting of the Management-Labor Policy Committees, December 2, 1942, Summary Minutes of the Regional, State and Area Management-Labor Policy Committees, 1942–1945, Twin Cities, Minnesota file, Records of the War Manpower Commission (hereafter WMC Records), RG 211, Box 199, NA.

8. "Labor Market Developments Report, Minneapolis–St. Paul Area," January 1943, Minneapolis file, USES Records, RG 183, Box 201, NA.

9. Ibid.

10. "Labor Market Developments Report, Minneapolis-St. Paul Area," January 1943 and October 1943, USES Records, RG 183, Box 201, NA. See Anderson, "Last Hired, First Fired."

11. Hotel and Restaurant Workers, Miscellaneous Workers local 665, was a desegregated union. See also the efforts of the CIO locally recorded in Henry Murray, "CIO Fights for Equal Rights," Minnesota State Industrial Union Council, *Directory and Annual Convention Brochure*, 17, and Private John Thomas, "The Brotherhood of Man: CIO for Race Equality," in Minnesota State Industrial Union Council, *Minnesota CIO Yearbook*, 19.

12. Regional files, Closed Cases, Region VIII, Committee on Fair Employment Practice, Federal Cartridge Company folder, Box 765, and Northern Pump Company folder, Box 766—both in Records of the Committee on Fair Employment

Practices, RG 228, NA. See Norrell, "Caste in Steel," on discrimination.

13. The dues check-off was instituted during World War II. It automatically deducted union dues from pay checks at closed shop firms.

14. In early March 1942, local UE officials reported that the FBI and the police department were obstructing the employment of union men in defense plants. Buford Eastman to Matles, March 2, 1942, FF 102; and Matles to Eastman, March 9, 1942, FF 99—both in UE Records, University of Pittsburgh.

15. Lichtenstein, *Labor's War at Home*, is perhaps the most extreme statement of this thesis.

16. Skold, "The Job He Left Behind," is particularly helpful here. See also Milkman, "Organizing the Sexual Division of Labor" and "Female Factory Labor and Industrial Structure."

17. For a good, thoughtful discussion of the lack of change during the war, see Milkman, "Organizing the Sexual Division of Labor" and *Gender at Work*, 96–98.

18. Fussell, *Wartime*, 149, gives the meaning of "victory girl" as a young woman who dated—and presumably gave sexual solace—to GIs. The use of the term by unions was intended to have a more neutral, desexualized meaning; one wonders what the GIs thought.

19. Nan Emanuel, "Sing a Song of Salvage," *Honeywell UE News*, August 10, 1942, FF 609D, UE Records, University of Pittsburgh. On the creation of Labor's Volunteers for Victory, see State of Minnesota, Office of Civil Defense, General Order 7, March 3, 1942, in Robley Dungleson Cramer Papers, Box 1, 1940 Correspondence file, MHS. On the parade, see mobilization leaflet, "I am an American Day Parade," local 1152, FF 691, UE Records, University of Pittsburgh; and "Labor Marches for Victory," in *Labor Volunteer for Victory*, July 1943, the newsletter of the Labor Coordinating Committee of the Minneapolis Defense Council; *UVG to GI Joe*—both in Labor Coordinating Committee file, CLUM Records, Box 13, MHS.

20. "To the War Bonds Ramparts—Modern Molly Pitchers," *Labor Review*, November 19, 1942; "Japan Smash My Union? I'll Smash Japan!" *Labor Review*, December 12, 1941; "Brother, I'm in—Every Pay Day!" *Labor Review*, December 5, 1941.

21. Lichtenstein, *Labor's War at Home*, 157–202; Tomlins, *The State and the Unions*, 252–81.

22. Tselos, "The Labor Movement in Minneapolis," 431–32. See also William Mauseth, IAM, to Julius Emspak, general secretary-treasurer, UE, August 27, 1937, FF 542; and Matles, director of organization, to Larry D. Kimmel, vice president, District 11, October 7, 1937, FF 105—both in UE Records, University of Pittsburgh.

23. "800 Laid off at Minneapolis Honeywell," *Labor Review*, December 27, 1929; U.S. National Labor Relations Board (hereafter NLRB), *Decisions and Orders*, vol. 33, June 27, 1941–August 7, 1941, 267.

24. "Don't Be Fooled! Look at the Record!," "The Door to Democracy on the

Job!," and "To the AFL, CIO and the Unemployed," Labor Handbills Collection, MHS. Also see Auerbach, *Labor and Liberty*.

25. NLRB, *Decisions and Orders*, vol. 33, 262–311; Exhibits 2049–51, U.S. Congress, Senate, Subcommittee on Education and Labor, *Report: Violations of Free Speech and the Rights of Labor*, vol. 15-A, Hearings, November 18, 1937, 5623–24.

26. NLRB, Case C-1769, *Decisions and Orders*, vol. 33, 26–70; "Don't Be Fooled!" Labor Handbills Collection, MHS.

27. NLRB, *Decisions and Orders*, vol. 33, 307–8; "UE-CIO-1145 Contract Signed with Honeywell Company," *Honeywell UE News*, September 25, 1942, FF 609D, UE Records, University of Pittsburgh. See also "Records Show Hundreds Have Joined CIO Since Election," *Honeywell UE News*, March 27, 1942, FF 609C, UE Records, which suggests that union strength is due in part to former AFL leaders in the upper floors.

28. See copies of the *Honeywell UE News* in the UE Records, University of Pittsburgh. Also, "Women Workers in Honeywell Realize the Value of Unionism," *Midwest Labor*, November 22, 1940.

29. NLRB, *Decisions and Orders*, vol. 33, 263–311, details the discrimination. Of the workers dismissed, a majority were found to be the victims of Honeywell's unfair labor practices. See also "Honeywell Employee Group Joins AFL; to Oppose CIO Unit," *Minneapolis Tribune*, July 25, 1941. On CIO protest of the firing, see Elsie Hoag, secretary of the corresponding committee of local 1145, to William McLain, October 12, 1940, FF 608; and Buford Eastman, president, District 11, UE, to Matles, July 18, 1941, FF 101—both in UE Records, University of Pittsburgh.

30. Ernest De Maio to Matles, January 26, 1942, FF 159, UE Records, University of Pittsburgh. De Maio states that the women in the AFL had been laid off, giving the UE an advantage. In subsequent letters, De Maio reveals that the AFL had been engaged in red-baiting and anti-Semitism, promoting factionalism in the union; he also made a request for a woman organizer (and evidently got his wish) to work on the Honeywell campaign, right before the switch in tactics noted later in the text. See De Maio to Matles, June 12, 1942 and July 7, 1942, both in FF 163, UE Records.

31. "You Were Mislead Once—Don't Be Mislead Again!" poster, enclosed in letter, Eastman to Matles, July 25, 1941, FF 101; Eastman to Matles, September 16, 1941, FF 102; "NLRB Decision Opens Way to New Honeywell Election," *Honeywell UE News*, April 24, 1942, FF 609C—all in UE Records, University of Pittsburgh. See also NLRB, *Decisions and Orders*, vol. 40, 633ff.; Case R-4053, Decision and Certification, *Decisions and Orders*, vols. 40 and 42, 1046–48.

32. "Production for Victory and Your Livelihood," n.d., CIO file, Box 7, CLUM Records; "Our Forefathers Fought in '76 for This" and "An Appeal to Reason," n.d., Labor Handbills Collection—all in MHS. These flyers also suggest the

Communist party influence in the UE. See Isserman, *Which Side Were You On?*, 9–14, 109–17. It is also worth noting that the Minneapolis Communist party organization during the war was named for Thomas Paine, and its publication was *The Appeal to Reason*.

33. "You Were Mislead Once—Don't Be Mislead Again," poster, enclosed in letter, Eastman to Matles, July 25, 1941, FF 101, UE Records, University of Pittsburgh. "An Appeal to Reason," and Handbill (June 8, 1941?), Labor Handbills Collection, MHS.

34. "It's a Woman's Right . . . to Change Her Mind," *Honeywell UE News*, June 26, 1942, FF 609D, UE Records, University of Pittsburgh.

35. Eastman, District 11 president, spoke of it as "trying different lines of thought" due to the "considerable criticism as to how [the election] was handled." See Eastman to Matles, September 16, 1941, FF 102; De Maio to Matles, Jaunuary 26, 1942, FF 159; De Maio to Matles, July 7, 1942, FF 164; and, on the woman organizer, De Maio to Matles, June 12, 1942, FF 163—all in UE Records, University of Pittsburgh.

36. "It's a Woman's Right . . . to Change Her Mind," *Honeywell UE News*, June 26, 1942, FF 609D, UE Records, University of Pittsburgh; "An Appeal to Reason," Labor Handbills Collection, MHS. See letter from De Maio to Matles, July 7, 1942, FF 163, UE Records, for a detailed discussion of the tactics, which included red-baiting and anti-Semitism.

37. "Betty Union Says," *TCOP UE News*, June 25, 1942, FF 691, UE Records, University of Pittsburgh; "Buy Union," *CIO News*, May 5, 1941; "It's the Latest Fashion," *CIO News*, March 12, 1938. On consumerism, see Marchand, *Advertising the American Dream*; on its Popular Front adaptation, see Dixler, "The Woman Question," 136–43. One could also speculate that wartime rationing created a hunger for goods that unionism could at least theoretically provide. On rationing and hunger, see Fussell, *Wartime*, 195–207. See also the reporting of union beauty contests in any labor newspaper, including that of the Teamsters. There is a tendency toward exotica in the coverage of women: see "Does Stunts for the CIO" (*CIO News*, September 17, 1938), about a woman acrobat and dancer; "Ladies in Masquerade" (*CIO News*, November 11, 1938), about a textile workers' organizing committee auxiliary and their parties; "Boost the CIO" (*CIO News*, August 5, 1940), about a "bevy of beauties" from Toledo who are giving "ooomph to that city's big CIO labor day jamboree"; and "Versatile" (*CIO News*, December 19, 1938) about "Pretty Betty Lowman, 24," a delegate of the CIO United Fisherman's Union, who was an author, musician, and athlete who sang while working on a Puget Sound fishing boat.

38. *TCOP UE News*, June 25, 1942, local 1152, FF 691, UE Records, University of Pittsburgh.

39. *TCOP UE News*, June 25, 1942, local 1152, FF 691, UE Records, University of Pittsburgh; "Buy Union," *CIO News*, March 4, 1940; "Everyone's in Good

Shape . . . But—" *CIO News*, May 5, 1941; "The Union Road to Love," *CIO News*, November 4, 1940. Unionism is put in consumer terms in "It's the Latest Fashion" (*CIO News*, March 12, 1938), where a retail employee is viewing department store windows displaying spring styles that represent CIO contracts. These also resonate with earlier images. See Ann Schofield, "From 'Sealskin and Shoddy' to 'the Pig-headed Girl,' " 112–24.

40. By May of 1942, women were about 40 percent of the Honeywell work force, an increase from previous years. By 1943, they represented 80 percent of the new hires, and Honeywell was one of the three major industrial employers of women. See Federal Security Board, Bureau of Employment Security, Reports and Analysis Division, Region VIII, June 24, 1942, "Status of Major War Projects," 10, Box 202; and "Labor Market Developments Report," January 1943, Minneapolis file, Box 201—both in USES Records, RG 183, NA.

41. "Moline Women Employees Receive 74 Cent Starting Rate," *Honeywell UE News*, June 12, 1942; "It's a Woman's Right . . . to Change Her Mind," *Honeywell UE News*, June 26, 1942; "UE-CIO Victory," *Honeywell UE News*, July 6, 1942; "Negotiations Move Forward for UE-CIO Union Contract," *Honeywell UE News*, August 25, 1942; "UE-CIO-1145 Contract Signed with Honeywell Company," *Honeywell UE News*, all in FF 609D, UE Records, University of Pittsburgh.

42. Notably Rupp, *Mobilizing Women for War*.

43. Honey, *Creating Rosie the Riveter*, esp. 5–9.

44. Ibid., pp. 149–81, 207–9, on the valorization of women's work during the war, especially as it affected working-class women. See also Gerstle, *Working-Class Americanism*, 278–309, on the malleability of language during the war.

45. "Onan Employees Speak to Onan Employees," *UE News*, published for Onan Employees, n.d. (1943?), DD 11–203, UE Records, University of Pittsburgh.

46. "Dear Sister," flyer, local 1139, February 4, 1943, DD 11-L200, UE Records, University of Pittsburgh.

47. Thomas Foley, UE field organizer, local 1139, telegram to Alice Smith, November 4, 1943, DD 11-L204; Foley to "Dear Onan Worker," November 22, 1943, DD 11-L200; Foley to De Maio, November 25, 1943, DD11-L204—all in UE Records, University of Pittsburgh.

48. Eastman, president district 11, to Matles, director of organization, December 23, 1941, FF 102; De Maio to Matles, July 7, 1942, FF 164; Robert Wishart to Matles, September 1942, FF 1626—all in UE Records, University of Pittsburgh.

49. Take, for example, a meeting of the local labor commission: "Mr. Cordner said he agreed all women should be under control, and asked the members if there was any objection to putting women under this classification. Mr. Welscher asked how it was thought to gain anything by control on women. Mr. Nord stated there was a great need now for women and it was impossible to get them into war plants without control." Minutes, Twin City Area Labor-Management Committee Meet-

ing, April 23, 1945, Management-Labor Policy Committee, Office of the Executive Secretary, Entry 18, Inventory 6, Summer Minutes, Twin Cities, Minnesota, WMC Records, RG 211, Box 199, NA. For employer response to women and veterans respectively, see Martha Ziegler, field inspector, office memorandum to Frieda Miller, director, Women's Bureau, May 8, 1945, Field Office files, Region IX, Records of the Women's Bureau, RG 86, Box 1395, NA.

50. Ziegler to Frieda Miller, May 8, 1945, Field Office files, Region IX, Records of the Women's Bureau, RG 86, Box 1395, NA.

51. Wurst dramatized the reasoning thus:

> Both the methods of the reactionaries and the attitudes of workers themselves tend to degrade women to take from them every vestige of dignity that is the inherent right of human beings.
>
> "But," an honest worker declares, "women don't seem to think right. They don't seem to get the idea."
>
> Most of us fail to recognize that those habits of thought and action that seem to be peculiar to women as a whole are merely the result of centuries of oppression that have been their lot. The solution of that problem lies in making women a part of the trade union movement. Then they will think as trade unionists.

See "Women in the Trade Unions," Minnesota State Industrial Union Council, *Directory and Annual Convention Brochure* (1940), 11.

52. For a suggestive study, see Martyna, "What Does 'He' Mean?"

Conclusion

1. Historical analyses of the New Deal, voluminous in the 1970s, have benefited from a sudden and prolific revival in an era when the state is being brought back into social history. For business reaction and benefits from the New Deal, see Barton Bernstein, "The New Deal"; and Hawley, *The New Deal and the Problem of Monopoly*. On the New Deal and its impact on labor and welfare, see Skocpol, "Political Response to Capitalist Crisis"; Vittoz, *New Deal Labor Policy*; Hodges, *New Deal Labor Policy*; Ann Shola Orloff, "The Political Origins," 65–80; Edwin Amenta and Theda Skocpol, "Redefining the New Deal," 81–122. For studies critical of labor's response to nationalization of labor relations, see Tomlins, *The State and the Unions*; Aronowitz, *False Promises*; Davis, *Prisoners of the American Dream*.

2. See Orloff, "The Political Origins," 65–80; Susan Ware, *Beyond Suffrage*; Scharf, *To Work and to Wed*; Barbara Nelson, "The Gender, Race, and Class Origins of Early Welfare Policy"; and Elizabeth Faue, "Women, Family, and Politics."

3. Milkman, "Organizing the Sexual Division of Labor"; Strom, "Challenging 'Woman's Place.' "

4. The crisis of masculinity is usually associated with World War I and the massive loss of life on the European front. I argue here that the notion must be extended to incorporate the depression as yet another manifestation of gender in contemporary crisis. See Fussell, *The Great War and Modern Memory*; Gilbert, "Soldier's Heart"; Perrot, "The New Eve and the Old Adam"; and Kent, "The Politics of Sexual Difference."

5. There is a curious parallel here with the other great economic crises of our history. As Suzanne Lebsock has shown, depressions, like wars, reorder gender roles. The depression of the 1850s represented a crisis for men of the propertied classes in Petersburg, Virginia. In the face of economic disaster, they relied on their wives as property holders and legatees. But this increase in the importance of women's economic and political role came at a price. Women lost both autonomy in the economic realm and public recognition of their economic and social role. Independent agencies of charity, founded by women in the early 19th century, were given sanction and public recognition only when men took over nominal authority. Recognition for women's work was denied. See Lebsock, *Free Women of Petersburg*.

6. Gabin, " 'They Have Placed a Penalty on Womanhood' "; Milkman, *Gender at Work*, 99–127, 130–44.

Bibliography

Manuscript Collections

Ithaca, New York
  Martin P. Catherwood Library. Cornell University.
    Amalgamated Clothing and Textile Workers of America.
      Twin City Joint Board Records.
    International Ladies' Garment Workers' Union Collection.
      Chicago Joint Board of the ILGWU Records.
      David Dubinsky Papers.
Madison, Wisconsin
  State Historical Society of Wisconsin.
    American Federation of Labor. Minnesota. Records.
Minneapolis, Minnesota
  Social Welfare History Archives. University of Minnesota.
    Family Welfare Association of Minneapolis Records.
    Helen Hall Papers.
    Young Women's Christian Association of Minneapolis Records.
Pittsburgh, Pennsylvania
  University of Pittsburgh Libraries.
    United Electrical, Radio, and Machine Workers of
    America Records.
St. Paul, Minnesota
  Minnesota Historical Society.
    Elmer Benson. Governor. Administrative Records.
    Douglas Alan Bruce Papers.
    Myrtle Cain Papers.
    Central Labor Union of Minneapolis Records.
    Citizens' Alliance of Minneapolis Records.
    Robley Dungleson Cramer Papers.
    Walter Frank Papers.
    Sander David Genis Papers.
    Douglas Hall Papers.
    Oscar and Madge Hawkins Papers.

Hennepin County Farmer-Labor Women's Club Records.
Labor Handbills Collection.
Arthur and Marian Le Sueur Papers.
Meridel Le Sueur Papers.
Minnesota Department of Labor and Industry Records.
Minnesota Public Safety Commission Records.
Northeast Neighborhood House Records.
Floyd B. Olson. Governor. Administrative Records.
St. Paul Trades and Labor Assembly Records.
Frances Howe Satterlee Papers.
Socialist Workers' Party Records.
Allen N. and Violet J. Sollie Papers.
Jean Spielman Papers.
Susie Stageberg Papers.
Harold Stassen. Governor. Administrative Records.
Roy Wier Papers.
Works Progress Administration. Minnesota. Records.
Washington, D.C.
United States. National Archives.
RG 9. Records of the National Recovery Administration.
RG 25. Records of the National Labor Relations Board.
RG 28. Records of the Post Office Department.
RG 60. Records of the Department of Justice.
RG 69. Records of the Works Progress Administration.
RG 86. Records of the Women's Bureau.
RG 183. Records of the United States Employment Service.
RG 211. Records of the War Manpower Commission.
RG 228. Records of the Committee on Fair Employment
Practices.
RG 257. Records of the Bureau of Labor Statistics. Family Dis-
bursements of Wage-earners and Salaried Clerical Workers.

Interviews and Transcripts

Elizabeth Banghart. Interview with the author. August 8, 1985, Minneapolis,
Minnesota.
Marguerite Belton. Interview with the author. May 20, 1985, Minneapolis,
Minnesota.
Wilbur Broms. Interview with the author. September 26, 1985, St. Paul, Min-
nesota.
Loretta DuFour. Interview with the author. June 20, 1985, Minnetonka, Min-
nesota.

Walter Frank. Interview with Lila Johnson and Donald Sofchalk. August 11, 1969, transcript at the Minnesota Historical Society.

Sander Genis. Interview with James Dooley. November 6, 1974, transcript at the Minnesota Historical Society.

Sander Genis. Interview with Martin Duffy. March 16, 1977, transcript at the Minnesota Historical Society.

Sander Genis. Interview with the author. June 17, 1985, St. Paul, Minnesota.

Myrtle Harris. Interview with James Dooley. July 9, 1975, transcript at the Minnesota Historical Society.

Hjordes Hedlund. Phone interview with the author. May 29, 1985.

Gertrude Larson. Interview with the author. September 17, 1985, Minneapolis, Minnesota.

Meridel Le Sueur. Interview with the author. July 28, 1989, Hudson, Wisconsin.

Grace Trost Neff. Interview with the author. July 17, 1985, Brooklyn Center, Minnesota.

Rose Seiler Palmquist. Interview with Mary Ellen Frank. June 1, 1977, Trade Union Woman in the Twentieth Century, microfilm collection.

Alan N. and Violet Johnson Sollie. Joint interview with Warren Gardner. August 24, 1974, transcript at the Minnesota Historical Society.

Newspapers

CIO News. Washington, D.C.
Farmer Labor Leader. Minneapolis.
Honeywell UE News. Minneapolis.
Justice. New York.
Midwest Labor. Duluth.
Minneapolis Journal. Minneapolis.
Minneapolis Labor Review. Minneapolis.
Minneapolis Spokesman. Minneapolis.
Minneapolis Star. Minneapolis.
Minneapolis Times. Minneapolis.
Minneapolis Tribune. Minneapolis.
Minnesota Leader. St. Paul.
Minnesota Union Advocate. St. Paul.
New Times. Minneapolis.
Nonpartisan Leader. St. Paul.
Northwest Organizer. Minneapolis.
The Organizer. Minneapolis.
Our Time. Minneapolis.
St. Paul Pioneer Press. St. Paul.
Strutwear Worker. Minneapolis.

TCOP UE News. Minneapolis.
United Action. Minneapolis.

Government Documents

Carpenter, Niles. *Immigrants and Their Children, 1920: A Study Based on Census Statistics Relative to the Foreign-Born and the Native White of Foreign or Mixed Parentage*. Census monograph 7. Washington, D.C.: GPO, 1927.

Edwards, Alba M. *Comparative Labor Statistics for the United States, 1870–1940*. Washington, D.C.: GPO, 1943.

Hauser, Philip M. *Workers on Relief in the United States in March 1935*. Vol. 1, *A Census of Usual Occupations*. Washington, D.C.: Works Progress Administration, 1938.

Hill, Joseph Adna. *Women in Gainful Occupations, 1870–1920*. Washington, D.C.: GPO, 1929.

Minneapolis. City Planning Commission. *A Survey of Housing Conditions*. Minneapolis, 1934.

Minnesota. Department of Labor and Industries. *Biennial Reports*. St. Paul, 1917–45.

Minnesota. Emergency Relief Administration. *Analysis and Report on Old Age Pension and Mothers' Allowance by Counties*. St. Paul, 1935.

————. *Women's Work in Minnesota under the Civil Works Administration and the Emergency Relief Administration*. St. Paul, 1935.

Minnesota. Minimum Wage Commission. *Biennial Report*, 2d. St. Paul, 1922.

Minnesota. State Council of Social Work. *A Study of Mothers' Pensions in Minnesota*. St. Paul, 1935.

Palmer, Gladys L., and Katherine D. Wood. *Urban Workers on Relief*, pt. 2. Washington, D.C.: Works Progress Administration, 1936.

U.S. Bureau of Labor Statistics. *Annual Report*, 4th, for 1888. *Working Women in Large Cities*. Washington, D.C.: GPO, 1889.

————. *Beneficial Activities of American Trade Unions*. Bulletin no. 465. Washington, D.C.: GPO, 1928.

————. *Unemployment in the United States*. Bulletin no. 195. Employment and Unemployment series no 2. Washington, D.C.: GPO, 1916.

U.S. Bureau of the Census. *Births, Stillbirths, and Infant Mortality Statistics*, 13th–22d annual reports for 1927–36. Washington, D.C.: GPO, 1930–38.

————. *Farm Population of the United States, 1920*. Census monograph. Washington, D.C.: GPO, 1927.

————. *12th Census of the United States, 1900: Statistics of Women at Work*. Washington, D.C.: GPO, 1907.

————. *13th Census of the United States, 1910. Population*. Vol. 4, *Occupational Statistics*. Washington, D.C.: GPO, 1912.

_____. *14th Census of the United States, 1920. Population.* Vol. 2, *General Report and Analytical Tables.* Washington, D.C.: GPO, 1922.

_____. *14th Census of the United States, 1920. Population.* Vol. 4, *Occupations.* Washington, D.C.: GPO, 1923.

_____. *15th Census of the United States, 1930. Population.* Vol. 3, *Reports by States.* Washington, D.C.: GPO, 1933.

_____. *15th Census of the United States, 1930. Population.* Vol. 4, *Occupations by States.* Washington, D.C.: GPO, 1933.

_____. *15th Census of the United States, 1930. Population.* Vol. 6, *Families; Reports by States.* Washington, D.C.: GPO, 1933.

_____. *15th Census of the United States, 1930. Unemployment. Unemployment Returns by Classes for States and Counties, for Urban and Rural Areas and for Cities with a Population of 10,000 or More.* 2 vols. Washington, D.C.: GPO, 1931.

_____. *16th Census of the United States, 1940. Internal Migration, 1935–1940: Social Characteristics of Migrants.* Washington, D.C.: GPO, 1946.

_____. *16th Census of the United States, 1940. Population.* Vol. 2, pt. 4, *Characteristics of the Population.* Washington, D.C.: GPO, 1943.

_____. *16th Census of the United States, 1940. Population.* Vol. 3, pt. 3, *The Labor Force: Occupation, Industry, Employment, Income.* Washington, D.C.: GPO, 1943.

_____. *16th Census of the United States, 1940. Population.* Vol. 4, pt. 3, *Characteristics by Age.* Washington, D.C.: GPO, 1943.

_____. *16th Census of the United States, 1940. Population and Housing. Families. General Characteristics.* Washington, D.C.: GPO, 1943.

_____. *17th Census of the United States, 1950. Population.* Vol. 2, *Special Reports.* Washington, D.C.: GPO, 1953–57.

_____. *Vital Statistics of the United States,* 1937–1940. Washington, D.C.: GPO, 1939–1943.

U.S. Congress. House of Representatives. *Investigation and Study of the Works Progress Administration: Hearings Before a Subcommittee.* 75th Cong., 3rd sess., 1939. Pt. 1. Washington, D.C.: GPO, 1940.

_____. Special Committee to Investigate Un-American Activities. *Hearings, Investigation of Un-American Propaganda Activities in the United States.* 75th Cong., 3rd sess. Washington, D.C.: GPO, 1938.

U.S. Congress. Senate. Subcommittee on Education and Labor. *Report: Violations of Free Speech and the Rights of Labor.* 77th Cong., 2d sess. Washington, D.C.: GPO, 1942.

U.S. Federal Emergency Relief Administration. *Unemployment Relief Census, October 1933.* Washington, D.C.: GPO, 1934.

U.S. National Labor Relations Board. *Decisions and Orders.* Vol. 33 (June 27, 1941–August 7, 1941). Washington, D.C.: GPO, 1942.

_____. *Decisions and Orders.* Vol. 40 (April 1, 1942–May 15, 1942). Washington, D.C.: GPO, 1942.

_____. *Decisions and Orders.* Vol. 42 (July 1, 1942–August 11, 1942). Washington, D.C.: GPO, 1942.

U.S. Office of the Administration of the Census. *Census of Partial Employment, Unemployment and Occupations, 1937. Final Report on Total and Partial Unemployment*. Washington, D.C.: GPO, 1938.

U.S. Works Progress Administration. Minnesota. *Divorce Records Study, Hennepin County, 1858–1940*. Minneapolis, 1941.

_____. *Industry in Minnesota*. Bulletin no. 30. Social Studies Research Materials Project. Minneapolis, 1940.

Contemporary Published Documents

"Brief Career of Minneapolis Committee Filled with Accomplishment." *Life and Labor* (October 1919): 271.

Citizens' Alliance of Minneapolis. *The Citizens' Alliance of Minneapolis: Law and Order and the Open Shop*. Minneapolis, 1927.

"Civil Liberties in Minneapolis." *New Republic* 105 (July 28, 1941): 103–4.

Dietrickson, Mary Watkins. "The Minimum Wage Situation in Minnesota." *Minnesota Woman Voter* (March 1926): 9.

Eastman, Daniel. "The Minneapolis 'Sedition' Trial." *New Republic* 105 (October 2, 1941): 503–4.

Farmer-Labor Women's Clubs of Minnesota. *Report of the Sixth State Convention, March 28, 1932*. St. Paul, 1932.

Farmer-Labor Women's Federation. *Farmer-Labor Women's Federation Annual, 1935–1936*. St. Paul, 1936.

_____. *A Woman's Political Primer*. St. Paul, 1936.

"Franklin Cooperative Creamery and Its Activities." *Monthly Labor Review* 31 (August 1930): 112–14.

Gallob, Ben. "The New Deal Cracks Down." *Black and White* 2 (January 1940): 17–19.

Hudson, Carlos. "Minneapolis—One Year Later." *Nation* 141 (October 30, 1935): 512–14.

International Ladies' Garment Workers' Union. *Report of the Proceedings of the 23rd Convention, 1937*. New York, 1937.

_____. Education Department. *Everybody Sings*. New York, 1934.

_____. *Garment Workers Speak*. New York, 1942.

_____. *Handbook of Trade Union Methods*. New York, 1937.

_____. *How to Conduct a Union Meeting*. New York, 1934.

_____. *Training for Union Service*. New York, 1940.

Kohler, Katherine M., and Walker A. Anderson. *A Social Survey of 20,000 Families Residing in 10 Minneapolis Settlement House Districts*. Minneapolis: Adult Education, 1934.

Le Sueur, Meridel. "I Was Marching." *New Masses* 12 (September 18, 1934): 16–18.

_____. "Murder in Minneapolis." *New Masses* 12 (August 7, 1934): 12–13.

_____. "What Happens in a Strike." *American Mercury* 33 (November 1934): 329–35.

_____. *Worker Writers.* St. Paul: Minnesota Worker Education, Works Progress Administration, 1935.

Levin, Harry. "Divided Front in Minnesota." *Nation* 145 (October 2, 1937): 346–48.

Macdonald, Dwight. "WPA Cuts—or Jail." *Nation* 150 (February 3, 1940): 120–23.

Minneapolis Union Education Center. Directing Committee. *Workers' Education.* Minneapolis, 1938.

Minnesota. State Industrial Union Council. *Directory and Annual Convention Brochure*, 3rd Convention. St. Paul, 1940.

_____. *Minnesota CIO Yearbook.* St. Paul, 1942.

_____. *Proceedings of the Annual Convention*, 1st–6th. St. Paul, 1937–42.

Munsingwear, Inc. *The Success of Doing Well.* Minneapolis, 1921.

_____. *Program of the Employment Relationship between Management and Employees of the Munsingwear Corporation.* Minneapolis, 1935.

Olson, Floyd B. *A Primer on Unemployment Insurance.* St. Paul, 1934.

"Revolt in the Northwest." *Fortune* 13 (April 1936): 112–19.

Ross, Anne. "Labor Unity in Minneapolis." *New Republic* 89 (July 15, 1934): 284–86.

_____. "Minnesota Sets Some Precedents." *New Republic* 80 (1934): 121–23.

Soltow, Herbert. "War in Minneapolis." *Nation* 80 (August 8, 1934): 160–61.

Stone, I. F. "The G-String Conspiracy." *Nation* 105 (July 26, 1941): 66–67.

"Strike Against the Government." *New Republic* 99 (July 29, 1939): 322.

"Twin Cities Progress toward League Organization." *Life and Labor* (July 1918): 152.

Van Kleeck, Mary. "Security for Americans, IV: The Workers' Unemployment and Pension Bill." *New Republic* 81 (December 12, 1934): 121–24.

Walker, Charles Rumford. "A Militant Trade Union. Minneapolis: Municipal Profile." *Survey Graphic* 26 (January 1937): 29–33.

_____. "Minneapolis: City of Tensions." *Survey Graphic* 25 (November 1936): 620–23, 633–34.

_____. "Minneapolis: Jim Hill's Empire." *Survey Graphic* 25 (October 1936): 549–55, 584–89.

Books, Articles, and Unpublished Studies

Agee, James, and Walker Evans. *Let Us Now Praise Famous Men*. 1939. Reprint. Boston: Houghton Mifflin, 1988.

Agulhon, Maurice. *Marianne into Battle: Republican Imagery and Symbolism in France, 1789–1880*. Cambridge and New York: Cambridge University Press, 1981.

————. "On Political Allegory, A Reply to Eric Hobsbawm." *History Workshop Journal* 8 (Autumn 1979): 167–73.

Alexander, Sally. "Women, Class and Sexual Differences in the 1830s and 1840s: Some Reflections on the Writing of a Feminist History." *History Workshop Journal* 17 (Spring 1984): 125–49.

Alexander, Sally, Anna Davin, and Eve Hostettler. "Labouring Women: A Reply to Eric Hobsbawm." *History Workshop Journal* 8 (Autumn 1979): 174–82.

Algren, Nelson. *Somebody in Boots*. New York: Vanguard Press, 1935.

Amenta, Edwin, and Theda Skocpol. "Redefining the New Deal: World War II and the Development of Social Provision in the United States." In *The Politics of Social Policy in the United States*, edited by Margaret Weir, Ann Shola Orloff, and Theda Skocpol, pp. 81–122. Princeton: Princeton University Press, 1988.

Anderson, Karen T. "Last Hired, First Fired: Black Women Workers in World War II." *Journal of American History* 69 (June 1982): 82–97.

————. *Wartime Women: Sex Roles, Family Relations, and the Status of Women in World War II*. Westport, Conn.: Greenwood Press, 1981.

Arendt, Hannah. *The Human Condition*. Chicago: University of Chicago Press, 1958.

Aronowitz, Stanley. *False Promises: The Shaping of American Working Class Consciousness*. New York: McGraw Hill, 1972.

Asher, Robert. "Radicalism and Reform: State Insurance of Workmen's Compensation in Minnesota, 1910–1933." *Labor History* 14 (Winter 1973): 19–41.

Asher, Robert, and Charles Stephenson, eds. *Labor Divided: Race and Ethnicity in U.S. Labor Struggles, 1835–1960*. Albany: SUNY Press, 1990.

Auerbach, Jerold. *Labor and Liberty: The LaFollette Committee and the New Deal*. Indianapolis: Bobbs-Merrill, 1966.

Baer, Judith A. *The Chains of Protection: The Judicial Response to Women's Labor Legislation*. Westport, Conn.: Greenwood Press, 1978.

Baker, Paula. "The Domestication of Politics: Women and American Political Society, 1780–1920." *American Historical Review* 89 (June 1984): 620–47.

Bakke, Edward Wight. *Citizens without Work: A Study of the Effects of Unemployment upon Workers' Social Relations and Practices*. New Haven: Yale University Press for the Institute of Human Relations, 1940.

Balbus, Isaac. *Marxism and Domination: A Neo-Hegelian, Feminist, Psychoanalytic Theory of Sexual, Political and Technological Liberation*. Princeton: Princeton University Press, 1982.

Banta, Martha. *Imaging American Women: Idea and Ideals in Cultural History*. New York: Columbia University Press, 1987.

Baron, Ava. "Questions of Gender: Deskilling and Demasculinization in the U.S. Printing Industry, 1830–1915." *Gender and History* 1 (Summer 1989): 178–99.

———. "Women and the Making of the American Working Class: A Study of the Proletarianization of Printers." *Review of Radical Political Economics* 14 (Fall 1982): 23–42.

Barrett, James R. "Unity and Fragmentation: Class, Race and Ethnicity on Chicago's East Side, 1900–1922." *Journal of Social History* 18 (Fall 1984): 37–55.

———. *Work and Community in the Jungle: Chicago's Packinghouse Workers, 1894–1922*. Urbana: University of Illinois Press, 1987.

Barrett, Michele. "Marxist-Feminism and the Work of Karl Marx." In *Feminism and Equality*, edited by Anne Phillips, pp. 44–61. Oxford: Basil Blackwell, 1987.

———. *Woman's Oppression Today: Problems in Marxist Feminist Analysis*. London: Verso Books, 1980.

Barrett, Michele, and Mary McIntosh. " 'The Family Wage': Some Problems for Socialists." *Capital and Class* 11 (1980): 51–73.

Beard, Mary R. *A Short History of the American Labor Movement*. New York: Macmillan, 1927.

Becker, Susan D. *The Origins of the Equal Rights Amendment: American Feminism Between the Wars*. Westport, Conn.: Greenwood Press, 1981.

Bell, Thomas. *Out of This Furnace*. 1941. Reprint. Pittsburgh: University of Pittsburgh Press, 1976.

Bender, Thomas. *Community and Social Change in America*. New Brunswick: Rutgers University Press, 1978.

Benenson, Harold. "The Community and Family Bases of U.S. Working Class Protest, 1880–1920: A Critique of the 'Skill Degradation' and 'Ecological' Perspectives." *Research in Social Movements, Conflict, and Change* 8 (1985): 109–32.

———. "Victorian Sexual Ideology and Marx's Theory of the Working Class." *International Labor and Working Class History* 25 (Spring 1984): 1–23.

Benhabib, Seyla, and Drucilla Cornell, eds. *Feminism as Critique: On the Politics of Gender*. Minneapolis: University of Minnesota Press, 1987.

Benson, Susan Porter. " 'The Clerking Sisterhood': Rationalization and the Work Culture of Saleswomen." *Radical America* 12 (March/April 1978): 41–55.

———. *Counter Cultures: Saleswomen, Managers and Customers in American Department Stores, 1890–1940*. Urbana: University of Illinois Press, 1986.

Bernstein, Barton J. "The New Deal: The Conservative Achievements of Liberal Reform." In *Towards a New Past: Dissenting Essays in American History*, edited by Barton J. Bernstein, pp. 263–88. New York: Pantheon Books, 1968.

Bernstein, Irving. *A Caring Society: A History of the American Worker, 1933–1941*.

Boston: Houghton Mifflin, 1986.

———. *The Lean Years: A History of the American Worker, 1919–1933*. Boston: Houghton Mifflin, 1960.

———. *The Turbulent Years: A History of the American Worker, 1933–1941*. Boston: Houghton Mifflin, 1970.

Bernstein, Michael A. *The Great Depression: Delayed Recovery and Economic Change in America, 1929–1939*. New York: Cambridge University Press, 1987.

Blackwelder, Julia Kirk. "Women in the Workforce: Atlanta, New Orleans and San Antonio 1930–1940." *Journal of Urban History* 4 (May 1978): 331–58.

———. *Women of the Depression: Caste and Culture in San Antonio, 1930–1940*. College Station, Tex.: Texas A & M University Press, 1984.

Blee, Kathleen. "The Impact of Family Settlement Patterns on the Politics of Lake Superior Communities, 1890–1920." Ph.D. dissertation, University of Wisconsin—Madison, 1982.

Blewett, Mary. *Men, Women and Work: Class, Gender and Protest in the New England Shoe Industry, 1780–1910*. Urbana: University of Illinois Press, 1988.

———. "The Union of Sex and Craft in the Haverhill Shoe Strike of 1895." *Labor History* 20 (Spring 1979): 352–75.

Bodnar, John E. *Immigration and Industrialization: Ethnicity in an American Mill Town, 1900–1940*. Pittsburgh: University of Pittsburgh Press, 1977.

———. "Immigration, Kinship and the Rise of Working Class Realism in Industrial America." *Journal of Social History* 14 (Fall 1980): 45–65.

———. *The Transplanted: A History of Immigrants in Urban America*. Bloomington: Indiana University Press, 1985.

———. *Workers' World: Kinship, Community and Protest in an Industrial Society, 1900–1940*. Baltimore: Johns Hopkins University Press, 1982.

Bolin, Winifred Wandersee. "The Economics of Middle-Income Family Life: Working Women during the Great Depression." *Journal of American History* 65 (June 1978): 60–74.

———. "Heating Up the Melting Pot: Settlement Work and Americanization in Northeast Minneapolis." *Minnesota History* 45 (Summer 1976): 58–74.

Braeman, John, Robert H. Bremner, and David Brody, eds. *The New Deal: The National Level*. Columbus: Ohio State University Press, 1975.

Brandes, Stuart. *American Welfare Capitalism, 1880–1940*. Chicago: University of Chicago Press, 1976.

Braverman, Harry. *Labor and Monopoly Capital: The Degradation of Work in the Twentieth Century*. New York: Monthly Review Press, 1974.

Brecher, Jeremy. *Strike!* San Francisco: Straight Arrow Press, 1972.

Brecher, Jeremy, Jerry Lombardi, and Jan Stackhouse, comps. *Brass Valley: The Story of Working People's Lives and Struggles in an American Industrial Region*. Philadelphia: Temple University Press, 1982.

Bridenthal, Renate, Atina Grossman, and Marion Kaplan, eds. *When Biology Be-*

came Destiny: Women in Weimar and Nazi Germany. New York: Monthly Review Press, 1984.

Bridges, Amy. *A City in the Republic: Antebellum New York and the Origins of Machine Politics.* Ithaca, N.Y.: Cornell University Press, 1987.

Briggs, Asa. "The Language of 'Class' in Early Nineteenth Century England." In *Essays in Labour History: In Memory of G. D. H. Cole,* edited by Asa Briggs and John Saville, pp. 43–73. London: Macmillan, 1968.

Brody, David. *Labor in Crisis: The Steel Strike of 1919.* Philadelphia: Lippincott, 1965.

———. *Workers in Industrial America: Essays on the Twentieth Century Struggle.* New York: Oxford University Press, 1980.

Buell, Carl J. *The Minnesota State Legislature of 1923.* St. Paul, 1923.

Buhle, Mari Jo. *Women and American Socialism, 1870–1920.* Urbana: University of Illinois Press, 1981.

Buhle, Paul. *Marxism in the United States: Remapping the History of the American Left.* London: Verso, 1986.

Burck, Jacob. *Hunger and Revolt: Cartoons by Burck.* New York: Daily Worker, 1935.

Burke, Kenneth. "Revolutionary Symbolism in America." In *American Writers' Congress,* edited by Henry Hart, pp. 87–94. New York: International Publishers, 1935.

Bush, Corlann Gee. " 'He Isn't So Cranky As He Used to Be': Agricultural Mechanization, Comparable Worth, and the Changing Farm Family." In *'To Toil the Livelong Day': America's Women at Work, 1780–1980,* edited by Carol Groneman and Mary Beth Norton, pp. 213–32. Ithaca, N.Y.: Cornell University Press, 1987.

Calhoun, Craig. "Community: Toward a Variable Reconceptualization for Comparative Research." *Social History* 5 (January 1980): 105–29.

———. *The Question of Class Struggle: Social Foundations of Popular Radicalism during the Industrial Revolution.* Chicago: University of Chicago Press, 1982.

Cameron, Ardis. "Bread and Roses Revisited: Women's Culture and Working Class Activism in the Lawrence Strike of 1912." In *Women, Work and Protest: A Century of U.S. Women's Labor History,* edited by Ruth Milkman, pp. 42–61. Boston: Routledge and Kegan Paul, 1985.

Campbell, D'Ann. *Women at War with America: Private Lives in a Patriotic Era.* Cambridge, Mass.: Harvard University Press, 1984.

Cantor, Milton, and Bruce Laurie, eds. *Class, Sex and the Woman Worker.* Westport, Conn.: Greenwood Press, 1977.

Carroll, Berenice, ed. *Liberating Women's History: Theoretical and Critical Essays.* Urbana: University of Illinois, 1976.

Carter, Patricia Anne. "Your Job or Your Marriage: Ultimatums for Cincinnati Women During the Great Depression." Paper presented at the annual meeting of the Social Science History Association, St. Louis, October 17, 1986.

Castells, Manuel. *The City and the Grassroots: A Cross-Cultural Theory of Urban Social Movements*. Berkeley: University of California Press, 1983.

_____. *The Urban Question: A Marxist Approach*. Translated by Alan Sheridan. Cambridge, Mass.: MIT Press, 1977.

Chafe, William. *The American Woman: Her Changing Social, Economic, and Political Role, 1920–1970*. New York: Oxford University Press, 1972.

Chrislock, Carl H. *The Progressive Era in Minnesota, 1899–1918*. St. Paul: Minnesota Historical Society Press, 1971.

Clive, Alan. "Women Workers in World War II: Michigan as a Test Case." *Labor History* 20 (Winter 1979): 44–72.

Coale, Ansley J., and Melvin Zelnik. *New Estimates of Fertility and Population in the United States*. Princeton: Princeton University Press, 1963.

Cobble, Dorothy Sue. " 'Practical Women': Waitress Unionists and the Controversies over Gender Roles in the Food Service Industry, 1900–1980." *Labor History* 29 (Winter 1988): 5–31.

_____. "Sisters in the Craft: Waitresses and their Unions in the Twentieth Century." Ph.D. dissertation, Stanford University, 1986.

Cohen, Lizabeth. "Encountering Mass Culture at the Grassroots: The Experience of Chicago Workers in the 1920s." *American Quarterly* 41 (March 1989): 6–33.

_____. "Learning to Live in the Welfare State: Industrial Workers in Chicago between the Wars, 1919–1939." Ph.D. dissertation, University of California at Berkeley, 1986.

Cohen, Miriam J. "From Workshop to Office: Italian Women and Family Strategies in New York City, 1900–1950." Ph.D. dissertation, University of Michigan, 1978.

Cohen, Ricki Carole Myers. "Fannia Cohn and the ILGWU." Ph.D. dissertation, University of Southern California, 1976.

Conk, Margo. "Accuracy, Efficiency, and Bias: The Interpretation of Women's Work in the U.S. Census of Occupations, 1890–1940." *Historical Methods* 14 (Spring 1981): 65–72.

_____. "Occupational Classification in the United States Census, 1870–1940." *Journal of Interdisciplinary History* 9 (Summer 1978): 111–30.

Conlin, Joseph, ed. *At the Point of Production: The Local History of the IWW*. Westport, Conn.: Greenwood Press, 1981.

Conner, Valerie Jean. "The Mothers of the Race in World War I: The National War Labor Board and Women in Industry." *Labor History* 21 (Winter 1979–1980): 31–54.

_____. *The National War Labor Board: Stability, Social Justice, and the Voluntary State in World War I*. Chapel Hill: University of North Carolina Press, 1983.

Conroy, Jack. *The Disinherited*. 1933. Reprint. New York: Hill and Wang, 1963.

Cooper, Patricia. *Once a Cigar-Maker: Men, Women and Work Culture in American Cigar Factories, 1900–1919*. Urbana: University of Illinois Press, 1987.

Corbin, David. *Life, Work and Rebellion in the Coal Fields: The Southern West Virginia Miners, 1880–1922*. Urbana: University of Illinois Press, 1981.

Cott, Nancy F. *The Grounding of Modern Feminism*. New Haven: Yale University Press, 1987.

Countryman, Edward. *A People in Revolution: The American Revolution and Political Society in New York, 1760–1790*. Baltimore: Johns Hopkins University Press, 1981.

Couvares, Frances G. "The Triumph of Commerce: Class Culture and Mass Culture in Pittsburgh." In *Working Class America: Essays on Labor, Community, and American Society*, edited by Michael Frisch and Daniel Walkowitz, pp. 123–52. Urbana: University of Illinois Press, 1982.

Cumbler, John T. *Working Class Community in Industrial America: Work, Leisure and Struggle in Two Industrial Cities, 1880–1930*. Westport, Conn.: Greenwood Press, 1979.

Dahlberg, Edward. *Bottom Dogs*. New York: Simon and Schuster, 1930.

Davis, Mike. *Prisoners of the American Dream: Politics and Economy in the History of the U.S. Working Class*. London: Verso, 1986.

————. "The Stop Watch and the Wooden Shoe: Scientific Management and the Industrial Workers of the World." *Radical America* 9 (January–February 1975): 69–95.

Dawley, Alan. *Class and Community: The Industrial Revolution in Lynn*. Cambridge, Mass.: Harvard University Press, 1976.

De Caux, Len. *Labor Radical: From the Wobblies to the CIO, a Personal History*. Boston: Beacon Press, 1970.

Deutsch, Sarah. *No Separate Refuge: Culture, Class, and Gender on an Anglo-Hispanic Frontier in the American Southwest, 1880–1940*. New York: Oxford University Press, 1987.

Dickinson, Jean Younger. *The Role of the Immigrant Woman in the U.S. Labor Force, 1890–1910*. New York: Arno Press, 1980.

Dixler, Elsa Jane. "The Woman Question: Women and the American Communist Party, 1929–1941." Ph.D. dissertation, Yale University, 1974.

Dobbs, Farrell. *Teamster Bureaucracy*. New York: Monad Press, 1977.

————. *Teamster Politics*. New York: Monad Press, 1975.

————. *Teamster Power*. New York: Monad Press, 1973.

————. *Teamster Rebellion*. New York: Monad Press, 1972.

Douglas, Paul. *Social Security in the United States*. New York: Whittlesey House, 1936.

Dublin, Thomas. "Rural-Urban Migrants in Industrial New England: The Case of Lynn, Massachusetts, in the Mid-Nineteenth Century." *Journal of American History* 73 (December 1986): 623–44.

————. *Women at Work: The Transformation of Work and Community in Lowell, Mass., 1826–1860.* New York: Columbia University Press, 1979.

Dubofsky, Melvyn. *We Shall Be All: A History of the IWW.* New York: Quadrangle Books, 1969.

Dye, Nancy Schrom. *As Equals and As Sisters: Feminism and Unionism in the Women's Trade Union League of New York.* Columbia: University of Missouri Press, 1979.

————. "Creating a Feminist Alliance: Sisterhood and Class Conflict in the New York Women's Trade Union League, 1903–1914." In *Class, Sex and the Woman Worker,* edited by Milton Cantor and Bruce Laurie, pp. 225–46. Westport, Conn.: Greenwood Press, 1977.

Easlea, Brian. *Science and Sexual Oppression: Patriarchy's Confrontation with Woman and Nature.* London: Weidenfeld and Nicolson, 1981.

Ebner, Michael. "The Passaic Strike of 1912 and the Two IWW's." *Labor History* 11 (Fall 1970): 452–66.

Elbert, Sarah. "Amber Waves of Grain: Women's Work in New York Farm Families." In *'To Toil the Livelong Day': America's Women at Work, 1780–1980,* edited by Carol Groneman and Mary Beth Norton, pp. 250–68. Ithaca, N.Y.: Cornell University Press, 1987.

Elder, Glen, Jr. *Children of the Great Depression: Social Change in Life Experience.* Chicago: University of Chicago Press, 1974.

Elmer, Manuel C. *A Study of Women in Clerical and Secretarial Work in Minneapolis, Minnesota.* Minneapolis: Women's Occupational Bureau, 1925.

Elshtain, Jean Bethke. "Antigone's Daughters." *Democracy* 2 (April 1982): 46–59.

Erenberg, Lewis A. *Steppin' Out: New York Nightlife and the Transformation of American Culture, 1890–1930.* Westport, Conn.: Greenwood Press, 1981.

Erickson, Hermann. "WPA Strike and Trials of 1939." *Minnesota History* 42 (Summer 1971): 202–14.

Evans, Sara M. *Personal Politics: The Roots of Women's Liberation in the Civil Rights Movement and the New Left.* New York: Knopf, 1979.

Evans, Sara M., and Harry Boyte. *Free Spaces: Sources of Democratic Social Change in America.* New York: Harper and Row, 1986.

Ewen, Elizabeth. *Immigrant Women in the Land of Dollars.* New York: Monthly Review Press, 1985.

Fantasia, Rick. *Cultures of Solidarity: Consciousness, Action, and Contemporary American Workers.* Berkeley: University of California Press, 1988.

Faue, Annamarie. " 'A Victory for One Is a Victory for All': A Case Study of Women's Participation in the Twin City Labor Union Campaigns of 1934–1936." Seminar paper, University of Minnesota, Spring 1981.

Faue, Elizabeth. "The 'Dynamo of Change': Gender and Solidarity in the American Labour Movement of the 1930s." *Gender and History* 1 (Summer 1989): 138–58.

———. "Paths of Unionization: Community, Bureaucracy and Gender in the Minneapolis Labor Movement of the 1930s." In *Work Engendered: Toward a New History of Men, Women and Work*, edited by Ava Baron. Ithaca, N.Y.: Cornell University Press, forthcoming in 1991.

———. "Women, Family and Politics: Farmer-Labor Women and Social Policy in the Great Depression." In *Women, Politics, and Change in Twentieth Century America*, edited by Louise Tilly and Pat Gurin, pp. 436–56. New York: Russell Sage, 1990.

———. "Women, Work and Community, Minneapolis, 1929–1946." Ph.D. dissertation, University of Minnesota, 1987.

———. "Women, Work and Protest in a Minneapolis Garment Factory, 1888." Paper presented at the annual meeting of the Social Science History Association, Bloomington, Ind., November 6, 1982.

Faue, Elizabeth, and Peter Rachleff, eds. *North Star Country Revisited: Essays in Regional Labor History*. St. Paul: Minnesota Historical Society Press, forthcoming.

Feldberg, Roslyn L. " 'Union Fever': Organizing among Clerical Workers, 1900–1930." *Radical America* 14 (May–June 1980): 53–67.

Filene, Peter. *Him/Her/Self: Sex Roles in Contemporary America*. 2d ed. Baltimore: Johns Hopkins University Press, 1986.

Filipelli, Ronald. "The United Electrical, Radio, and Machine Workers of America, 1933–1949: The Struggle for Control." Ph.D. dissertation, Pennsylvania State University, 1970.

Fine, Sidney. *Sitdown: The General Motors Strike of 1936–37*. Ann Arbor: University of Michigan Press, 1970.

Fink, Leon. "Looking Backward: Reflections on Working Class Culture and the Conceptual Dilemmas of the New Labor History." In *Perspectives in American Labor History: Towards a Synthesis*, edited by J. Carroll Moody and Alice Kessler-Harris, pp. 5–29. DeKalb, Ill: Northern Illinois University Press, 1989.

———. "The New Labor History and the Powers of Historical Pessimism: Consensus, Hegemony and the Case of the Knights of Labor." *Journal of American History* 75 (June 1988): 115–36.

———. *Workingmen's Democracy: The Knights of Labor in Local Politics, 1886–1896*. Urbana: University of Illinois Press, 1982.

Fitzgerald, Robert. *Art and Politics: Cartoonist of the Masses and the Liberator*. Westport, Conn.: Greenwood Press, 1973.

Flynn, Elizabeth Gurley. *The Rebel Girl: An Autobiography*. New York: International Publishers, 1955.

Foner, Eric. "Class, Ethnicity, and Radicalism in the Gilded Age: The Land League and Irish America." *Marxist Perspectives* 1 (Summer 1978): 6–55.

Foner, Philip. *Organized Labor and the Black Worker, 1619–1981*. 2d ed. New York: International Publishers, 1981.

———. *Women and the American Labor Movement*. 2 vols. New York: Free Press, 1979–80.

Foster, Mary Dillon. *Who's Who among Minnesota Women: A History of Woman's Work in Minnesota from Pioneer Days to Date*. St. Paul, 1923.

Frank, Dana. "Housewives, Socialists, and the Politics of Food: The 1917 New York Cost-of-Living Protests." *Feminist Studies* 11 (Summer 1985): 255–86.

———. " 'The Labor Woman Fights at the Point of Consumption': Gender, Consumer Organizing, and the Seattle Labor Movement, 1919–1928." Paper presented at the Seventh Berkshire Conference on Women's History, Wellesley College, Wellesley, Mass., June 21, 1987.

Fraser, Avronne, and Sue E. Holbert. "Women in the Minnesota Legislature." In *Women of Minnesota: Selected Biographical Essays*, edited by Barbara Stuhler and Gretchen Kreuter, pp. 247–79. St. Paul: Minnesota Historical Society Press, 1977.

Fraser, Steve. "From the 'New Unionism' to the New Deal." *Labor History* 25 (Summer 1984): 405–30.

———. "Industrial Democracy in the 1980s." *Socialist Review* 72 (November–December 1983): 99–122.

Fraser, Steve, and Gary Gerstle, eds. *The Rise and Fall of the New Deal Order*. Princeton: Princeton University Press, 1989.

Freedman, Estelle. "Separatism as Strategy: Female Institution Building and American Feminism, 1870–1930." *Feminist Studies* 5 (Fall 1979): 512–29.

Friedlander, Peter. *The Emergence of a UAW Local, 1936–1939: A Study in Class and Culture*. Pittsburgh: University of Pittsburgh Press, 1975.

Frisch, Michael, and Daniel Walkowitz, eds. *Working Class America: Essays on Labor, Community, and American Society*. Urbana: University of Illinois Press, 1982.

Fussell, Paul. *The Great War and Modern Memory*. New York: Oxford University Press, 1975.

———. *Wartime: Understanding and Behavior in the Second World War*. New York: Oxford University Press, 1989.

Gabaccia, Donna. "Neither Padrone Slaves nor Primitive Rebels: Sicilians on Two Continents." In *'Struggle a Hard Battle': Essays on Working Class Immigrants*, edited by Dirk Hoerder, pp. 95–120. DeKalb, Ill.: Northern Illinois University Press, 1986.

Gabin, Nancy. " 'They Have Placed a Penalty on Womanhood': The Protest Actions of Women Auto Workers in Detroit Area Locals, 1945–1947." *Feminist Studies* 8 (Summer 1982): 373–98.

———. "Women Workers and the U.A.W. in the Post World War II Period." *Labor History* 21 (Winter 1979–1980): 5–30.

Gabler, Edward. *The American Telegrapher: A Social History, 1860–1900*. New Brunswick, N.J.: Rutgers University Press, 1988.

Galenson, Walter. *The CIO Challenge to the AFL*. Cambridge, Mass.: Harvard University Press, 1960.

Geertz, Clifford. *The Interpretation of Culture: Selected Essays*. New York: Basic Books, 1973.

Gerstle, Gary. "The Mobilization of the Working Class Community: The Independent Textile Union in Woonsocket, 1931–1946." *Radical History Review* 17 (Spring 1978): 161–72.

———. "The Politics of Patriotism: Americanization and the Rise of the CIO." *Dissent* (Winter 1986): 84–92.

———. *Working-Class Americanism: The Politics of Labor in a Textile City, 1914– 1960*. Cambridge: Cambridge University Press, 1989.

Gieske, Millard. *Minnesota Farmer Laborism: The Third Party Alternative*. Minneapolis: University of Minnesota Press, 1979.

Gilbert, Sandra. "Soldier's Heart: Literary Men, Literary Women and the Great War." *Signs: A Journal of Women in Culture and Society* 8 (Spring 1983): 422– 50.

———. " 'This Is My Rifle, This Is My Gun': World War II and the Blitz on Women." In *Behind the Lines: Gender and the Two World Wars*, edited by Margaret Higonnet et al., pp. 227–59. New Haven: Yale University Press, 1987.

Gilbert, Sandra, and Susan Gubar. *No Man's Land: The Place of the Woman Writer in the Twentieth Century*. 2 vols. New Haven: Yale University Press, 1987–89.

Gjerde, Jon. *From Peasants to Bourgeoisie: The Migration from Balestrand, Norway, to the Upper Midwest*. Cambridge: Cambridge University Press, 1985.

Gluck, Sherna. *Rosie the Riveter Revisited: Women, the War and Social Change*. Boston: Twayne Publishers, 1987.

———, ed. *From Parlor to Prison: Five American Suffragists Talk about Their Lives*. New York: Vintage, 1976.

Göbel, Thomas. "Becoming American: Ethnic Workers and the Rise of the CIO." *Labor History* 29 (Spring 1988): 173–98.

Goldin, Claudia. "The Changing Economic Role of Women: A Quantitative Approach." *Journal of Interdisciplinary History* 13 (Spring 1983): 707–33.

———. "Female Labor Force Participation: The Origin of Black and White Differences, 1870 and 1880." *Journal of Economic History* 37 (March 1977): 87– 108.

———. *Understanding the Gender Gap: An Economic History of American Women*. New York: Oxford University Press, 1990.

———. "The Work and Wages of Single Women, 1870 to 1920." *Journal of Economic History* 40 (March 1980): 81–88.

Golin, Steve. "Defeat Becomes Disaster: The Paterson Strike of 1913 and the Decline of the IWW." *Labor History* 24 (Spring 1983): 223–48.

Gordon, Albert I. *Jews in Transition*. Minneapolis: University of Minnesota Press, 1949.

Gordon, David M., Richard Edwards, and Michael Reich. *Segmented Work, Divided Workers: The Historical Transformation of Labor in the United States.* Cambridge: Cambridge University Press, 1982.

Gordon, Linda. *Woman's Body, Woman's Right: A Social History of Birth Control in America.* New York: Grossman Publishers, 1976.

Gordon, Michael A. "The Labor Boycott in New York City, 1880–1886." *Labor History* 16 (Spring 1975): 185–229.

Gorn, Elliot. " 'Goodbye Boys, I Die a True American': Homicide, Nativism, and Working Class Culture in Antebellum New York." *Journal of American History* 74 (September 1987): 388–410.

Gould, Leslie, and Carol Hurd Green. "Mary Heaton Vorse." In *Notable American Women: The Modern Period,* edited by Edward T. James, Janet Wilson James, and Paul Boyer, pp. 712–14. Cambridge, Mass.: Harvard University Press, Belknap Press, 1980.

Granhus, Odd-Stein. "Scandinavian-American Socialist Newspapers with Emphasis on the Norwegian Contribution and E. L. Mengshoel's *Gaa Paa / Folkets Rost.*" In *Essays on the Scandinavian-North American Radical Press, 1880–1930,* edited by Dirk Hoerder, pp. 78–99. Bremen, W. Ger.: Labor Newspaper Preservation Project, University of Bremen, 1984.

Green, James R. *The World of the Worker: Labor in Twentieth Century America.* New York: Hill and Wang, 1980.

———, ed. *Workers' Struggles, Past and Present: A Radical America Reader.* Philadelphia: Temple University Press, 1983.

Greene, Victor. *The Slavic Community on Strike: Immigrant Labor in Pennsylvania Anthracite.* Notre Dame, Ind.: Notre Dame University Press, 1968.

Greenwald, Maurine Weiner. *Women, War and Work: The Impact of World War I on Women Workers in the United States.* Westport, Conn.: Greenwood Press, 1980.

Grob, Gerald. *Workers and Utopia: A Study in Ideological Conflict in the American Labor Movement, 1865–1900.* Evanston, Ill.: Northwestern University Press, 1961.

Groneman, Carol, and Mary Beth Norton, eds. *'To Toil the Livelong Day': America's Women at Work, 1780–1980.* Ithaca, N.Y.: Cornell University Press, 1987.

Gutman, Herbert. *Work, Culture, and Society in Industrializing America.* New York: Random House, 1976.

Hall, Jacquelyn Dowd. "Disorderly Women: Gender and Labor Militancy in the Appalachian South." *Journal of American History* 73 (September 1986): 354–82.

Hall, Jacquelyn Dowd, Robert Korstad, and James Leloudis. "Cotton Mill People: Work, Community and Protest in the Textile South, 1880–1940." *American Historical Review* 91 (April 1986): 245–86.

Hall, Jacquelyn Dowd, James Leloudis, Robert Korstad, Mary Murphy, Lu Ann Jones, and Christopher B. Daly. *Like a Family: The Making of the Cotton Mill World.* Chapel Hill: University of North Carolina Press, 1987.

Hanagan, Michael. "Proletarian Families and Social Protest: Production and Reproduction as Issues of Social Conflict in 19th Century France." In *Work in France: Representations, Meaning, Organization and Practice*, edited by Steven Laurence Kaplan and Cynthia J. Koepp, pp. 418–56. Ithaca, N.Y.: Cornell University Press, 1986.

Harding, Vincent. *There Is a River: The Black Struggle for Freedom in America*. New York: Vintage, 1981.

Hareven, Tamara. *Family Time, Industrial Time: The Relationship Between Family and Work in a New England Industrial Community*. Cambridge and New York: Cambridge University Press, 1982.

————, ed. *Transitions: The Family and the Life Course in Historical Perspective*. New York: Academic Press, 1978.

Harris, Abram L. *The Negro Population in Minneapolis; A Study in Race Relations*. Minneapolis: Urban League and Phillis Wheatley House, 1926.

Hartmann, Heidi. "Capitalism, Patriarchy and Job Segregation by Sex." *Signs: A Journal of Women in Culture and Society* 1, no. 3, pt. 2 (Spring 1976): 137–70.

Hartmann, Susan. *The Home Front and Beyond: American Women in the 1940s*. Boston: Twayne Publishers, 1982.

Hartsough, Mildred. *The Twin Cities as a Metropolitan Market*. Studies in Social Science, no. 8. Minneapolis: University of Minnesota Research Publications, 1925.

Hausen, Kärin. "The German Nation's Obligations to the Heroes' Widows of World War I." In *Behind the Lines: Gender and the Two World Wars*, edited by Margaret Higgonet et al., pp. 126–40. New Haven: Yale University Press, 1987.

Hawley, Ellis. *The Great War and the Search for a Modern Social Order: A History of the American People and Their Institutions*. New York: St. Martin's Press, 1979.

————. *The New Deal and the Problem of Monopoly*. Princeton: Princeton University Press, 1966.

Haydu, Jeffrey. *Between Craft and Class: Skilled Workers and Factory Politics in the United States and Britain, 1890–1922*. Berkeley: University of California Press, 1988.

Haynes, John. *Dubious Alliance: The Making of Minnesota's DFL Party*. Minneapolis: University of Minnesota Press, 1984.

Hearn, Jeff. *The Gender of Oppression: Men, Masculinity, and the Critique of Marxism*. New York: St. Martin's Press, 1988.

Helmbold, Lois R. "Beyond the Family Economy: Black and White Working Class Women during the Great Depression." *Feminist Studies* 13 (Fall 1987): 629–56.

————. "Downward Occupational Mobility during the Great Depression: Urban Black and White Working Women." *Labor History* 29 (Spring 1988): 135–72.

————. "Making Choices, Making Do: Black and White Working Class Women's Lives during the Great Depression." Ph.D. dissertation, Stanford University, 1982.

Henry, Alice. *Trade Union Woman*. New York: Appleton, 1915.

Herbst, Josephine. *Rope of Gold*. 1939. Reprint. Old Westbury, N.Y.: Feminist Press, 1983.

Hershberg, Theodore, ed. *Philadelphia: Work, Space, Family, and Group Experience in the Nineteenth Century*. New York: Oxford University Press, 1981.

Hess, Stephen, and Milton Kaplan. *The Ungentlemanly Art: A History of American Political Cartoons*. Rev. ed. New York: Macmillan, 1975.

Hewitt, Nancy. " 'The Voice of Virile Labor': Labor Militancy, Community Solidarity, and Gender Identity among Tampa's Latin Workers." In *Work Engendered: Toward a New History of Men, Women and Work*, edited by Ava Baron. Ithaca, N.Y.: Cornell University Press, forthcoming in 1991.

Hicks, Granville, Joseph North, Michael Gold, Paul Peters, Isador Schneider, and Alan Calmer, eds. *Proletarian Literature of the United States: An Anthology*. New York: International Publishers, 1935.

Higham, John. *Strangers in the Land: Patterns of American Nativism, 1860–1925*. New York: Atheneum, 1977.

Higonnet, Margaret Randolph, Jane Jenson, Sonya Michel, and Margaret Collins Weitz, eds. *Behind the Lines: Gender and the Two World Wars*. New Haven: Yale University Press, 1987.

Hills, Patricia. "John Sloan's Images of Working Class Women: A Case Study of the Roles and Interrelationships of Politics, Personality, and Patrons in the Development of Sloan's Art." *Prospects* 5 (1980): 157–96.

Hobsbawm, Eric. "Man and Woman in Socialist Iconography." *History Workshop Journal* 6 (Autumn 1978): 121–38.

Hodges, James A. *New Deal Labor Policy and the Southern Cotton Textile Industry, 1933–1941*. Knoxville: University of Tennessee Press, 1986.

Hoerder, Dirk, ed. *'Struggle a Hard Battle': Essays on Working Class Immigrants*. DeKalb, Ill.: Northern Illinois University Press, 1986.

Holmquist, June Denning, ed. *They Chose Minnesota: A Survey of the State's Ethnic Groups*. St. Paul: Minnesota Historical Society Press, 1981.

Honey, Maureen. *Creating Rosie the Riveter: Class, Gender and Propaganda During World War II*. Amherst: University of Massachusetts Press, 1984.

————. "The Working Class Woman and Recruitment Propaganda during World War II: Class Differences in the Portrayal of War Work." *Signs: A Journal of Women in Culture and Society* 8 (Summer 1983): 672–87.

Howard, Donald S. *The Works Progress Administration and Federal Relief Policy*. New York: Russell Sage, 1943.

Hunt, Lynn. *Politics, Culture and Class in the French Revolution*. Berkeley: University of California Press, 1984.

Hutchins, Grace. *Women Who Work*. New York: International Publishers, 1934.

Hyman, Colette. "Labor Organizing and Female Institution-Building: The Chicago Women's Trade Union League, 1904–1924." In *Women, Work and Protest: A Century of U.S. Women's Labor History*, edited by Ruth Milkman, pp. 22–41. Boston: Routledge and Kegan Paul, 1985.

———. "Political Theater, Popular Front Politics, and the Minneapolis Theater Union, 1935–1938." In *North Star Country Revisited: Essays in Regional Labor History*, edited by Elizabeth Faue and Peter Rachleff. St. Paul: Minnesota Historical Society Press, forthcoming.

Isserman, Maurice. *Which Side Were You On? The American Communist Party during World War II*. Middletown, Conn.: Wesleyan University Press, 1982.

Jacoby, Robin Miller. "The Women's Trade Union League and American Feminism." In *Class, Sex and the Woman Worker*, edited by Milton Cantor and Bruce Laurie, pp. 203–24. Westport, Conn.: Greenwood Press, 1977.

———. "The Women's Trade Union League School for Women Organizers, 1914–1926." In *Sisterhood and Solidarity: Workers' Education for Women, 1914–1984*, edited by Joyce Kornbluh and Mary Frederickson, pp. 3–35. Philadelphia: Temple University Press, 1984.

Jacoby, Sanford M. *Employing Bureaucracy: Managers, Unions and the Transformation of American Industry, 1900–1945*. New York: Columbia University Press, 1985.

Jameson, Elizabeth. "Imperfect Unions: Class and Gender in Cripple Creek, 1894–1904." In *Class, Sex and the Woman Worker*, edited by Milton Cantor and Bruce Laurie, pp. 166–202. Westport, Conn.: Greenwood Press, 1977.

Janiewski, Dolores. *Sisterhood Denied: Race, Gender, and Class in a New South Community*. Philadelphia: Temple University Press, 1985.

Jensen, Joan. "All the Pink Sisters: The War Department and the Feminist Movement of the 1920s." In *Decades of Discontent: The Women's Movement, 1920–1940*, edited by Lois Scharf and Joan Jensen, pp. 199–222. Westport, Conn.: Greenwood Press, 1983.

Jensen, Joan, and Sue Davidson, eds. *A Needle, a Bobbin, a Strike: Women Needleworkers in America*. Philadelphia: Temple University Press, 1984.

Jones, Gareth Stedman. *Languages of Class: Studies in English Working Class History, 1832–1982*. Cambridge: Cambridge University Press, 1982.

Jones, Jacquelyn. *Labor of Love, Labor of Sorrow: Black Women, Work and the Family*. New York: Basic Books, 1985.

Kaplan, Temma. "Female Consciousness and Collective Action: The Case of Barcelona, 1910–1918." *Signs: A Journal of Women in Culture and Society* 7 (Spring 1982): 545–66.

Karger, Howard Jacobs. "The Phillis Wheatley House: A History of the Minneapolis Black Settlement House, 1924 to 1940." *Phylon* 47 (December 1986): 79–90.

Katznelson, Ira. *City Trenches: Urban Politics and the Patterning of Class in the United States*. Chicago: University of Chicago Press, 1981.

Kazin, Michael. "A People Not a Class: Rethinking the Political Language of the

Modern U.S. Labor Movement." In *The Year Left*, edited by Mike Davis and Michael Sprinker, pp. 257–86. London: Verso, 1987.

Kealey, Gregory, and Bryan Palmer. *'Dreaming of What Might Be': The Knights of Labor in Ontario, 1880–1900*. Cambridge: Cambridge University Press, 1982.

Keen, Sam. *Faces of the Enemy: Reflections on the Hostile Imagination*. New York: Harper and Row, 1986.

Kempton, Murray. *Part of Our Time: Some Ruins and Monuments of the 1930s*. New York: Simon and Schuster, 1955.

Kenneally, James. *Women and American Trade Unions*. St. Albans, N.Y.: Eden Press Women's Publications, 1978.

Kent, Susan K. "The Politics of Sexual Difference: World War I and the Demise of British Feminism." *Journal of British Studies* 27 (July 1988): 232–53.

Kerber, Linda K. *Women of the Republic: Intellect and Ideology in Revolutionary America*. Chapel Hill: University of North Carolina Press, 1980.

Kessler-Harris, Alice. "The Debate Over Equality for Women in the Workplace: Recognizing Differences." *Women and Work, an Annual Review* 1 (1985): 141–61.

———. "Gender Ideology in Historical Reconstruction: A Case Study from the 1930s." *Gender and History* 1 (Spring 1989): 31–49.

———. *Out to Work: A History of Wage-Earning Women in the United States*. New York: Oxford University Press, 1982.

———. "Problems of Coalition-Building: Women and Trade Unions in the 1920s." In *Women, Work and Protest: A Century of U.S. Women's Labor History*, edited by Ruth Milkman, pp. 110–38. Boston: Routledge and Kegan Paul, 1985.

———. "Rose Schneiderman and the Limits of Trade Unionism." In *Labor Leaders in America*, edited by Melvyn Dubofsky and Warren Van Tine, pp. 160–84. Urbana: University of Illinois Press, 1987.

———. "Where Are the Organized Women Workers?" *Feminist Studies* 3 (Fall 1975): 92–110.

———. "Women, Work and the Social Order." In *Liberating Women's History: Theoretical and Critical Essays*, edited by Berenice Carroll, pp. 330–43. Urbana: University of Illinois, 1976.

Keyssar, Alexander. *Out of Work: The First Century of Unemployment in Massachusetts*. Cambridge and New York: Cambridge University Press, 1985.

King, Miriam, and Steven Ruggles. "American Immigration, Fertility, and Race Suicide at the Turn of the Century." *Journal of Interdisciplinary History* 20 (Winter 1990): 347–69.

Klehr, Harvey. *The Heyday of American Communism: The Depression Decade*. New York: Basic Books, 1984.

Klein, Philip. *The Burden of Unemployment: A Study of Unemployment Relief Measures in Fifteen American Cities, 1921–22*. New York: Russell Sage Foundation, 1923.

Kleinberg, Susan J. "Technology's Stepdaughters: The Impact of Industrialization upon Working Class Women, Pittsburgh, 1865–1890." Ph.D. dissertation, University of Pittsburgh, 1973.

Koch, Raymond L. "The Development of Public Welfare Relief Programs in Minnesota, 1929–1941." Ph.D. dissertation, University of Minnesota, 1967.

————. "Politics and Relief in Minneapolis during the 1930s." *Minnesota History* 41 (Winter 1968): 153–70.

Kocka, Jürgen. *White Collar Workers in the United States, 1890–1940: A Social-Political History in Comparative Perspective.* Beverly Hills: Sage Publications, 1980.

Komarovsky, Mirra. *The Unemployed Man and His Family: The Effect of Unemployment on the Status of the Man in 59 Families.* New York: Dryden Press for the Institute for Social Research, 1940.

Kornbluh, Joyce L., ed. *Rebel Voices: An IWW Anthology.* 2d ed. Chicago: Charles H. Kerr, 1988.

Kornbluh, Joyce L., and Mary Frederickson, eds. *Sisterhood and Solidarity: Workers' Education for Women, 1914–1984.* Philadelphia: Temple University Press, 1984.

Korth, Philip A., and Margaret R. Beegle. *'I Remember Like Today': The Auto-Lite Strike of 1934.* East Lansing: Michigan State University Press, 1988.

Krause, Paul. "Labor Republicanism and 'Za Chlebom': Anglo-Americans and Slavic Solidarity in Homestead." In *'Struggle a Hard Battle': Essays on Working Class Immigrants*, edited by Dirk Hoerder, 121–42. DeKalb, Ill.: Northern Illinois University Press, 1986.

Kwolek-Folland, Angel. "The Business of Gender: The Redefinition of Male and Female and the Modern Business Office in the United States, 1880–1930." Ph.D. dissertation, University of Minnesota, 1987.

Lamphere, Louise. "Fighting the Piece Rate System: New Dimensions of an Old Struggle in the Apparel Industry." In *Case Studies in the Labor Process*, edited by Andrew Zimbalist, pp. 257–76. New York: Monthly Review Press, 1979.

————. *From Working Mothers to Working Daughters: Immigrant Women in a New England Industrial Community.* Ithaca, N.Y.: Cornell University Press, 1987.

Landes, Joan. *Women and the Public Sphere in the Age of the French Revolution.* Ithaca, N.Y.: Cornell University Press, 1988.

Lane, A. T. *Solidarity or Survival? American Labor and European Immigrants, 1830–1924.* Westport, Conn.: Greenwood Press, 1986.

Langer, Elinor. *Josephine Herbst: The Story She Could Never Tell.* New York: Little, Brown, 1984.

Lasky, Marjorie Penn. " 'Where I Was a Person': The Ladies' Auxiliary in the 1934 Minneapolis Truckers Strike." In *Women, Work and Protest: A Century of U.S. Women's Labor History*, edited by Ruth Milkman, pp. 181–205. Boston: Routledge and Kegan Paul, 1985.

Laslett, Barbara. "Production, Reproduction and Social Change: The Family in Historical Perspective." In *The State of Sociology*, edited by Frank J. Short, pp. 239–58. Beverly Hills: Sage Publications, 1981.

Laurie, Bruce. *Artisans into Workers: Labor in Nineteenth Century America*. New York: Noonday Press, 1989.

Leab, Daniel J. " 'United We Eat': The Creation of the Unemployed Councils in 1930." *Labor History* 8 (Fall 1967): 300–315.

Lebergott, Stanley. "Labor Force, Employment and Unemployment, 1929–1939: Estimating Methods." *Monthly Labor Review* 67 (July 1948): 50–53.

Lebsock, Suzanne. *Free Women of Petersburg: Status and Culture in a Southern Town, 1784–1860*. New York: Norton, 1984.

Lee, Everett S., et al. *Methodological Considerations and Reference Tables*. Vol. 1 of *Population Redistribution and Economic Growth in the United States, 1870–1950*, prepared under the direction of Simon S. Kuznets and Dorothy Swaine Thomas. Philadelphia: American Philosophical Society, 1957–1964.

Leed, Eric. *No Man's Land: Combat and Identity in World War I*. Cambridge: Cambridge University Press, 1979.

Leidenberger, Georg. "Reformers and Revolutionists: The Socialist Party in Minnesota." Honors thesis in History, Macalester College, 1987.

Lerner, Elinor. "Family Structure, Occupational Patterns and Support for Women's Suffrage." In *Women in Culture and Politics: A Century of Change*, edited by Judith Friedlander, Blanche Wiesen Cook, Alice Kessler-Harris, and Carroll Smith-Rosenberg, pp. 223–36. Bloomington: Indiana University Press, 1986.

Le Sueur, Meridel. *Crusaders: The Radical Legacy of Marian and Arthur Le Sueur*. New York: Blue Heron Press, 1955.

―――. *The Girl*. Minneapolis: West End Press, 1978.

―――. *North Star Country*. 1946. Reprint. Lincoln: University of Nebraska Press, 1984.

―――. *Ripening: Selected Work, 1927–1980*. Edited with an Introduction by Elaine Hedges. Old Westbury, N.Y.: Feminist Press, 1982.

―――. *Salute to Spring*. New York: International Publishers, 1940.

―――. "Sequel to Love." 1935. Reprinted in *Writing Red: An Anthology of American Women Writers, 1930–1940*, edited by Charlotte Nekola and Paula Rabinowitz, pp. 36–38. New York: Feminist Press at CUNY, 1987.

Leuchtenburg, William E. *Franklin D. Roosevelt and the New Deal, 1932–1940*. New York: Harper and Row, 1963.

―――. "The New Deal and the Analogue of War." In *Change and Continuity in Twentieth Century America*, edited by John Braeman, Robert H. Bremner, and Everett Walters, pp. 81–144. Columbus: Ohio State University Press, 1964.

Levine, Susan. " 'Honor Each Noble Maid': Women Workers and the Yonkers Carpet Weavers' Strike of 1885." *New York History* 62 (April 1981): 152–76.

―――. *Labor's True Woman: Carpet Weavers and Labor Reform in the Gilded Age*. Philadelphia: Temple University Press, 1984.

―――. "Labor's True Woman: Domesticity and Equal Rights in the Knights of Labor." *Journal of American History* 70 (September 1983): 323–39.

Lichtenstein, Nelson. *Labor's War at Home: The CIO in World War II*. Cambridge and New York: Cambridge University Press, 1982.

Lichtman, Sheila Tropp. "Women at Work, 1941–1945: Wartime Employment in the San Francisco Bay Area." Ph.D. dissertation, University of California at Davis, 1981.

Lintelman, Joy. " 'More Freedom, Better Pay': Single Swedish Immigrant Women in America, 1880–1920." Ph.D. dissertation, University of Minnesota, 1991.

Lubove, Roy. *The Struggle for Social Security*. Cambridge: Harvard University Press, 1968.

Lynd, Alice, and Staughton Lynd, comps. *Rank and File: Personal Histories by Working Class Organizers*. Boston: Beacon Press, 1973.

Lynd, Robert S., and Helen Merrell Lynd. *Middletown: A Study in Contemporary American Culture*. New York: Harcourt, Brace, 1929.

————. *Middletown in Transition: A Study in Cultural Conflicts*. New York: Harcourt, Brace, 1937.

McKenney, Ruth. *Industrial Valley*. New York: Harcourt, Brace, 1939.

MacLean, Nancy. *'The Culture of Resistance': Female Institution-Building in the International Ladies' Garment Workers Union, 1905–1925*. Michigan Occasional Papers in Women's Studies, no. 21. Ann Arbor: University of Michigan, 1982.

Marchand, Roland. *Advertising the American Dream: Making Way for Modernity, 1920–1940*. Berkeley: University of California Press, 1985.

Mark-Lawson, Jane, Mike Savage, and Alan Warde. "Gender and Local Politics: Struggles over Welfare Policies, 1918–1939." In *Localities, Class, and Gender*, edited by Lancaster Regionalism Group, pp. 195–215. London: Pion Press, 1985.

Marling, Karal Ann. "A Note on New Deal Iconography: Futurology and the Historical Myth." *Prospects* 4 (1979): 421–41.

Martyna, Wendy. "What Does 'He' Mean? Use of the Generic Masculine." *Journal of Communication* 28 (Winter 1978): 131–38.

Mason, Karen M. "Feeling the Pinch: The Kalamazoo Corsetmakers' Strike of 1912." In *'To Toil the Livelong Day': America's Women at Work, 1780–1980*, edited by Carol Groneman and Mary Beth Norton, pp. 141–60. Ithaca, N.Y.: Cornell University Press, 1987.

Mason, Tim. "The Domestication of Female Socialist Icons: A Reply to Eric Hobsbawm." *History Workshop Journal* 7 (Spring 1979): 170–75.

————. "Women in Germany, 1925–1940: Family, Welfare and Work." *History Workshop Journal* 1 (Spring 1976): 74–113; (Autumn 1976): 5–32.

May, Elaine Tyler. *Great Expectations: Marriage and Divorce in Post-Victorian America*. Chicago: University of Chicago Press, 1980.

————. "The Pressure to Provide: Class, Consumerism, and Divorce in Urban America." In *The American Family in Social-Historical Perspective*, 3rd ed., edited by Michael Gordon, pp. 154–68. New York: St. Martin's Press, 1983.

May, Martha. "Bread before Roses: American Workingmen, Labor Unions, and the Family Wage." In *Women, Work and Protest: A Century of U.S. Women's Labor History*, edited by Ruth Milkman, pp. 1–21. Boston: Routledge and Kegan Paul, 1985.

Mayer, George H. *The Political Career of Floyd B. Olson*. Minneapolis: University of Minnesota Press, 1951.

Melosh, Barbara. "Peace on Demand: Anti-War Drama in the 1930s." *History Workshop Journal* 22 (Autumn 1986): 70–88.

Meyerowitz, Joanne J. *Women Adrift: Independent Wage Earners in Chicago, 1880–1930*. Chicago: University of Chicago Press, 1988.

Michels, Roberto. *Political Parties: A Sociological Study of the Oligarchical Tendencies of Modern Democracy*. New York: Free Press, 1962.

Milkman, Ruth. "American Women and Industrial Unionism during World War II." In *Behind the Lines: Gender and the Two World Wars*, edited by Margaret Higgonet et al., pp. 168–81. New Haven: Yale University Press, 1987.

———. "Female Factory Labor and Industrial Structure: Control and Conflict over 'Woman's Place' in Auto and Electrical Manufacturing." *Politics and Society* 12 (1983): 159–204.

———. *Gender at Work: The Dynamics of Job Segregation by Sex during World War II*. Urbana: University of Illinois Press, 1987.

———. "Organizing the Sexual Division of Labor: Historical Perspectives on Women's Work and the American Labor Movement." *Socialist Review* 49 (January–February 1980): 95–150.

———. "Redefining 'Women's Work': The Sexual Division of Labor in the Auto Industry during World War II." *Feminist Studies* 8 (Summer 1982): 359–72.

———. "Women's Work and the Economic Crisis: Some Lessons from the Great Depression." *Review of Radical Political Economics* 8 (Spring 1976): 73–97.

———, ed. *Women, Work and Protest: A Century of U.S. Women's Labor History*. Boston: Routledge and Kegan Paul, 1985.

Miller, Marc. "Working Women and World War II." *New England Quarterly* 53 (March 1980): 42–61.

Miller, Roberta Balstad. *City and Hinterland: A Case Study of Urban Growth and Regional Development*. Westport, Conn.: Greenwood Press, 1979.

Millikan, William. "Defenders of Business: The Minneapolis Civic and Commerce Association versus Labor during World War I." *Minnesota History* 50 (Spring 1986): 3–17.

———. "World War I in Minneapolis: An Ideological Battleground." In *North Star Country Revisited: Essays in Regional Labor History*, edited by Elizabeth Faue and Peter Rachleff. St. Paul: Minnesota Historical Society Press, forthcoming.

Mills, C. Wright. *The New Men of Power: America's Labor Leaders*. New York: Harcourt, Brace, 1948.

_____. *White Collar: The American Middle Class*. New York: Oxford University Press, 1951.

Milton, David. *The Politics of U.S. Labor from the Great Depression to the New Deal*. New York: Monthly Review Press, 1982.

Mink, Gwendolyn. *Old Labor and New Immigrants in American Political Development: Union, Party, and State, 1875–1920*. Ithaca, N.Y.: Cornell University Press, 1986.

Minnesota Federal Writers' Project. *Bohemian Flats*. Minneapolis: University of Minnesota Press, 1941.

_____. *Minneapolis: The Story of a City*. St. Paul: Works Progress Administration, 1940.

_____. *WPA Guide to Minnesota*. 1938. Reprint. St. Paul: Minnesota Historical Society, 1986.

Mitchell, Margaret. "The Effects of Unemployment on the Social Condition of Women and Children in the 1930s." *History Workshop* 19 (Spring 1985): 105–27.

Modell, John. "Changing Risks, Changing Adaptions: American Families in the Nineteenth and Twentieth Centuries." In *Kin and Communities: Families in America*, edited by Allen J. Lichtman and Joan R. Challenor, pp. 119–44. Washington, D.C.: Smithsonian Institution Press, 1979.

_____. "Mobility and Industrialization: Countryside and City in Nineteenth-Century Rhode Island." In *Essays from the Lowell Conference on Industrial History, 1980 and 1981*, edited by Robert Weible, Oliver Ford, and Paul Marion, pp. 86–109. Lowell: The Conference, 1981.

_____. "Patterns of Consumption, Acculturation, and Family Income Strategies in Late Nineteenth-Century America." In *Family and Population in Nineteenth-Century America*, edited by Tamara Hareven, pp. 206–40. Princeton: Princeton University Press, 1978.

_____. "Public Griefs and Personal Problems: An Empirical Inquiry into the Impact of the Great Depression." *Social Science History* 9 (Fall 1985): 399–428.

Modell, John, and Tamara K. Hareven. "Urbanization and the Malleable Household: An Examination of Boarding and Lodging in American Families." *Journal of Marriage and the Family* 35 (August 1973): 467–79.

Montgomery, David. *Beyond Equality: Labor and the Radical Republicans*. New York: Knopf, 1967.

_____. *The Fall of the House of Labor: The Workplace, the State and Labor Activism, 1865–1925*. Cambridge: Cambridge University Press, 1987.

_____. "The Farmer Labor Party." In *Working for Democracy: American Workers from the Revolution to the Present*, edited by Paul Buhle and Alan Dawley, pp. 73–82. Urbana: University of Illinois Press, 1985.

_____. *Workers' Control in America: Studies in the History of Work, Technology, and Labor Struggles*. Cambridge: Cambridge University Press, 1979.

Montgomery, David, and Ronald Schatz. "Facing Layoffs." In *Workers' Control in America*, by David Montgomery, pp. 139–52. Cambridge: Cambridge University Press, 1979.

Moody, J. Carroll, and Alice Kessler-Harris, eds. *Perspectives on American Labor History: Toward a Synthesis*. DeKalb, Ill.: Northern Illinois University Press, 1989.

Moody, Kim. *An Injury to All: The Decline of American Unionism*. London: Verso, 1988.

Morawska, Ewa. *For Bread with Butter: The Life Worlds of East Central Europeans in Johnstown, Pennsylvania, 1890–1940*. Cambridge: Cambridge University Press, 1985.

Munsingwear Corporation. *The Story of Munsingwear*. Minneapolis, 1964.

Murray, Robert K. *Red Scare: A Study in National Hysteria, 1919–1920*. Minneapolis: University of Minnesota Press, 1955.

Nash, Gerald D. "Franklin D. Roosevelt and Labor: The World War I Origins of Early New Deal Policy." *Labor History* 1 (Winter 1960): 39–52.

National Federation of Settlements and Neighborhood Centers. Unemployment Committee. *Case Studies of Unemployment*. Philadelphia: University of Pennsylvania Press, 1931.

Nekola, Charlotte, and Paula Rabinowitz, eds. *Writing Red: An Anthology of American Women Writers, 1930–1940*. New York: Feminist Press at CUNY, 1987.

Nelson, Barbara. "The Gender, Race, and Class Origins of Early Welfare Policy and the Welfare State: A Comparison of Workmen's Compensation and Mothers' Aid." In *Women, Politics, and Change in Twentieth Century America*, edited by Louise Tilly and Pat Gurin, pp. 413–35. New York: Russell Sage, 1990.

Nelson, Bruce. " 'Pentecost' on the Pacific: Maritime Workers and Working Class Consciousness in the 1930s." *Political Power and Social Theory* 4 (1984): 141–82.

————. "Unions and the Popular Front: The West Coast Waterfront in the 1930s." *International Labor and Working Class History* 30 (Fall 1986): 59–78.

————. *Workers on the Waterfront: Seamen, Longshoremen, and Unionism in the 1930s*. Urbana: University of Illinois Press, 1988.

Nelson, Daniel. "The CIO at Bay: Labor Militancy and Politics in Akron, 1936–1938." *Journal of American History* 71 (December 1984): 565–86.

————. "Origins of the Sit-Down Era: Worker Militancy and Innovation in the Rubber Industry, 1934–1938." *Labor History* 23 (Spring 1982): 198–225.

Nelson, Steve, James Barrett, and Rob Ruck. *Steve Nelson, American Radical*. Pittsburgh: University of Pittsburgh Press, 1981.

Nicholson, Linda J. *Gender and History: The Limits of Social Theory in the Age of the Family*. New York: Columbia University Press, 1986.

Nielsen, Kim E. "Who Were Those Farmer Radicals? The Douglas County Farm Holiday Association." *Minnesota History* 51 (Fall 1989): 270–80.

Nord, David Paul. "Minneapolis and the Pragmatic Socialism of Thomas Van Lear." *Minnesota History* 45 (Spring 1976): 2–10.

————. "Socialism in One City: A Political Study of Minneapolis in the Progressive Era." M.A. thesis, University of Minnesota, 1972.

Norrell, Robert J. "Caste in Steel: Jim Crow Careers in Birmingham, Alabama." *Journal of American History* 73 (December 1986): 669–94.

Norwood, Stephen H. *Labor's Flaming Youth: Telephone Operators' and Worker Militancy, 1878–1923*. Urbana: University of Illinois Press, 1990.

Odets, Clifford. *Three Plays: Awake and Sing, Waiting for Lefty, and Till the Day I Die*. New York: Random House, 1935.

Oestreicher, Richard J. *Solidarity and Fragmentation: Working People and Class Consciousness in Detroit, 1875–1900*. Urbana: University of Illinois Press, 1986.

————. "Urban Working Class Political Behavior and Theories of American Electoral Politics, 1870–1940." *Journal of American History* 74 (March 1988): 1257–86.

Olsen, Tillie (Lerner). "The Iron Throat." *Partisan Review* 1 (May–June 1934): 3–9.

————. "The Strike." *Partisan Review* 1 (September–October 1934): 3–9.

————. *Yonnondio from the Thirties*. New York: Dell, 1974.

O'Neill, William L., ed. *Echoes of Revolt: The Masses, 1911–1917*. Introduction by Irving Howe. Afterword by Max Eastman. Chicago: Quadrangle Books, 1966.

Oppenheimer, Valerie Kincaide. *The Female Labor Force in the United States*. Berkeley: Institute for International Studies, University of California, 1970.

Orloff, Ann Shola. "The Political Origins of America's Belated Welfare State." In *The Politics of Social Policy in the United States*, edited by Margaret Weir, Ann Shola Orloff, and Theda Skocpol, pp. 65–80. Princeton: Princeton University Press, 1988.

Pahl, Thomas L. "The G-String Conspiracy." *Labor History* 8 (Winter 1967): 30–51.

Painter, Nell Irvin. *The Narrative of Hosea Hudson: His Life as a Negro Communist in the South*. Cambridge: Cambridge University Press, 1977.

————. *Standing at Armageddon: The United States, 1877–1919*. New York: Norton, 1987.

Palmer, Bryan D. *Descent into Discourse: The Reification of Language and the Writing of Social History*. Philadelphia: Temple University Press, 1990.

Panofsky, Erwin. *Meaning in the Visual Arts*. New York: Doubleday, 1955.

Parkin, Frank. *Marxism and Class Theory: A Bourgeois Critique*. New York: Columbia University Press, 1979.

Pateman, Carole. "Feminist Critiques of the Public/Private Dichotomy." In *Feminism and Equality*, edited by Anne Phillips, pp. 103–26. Oxford: Basil Blackwell, 1987.

Patterson, James T. *The New Deal and the States: Federalism in Transition*. Princeton: Princeton University Press, 1969.

Peiss, Kathy. *Cheap Amusements: Working Women and Leisure in Turn-of-the-Century New York.* Philadelphia: Temple University Press, 1986.

Pells, Richard H. *Radical Visions and American Dreams: Culture and Social Thought in the Depression Years.* New York: Harper and Row, 1973.

People's Centennial Book Committee. *The People Together.* St. Paul, 1958.

Perrot, Michelle. "The New Eve and the Old Adam: French Women's Condition at the Turn of the Century." In *Behind the Lines: Gender and the Two World Wars,* edited by Margaret Higgonet et al., pp. 51–60. New Haven: Yale University Press, 1987.

Pesotta, Rose. 1944. Reprint. *Bread Upon the Waters.* Introduction by Ann Schofield. New York: ILR Press, 1987.

Philippe, Robert. *Political Graphics: Art as Weapon.* New York: Abbeville Press, 1981.

Piven, Frances Fox, and Richard Cloward. *Poor People's Movements: Why They Succeed, How They Fail.* New York: Vintage, 1977.

Pratt, Linda Ray. "Woman Writer in the CP: The Case of Meridel Le Sueur." *Women's Studies* 14 (1988): 247–64.

Preis, Art. *Labor's Giant Step.* New York: Pioneer Press, 1964.

Preston, William. *Aliens and Dissenters: Federal Suppression of Radicals, 1903–1933.* Cambridge, Mass.: Harvard University Press, 1963.

Prude, Jonathan. *The Coming of the Industrial Order: Town and Factory Life in Rural Massachusetts, 1810–1860.* Cambridge: Cambridge University Press, 1983.

Pruitt, Mary Christine. "'WOMEN UNITE!' The Modern Women's Movement in Minnesota." Ph.D. dissertation, University of Minnesota, 1988.

Qualey, Carlton C., and Jon A. Gjerde. "The Norwegians." In *They Chose Minnesota: A Survey of the State's Ethnic Groups,* edited by June Denning Holmquist, pp. 220–47. St. Paul: Minnesota Historical Society Press, 1981.

Quam, Lois, and Peter Rachleff. "Keeping Minneapolis an Open Shop Town: The Citizens' Alliance in the 1930s." *Minnesota History* 50 (Fall 1986): 105–17.

Quataert, Jean. "Women's Work and Worth: The Persistence of Stereotype Attitudes in the German Free Trade Unions, 1890–1929." In *The World of Women's Trade Unionism: Comparative Historical Essays,* edited by Norbert C. Soldon, pp. 93–124. Westport, Conn.: Greenwood Press, 1985.

Quick, Paddy. "Rosie the Riveter: Myths and Realities." *Radical America* 9 (July 1975): 115–31.

Quin, Mike. *The Big Strike.* 1949. Reprint. New York: International Publishers, 1979.

Rabinowitz, Paula. "Female Subjectivity in Women's Revolutionary Novels of the 1930s." Ph.D. dissertation, University of Michigan, 1986.

――――. "Maternity as History: Gender and the Transformation of Genre in *The Girl.*" *Contemporary Literature* 29 (Winter 1988): 538–48.

Rachleff, Peter J. *Black Labor in the South: Richmond, Virginia, 1865–1890.* Philadelphia: Temple University Press, 1984.

Radosh, Ronald. "A Radical Critique: The Myth of the New Deal." In *A New History of Leviathan: Essays on the Rise of the American Corporate State*, compiled by Ronald Radosh and Murray Rothbard, pp. 146–87. New York: Dutton, 1972.

Reid, Bill G. "John Baer, Non-Partisan League Cartoonist and Congressman." *North Dakota History* 44 (Winter 1977): 4–13.

Richardson, Ruth. " 'In the Posture of a Whore': A Reply to Eric Hobsbawm." *History Workshop Journal* 14 (Autumn 1982): 132–37.

Roediger, David, and Franklin Rosemont, eds. *Haymarket Scrapbook*. Chicago: Charles H. Kerr, 1986.

Rosemont, Franklin. "A Short Treatise on Wobbly Cartoons." In *Rebel Voices: An I.W.W. Anthology*, 2d ed., edited by Joyce L. Kornbluh, pp. 424–43. Chicago: Charles H. Kerr, 1988.

Rosenfelt, Deborah. "From the Thirties: Tillie Olsen and the Radical Tradition." *Feminist Studies* 7 (Fall 1981): 370–406.

Rosenhaft, Eve. *Beating the Fascists? The German Communist Party and Political Violence, 1929–1933*. Cambridge: Cambridge University Press, 1983.

Rosenzweig, Roy. *Eight Hours for What We Will: Workers and Leisure in an Industrial City, 1870–1920*. Cambridge and New York: Cambridge University Press, 1985.

Rosheim, David. *The Other Minneapolis, or the Rise and Fall of the Gateway, the Old Minneapolis Skid Row*. Maquoketa, Iowa: Andromeda Press, 1978.

Ross, Carl. "Labor Radicalism in the 1930s." Paper presented at the annual meeting of the Minnesota Historical Society, St. Paul, Minnesota, October 27, 1985.

Rotella, Elyce. *From Home to Office: U.S. Women at Work, 1870–1930*. Ann Arbor: University of Michigan Research Press, 1981.

Roth, Henry. *Call It Sleep*. New York: Robert O. Ballou, 1935.

Rubin, Lillian. *Worlds of Pain: Life in the Working Class Family*. New York: Basic Books, 1978.

Rubinstein, Annette T. "The Radical American Theatre of the Thirties." *Science and Society* 50 (Fall 1986): 300–320.

Rudé, George. *The Crowd in History, 1730–1848*. New York: Wiley, 1964.

Ruggles, Steven. *Prolonged Connections: The Rise of the Extended Family in the Nineteenth Century*. Madison: University of Wisconsin Press, 1987.

Rupp, Leila. *Mobilizing Women for War: German and American Propaganda*. Princeton: Princeton University Press, 1978.

Salerno, Salvatore. *Red November, Black November: Culture and Community in the Industrial Workers of the World*. Albany: SUNY Press, 1989.

Salzman, Jack, and Barry Wallenstein, eds. *Years of Protest*. New York: Pegasus, 1967.

Schacht, John N. *The Making of Telephone Unionism, 1920–1947*. New Brunswick, N.J.: Rutgers University Press, 1985.

———. "Toward Industrial Unionism: Bell Telephone Workers and Company Unions, 1919–1937." *Labor History* 16 (Winter 1975): 5–36.

Schafer, Robert. "The Educational Activities of the Garment Unions." Ph.D. dissertation, Teachers' College, 1951.

Scharf, Lois. *To Work and to Wed: Female Employment, Feminism, and the Great Depression.* Westport, Conn.: Greenwood Press, 1980.

Scharf, Lois, and Joan Jensen, eds. *Decades of Discontent: The Women's Movement, 1920–1940.* Westport, Conn.: Greenwood Press, 1983.

Schatz, Ronald W. *The Electrical Workers: A History of Labor at G.E. and Westinghouse, 1923–1960.* Urbana: University of Illinois Press, 1983.

Schleuning, Neala. *America, Song We Sang Without Knowing: The Life and Ideas of Meridel Le Sueur.* Mankato: Little Red Hen Press, 1983.

Schmid, Calvin. *Social Saga of Two Cities: An Ecological and Statistical Study of Social Trends in Minneapolis and St. Paul.* Minneapolis: Bureau of Social Research, 1938.

Schofield, Ann. "From 'Sealskin and Shoddy' to 'the Pig-headed Girl': Patriarchal Fables for Workers." In *'To Toil the Livelong Day': America's Women at Work, 1780–1980,* edited by Carol Groneman and Mary Beth Norton, pp. 112–24. Ithaca, N.Y.: Cornell University Press, 1987.

———. "Rebel Girls and Union Maids: The Woman Question in the Journals of the A.F.L. and I.W.W., 1905–1920." *Feminist Studies* 9 (Summer 1983): 335–58.

———. "The Rise of the Pig-Headed Girl: An Analysis of the American Labor Press for Their Attitudes toward Women." Ph.D. dissertation, SUNY— Binghampton, 1980.

Schwartz, Bonnie Fox. *The Civil Works Administration, 1933–1934: The Business of Emergency Employment in the New Deal.* Princeton: Princeton University Press, 1984.

Schweitzer, Mary M. "World War II and Female Labor Force Participation Rates." *Journal of Economic History* 40 (March 1980): 89–95.

Scimé, Joy A. "Section 213 of the 1932 Economy Act: Government Policy, Working Women, and Feminism." Paper presented at the annual meeting of the American Society for Legal History, Baltimore, 1983.

Scott, Joan Wallach. *Gender and the Politics of History.* New York: Columbia University Press, 1988.

———. "Men and Women in the Parisian Garment Trades: Discussions of Family and Work in the 1830s and 1840s." In *The Power of the Past: Essays for Eric Hobsbawm,* edited by Pat Thane, Geoffrey Crossick, and Roderick Floud, pp. 67–93. Cambridge: Cambridge University Press, 1983.

———. "On Language, Gender and Working Class History." *International Labor and Working Class History* 31 (Spring 1987): 1–13, 39–45.

Segner, Paul. *Minneapolis Unemployed: A Description and Analysis of the Resident Relief Population in the City of Minneapolis, 1900–1937*. 2 vols. Minneapolis: Works Progress Administration, 1937.

Seidman, Joel. "Democracy in Labor Unions." *Journal of Political Economy* 61 (June 1953): 220–31.

———. *The Needle Trades*. New York: Farrar and Rinehart, 1942.

Seller, Maxine Schwartz. "The Uprising of the 20,000: Sex, Class, and Ethnicity in the Shirtwaist Makers' Strike of 1909." In *'Struggle a Hard Battle': Essays on Working Class Immigrants*, edited by Dirk Hoerder, pp. 254–79. DeKalb, Ill.: Northern Illinois University Press, 1986.

Sewell, William H., Jr. "Visions of Labor: Illustrations of the Mechanical Arts before, in, and after Diderot's *Encyclopédie*." In *Work in France: Representations, Meaning, Organization and Practice*, edited by Steven Laurence Kaplan and Cynthia J. Koepp, pp. 258–86. Ithaca, N.Y.: Cornell University Press, 1986.

———. *Work and Revolution in France: The Language of Labor from the Old Regime to 1848*. Cambridge: Cambridge University Press, 1980.

Seymour, Helen. *When Clients Organize*. Chicago: Public Welfare Association, 1937.

Shaffer, Robert. "Women and the Communist Party, U.S.A., 1930–1940." *Socialist Review* 45 (May–June 1979): 73–118.

Shaver, Michelle J. "Roles and Images of Women in World War I Propaganda." *Politics and Society* 5 (1975): 469–89.

Shikes, Ralph E., and Steven Heller. "The Art of Satire: Painters as Caricaturists and Cartoonists from Delacroix to Picasso." *Print Review* 19, special issue (1984).

Shorter, Edward, and Charles Tilly. *Strikes in France, 1830–1968*. New York: Cambridge University Press, 1974.

Simirenko, Alex. *Pilgrims, Colonists, and Frontiersmen: An Ethnic Community in Transition*. New York: Free Press, 1964.

Skocpol, Theda. "Political Response to Capitalist Crisis: Neo-Marxist Theories of the State and the Case of the New Deal." *Politics and Society* 10 (1980): 155–201.

Skold, Karen Beck. "The Job He Left Behind: American Women in the Shipyards during World War II." In *Women, War and Revolution*, edited by Carol R. Berkin and Clara M. Lovett, pp. 55–76. New York: Holmes and Meier, 1980.

Slessinger, Tess. *The Unpossessed*. 1939. Reprint. Old Westbury, N.Y.: Feminist Press, 1984.

Smedley, Agnes. *Daughter of Earth*. New York: Coward-McCann, 1929.

Smith, Bonnie G. *Changing Lives: Women in European History Since 1700*. Lexington, Mass.: D. C. Heath, 1989.

Smith, Daniel Scott. "Historical Change in the Household Structure of the Elderly in Economically Developed Societies." In *Aging, Stability, and Change in the Family*, edited by Robert Fogel, Elaine Hatfield, Sara B. Kiesler, and Ethel Shanas, pp. 91–114. New York: Academic Press, 1979.

Smith, Judith E. *Family Connections: A History of Italian and Jewish Immigrant Lives*. Albany: SUNY Press, 1985.

———. "The 'New Woman' Knows How to Type: Some Connections between Sexual Ideology and Clerical Work, 1900–1930." Paper presented at the Berkshire Conference on Women's History, Smith College, 1974.

———. "The Transformation of Family and Community Culture in Immigrant Neighborhoods, 1900–1940." In *Labor History and the New England Working Class*, edited by Donald H. Bell and Herbert Gutman, pp. 159–84. Urbana: University of Illinois Press, 1986.

Sorenson, Helen. *The Consumer Movement: What It Is and What It Means*. New York: Harper and Row, 1941.

Srole, Carole. " 'A Position That God Has Not Particularly Assigned to Men': The Feminization of Clerical Work, Boston, 1860–1915." Ph.D. dissertation, University of California—Los Angeles, 1984.

Stansell, Christine. *City of Women: Sex and Class in New York, 1789–1860*. New York: Knopf, 1986.

———. "The Origins of the Sweatshop." In *Working Class America: Essays on Labor, Community, and American Society*, edited by Michael Frisch and Daniel Walkowitz, pp. 78–103. Urbana: University of Illinois Press, 1982.

———. "A Response to Joan Scott." *International Labor and Working Class History* 31 (Spring 1987): 24–29.

Starr, Karen. "Fighting for the Future: Farm Women of the Nonpartisan League." *Minnesota History* 48 (Summer 1983): 255–62.

Stipanovich, Joseph. *City of Lakes: An Illustrated History*. Woodland, Calif.: Winsor Publishing Co., 1982.

Straub, Eleanor F. "U.S. Government Policy toward Civilian Women during World War II." *Prologue* 5 (1973): 240–53.

Stricker, Frank. "Affluence for Whom? Another Look at the Affluent 1920s." *Labor History* 24 (Winter 1983): 5–33.

Strom, Sharon Hartman. "Challenging 'Woman's Place': Feminism, the Left and Industrial Unionism in the 1930s." *Feminist Studies* 9 (Summer 1983): 359–86.

———. "We're No Kitty Foyles: Organizing Office Workers for the Congress of Industrial Organizations, 1937–1950." In *Women, Work and Protest*, edited by Ruth Milkman, pp. 206–34. Boston: Routledge and Kegan Paul, 1985.

Strong, Anna Louise. *My Native Land*. New York: Viking, 1940.

Susman, Warren I. *Culture as History: The Transformation of American Society in the Twentieth Century*. New York: Pantheon Books, 1984.

Swados, Henry. *The American Writer and the Great Depression*. Indianapolis: Bobbs-Merrill, 1969.

Taeuber, Conrad, and Irene Taeuber. *The Changing Population of the United States*. New York: Wiley, 1958.

Tax, Meredith. *The Rising of the Women: Feminist Solidarity and Class Conflict, 1880–1917.* New York: Monthly Review Press, 1981.

Taylor, Barbara. *Eve and the New Jerusalem: Socialism and Feminism in the 19th Century.* New York: Pantheon Books, 1983.

————. " 'The Men Are as Bad as Their Masters': Socialism, Feminism, and Sexual Antagonism in the London Tailoring Trade in the 1830s." *Feminist Studies* 5 (Spring 1979): 27–40.

Taylor, Thomas. "The Transition to Adulthood in Comparative Perspective: Professional Men in Germany and the United States at the Turn of the Century." *Journal of Social History* 21 (Summer 1988): 635–58.

Tentler, Leslie. *Wage Earning Women: Industrial Work and Family Life in the United States, 1900–1930.* New York: Oxford University Press, 1978.

Therborn, Goran. *The Ideology of Power and the Power of Ideology.* New York: Schocken Books, 1980.

Theweleit, Klaus. *Male Fantasies.* 2 vols. Minneapolis: University of Minnesota Press, 1987–89.

Thompson, Edward P. "Eighteenth Century English Society: Class Struggle without Class?" *Social History* 3 (May 1978): 133–65.

————. *The Making of the English Working Class.* New York: Vintage, 1960.

————. "The Moral Economy of the English Crowd in the Eighteenth Century." *Past and Present* 50 (February 1971): 76–136.

Thorkelson, Nick. "Cartooning." *Radical America* 13 (March–April 1979): 27–52.

Thornthwaite, C. Warren. *Internal Migration in the United States.* Philadelphia: University of Pennsylvania Press, 1934.

Tickner, Lisa. *The Spectacle of Women: Imagery of the Women's Suffrage Campaign, 1907–1914.* Chicago: University of Chicago Press, 1988.

Tilly, Charles. *From Mobilization to Revolution.* Reading, Mass.: Addison-Wesley, 1978.

Tilly, Louise A. "The Food Riot as a Form of Political Conflict in France." *Journal of Interdisciplinary History* 2 (Summer 1971): 23–58.

————. "Paths of Proletarianization: Organization of Production, Sexual Division of Labor, and Women's Collective Action." *Signs: A Journal of Women in Culture and Society* 7 (Winter 1981): 400–417.

Tobias, Sheila, and Lisa Anderson. "What Really Happened to Rosie the Riveter: Demobilization and the Female Labor Force, 1944–1947." *MSS Modular Publications* module 9 (1974): 1–36.

Tomlins, Christopher L. "AFL Unions in the 1930s: Their Performance in Historical Perspective." *Journal of American History* 65 (March 1979): 1021–42.

————. *The State and the Unions: Labor Relations, Law and the Organized Labor Movement in America, 1880–1960.* New York: Cambridge University Press, 1985.

Traugott, Mark. "Reconceiving Social Movements." *Social Problems* 26 (1978): 38–49.

Trey, Joan E. "Women in the War Economy—World War II." *Review of Radical Political Economics* 4 (Spring 1972): 40–57.

Trolander, Judith. *The Settlement House during the Great Depression*. Detroit: Wayne State University Press, 1975.

Tselos, George. "The Labor Movement in Minneapolis in the 1930s." Ph.D. dissertation, University of Minnesota, 1970.

————. "Self-Help and Sauerkraut: The Organized Unemployed, Inc., of Minneapolis." *Minnesota History* 45 (Winter 1977): 306–20.

Turbin, Carole. "And We Are Nothing But Women: Irish Working Women in Troy." In *Women of America: A History*, edited by Carol Berkin and Mary Beth Norton, pp. 202–22. Boston: Houghton Mifflin, 1979.

————. "Reconceptualizing Family, Work and Labor Organizing in Troy, 1860–1890." *Review of Radical Political Economics* 16 (Spring 1984): 1–16.

Turner, Victor. *Dramas, Fields and Metaphors: Symbolic Action in Human Society*. Ithaca, N.Y.: Cornell University Press, 1974.

Ulman, Lloyd. *The Rise of the National Union*. Cambridge, Mass.: Harvard University Press, 1955.

Urgo, Joseph R. "Proletarian Literature and Feminism: The Gastonia Novels and Feminist Protest." *Minnesota Review* n.s. 24 (Spring 1985): 64–84.

Vaile, Roland. *The Impact of the Depression upon Business Activity and Real Income in Minnesota*. University of Minnesota Studies in Economics and Business, no. 8. Minneapolis: University of Minnesota Press, 1933.

Valelly, Richard Martin. *Radicalism in the States: Minnesota's Farmer Labor Party and the American Political Economy*. Chicago: University of Chicago Press, 1989.

————. "State-Level Radicalism and the Nationalization of American Politics: The Case of the Minnesota Farmer Labor Party." Ph.D. dissertation, Harvard University, 1984.

Valesh, Eva. "Wage Working Women." *American Federationist* 13 (December 1906): 463–67.

————. "Women and Labor." *American Federationist* 2 (February 1896): 221–23.

Verba, Sidney, and Kay L. Schlozman. "Unemployment, Class Consciousness and Radical Politics: What Didn't Happen in the 1930s." *Journal of Politics* 39 (1977): 291–323.

Vittoz, Stanley. *New Deal Labor Policy and the American Industrial Economy*. Chapel Hill: University of North Carolina Press, 1986.

Von Blum, Paul. *The Critical Vision: A History of Social and Political Art in the U.S.* Boston: South End Press, 1982.

Vorse, Mary Heaton. *Footnote to Folly: Reminiscences of Mary Heaton Vorse*. New York: Farrar and Rinehart, 1935.

————. *Labor's New Millions*. New York: Modern Age Books, 1938.

————. *Rebel Pen: Selected Writings*. Edited by Dee Garrison. Old Westbury, N.Y.:

Feminist Press, 1985.

Walker, Charles Rumford. *American City: A Rank and File History*. New York: Farrar and Rinehart, 1937.

Walkowitz, Daniel J. " 'Fudge Alone Does Not Work!': Work, Gender and the Mystification of Professional Workers—Social Workers at Work in the 1920s." Paper presented at the annual meeting of the American Historical Association, Washington, D.C., December 29, 1987.

_____. *Worker City, Company Town: Iron and Cotton Workers Protest in Cohoes, New York, 1855–1885*. Urbana: University of Illinois Press, 1978.

_____. "Working Class Women in the Gilded Age: Factory, Community and Family Life among Cohoes, N.Y., Cotton Workers." *Journal of Social History* 5 (Summer 1972): 464–90.

Wandersee, Winifred. *Women's Work and Family Values, 1920–1940*. Cambridge, Mass.: Harvard University Press, 1980.

Ware, Norman. *The Labor Movement in the United States, 1860–1895*. New York: Appleton, 1929.

Ware, Susan. *Beyond Suffrage: Women in the New Deal*. Cambridge, Mass.: Harvard University Press, 1981.

_____. *Holding Their Own: American Women in the 1930s*. Boston: Twayne Publishers, 1982.

Warner, Marina. *Monuments and Maidens: The Allegory of the Female Form*. New York: Atheneum, 1985.

Warner, Sam Bass. *The Private City: Philadelphia in Three Periods of Its Growth*. Philadelphia: University of Pennsylvania Press, 1968.

_____. *Streetcar Suburbs: The Process of Growth in Boston, 1870–1900*. Cambridge, Mass.: Harvard University Press, 1962.

Weber, Adna Ferrin. *The Growth of Cities: A Study in Statistics*. New York: Macmillan, 1899.

Weiner, Lynn. *From Working Girl to Working Mother: The Female Labor Force in the United States, 1820–1980*. Chapel Hill: University of North Carolina Press, 1985.

_____. "Our Sisters' Keepers: The Minneapolis Woman's Christian Association and Housing for Working Women." *Minnesota History* 46 (Summer 1979): 189–200.

Weinstein, James M. *The Decline of Socialism in America, 1912–1925*. New York: Monthly Review Press, 1967.

Weir, Margaret, Ann Shola Orloff, and Theda Skocpol, eds. *The Politics of Social Policy in the United States*. Princeton: Princeton University Press, 1988.

Wellman, Barry, and Barry Leighton. "Networks, Neighborhoods, and Communities: Approaches to the Study of the Community Question." *Urban Affairs Quarterly* 14 (March 1979): 363–90.

Westwood, Sallie. *All Day, Every Day: Factory and Family in the Making of Women's*

Lives. Urbana: University of Illinois Press, 1985.

White, Hayden. *Tropics of Discourse: Essays in Cultural Criticism*. Baltimore: Johns Hopkins University Press, 1978.

Wilentz, Sean. "Against Exceptionalism: Class Consciousness and the American Labor Movement, 1780–1920." *International Labor and Working Class History* 26 (Fall 1984): 1–24.

————. *Chants Democratic: New York City and the Rise of the American Working Class*. New York: Oxford University Press, 1984.

Williams, Raymond. *Marxism and Literature*. New York: Oxford University Press, 1977.

Willis, Paul. "Shop Floor Culture, Masculinity and the Wage Form." In *Working Class Culture: Studies in History and Theory*, edited by John Clarke, Chas Crichter, and Richard Johnson, pp. 185–98. New York: St. Martin's Press, 1979.

Wong, Susan. "From Soul to Strawberries: The ILGWU and Workers' Education, 1914–1980." In *Sisterhood and Solidarity: Workers' Education for Women, 1914–1984*, edited by Joyce L. Kornbluh and Mary Frederickson, pp. 38–74. Philadelphia: Temple University Press, 1984.

Wright, Erik Olin. *Class Structure and Income Determination*. New York: Academic Press, 1979.

————. "Women in the Class Structure." *Politics and Society* 17 (March 1989): 35–66.

Yans-McLoughlin, Virginia. *Family and Community: Italian Immigrants in Buffalo, 1880–1930*. Urbana: University of Illinois Press, 1978.

Young, Art. *The Best of Art Young*. New York: Vanguard Press, 1936.

Youngdale, James. *Populism: A Psychohistorical Approach*. Port Washington, N.Y.: Kennikat Press, 1975.

Zelizer, Viviana A. *Pricing the Priceless Child: The Changing Social Value of Children*. New York: Basic Books, 1985.

Zieger, Robert H. "The Limits of Militancy." *Journal of American History* 63 (December 1976): 646–56.

Zimmerman, Carle C. "The Migration to Towns and Cities." *American Journal of Sociology* 32 (November 1926): 450–55.

Zugsmith, Leane. *A Time to Remember*. New York: Random House, 1936.

Zurier, Rebecca. *Art for the Masses: A Radical Magazine and its Graphics*. Philadelphia: Temple University Press, 1988.

Index

ACW. *See* Amalgamated Clothing
  Workers
AFL. *See* American Federation of
  Labor
Aid for Dependent Children (ADC),
  133–34, 147, 149, 154–55, 160,
  162
Amalgamated Clothing Workers, 106,
  128–29
American City, 1–2
American Federation of Full-Fash-
  ioned Hosiery Workers, 117, 120–
  21. *See also* Strutwear Company
American Federation of Labor (AFL),
  9–10, 12, 51, 95, 127, 143–45,
  176–77, 182–86; rivalry with CIO,
  127–31, 143–45
Anti-Semitism, 127, 158–59, 246
  (n. 30)
Artisans, 4–6, 15; artisanal republi-
  canism, 93–94
Asunma, Sigrid, 147, 162–64

Beard, Mary, xiv
Being outside, fetish of, 1, 20
Belor, John, 79–82
Belton, Marguerite, 25, 104–6, 108
Blacks (African Americans), 30, 32,
  143, 162, 171–74; migration, 7, 30;
  women, 28–30; female labor force
  participation, 33–34, 196, 199
Bloody Friday (July 21, 1934), 73, 79–
  82. *See also* Truckers' strike of 1934
Boston Tea Party, 75

Boulevard Frocks, 128–30
Boycotts, 6, 9, 12, 55–56, 127–28
Broms, Claire Strong, 123
Brontë, Charlotte, xv
Buccaneers, xviii
Bureaucratic unions, 4, 12–15, 126–
  31, 137–41, 145–46; and women,
  145–46

Cain, Myrtle, 47, 53, 56–57, 66–68,
  111–13
Capital, xiii–xiv, 127, 189–93; indus-
  trial capitalism, 5–6; depictions of,
  74–76, 82–83
Central Labor Union of Minneapolis,
  123, 148, 150, 177
Chicago, Illinois, 27, 42, 131
Child Protective Association, 115
Children, 2–3, 41, 75–76, 83–91,
  115–16
CIO. *See* Congress of International
  Organizations
CIO News, 75
Citizens' Alliance of Minneapolis, 55–
  56, 64, 72–73, 119–20, 130, 180,
  189; depictions of, 74–76, 82–83
City, great mysteries of, 61
Civil Works Administration, 153
Class, social theories of, 15–18, 98–
  99. *See also* Solidarity
Clerical workers, 8, 22, 27–28, 38–40,
  53–54, 123–24. *See also* Stenogra-
  phers, Bookkeepers, and Tax Ac-
  countants local 17661

Communist party, 19, 55, 64–66, 115, 119–20, 142, 247 (n. 32)

Community, 8–9, 30–32, 208–9 (n. 60)

Community-based unionism, xiii, 1–7, 11–18, 48–50, 69–71, 101, 126–31, 168–69; definition of, 4

Congress of Industrial Organizations (CIO), 12, 44, 75, 127, 130–31, 139–41, 144–45, 176, 180–82, 188. *See also* Amalgamated Clothing Workers; Textile Workers union; United Electrical, Radio and Machine Workers of America

Consumerism, 182–86, 247–48 (nn. 37, 39)

Consumption, politics of, 5, 54–55, 83–84, 88, 113–14, 227 (n. 40), 246 (n. 30). *See also* Boycotts

Davis, Tom, 162–64

De Caux, Len, 75, 221 (n. 18)

Detroit, Michigan, 19, 58, 114, 217 (n. 51)

Divorce, 21, 41

Dobbs, Farrell, 74, 115

Dubinsky, David, 106, 107, 129, 131

DuFour, Loretta, 104, 108, 128, 137

Duluth, Minnesota, 112, 157–58

Dunne, Miles, 142

Dunne, Vincent, 72

Dynamite, bricks of patent, 63

Dynamo of change, 69, 72–73

Economic crisis, 58–63, 104, 136–38, 161. *See also* Great Depression

Economic system: diseases of, 58

Emergency Relief Administration, 153

Equal pay, 177, 186–87

Ethnicity, 20, 50–51, 64–65, 119–122; ethnic division, 6–8, 28–29, 50

Exclusion, 9, 14

Fagerhaugh, Peter, 117, 229 (n. 65)

Family: as symbol, 14, 45–46, 83–92, 97–99; economy, 5, 12, 41–45, 60–61; wage, 9–10, 13–14, 53

Farmer-Labor movement, 12, 19–20, 48, 58, 67–68, 71, 123–25, 190–91; ideology, 89–90, 98. *See also* Hennepin County Farmer-Labor Women's Club

Farmer-Labor party, 55–57, 101, 110–16, 141–42, 148–54, 166–67, 190–91

Farm Holiday Association, 113–14, 120

Fate, Gods of, 82

Federal Emergency Relief Administration (FERA), 111

Federal Workers Section (FWS) of General Drivers' local 574, 115–16, 132–34, 147, 155, 161–64. *See also* Sewing project; WPA strike

Female labor force, 8, 32–34, 36–38, 169–74, 199–201, 212 (nn. 34, 36, 40, 41), 213 (n. 54), 249 (n. 51)

Fertility, 32–34, 41–42

Finkelstein, Michael, 130, 135

Flaherty, Jewell, 123, 142, 144

"Forgotten man," 98

"Forgotten woman," 13–14, 61–62, 218 (n. 70)

Frankenstein, 74, 221 (n. 18)

Franklin Cooperative Creamery, 56, 123

Fraternal organizations, 7, 113

Funerals, mass, 18, 73, 80–81, 119, 169

FWS. *See* Federal Workers Section of General Drivers' local 574

Garment industry, 23, 124–35, 151–52, 171–72; strikes, 56, 116–22; workers, 101–4. *See also* Amalga-

mated Clothing Workers; International Ladies Garment Workers' Union; Munsingwear Company; Sewing project; Strutwear Company
Gateway District, 23, 40–41, 60–61. *See also* Truckers' strike of 1934
Geldman, Max, 158, 160–61
General Drivers' local 574/544, 19, 66, 69–78, 100–101, 121, 127–29, 142–44
Genis, Sander, 106–7, 126, 128–31
Glotzbach, Linus, 157, 161
Grant, Ulysses S., 74–75
Great Depression, 38–46, 58–63, 189–93; images of, 90. *See also* Economic crisis

Hagiography, 78–83
Harris, Myrtle, 106–7, 120, 125, 142, 161
Hawkins, Oscar, 100, 118–19
Hennepin County Farmer-Labor Women's Club, 112–13, 120, 136, 149–50
Holmes, Clara (Dunne), 72, 115
Honeywell Regulator Company, 169, 176, 179, 188, 248 (n. 40); organization of, 180–87
Hotel and Restaurant Workers Miscellaneous Workers' local 665, 120–21
Household Helpers' Union, 54
Households, female-headed, 41–42, 135–36
Housewives' Union, 123
Huber, Florence Strong, 123–24, 141–42, 226–27 (n. 31)

Ideology, 6–10, 12–14, 16, 19, 69–99, 101. *See also* Masculinity: cult of; Representations
ILGWU. *See* International Ladies Garment Workers' Union

Immigrants, 7, 10–11, 28–29, 50, 197; women's labor force participation, 33–34; unemployment, 60
Industrial Workers of the World (IWW), 10–11, 51–52, 94–95, 206–7 (n. 40)
International Association of Machinists (IAM), 127
International Ladies Garment Workers' Union (ILGWU), 86–97, 101–16, 123, 126–31, 135, 137–39, 151; education, 109–10, 137–39; Twin Cities Joint Board, 109–10, 139
IWW. *See* Industrial Workers of the World

Jane Eyre, xv
Johnson, Violet, 144, 226–27 (n. 31), 230 (n. 80)
Justice (ILGWU), 96–97

Kessler-Harris, Alice, xiv, 235 (n. 54), 235–36 (n. 63)
Knights of Labor, 6–9
Knutson, Evelyn, 181–82
Kohn, Minnie, 147–48, 158, 162–64

Labor history, xiii, 15–16
Labor movement: decline, xiii, 191–93; male dominance, xiv, 6, 7, 14, 16, 39, 67, 139, 175; and women, 1, 4–10, 12–13, 47–53, 69–99, 108–10, 166–69, 182–88, 190–93, 249 (n. 51); competition between sexes in, 8, 14, 140. *See also* Women's auxiliaries
Labor union membership, 51–52, 175
Lawrence, Massachusetts, 3, 11, 94, 217 (n. 51), 220 (n. 3)
Le Sueur, Marian, 57, 69, 89–90, 111–14, 120, 124–25, 226–27 (n. 31)

Le Sueur, Meridel, xiv, xx, 1, 20, 21, 23, 38, 45–46, 61–62, 64–65, 124–25, 226 (n. 23)
Life and Labor, 10
Life course, 32–41, 53; work as part of, 36–38
Lowell, Massachusetts, 6, 217 (n. 51)
Lundeen, Ernest, 149

Mahoney, William, 56
Making of the English Working Class, The, 15–16
Marriage, 32–34, 41, 211 (nn. 31, 32, 33)
Married women, 33–34, 42–45, 148–51, 201
Masculinity: cult of, 83; social construction of, 73–76, 82–83, 93–97, 218 (n. 70); crisis of, 166, 191, 250 (n. 4)
Maternalism, 80, 83–89
Mauseth, William, 181
Mayville, Harry, 181
Memory, 67–68, 69, 71, 97–99, 165–67
Migration, 21, 23–28, 32, 198, 209 (n. 5), 209–10 (n. 10), 210 (n. 12); black migration, 7, 30; as obstacle to solidarity, 8–9
Milwaukee, Wisconsin, 117
Minimum wage law, 54, 151–52
Minneapolis, Minnesota: exceptionalism, 18–20, 22; migration to, 23–28; demography, 28–30, 195–97; neighborhoods, 28–32; labor community before World War I, 50–53; impact of the depression on, 58–63; World War II, 169–74
Minneapolis Theater Union, 115–16, 125
Minneapolis Trades and Labor Assembly, 52, 54
Minnesota: Iron Range, 11, 51; regional economy, 23–28, 39–41, 51, 134–36
Minnesota Commission of Public Safety (World War I), 52
Moline Company, 170, 179
Montgomery, David, xiii, 16
Munsingwear Company (Northwest Knitting), 28, 130–31, 152, 171, 172

National Labor Relations Board (NLRB), 12–13, 126, 181–82, 186, 189
National Recovery Administration (NRA), 104–7, 117–18, 128, 130
National War Production Board, 177
National Woman's party, 53, 67
Native Americans, 61, 126
Nativism, 3, 6–8, 28–29, 50
Ness, Henry, 2, 73, 78–81
New Deal, 13–14, 113, 148, 166–67, 189–92
New York City, 6, 101, 114
Non-Partisan League, 47, 51, 55–56, 111
Nonunion workers, 75–76
Northeast Settlement House, 30, 49, 60–61, 142–43
Northwest Organizer, 73, 118, 161
"NRA babies," 101, 138. *See also* National Recovery Administration

Office workers. *See* Clerical workers
Olson, Floyd B. (governor), 111, 148
Open shop, 3, 12, 79

Palmer raids, 12
Patriotism, 49–50, 169, 182–87
Perlstein, Meyer, 129–31, 138
Persistence, bull-headed, 75
Philadelphia, Pennsylvania, 6, 7, 42, 101
Piecework, 104, 138

Politics, 108–16, 119–20, 124–25, 132–36, 152–57, 165–67; and the state, 73, 148–54. *See also* Farmer-Labor movement; Hennepin County Farmer-Labor Women's Club; Social reproduction; State, the; Women's League against the High Cost of Living

Popular Front, 14, 18, 83–85, 89–90, 111, 141, 154, 222–23 (n. 45)

Prosperity, illusion of, 58

Prostitute press, 74, 78

Prostitution, 21, 24, 90, 92, 136

Protective legislation, 151–52

Public-private dichotomy, 15–16, 204–5 (n. 16)

Racism, xv, 3–4, 7, 9, 171–74

Ramsey County Welfare Board, 135–36

Relief, 59–60, 63–66, 72–73; politics of, 110–16, 119–20, 132–36, 152–57, 165–67. *See also* Works Progress Administration; WPA strike

Representations: labor, 11, 14, 19, 65, 69–99, 115–16, 153; republican womanhood, 14, 83–85, 93–94; male, 73–76, 82–83, 93–97; women workers, 76–78; female, 83–99, 156, 158, 162–64, 166–67, 214 (n. 59), 222–23 (n. 45), 247 (n. 37)

Republican ideology, 17, 86–88, 93–94, 178, 205 (n. 19)

Roosevelt recession (1937), 134–36

Rosie the Riveter, 174–76, 186–87

St. Paul, Minnesota, 105–6, 112, 123, 138, 157

Saints, secular, 78–81

Sammele, Jennie, 123, 142

San Francisco general strike, 72

SBTA. *See* Stenographers, Bookkeepers, and Tax Accountants local 17661

Schneider, Leah, 109, 130

Scholl, Marvel, 72, 115–16, 162

Schroth, Josephine, 123

Seestrom, Selma, 113, 120, 142, 230 (n. 80)

Seiler, Rose, 142–44

Seventh Street Club for Girls, 24, 27, 62–64

Sewing project (WPA), 132–33, 155–56. *See also* Federal Workers Section of General Drivers' local 574; Works Progress Administration

Sexual difference, 89–90, 97–99. *See also* Masculinity: cult of; Representations

Sexual division of labor, 8, 22, 117, 133, 139, 141, 166

Sexuality, 16–17, 21–22, 53–54, 63, 66–67, 83, 245 (n. 18)

Skilled workers, 6, 7, 9, 13

Skoglund, Karl, 72

Socialism, 16, 18, 51

Socialist party, 20, 50–52, 55, 115, 215 (n. 14)

Social reproduction, 9, 204 (n. 13), 208 (n. 58); politics of, 5, 15, 51, 54–55, 83–84, 88, 113–14, 227 (n. 40)

Social Security, 13, 148–49

Sodom and Gomorrah, 21, 24

Solidarity, 3, 8–10, 12–18, 69–99, 159–60, 161–67; labor, 7, 17–18, 97–99; craft, 9–10, 93–95, 121–22; gender, 12–13, 166–67

Sport, metaphors of, 74–75

Stageberg, Susie, 47, 189

Stassen, Harold (governor), 154–56

Stassen Slave Labor Act, 155

State, the, 73, 148–54. *See also* New Deal; Politics; Protective legislation; Relief

Stenographers, Bookkeepers, and Tax Accountants local 17661, 115, 122–24, 141–45
Strikes, 1–2, 47–54, 56, 72–83, 100–101, 116–22, 147–48, 156–61, 165–67
Strutwear Company, 100–101, 116–22, 127, 129–30, 139–41, 163; plant, 28; strike (1936), 100–101, 116–22, 228 (n. 52), 241 (n. 48). *See also* American Federation of Full-Fashioned Hosiery Workers

Teamsters. *See* General Drivers' local 574/544
Telephone workers: 1918 strike, 47–54, 71
Textile Workers union, 130–31
Thompson, E. P., 15
Toledo, Ohio, 72, 217 (n. 51)
Trotsky, Leon, 2
Trotskyists, 115, 144–45, 161
Truckers' strike of 1934, 1–2, 72–83
Twin City Ordnance Plant, 169–70, 171, 174, 188
TWOC. *See* Textile Workers union

UE. *See* United Electrical, Radio, and Machine Workers of America
Unemployed: organizations, 64–66, 143. *See also* Federal Workers Section of General Drivers' local 574; Relief: politics of; Workers' Alliance
Unemployment, 14, 22, 58–59, 136–37, 217 (nn. 51, 52); women, 62–63
Unions. *See* Bureaucratic unions; Community-based unionism; Labor movement; individual unions
Unitarian Society, 114
United Action, 85–89
United Electrical, Radio, and Machine Workers of America (UE), 127, 180–87

United States Employment Service (USES), 170

Van Lear, Thomas, 51–52, 56
Violence: images of, 73–75
Vorse, Mary Heaton, xiv, 1–3, 100, 204 (nn. 7, 11)

Wagner Act, 189
Waitresses union, 54–55
Walker, Charles Rumford, 1–3, 21, 58, 69–71, 203–4 (n. 3)
Who's Getting Excited?, 126
Woman suffrage, 51, 57
Women's auxiliaries, 3, 7, 12–13, 72, 83–89, 106, 113, 115, 139–41
Women's Emergency Brigade (Flint), 3, 139
Women's history, xiii, 168–69
Women's League against the High Cost of Living, 113–14, 116, 120, 227 (n. 40)
Women's Occupational Bureau, 62–63
Women's Trade Union League (WTUL), 10, 53–54
Women workers. *See* Female labor force
Woodrum Act (1939), 154–57, 159–61
Workers' Alliance, 132–34, 136, 155, 157
Workers' education, 109–10, 137–38, 204 (n. 7), 226 (n. 23)
Working-class culture, 1–2, 4–12, 50–53, 69–99, 118–19
Works Progress Administration (WPA), 19, 38, 119–20, 132–34, 154–57. *See also* Woodrum Act; WPA strike
World War I, 11, 29, 30, 40–41, 47–48, 52–53, 56, 61, 66–68, 82, 93, 104, 117, 189, 222 (n. 34); veterans of, 41, 74, 80–81

World War II, 19, 38, 168–93; economy, 169–74; labor force, 170–74; gender ideology, 174–80, 182–87; unions, 174–88, 248–49 (n. 49); impact, 189–93
WPA. *See* Works Progress Administration
WPA strike (1939), 147–48, 156–61, 165–67; trial, 161–64

WTUL. *See* Women's Trade Union League

Young Women's Christian Association (YWCA), 24, 30

Ziegler, Martha, 188
Zuk, Mary, 114